高等学校应用型特色规划教材

国际商务英语
(第 3 版)

火树钰　主　编

郑宗璋　火宗玮　副主编

清华大学出版社
北　京

内 容 简 介

本书为国际商务英语应用型特色教材。

以往商务英语教材中电报、电传往往占很大篇幅,现已淘汰不用,本书予以删除,增加了电邮、传真、电子交换等内容。另外,本书按照外贸业务中涉及的各个环节的先后顺序来编排各个章节及专题,用中英文对照的形式加以表现,内容实用、全面,也有利于读者深刻理解,切实掌握及正确应用。本书还应用国际商务英语中最常见的 400 个汉译英句子进行英语语法、句法、句型及习惯用语等的剖析与讲解,有利于读者理解、模拟及应用,提高汉译英的能力。

本书可供外贸专业的学生学习国际商务英语使用,也可供外贸、经贸实务工作者阅读参考。

图书在版编目(CIP)数据

国际商务英语/火树钰主编. —3 版. —北京:清华大学出版社,2018(2023.7重印)
(高等学校应用型特色规划教材)
ISBN 978-7-302-50177-0

Ⅰ. ①国… Ⅱ. ①火… Ⅲ. ①国际商务—英语—高等学校—教材 Ⅳ. ①F740

中国版本图书馆 CIP 数据核字(2018)第 112408 号

责任编辑:杨作梅
装帧设计:李 坤
责任校对:吴春华
责任印制:杨 艳
出版发行:清华大学出版社
　　　　　网　　　址:http://www.tup.com.cn, http://www.wqbook.com
　　　　　地　　　址:北京清华大学学研大厦 A 座　　　邮　　编:100084
　　　　　社 总 机:010-83470000　　　　　　　　　邮　　购:010-62786544
　　　　　投稿与读者服务:010-62776969, c-service@tup.tsinghua.edu.cn
　　　　　质量反馈:010-62772015, zhiliang@tup.tsinghua.edu.cn
　　　　　课件下载:http://www.tup.com.cn, 010-62791865
印 装 者:三河市君旺印务有限公司
经　　销:全国新华书店
开　　本:185mm×260mm　　　印　张:20.5　　　字　数:498 千字
版　　次:2008 年 9 月第 1 版　2018 年 7 月第 3 版　　印　次:2023 年 7 月第 6 次印刷
定　　价:59.00 元

产品编号:076274-02

前　言

　　本书在第 2 版基础上进行了修订。第 2 版至今已重印了 10 次。本书特色表现为以下几点。

　　(1) 全书使用中英文对照的形式，方便学生通过中英文对照，全面、深刻地理解国际商务英语的各个环节与程序。

　　(2) 书中将国际商贸的各个环节与内容通过书信形式加以表现，体裁丰富多样，有利于扩大学生实用商贸知识面，也有利于学生对英语知识的掌握。

　　(3) 对信函、E-mail、传真的书写格式等也详细、严谨地加以举例图示，有利于学生在以后的实践工作中正确地使用相应的形式与客户进行交流。

　　(4) 每章后面的单词表及附注中都列出该章的有关同义词、近义词、重要词组及没有讲到的一些重要商务活动的句子，以资补缺。

　　为了避免学生在进行国际交流时由于对英语的语法、句法等方面的基础知识以及汉译英的翻译手法掌握不够，不能正确、清楚地表达自己的意思，这次再版时对一些英汉句子的对译方法及英语语法知识进行了详细的剖析与讲解，希望学生能通过分析、研究与熟读相关用法来进行模拟与实践，可以快速提高自己汉译英的能力，从而在从事国际经贸业务时能够自如地运用英语进行交流。

　　由于水平所限，书中难免存在不足之处，欢迎批评指正。

编　者

目　　录

Chapter 1　Basic Knowledge of Business English Letter Writing
商务英语书信写作基础知识

Learning Objectives:

- Understand the structure of a business English letter.
- Know the importance of standardizing the business English letter writing.
- Learn the designing of an elegant letterhead, a standardized inside address and a perfect letter body.
- Master the correct arrangement of various parts of a letter.

学习目标：

- 了解商务英语书信的结构。
- 认识商务英语书信书写标准化的重要性。
- 学习设计美观的信头、标准的信内地址以及信函正文。
- 掌握信函各部分的正确安排。

Ⅰ．The Aim of Learning International Business English

In order to do excellent international trading work, it is necessary to keep good communications with others for offering a perfect understanding between each other. After getting necessary, correct and prompt information, the businessmen can come into contact with their partners involved and make their business concluded. Businessmen should be keen on promoting mutually beneficial business arrangements and on making quick and correct reactions to the business information.

一、学习国际商务英语的目的

要做好国际贸易工作，必须与人进行良好的沟通，以便能很好地了解彼此。在获得必要、准确、及时的信息之后，商务人员能与其交易方建立联系并完成交易。商务人员必须积极促进互利的商务部署，并对商务信息做出迅速、正确的反应。

Ⅱ．The Keys of Learning Good Business English

In order to learn good business English, only equipping yourselves with business knowledge is not practicable. The solid English foundation and certain ability of translating from English into Chinese and from Chinese into English are both required. Therefore, it is necessary for the readers to remember the words, phrases and sentence patterns in foreign trade from the early beginning of Chapter 1. Write them down in your notebook, put it in your pocket and take it along with you anywhere in order to recite the words, phrases and sentence patterns anytime you are free. When you use your business English in your letter writing, don't create the words, phrases and sentences by yourselves, try your best just to imitate and to follow the good English usage. As you know, your skill comes from practices and your successes arrive only when your conditions are ripe.

二、学好商务英语的关键

要学好商务英语，光有商务知识是不够的，还得有扎实的英语基础知识和一定的英译汉、汉译英能力。因此，读者从本章开始就需要记忆外贸方面的词汇、词组和句型。把它们记在一个小本上随身带着，只要有空就拿出来背诵，在书写商务书信时，不要自己创造词句，而要尽量模仿造句，学着使用地道的英语。只有通过练习才能逐渐水到渠成。

Ⅲ. The Thirteen Trade Terms in International Trade

The telegrams and telexes have now fallen into disuse, but some abbreviations and abbreviated words are still remaining in use. The following thirteen trade terms must be mastered. They are classified according to the places of delivery.

三、国际贸易中的十三种贸易术语

在国际贸易中，电报、电传现在都已淘汰，但一些个别的缩略语、缩写词还在使用。以下列出的十三种贸易术语必须掌握，它们是根据交货地点来分类的。

(1) Deliveries are effected inland or at the ports of the exporting country　在出口国内地或港口交货者

EXW (Ex Works)　工厂交货

FCA (Free Carrier)　货交承运人

FAS (Free Alongside Ship)　船边交货

FOB (Free on Board)　船上交货

CFR (Cost and Freight)　成本加运费

CIF (Cost, Insurance and Freight)　成本、保险和运费

(In the previous time CIF was translated as "到岸价", but in fact "到岸价" does not include the premium, so at present translating CIF into "CIF 价" is OK.)

(以前 CIF 有译成"到岸价"的，但实际上到岸价不包括保险费，所以现在将 CIF 译成"CIF 价"就可以。)

CPT (Carriage Paid to)　运费付至

CIP (Carriage and Insurance Paid to)　运费、保险付至

(2) Deliveries are effected inland, at the frontier or at the ports of the importing country 在进口国内地、边境或港口完成交货者

DAF (Delivered at Frontier)　边境交货

DES (Delivered Ex Ship)　目的港船上交货

DEQ (Delivered Ex Quay)　目的港码头交货

DDU (Delivered Duty Unpaid)　未完税交货

DDP (Delivered Duty Paid)　完税后交货

Ⅳ. Structure of Business English Letters

There are 13 parts of the Business Letter as follows:

(1)　Letterhead;

(2)　Reference and Date;

(3)　Inside Address;

(4)　Attention Line;

(5)　Salutation;

(6)　Subject Line;

(7)　Body:

① Opening or Introduction;　② Details;　③ Response or Action;　④ Close;

(8)　Complimentary Close;

(9)　Signature;

(10) Initials;

(11) Enclosure;

(12) Carbon Copy;

(13) Postscript.

四、商务英语书信的结构

商务书信由以下 13 个部分组成：

(1)　信头；

(2)　编号和日期；

(3)　信内地址；

(4)　经办人行；

(5)　称呼；

(6)　事由行；

(7)　正文：

① 开头或引言；② 具体事项；③ 反应或行动；④ 结尾；

(8)　结尾敬语；

(9)　签名；

(10) 姓名首字母；

(11) 附件；

(12) 复写副本(抄送)；

(13) 附言。

Good learning of writing various parts of English business letters is very important. Only after mastering the correct writing can you strengthen the good impression your corporation gives to the outside world and increase its prestige. It is also beneficial to raise the position and the trust of your corporation in the international field and in the business circle.

掌握商务书信各个部分的写法是十分重要的。只有掌握了正确的书写方法才能提升公司对外的形象和声誉，并有助于提高公司在国际上和商务领域中的地位与信任度。

V. The Ways of Using the Writing Parts and Their Standardized Designs

1. Letterhead

Letterhead includes the sender's name, postal address, post code, telephone number, fax number, E-mail address, etc. Usually big firms engage experts to design their attractive letter paper, with their well-balanced letterheads, sometimes even with trademarks pre-printed on it in order to strengthen their firms' impression and enhance their firms' prestige. The best way is to print the letterhead in the up-center, because the letterhead printed in the up-center will offer a well-balanced appearance to others, and using different forms and sizes of both English alphabets and Chinese characters will especially show a very smart and wonderful design of the letterhead.

See Examples (1) and (2).

Example (1)

China National Light Industrial Products Imp. & Exp. Co.

82 Donganmen Street, Beijing, China

Tel: ******   Fax: ******

E-mail: ********   Post Code: ******

Example (2)

1242   West Lafayette Rd., Indianapolis, IN 46268, USA

Tel: ******   Fax: ******

E-mail: *******   Post Code: ******

Using this design will enable the writer to put the firm's name, postal address and all the communicating information in four lines and not to occupy too many lines of the letter paper. In the following Example (3) sometimes letterhead is printed at the left margin of the sheet of letter

paper. Such design can often be found in the full-blocked style or semi-blocked style of letter writing.

Example (3)

Jameson & Sons Ltd.
　34 Madison Square
　　Melbourne, Australia
　　　Tel: *******　　E-mail: *******
　　　Fax: *******　　Post Code: *******

　　In this design, in order not to occupy too many lines in the letterhead, E-mail address and Fax number have to be omitted, thus the inconvenience in using modern communicating techniques will be resulted in. And if you type all of the numbers below the address, your letterhead will be long enough to occupy nearly a quarter of your sheet of paper. So the best design of letterhead writing does not belong to this kind.

　　In Example (4) sometimes you can find that the letterhead is put at the right margin of the sheet of letter paper. Such design will bring you much difficulty in offering good balance, especially when the letterhead is too long to put into some short lines and will as well show you a long list of communicating numbers and figures.

Example (4)

M.D. Edward & Co., Ltd.
36 Tower Street
Toronto 4, Canada
Tel: ******　　E-mail: ******
Fax: ******　　Post code: ******

五、书信各部分的书写方法及标准设计

1.　信头

　　信头包括发信人的姓名、地址、邮编、电话号码、传真号码、邮政编码和电子邮件地址等。通常大公司会请专业人员设计好看的信笺，上面印有比例匀称的信头，有时也预印上公司的商标，以便加深客户对公司的印象，提高公司的声誉。最好的方法是将信头印在信纸正上方中央，因为印在正中央的信头会给人一种非常协调的视觉感受。使用不同字体和字号的英文字母和汉字尤其会使设计的信头显得巧妙而大方。如例(1)、例(2)。

　　使用这种设计可以将公司名称、地址以及所有联系方式信息分四行排列，而不会占用信纸太多行数。在下面的例(3)中有时信头印在信纸的左侧边缘，这种设计常见于全齐头式或半齐头式的书信中。

　　在例(3)中，为了使信头不占太多的行数，E-mail 地址和传真号码就不得不省略，这样，

现代通信技术的使用就显得很不方便。如果把所有号码都写在地址下面，那么信头就将会占信纸的 1/4 了。因此，这不是一种最佳的设计。

在例(4)中有时信头位于信纸的右侧边缘，这样的设计在保持整体协调上会有很大的难度，特别是当信头太长而不能置于短行中以及列出一长列通信号码和数字时。

2. Reference and Date

In business correspondence, reference will be given by a firm to another. Reference may include a file number, departmental code, or the initials of the signer, followed by that of the typist of the letter. They are marked as " Our Ref: *** " and " Your Ref:*** " to avoid confusion.

See Examples (1) and (2).

Example (1)

Your Ref: JVD/ZH

Our Ref: WDC/LF

Example (2)

Our Ref: SEL/SY

Your Ref: No. 145/170

The dates should be typed in full, but some of the English names of the months may be abbreviated, such as Jan.=January, Feb.=February, Aug.=August, Sept.=September, Oct.=October, Nov.=November, Dec.=December. The -th,-st,-nd and-rd that follow the day may be omitted such as, "6 June" for "6th June", "May 1" for "May 1st". Don't use the all-number form. The American practice is to write the date in the order of month, day and year as 3/8/2005 or 03/08/2005, but the British practice is written in the order of day, month and year, as 8/3/2005 or 08/03/2005. So using all-number form to express the date will make the letter date thrown into confusion.

2. 编号和日期

在商务通信中，公司之间会相互提供编号。编号包括存档号、部门代码或签名人的首字母，后面紧接着打字员的首字母。这些都以"我方编号：***"及"你方编号：***"来标示，以免混淆，如例(1)和例(2)。

日期应该全部拼写出来，但某些月份的英文名字可以用缩写形式：如 1 月用 Jan.，2 月用 Feb.，8 月用 Aug.，9 月用 Sept.，10 月用 Oct.，11 月用 Nov.，12 月用 Dec.。日期后的-th, -st, -nd 及-rd 均可省略，如 6 月 6 日可写成"June 6"，而不是"June 6th"；5 月 1 日写成"May 1"，而不是"May 1st"；但不要采用全数字形式。美式的日期写法是以月/日/年为序，即月份在前，如 03/8/2005 或 03/08/2005，即 2005 年 3 月 8 日；而英式的日期写法是以日/月/年为序，即日期在前，如"8/3/2005"或"08/03/2005"，即 2005 年 3 月 8 日。因此，使用全数字形式来表示日期容易发生混淆。

3. Inside Address

Generally, the inside address should include the receiver's name and title, company name, street address, city, state (province), post-code, and country (if necessary). They are typed at the upper left-hand margin of the sheet, starting two to three lines below the last line of the letterhead.

See Examples (1) and (2).

Example (1)

China National Light Industrial Products Imp. & Exp. Co.

82 Donganmen Street, Beijing, China

Tel: ******   Fax: ******

E-mail ********   Post Code: ******

4 June, 2005

Mr. Walter Roberts
Sales Manager
Mid-West Imp. & Exp. Inc.
12 East Tenth Street
Chicago, IL 60687, USA.

Example (2)

1242 West Lafayette Rd., Indianapolis, IN 46268, USA

Tel: ******   Fax: ******

E-mail: ********   Post Code: ******

5 May, 2005

The Manager
Star Stores
101 High Street
Fulham
London SW6, 3BA
England, UK

3.　信内地址

通常信内地址包括收信人的姓名和头衔、公司名称、街道、市、州(省)、邮编及国家(如果需要的话)。它们均位于信纸的左上侧边缘，在信头最后一行下的 2～3 行处，如例(1)和例(2)。

4.　Attention Line

Attention line is used when the writer of a letter addressed to an institution or an organization wishes to direct the letter to a specific individual or specific department. It is generally placed between the inside address and the salutation, underscored or not underscored and is centered over the body of the letter. If it is used in the full block format, it will be typed at the left-hand margin.

Example

Attention: Export Department

Dear Sirs,

4. 经办人行

当写信人希望自己写给某个特定的机构或组织的信直接送达该人或该部门时，可以使用经办人行。此行通常置于信内地址和称呼之间，文字下面使用或不使用画线均可，在正文上方居中位置。如果采用全齐头式，则经办人行应位于左侧边缘。

5. Salutation

Salutation is placed two lines below the inside address. The salutation is "Gentlemen" if the letter is addressed to an organization, even if there is an attention line directing the letter to a particular individual within that organization.

In business correspondence, the most commonly used salutation forms are:

Dear Sirs, (British Style)

Gentlemen: (American Style)

Dear Sir,

Dear Madam:

Dear Mr. Brown:

Whether married or unmarried, a woman is always addressed as "Dear Madam", never as "Dear Miss". The Americans prefer to use "Gentlemen" while the British use "Dear Sirs".

Even when the firm's name is the name of a single individual, the salutation of plural form is preferred, such as:

Example

John Norris Inc.   (Date)
O' Sallivan Building
Baltimore, MD 10026
USA.

Gentlemen:

In writing to a firm consisting of both men and women, or even to a firm consisting of women alone, the salutation of "Gentlemen" is preferably used.

The salutation of "Dear Sirs" is followed by a comma and "Gentlemen" is followed by a colon.

5. 称呼

称呼位于信内地址下两行处，如果写信给某个机构，即使经办人行指明将信送至该机构内某个人，称呼仍使用"先生"的复数(Gentlemen)。

在商业信件中最常用的称呼有：

Dear Sirs, (英式)

Gentlemen: (美式)

Dear Madam:

Dear Mr. Brown:

女性不管婚否均被称为"Dear Madam"，不要用"Dear Miss"。另外，美国人喜欢用"Gentlemen"，而英国人喜欢用"Dear Sirs"。

即使公司的名称是某个人的名字，称呼也倾向于使用复数形式，如示例所示。

当写信给既有男性员工也有女性员工的公司时，或写给只有女性员工的公司时，使用Gentlemen 的称呼更合适。

"Dear Sirs"的称呼后常用逗号，"Gentlemen"后常用冒号。

6.   Subject Line

Subject line is actually the central idea of a letter. It is inserted between the salutation and the body of the letter. If the letter is in the full block form, it is placed at the left-hand margin. In other styles, it is centered over the body of the letter. In order to invite the receiver's attention, it is usually underlined. In front of it "Re:" or "Subj:" is written as the following examples.

Example (1)

　　　　Dear Sirs,
　　　　　　　Re: Women's Blouses

Example (2)

　　　　Gentlemen:
　　　　　　　Subj: Tin Foil Sheets

Sometimes, the subject line can be underscored.

6.   事由行

事由行实际上是一封信的中心思想，位于称呼和正文之间。如果信是全齐头式，事由行就放在信的左侧边缘；在其他格式中，则位于信的正中。为了引起收信人的注意，通常在其下加下画线，在前面写"Re:"或"Subj:"。

如例(1)和例(2)。

有时，对事由行可予以特别强调。

7.   Body

This part is the most important one in business correspondence. The body of the letter generally consists of four essential parts.

1) Opening (or Introduction)

The opening is actually the background of this letter. It indicates the referring letter, contract or letter of credit to which response will be made.

2) Details

The details refer to the enquires, problems, requirements, etc. which will be put forth by the letter. Some relative details will be illustrated in this part.

3) Response (or Action)

In this part the expected response or possible decision will be expressed here.

4) Close

In this part a short close must be made politely. Attention must be paid to the keeping of friendly relations between the letter writer and the letter receiver. Business development should not be hindered by a discourteous letter close.

In writing the body of the letter you must always ask yourself about the purpose of writing this letter. You must always consider the best ways of accomplishing your hope and conveying your ideas to your correspondent. Try your best to streamline your letter and use short sentences and short paragraphs for giving your correspondent a brief letter to read fast. Start a new paragraph for each point you wish to stress and make your letter to be read easily and clearly and as well inspire the action or response you desire.

7. 正文

这是商务信件中最重要的一个部分。信的正文一般包括四个基本部分。

1) 开头(或引言)

开头实际上是信的背景，指出了有待回复的信函、合同或信用证。

2) 具体事项

具体事项会谈到信函提出的询价单、问题或要求等。有关的细节将在这部分阐述。

3) 回应(或行动)

这一部分必须有一个将表达期望的回应或可能的决策。

4) 结尾

这一部分必须有一个简短的语气客气的结尾。要注意保持写信人与收信人之间的友好关系。业务的发展不要因为一个不客气的结尾而受到阻碍。

在书写正文时，应该始终围绕写信的目的展开。写信人必须始终考虑以最好的方法来构建期望，并将自己的想法传达给客户。要尽最大的努力简化信函的内容，并使用短句和简短的段落，使客户能收到一封言简意赅的书信。每强调一点都新起一段，这样可以使信易读、清晰，并且可以激发出希望的行动或反应。

8. Complimentary Close

Complimentary Close is used to provide the letter a courteous ending. The correct position for complimentary close is two spaces below the body of the letter to the right side of the page, in line with the date block at the top.

In business correspondence, "Yours truly" is the style used most frequently. Here are some more styles which can be used: Yours sincerely, Sincerely yours, Yours faithfully, Faithfully yours.

If continuation sheets are needed, plain paper of the same quality as the letterhead must be used and typed with a heading to show the following:

(1)　The number of the sheet (in the center of the page);

(2)　The name of your correspondent (on the left-hand side);

(3)　The date of the letter (on the right-hand side).

Example

— P2 —

China Foodstuffs I/E Corp.   1 May, 2005

8.　结尾敬语

结尾敬语是书信的一个礼貌结尾。结尾敬语的正确位置是正文下的第 2 行的右边缘，与顶部的日期对齐。

在商务信件中"Yours truly"是最常用的。这里还有其他一些常用的形式，如 Yours sincerely, Sincerely yours 等。

如果需要续页，则应使用与信头所在页质量相同的纸张，并且要带有信头，显示以下内容：

(1)　页码(信纸中央)；

(2)　收信人姓名(信的左侧)；

(3)　信的日期(信的右侧)。

9. Signature

The signature is the signed name of the person writing the letter. It is signed by hand in black or blue ink. Since the hand-written signature is illegible, the name of the signer should be typed below the signature. The name should be written out in full, as initials may be misleading or confusing. It is common to have the writer's name typed several lines below the complimentary close, leaving space between for the hand-written signature, followed by his job title or position.

If the writer writes the letter for his firm, not for himself, he should type the name of his firm in capital letters below the complimentary close, followed by his signed name right below it.

Example

Sincerely yours,

China National Machinery Imp. & Exp. Co.

Signature (hand-signed)

Li Ming-yu (typed)

Sales Manager

---

9. 签名

签名是写信人所签的名字。签名通常用黑墨水笔或蓝墨水笔手写。由于手写的签名难以辨认，签名人的名字应该打印在所签名字的下面。名字应该全部写出，因为仅写首字母可能会引起误导或混淆。通常将写信人的名字打在结束语下面几行的位置上，中间留出一定的空间以供手写签名，签名人的头衔或职务紧随打印签名之后。

如果写信人是为其公司写信而不是为个人，就应该在结束语下面打出公司名称的大写字母(或首字母大写)，其手写签名在其下面。

10. Initials

The initials line firstly show the name of the dictator of the letter, and secondly shows the typist of the letter. In the initial line, the dictator's name should appear before the typist's. And one method of the following four may be used:

WT/FM　　　　　WT:FM　　　　WT-FM　　　　WT/fm

Occasionally the full name of the dictator is used, followed by the typist's initials, as:

Wu Tong /sm

Nowadays the business letters are often written and typed by the businessmen themselves in a corporation. In this case this line is not necessary to be typed after the signature.

10. 姓名首字母

在这行中应首先列出信件口授人的首字母，其次是打字人的首字母。在该行中，口授人的姓名应放在打字人姓名之前。可以选用下列四种写法中的任意一种。

WT/FM　　　WT:FM　　　　WT-FM　　　　WT/fm

有时也使用口授人的全名，后面跟打字人的姓名首字母，如 Wu Tong/sm。

现在的商务信件经常由公司的商务人员自己书写和打印。在这种情况下，签名后就不必打上该行。

11. Enclosure

If it is necessary to enclose something with the letter, such as a photo, a bill, a cheque or a brochure, attention should be called to it by writing "Enclosure" or "Enclosures" below the signature in the lower left-hand corner.

Enclosures: A. 2005 Price List

　　　　　　B. 2005 Catalogue

Encls: 2 Cheques

Enc. Under Separate Cover

11. 附件

如果需要随信附寄照片、账单、支票、小册子等，则必须在左下角的签名下写上"Enclosure"或　"Enclosures"以引起收信人的注意。例如：

　　附件(复数)：A. 2005 年价格单
　　　　　　　　B. 2005 年商品目录
附件(复数)：支票两张
附件：另封邮寄

12. Carbon Copy

There are two types of carbon copy notation. One is indicated by "CC" followed by the names of the "CC" receiver. This notation is typed both on the original and the carbon copies, as,

CC: Shanghai Branch

The other type of CC notation is to type "bcc" only on the copy, not on the original letter, as,

bcc: Mr. John Black

For convenience of mailing and filing, full names and addresses are better to be given. CC can also be written as C.C. or cc.

12. 复写副本

复写副本的标记有两种。一种是在 CC 标记后写副本收件人的姓名。该标记显示在原本和副本上，如：

CC：上海分行

另一种复写副本标记 bcc，该标记只显示在副本上，如：

bcc：琼斯先生

为了邮寄和存档方便，最好写出全名和完整的地址。复写副本可以写成 C.C.或 cc。

13. Postscript

When the letter writer forgets to mention or to emphasize something in his letter, he may add his postscript two spaces below the CC notation, as,

P.S.　The catalogue will be airmailed to you under separate cover.

However, the adding of a "P.S." will show that the writer's letter is lack of good planning and well consideration, so the adding of a "P.S." should be avoided as far as possible.

Below is a complete business letter including the above-mentioned thirteen parts.

13. 附言

当写信人忘记在信中提及或强调某事，写信人可以在 CC 标记下的两行处加上附言，前面冠以 P.S.(或 PS)，如：

P.S.　产品目录将于明天另封邮寄你方。

但是，添加附言表明写信人在书写时缺少周密的计划和全面的考虑，所以应尽可能避免添加附言。

下面是一封包含了以上 13 个部分的完整的商务信函。

China National Light Industrial Products Imp. & Exp. Co.

82 Donganmen Street, Beijing, China

Tel: ******   Fax: ******
E-mail: ********   Post Code: ******

4 June, 2005

Our Ref. No.: ****
Mr. Walter Roberts
Sales Manager
Mid-West Imp. & Exp. Inc.
12 East Tenth Street
Chicago, Illinois 60687, USA

Attention: Import Department

Dear Sirs,

Chinese Color TV Sets

Thank you for your inquiry of Oct.10 about our Color TV Sets. Here we enclose our catalogues and price list for your reference.

In case of your requiring further information, please fax us. We look forward to hearing from you soon.

Yours sincerely,
(Signature)
Wang Ming
International Electronic Machines

书信译文：

感谢你方 10 月 10 日关于我方彩色电视机的询价。我方现附寄几份产品目录及一份价格单，供你方参考。

如你方需要进一步的信息资料，请传真我方。我方盼望你方尽快回音。

Exercises

Ⅰ. Design a letterhead with the following address (用下列地址设计一个信头).

Shanghai Import and Export Commodity Inspection Bureau
No. 13 Zhongshan Road, Shanghai, China
(With the numbers of Tel, Fax, E-mail and Post Code)

Ⅱ. Design an inside address with the following address (用下列地址设计一个信内地址).

China National Light Industrial Products Import and Export Corp. Guangzhou Branch
No. 87 The Bund, Guangzhou, China

Chapter 2　Business Writing and Envelope Addressing
商务书信和书写信封

Learning Objectives:

- Understand the language characteristics of business writing.
- Master the styles of business letters.
- Get familiar with the letter body writing.
- Learn the ways of designing the envelope addressing.

学习目标：

- 理解商务书信的语言特点。
- 掌握商务书信的格式。
- 熟悉信件正文的书写。
- 学会设计信封地址。

I．The Seven Principles of Writing English Business Letters

There are seven principles which must be observed in writing English business letters. Since all these seven principles are begun with the letter "C", we can call them the "7C's".

一、书写英语商务书信的七个原则

书写商务书信时要遵循七个原则。因为七个原则的英文都是以"C"打头，所以也可称为"7C's"。

1.　Consideration

In preparing every piece of information and before taking every step, you must always keep your reader in mind and think about your opposite side. There is an old saying: "Put yourself into the reader's shoes." It means that you must always show your consideration for your correspondents.

1.　顾及他人

准备每一条信息，以及采取每一个步骤前，都要想到收信人，有句老话："Put yourself into the reader's shoes."意思是要随时设身处地地为对方着想。

2.　Courtesy

When writing to your correspondents, it is necessary for you not only to be polite, but also to be sincere and tactful, thoughtful and appreciative. It is also a kind of courtesy for the tradesmen to answer the letters and the enquiries promptly. Any delay in dealing with the matters is discourteous.

2. 谦恭有礼

给对方写信时不仅要谦恭有礼，而且要真挚诚恳、机智得体、善于思辨。对于对方的任何来信或咨询都要及时回复，否则是不礼貌的。

3. Clarity

The writer should express his aims, ideas and requirements clearly not only by distinct and understandable wordings, but also by correct phrases, tenses, voices and sentence structures in order not to be misunderstood or misinterpreted. Writing letters to and fro for enquiring about the same thing will enable you to miss business opportunities.

3. 清晰明朗

写信人不仅要用清晰明朗的用语明确地表达自己的目的、意思与要求，而且要用准确的词语、时态、语态及句子结构来正确地表达自己的意思，不能使对方产生曲解或误解。写信时来回询问同一件事情是会贻误商机的。

4. Conciseness

A letter written with wordiness or redundancy will not be welcomed in the business circle. The business field is just like a battle field. The aim of doing business is to gain profits from fighting a quick battle to force a quick decision in winning over the business opportunities. In writing letters, the sentences you use must be brief and to the point.

4. 简洁扼要

冗长累赘的书信在商界是不受欢迎的。商场如战场，速战速决争取商机以获得最大利润是进行商务的目的，写信时句子要简洁扼要。

5. Concreteness

The enquiries of others about something and your answers to the others' letters must be made with reality and concreteness. Any ambiguous and vague words must not be used and the information must be supplied with definiteness and concreteness.

5. 具体实在

咨询他人或回复他人都必须具体实在，不能含糊其辞。提供信息必须具体、明确。

6. Completeness

The business letters must consist of complete and intact information. The incomplete information will fail to enable the tradesmen to seize the business opportunities of doing mutually beneficial trades.

6.　完整无缺

商务信函必须包括完整无缺的信息，信息不完整就无法抓住商机并进行互利的贸易。

7.　Correctness

Holding some important and beneficial information in hand, but at the same time with lacking of correct skills and certain level to express it in writing will not make you enable to achieve your aim of conveying the business opportunities to others. Therefore learning good English, studying well the English grammar and English syntax and mastering good business English are very important for your achieving this goal. Whenever you are writing letters, faxing or E-mailing, you must check the typings of figures, types, specifications, etc. again and again before sending them out in order not to make any mistakes which will bring injuries to your business.

7.　准确无误

有重要而有益的信息却缺乏正确的表达技巧和一定的写作水平，也达不到传递商机的目的，所以学好英语，学好英语的语法、句法知识，掌握商务英语还是十分重要的。无论写信、发传真还是发送电子邮件，对打好的数字、型号、规格等在发送前都要再三校对，以避免因出错而造成生意上的损失。

Ⅱ．The Styles of Business English Letters

There are several styles of business letters. The main styles of them are Full-blocked style, Semi-blocked style, Indented style, Modified style, and Simplified style.

商务英语书信有几种格式，其中主要有全齐头式、半齐头式、缩行式、混合式和简化式。

二、商务英语书信的格式

It is very important for the businessmen to master various styles of writing English business letters and the correct ways of writing. The applying of correct, well-laid-out, smart and tasteful styles can not only show the high level and high quality of the businessmen's English letter writing, but also beneficial to the raise of the impression, prestige, position and confidence of the business institution you represent in the society, in the domestic and international business fields.

商务人员掌握商务英语书信的各种格式及其准确的书写方法是十分重要的。准确、整齐、美观、大方的格式应用不仅显示了商务人员在英文信函写作方面的高水平和高素质，而且有利于提高商务人员所代表的商务机构在社会上以及国内外商务领域中的形象、声誉、地位和信任度。

1. Full-blocked style

This style is rather modern and is widely used in business letter writing. The following letter is written with pre-printed letterhead and with all the thirteen parts of a business letter included. The letter is shown in the following way in order that the readers may get familiar with all the names and positions of various parts of a business letter. See Letter (1).

Letter (1)

John Smith & Sons Co.

180 Edwards Street, Sydney, Australia

Tel: ******   E-mail: ******

Fax: ******   Post Code: ******

18 March, 2015

Mr. ***

General Manager

China National Machinery Imp. & Exp. Corp.

Erligou, Haidian District

Beijing, China

Our Ref. No.   ******

Attention: General Manager

Dear Mr. Wang,

Re: Establishing Business Relationship

Your name and good experiences of managing the import and export businesses in the line of industrial machinery have been known to us for a long time, but it's a great regret that we have not yet established definite business relationship between us.

As you know, it is our policy to trade with the people of all countries on the basis of equality and mutual benefit. Our firm has been keeping long direct relations with our competitive domestic manufacturers. We believe the establishing of our business relationship will greatly help the economic development of our two nations.

We hope to receive your reply as soon as possible.

Yours sincerely,

John Smith & Sons Co.

Signature (hand-signed)

James Mccarthy (typed)

WY/FG

Encl.: A pamphlet.

CC: Our Branch

P.S. We will airmail under separate cover some catalogues of our firm tomorrow.

Note: In case the writer uses the letter paper with no printed letterhead, the letterhead is placed at the left-hand margin. In some business letters the attention line and the subject line are sometimes omitted. And the parts of "Encl", "CC" and "P. S." are typed only if it is necessary. See letter (2).

1. 全齐头式

这种格式非常现代，被广泛运用于商务书信的写作中。下面这封信的信头是预先印刷的，商务书信的所有 13 个部分都包括在内，该信采用这种方式，目的是使读者熟悉商务信函不同部分的名称和地位。见信件(1)。

信件(1)

约翰·史密斯父子公司

澳大利亚 悉尼 爱德华大街 180 号

电话：******　　　　E-mail：******

传真：******　　　　邮编：******

2015 年 3 月 18 日

***先生

总经理

中国机械进出口公司

中国北京市海淀区二里沟

我方编号：******

经办人：总经理

亲爱的王先生：

事由：建立业务关系

我方久闻您的大名，知道贵公司在工业机械进出口管理方面的经验非常丰富，但遗憾的是，我们之间尚未确立业务关系。

正如你们所知，我们的政策是在平等互利的基础上与世界各地的人民进行贸易。我方与我国富有竞争力的制造商一直保持着长久且密切的联系。我方相信建立彼此之间的业务关系将大大有助于两国经济的发展。

希望尽快收到您的回复。

约翰·史密斯父子公司
签名：
（手签）
James Mccarthy（打印）

WY/FG
附件：一份小册子
抄至：各公司

附言：明天我们将另外空邮一些我公司的产品目录。

注意：如果写信人使用的是没有印刷信头的信纸，则将信头置于左侧边缘。有些商务信件的经办人行和事由行有时会省略，附件、复写副本及附言只在需要时添加，如信件(2)所示。

Letter (2)

John Smith & Sons Co.
180 Edward Street, Sydney
SW 6008, Australia
Tel: ******   Fax: ******
E-mail: ******   Post Code: *******

1 March, 2015

Mr. ***
General Manager
China Machinery Imp. & Exp. Corp.
Erligou, Haidian District
Beijing, China.

Our Ref. No. WHJ 0068.

Dear Mr. Wang,

Your name and good experiences of managing the import and export businesses in the line of industrial machinery have been known to us for a long time, but it's a great regret that we have not yet established definite business relationship between us.

As you know, it is our policy to trade with the people of all countries on the basis of equality and mutual benefit. Our firm has been keeping long direct relations with our competitive domestic manufacturers. We believe the establishing of our business relationship will greatly help the economic development of our two nations.

We hope to receive your reply as soon as possible.

Yours sincerely,
John Smith Sons Co.
Signature(hand-signed)
James Mccarthy (typed)

信件(2)

约翰·史密斯父子公司

澳大利亚悉尼 SW6008 爱德华大街 180 号
电话：******　　传真：******
E-mail：******　　邮编：*******

2015 年 3 月 1 日
***先生
总经理
中国机械进出口公司
中国北京市海淀区二里沟

我方编号：WHJ0068

亲爱的王先生：(信函译文同信件(1)的译文，此处省略。)

2. Semi-blocked style

The semi-blocked style is similar to the full-blocked style except that the date, the complimentary close and the signature are typed on the right side in line with the date and with the attention line and the subject line in the middle of the page.

Letter (3)

Overseas Trading Co.

153 Market Street, London, EC 3, E, UK

Tel: ******   E-mail: ******

Fax:******   Post Code: ******

August 8, 2015

Your Ref. No.: ******

China National Light Industrial Products
Import and Export Corporation

82 Donganmen Street

Beijing, China

Dear Sirs,

Re: Expediting the Delivery of the Goods

With reference to our 2,000 dozen cotton blouses under our Sales Confirmation No. B145, we think it is our duty to remind you that the date of delivery is approaching, but we still haven't received your Shipping Advice. Since our L/C has already been opened for one month, please expedite the delivery of the goods to meet the urgent needs of our customers.

In addition, we would like to inform you that any delay in delivery of our goods will effect the prospective business relationship between us.

Looking forward to your prompt reply.

Sincerely yours,

Overseas Trading Co.

Signature (hand-signed)

Signature (typed)

2. 半齐头式

半齐头式的日期、结束语及签名打印在右侧边缘与日期对齐外，经办人行及主题行打在信纸中央，其他均与全齐头式相同。

信件(3)

海外贸易公司

英国伦敦 EC3 市场街 153 号

电话: ******　　　E-mail: ******

传真: *****　　　　邮编: ******

2015 年 8 月 8 日

你方编号：******

中国轻工业产品进出口公司
中国北京东安门大街 82 号

先生：

<u>关于：催促交货</u>

关于我方第 B145 号销售确认书名下 2000 打女棉衬衣，我方认为有责任提醒你方：交货日期已经临近，但我方迄今尚未收到你方装运的通知。由于我方信用证已于一个月前开出，请尽快交货，以满足我方顾客的迫切需要。

此外，我方通知你方，交货的任何耽搁必将影响我们之间未来的业务关系。

盼望你方迅速回复。

海外贸易公司
签名(手签)
签名(打印)

Notes：

(1) In writing the inside address, if the name of the firm is too long to be combined into a single line, it may be placed into two lines with the commodities which it engages in not to be separated from each other and not to be arranged into the next line to continue the writing of the firm's name. For finishing the writing of the firm's name the second line must be indented for two spaces. For example:

The correct writing:

China National Light Industrial Products
Import & Export Corporation

China National Cereals, Oils and Foodstuffs
Import & Export Corporation

注意：

（1）在写信内地址时，如果公司名称太长、单行不能写完时，可以分成两行，但名称中公司所经营的商品不能分割，不能延长到下一行写完公司名称。如果要在第二行继续写完公司名称，则必须空两格，例如：

正确的写法：

China National Light Industrial Products
Import & Export Corporation

China National Cereals, Oils and Foodstuffs
Import & Export Corporation

Here, "Light Industrial Products" are not separated and the indenting of the "Import and Export Corporation" makes the reader understand at once that this line is the continuation of the receiver's address.

It is better not to arrange the line as follows:

China National Light Industrial
Products Import and Export Corporation

China National Cereals, Oils
and Foodstuffs Import and Export Corporation

这里的"轻工业产品"是不分的，在"进出口公司"前空两格，可以使收信人马上知道，这一行是收信人地址的继续。

最好不要写成下面的形式：

China National Light Industrial
Products Import and Export Corporation

China National Cereals, Oils
and Foodstuffs Import and Export Corporation

（2）If the firm's name is too long, it may be abbreviated as follows:
Import & Export Corp.

Imp. & Exp. Co.

I/E Co.

(2)　如果公司的名称太长，可以缩写成以下形式：

Import & Export Corp.

Imp. & Exp. Co.

I/E Co.

(3)　The names of the countries may as well be abbreviated, for example:

Britain as U.K. (UK)

America as U.S.A. (USA)

People's Republic of China as PRC

(3)　国家名也可缩写，例如：

Britain 缩写为 U.K. (UK)

America 缩写为 U.S.A. (USA)

People's Republic of China 缩写为 PRC

The necessity of using abbreviations depends upon their layout. A well balanced address will be more preferable and will bring about more favorable impression of the writer's firm to the other organizations and institutions. If there are too many lines in the inside address, you may use the abbreviation form of the countries to cut down one of its lines, especially when the name and the title of the inside address are used simultaneously, they can be written in a single line. For example:

(Mr. ***)

General Manager

Xi'an Electric Machinery Imp. & Exp. Co.

Fengdeng Road, Xijiao, Xi'an

Shaanxi, PRC

The above address may be confined into three lines:

(Mr. ***), General Manager

Xi'an Electric Machinery Imp. & Exp .Corp.

Fengdeng Road, Xi'an, Shaanxi, China.

是否需要使用缩写方式取决于其设计。一个布局匀称的地址是更为可取的，并且会使其他组织机构对自己的公司产生更好的印象。若信内地址行数太多，可以使用国家名的缩写来压缩一行，特别是信内地址中的姓名和头衔同时使用时，它们可书写于同一行中。例如：

(***先生：)

总经理

中华人民共和国陕西省

西安市西郊丰登路

西安电力机械进出口公司

上述地址可以缩为 3 行：

***先生，总经理
中国陕西西安丰登路
西安电力机械进出口公司

(4)　If the letter is not too long, you may adopt double line-spacing for each paragraph. As shown in the above letters of (1)(2).

(4)　如果信件不太长，可以如前面的信件(1)(2)所示，在每段之间空一行。

3.　Indented Style

The indented style is traditional. In this style, each line of the inside name and address and as well the first line of each paragraph are indented for two or several spaces. The date is on the right hand side with the complimentary close and the signature kept in line with the date.

Letter (4)

ABC Computer Corp.

19 Hampton Road

London　　SW113SH

Tel:******　　　E-mail:******

Fax:******　　　Post Code:******

August 1, 2015

Your Ref: ******
Our Ref:******

P&H Company

8000 Lincoln Avenue

New York, NY 11222，USA

Dear Sirs,

　　Mr. James Scott, president of our Corp. and Mr. Bill Smith, Marketing Manager, would like to visit New York to continue our discussion on the joint venturing of electronic computers. They are planning to leave London in the middle of September and to stay in New York about 3-4 days.

　　Would you please let us know your opinion on this planned visit? If their visit is agreeable and is convenient for you, please request your Embassy here to issue them the necessary visa. We would be very glad if you would offer us your suggestion on their itinerary.

> Best regards to you.
>
> Yours faithfuly,
> **ABC Computer Corp.**
> (signature)

3.　缩行式

缩行式是传统的书信形式。用这种格式写信，信内姓名和地址以及每一段的起始行均要缩进两格或两格以上。日期位于右上方，结尾敬语和签名与日期对齐。

信件(4)

> **ABC 计算机公司**
> 汉普顿路 19 号
> 伦敦　SW113SH
>
> 电话：******　　　　E-mail：******
> 传真：******　　　　邮编：******
>
> 2015 年 8 月 1 日
>
> 你方编号：******
> 我方编号：******
>
> **P/H 公司**
> 林肯大道 8000 号
> 纽约市(邮编 NY 11222)，美国
>
> 先生：
> 　　我公司总裁詹姆士·司考脱先生及销售经理比尔·史密斯先生将前往纽约，以继续我们之间有关合资经营电子计算机的商讨。他们计划于 9 月中旬离开伦敦，并在纽约停留 3～4 天。
>
> 　　你方对此次计划来访有何意见，请告知我方。如果此行能获得你方同意，对你方亦无不便之处，请你方要求驻此地大使馆给他们发放必要的签证。我方很乐意听取你方对此次日程方面的建议。
>
> 　　谨致问候！
>
> **ABC 计算机公司**
> (签名)

4. Modified Style

The modified style is similar to the indented style. In this style the inside name and address are typed in blocked style with the first line of each paragraph forming the body of the letter indented for two or several spaces. The complimentary close and the signature are also on the right hand side in line with the date.

Letter (5)

International Laser Machines

1242 West Lafayette Rd. , Indianapolis, IN 46268, U.S.A.

| Tel: ****** | E-mail: ****** |
| Fax: ****** | Post Code: ****** |

April 1, 2015

Our Ref. No: ******

The Singapore Lasers Co.
92 Napier Road
Singapore 3806

Dear Sirs,

We are arranging to attend the International Fair of 2015 which will be held in New York City from May 2 to May 12.

We have been informed that more than 200 companies will present their products in that Fair and a series of very modern and important technical lectures will be given to the customers coming from various parts of the world.

We hope that you would like to pay a visit to that Fair. It will be a great pleasure for us to get the opportunity of meeting you at that Fair and discussing with you on our joint venture of the most advanced laser machines in the world.

Look forward to hearing from you soon.

Your friendly
International Laser Machines
(Signature)

---

4. 混合式

混合式与缩行式类似。这种形式的信件中，信内的姓名和地址用齐头式，而且正文每一段的第一行均缩进两格或两个空格以上。结尾敬语及签名也在右侧且与日期对齐。

信件(5)

国际激光机公司

美国印第安纳州拉法叶西路 1242 号(IN 46268)

电话：******   E-mail：*******

传真：******   邮编：******

2015 年 4 月 1 日

我方编号：******

新加坡激光公司

新加坡 3806

纳波路 92 号

先生：

我方正安排出席 5 月 2 日到 5 月 12 日在纽约举行的 2015 年国际展览会。

我方获悉将有 200 多个公司在交易会上展示他们的产品，并将为来自世界各地的用户举行一系列非常现代的、重要的科技讲座。

我方希望你方愿意去参加该展览会。如果能有机会在该展览会上与你方会晤，并与你方讨论世界上最先进的激光机的合资经营问题，我方将感到十分荣幸。

盼望不久收到你方佳音。

国际激光机公司

(签名)

---

5. Simplified Style

Nowadays, it has become fashionable to use the simplified style. In this style, all parts of a letter are typed at the left margin. It makes the letter typing quickened. Also, the salutation and complimentary close are omitted, which makes the letter typing simplified, and the writer's name is typed in capital letters four lines below the last line of the letter body.

Letter (6)

Singapore Laser's Co.

92 Napier Road,

Singapore 3806

April 8, 2015.

Your Ref. No: ******

Our Ref. No: ******

Mr. Thompson, General Manager

International Laser Machines

1242 West Lafayette Rd.

Indianapolis, IN 46268, USA

We are pleased to inform you that we have already received an invitation to the International Fair of 2015 which is to be held in New York City from May 2 to May 12. We would like to attend that Fair and would arrive in New York 2 days earlier than the Opening Ceremony of that Fair.

It would be also a great pleasure for us to get the opportunity of visiting the International Fair and discussing with you on our future joint venturing of our laser machines.

JOHN SMITH, SALES MANAGER

5. 简化式

现在使用简化式写信已很流行，因为在这种格式中，信件的所有部分都排列在左侧，使得打信速度加快；另外称呼和结尾敬语省略，使打信更简单。写信人的姓名用大写字体，放在正文最后一行下面第 4 行。

信件(6)

新加坡激光机公司

纳波路 92 号

新加坡 3806

2015 年 4 月 8 日

你方编号：******

我方编号：******

总经理汤姆森先生

国际激光机公司

美国印第安纳州拉法叶西路 1242 号(IN 46268)

我方有幸通知你方，我方已收到将于 5 月 2 日至 5 月 12 日在纽约市举行的 2015 年国际展览会的邀请函。我公司将参加该展览会，并在该交易会开幕式的前两天到达纽约。

若能获得机会出席该国际商品交易会，并和你方商讨双方合资经营激光机的事宜，将使我方甚感荣幸。

销售经理　约翰·史密斯

III. Ways of English Envelope Addressing and Their Standardized Designs

It is better for the first learners of English envelope addressing to design and arrange the envelope addressing according to the following procedures:

(1)　Use your pencil and ruler to divide the envelope into four equivalent quadrants with dotted lines according to the necessary number and length of the lines.

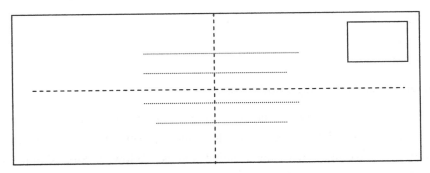

(2)　Fix the starting points and finishing points of each line properly according to the length of the address and to the lines in need to make your addressing well balanced and symmetrized (Note: Good balancing and symetrizing are very difficult to do well, so you must for the first step to practise with your pencil).

(3)　Address the envelope with your pencil firstly.

(4)　Trace in black or blue ink over the envelope words written with pencil after your feeling satisfied with your envelope addressing.

(5)　Brush away the pencil dotted line and pencil marks with your rubber.

(6)　When you address the envelope in American style, you must make sure which is the address of the sender and which is the address of the receiver. Don't make these two addresses transposed. In this way, your letter will not reach into your partner's hand.

三、信封书写的方法及信封的标准设计

初学书写信封者最好按照下列步骤设计和安排信封的书写：

(1) 用铅笔和尺子将信封分成等面积的四个部分，根据所需行数和长度用铅笔画出虚线线条。

(2) 根据地址长度及所需行数标好每行的起始点及结束点，使地址均衡匀称(注意均衡匀称较难做到，所以开始时最好用铅笔来实践)。

(3) 先用铅笔写地址。

(4) 在对所写的信封地址感到满意后，再在铅笔所写地址上用蓝色或黑色笔写出。

(5) 用橡皮将虚线及铅笔字迹擦掉。

(6) 在写美式信封地址时，必须确定收信人地址和发信人地址，不要将两个地址颠倒，以致收信人收不到信。

Ⅳ. The Styles of English Envelope Addressing

There are two styles of envelope addressing:

(1) The British style;

(2) The American style.

四、信封书写的种类

有两种书写信封的方法：

(1) 英式信封；

(2) 美式信封。

1. The British style envelope addressing

The receiver's address should be started 4 or 5 spaces to the left of the center of the envelope. The first line should be the name or title of the receiver. The second line is the name of the corporation or institution with the detailed address followed. First should come the number of the house, the name of the street or road, then appear the names of the city, the province, the state or country. If you must type five lines to finish your addressing, it is better for you to type two lines above the central line and the other three lines below it in order to pay a favorable and well-balanced impression to the others. In addition, if your address lines are long, start your lines more than 4 to 5 spaces to the left center of the envelope, and if your address lines are short, you can arrange your lines with less spaces to it. In addition, in English style the sender's address is written on the envelope flap.

You can design your envelope addressing both in indented style and in block style. If the address of the receiver is typed in indented style, the addressing style of the sender typed on the envelope flap should be kept in matching with that of the receiver.

British Envelope Addressing (1)——BLOCK STYLE

Mr. Walter Roberts
Sales Manager
Mid-West Import & Export Corporation
12 East Tenth Street
Chicago, IL 60687
United States of America

British Envelope Flap Addressing (1)

New Asia Inc.
38 Napier Road
Singapore 1025

British Envelope Addressing (2)——INDENTED STYLE

Mr. Zhang Zhongming

General Manager

China National Machinery Imp. & Exp. Corp.

Erligou, Haidian District, Post Code ****

Beijing, People's Republic of China

British Envelope Flap Addressing (2)

The Pakistan Trading Company
15 Broad Street
Karachi, Pakistan

1. 英式信封地址

英式信封是将收信人地址放在信封的正中央，把发信人的地址放在信封的封口上。英语学习者最好将信封用虚线分成等面积的四部分。用铅笔在信封上画出虚线，以便在写完信封后可以用橡皮擦掉虚线。

画有虚线的信封见英语虚线信封。

收信人的地址应从信封中央向左第四或第五个空格处开始写。第一行应为收信人的姓名或头衔，第二行是公司或机构的名称，后跟详细地址。首先写房间号码、街道名称，然后是城市、省、州以及国家。如果必须用五行写完地址，最好将第一、二行打在中线之上，第三、四、五行打在中线之下，以便给人一种匀称美观的效果。此外，如果地址行很长，可从信封中央向左 4～5 个以上的空格处写起。如果地址行较短，可以从信封中央向左少几个空格处起写。此外，发信人地址可以写在信封封口上。

可以用缩行式或齐头式设计信封。如果收信人地址用缩行式，那么封口上的发信人的地址书写时应该与收信人地址的书写格式一致。

英式信封地址(1)——齐头式 (译文略)

英式信封封口地址(1)(译文略)

英式信封地址(2)——缩行式 (译文略)

英式信封封口地址(2)(译文略)

2. The American Style Addressing

In using American style to type the envelope, you must type the sender's address on the upper left corners with the receiver's address typed a little lower than that of the English style.

Sometimes the name of the corporation or the institution is rather long and shifting to the next line to finish the addressing is necessary, then you must indent for two spaces in block style, see American Envelope Addressing (1); and four spaces in indented style, see American Envelope Addressing (2). This rule is as well applicable to the British envelope addressing.

American Envelope Addressing (1)——BLOCK STYLE

Billboard Inc.
999 Broadway
Metropolis, NY 11222, U.S.A.

　　　　Mr. Li Mingwei, General Manager
　　　　China National Light Industrial Products
　　　　　Import & Export Corporation
　　　　82, Donganmen Street
　　　　Beijing, ****, China**

American Envelope Addressing (2)——INDENTED STYLE

Billboard Inc.
999 Broadway
Metropolis, NY 11222, U.S.A.

Mr. Li Mingwei, General Manager
China National Light Industrial Products
Import & Export Corporation
82, Donganmen Street
Beijing, ******, China

---

2. 美式信封地址

美式信封必须将发信人地址放在信封的左上角，收信人的地址则应该比英式信封的收信人地址稍低一些。

有时公司或机构的名称相当长，必须移至下一行写完地址，那么用齐头式时必须缩进两格，参见美式信封地址(1)；用缩行式则必须缩进四格，参见美式信封地址(2)。这种缩行规则也适用于英式信封地址。

美式信封地址(1)——齐头式(译文略)

美式信封地址(2)——缩行式(译文略)

Exercises

Ⅰ. Use the letterhead and inside address which you designed in your exercises of Chapter One to write four short letters in different styles. If possible, type these letters with your computer. (用在第1章练习中设计的信头和信内地址写四封不同格式的短信函，并用电脑打印出来。)

Ⅱ. Design four styles of envelope addressing in the ways you learnt from your textbook and type them with your computer. (用教材中所学的方法，设计四个不同格式的信封，并用电脑打印出来。)

Chapter 3   Establishing Business Relations
建立业务关系

Learning Objectives:

- Master the ways of introducing your own company.
- Understand the necessity of praising the other companies for establishing good business relationship with them.
- Know various kinds of business relations in business world.

学习目标：

- 掌握介绍自己公司的方法。
- 理解为了与其他公司建立良好的业务关系而赞扬对方的必要性。
- 认识商界中的各种商务关系。

I . The Origin of Establishing Business Relations

In doing international trade, the tradesmen often face the problem of the long distance of thousands upon thousands of miles from the location of the importer's country to that of the exporter's. In this case, the country which needs to do international trade must at first establish its business relations with other countries.

Writing letters to the new customers with the aim of establishing business relations is the conventional activity of business communicating. It is a very important measure both for the newly-established corporations and for the old ones wishing to expand their business scope and their turnover to establish business relations with some prospective business institutions.

一、建立业务关系的理由

在国际贸易中，进口商的国家和出口商的国家往往相隔千万里，因此要进行国际贸易的国家之间必须首先建立业务关系。

写信给新客户以建立业务关系是商务通信中的常规活动，对于新成立的公司或希望扩大业务范围及营业额的公司而言，与一些有发展前景的商业机构建立业务关系是非常重要的举措。

II . The Channels of Establishing Business Relations

The importer and the exporter will find their channels of understanding each other as follows:

(1) Self-introduction or introduction carried on by friends.

(2) The banker's offering the name and address of the exporter.

(3) The chamber of commerce in every city and town of the western countries is the tradesmen's organizations. One of their duties is to get information and to seek new business opportunities for its members.

(4) The Commercial Councilor's Office subordinated to the Embassy of a certain country.

(5) The media of the newspapers, magazines and television.

(6) The commodity fairs, the international fairs and the exchangings of the business delegations.

二、建立业务关系的渠道

进口商和出口商了解彼此的渠道如下。

(1) 自我介绍或由朋友介绍。

(2) 由银行提供出口商的名称和地址。

(3) 西方国家每个城镇的商会是一个生意人的组织，其任务之一就是为其成员获取信息以及寻找新的商机。

(4) 各国大使馆下属的商务参赞处。

(5) 报纸、杂志、电视等媒体。

(6) 交易会、博览会及商务代表团的互访。

III. Learning Some Situations before Communicating with the Customers

The following situations of the new customers must be investigated before communicating with them:

(1) Financial affairs.

(2) Business activities, their business scope and their management capability.

(3) Business trustworthiness and credit.

(4) In writing such kinds of business letters, the tradesman usually makes self-introduction first or explains through whom he has got the information. Then he expresses his aim and intention of his writing the letter. At the same time he introduces the business scope, the items they are engaged in, the branch institutions and their trustworthiness and credit. In the necessity of importing products from them, put forward your requirements and ask them to send you samples, price list, catalogue, etc.

三、与客户沟通前熟悉情况

和新客户通信前要了解对方下列情况：

(1) 资金财务情况。

(2) 业务活动、业务范围及经营能力。

(3) 商务诚信。

(4) 书写商务信件时一般先进行自我介绍，或说明通过谁得到信息，然后说明写信的目的和意图，并介绍自己公司的业务范围、经营项目、分支机构、信用状况及信誉等。如果需从对方进口产品，则往往会提出要求，索取样品、价格单、产品目录等。

IV. Letter Examples

1. Establishing Import and Export Business Relations

Dear Sirs,

Re: Establishing Import and Export Business Relations

Your Commercial Councilor's Office has recommended you to us as a firm of good standing and reliability in the line of light industrial products and advised us that you are interested in establishing import and export business relations with other countries for marketing various light industrial products on the basis of equality and mutual benefit.

We have many years' experiences in foreign trading and the long established direct factory connections allow us to become the most competitive firm in our line.

In order to give you a general idea of our various kinds of commodities now available for export, we enclose here a brochure and a price list, from which you will know that our products are of high quality and our prices are the most competitive in the world. We are writing you in the hope of establishing business relations between us. We are expecting that you will send us your catalogues of the products available for export, your price-list, etc. Once we are in need of importing your products, we can contact you directly.

We are looking forward to receiving your early reply.

Yours faithfully,

四、信件实例

1. 建立进出口业务关系

关于：建立进出口业务关系

承蒙贵国商务参赞处向我公司介绍，贵公司的轻工业产品在行业中享有盛名、品质卓越，并告知我们，贵公司有意在平等互利的基础上和其他国家建立进出口业务关系，以经销各种轻工业产品。

我公司有多年从事外贸工作的经验，长期以来与生产厂家建立起来的直接关系使我们成为行业中最有竞争力的公司。

为了使贵公司对我公司现在可供出口的各种产品有一个全面的了解，在此附上一本小册子及一份价格单。从这些材料贵公司将会了解，我们的产品是高质量的，而我们的价格在世界上也最有竞争力。我们希望通过这封信建立起我们之间的业务关系，希望贵公司能寄来可供出口产品的目录、价格单等。一旦我公司需要进口贵公司的产品，即可进行直接联系。

盼望早日收到贵公司的回复。

Words and Expressions

recommend	*v.* 推荐，介绍
firm	*n.* 公司，商号
reliability	*n.* 可靠性
relationship/relation	*n.* 关系
equality	*n.* 平等
establish	*v.* 建立
connection	*n.* 联系
competitive	*a.* 有竞争力的
available	*a.* 可用的，可得到的
availability	可用性，效力
brochure	*n.* 小册子(法)，意同英语中的 pamphlet (小册子)，常用来介绍一种或一类商品
price list	价格单，价目表
look forward to	渴望，盼望
Commercial Councilor's Office	商务参赞处
light industrial products	轻工业产品
mutual benefit	互利
available power	可用功率
available fertilizer	有效肥料
available for export	可供出口

Notes

(1) recommend　*v.* 推荐，介绍

　　introduce　*v.* 介绍

　　introduction　*n.* 序言

　　recommendation　*n.* 推荐信，介绍信

(2) firm　商号，商店，公司

　　corporation　(美)公司，行会，商会

　　private(ly)-owned corporation　私有公司

　　nonprofit corporation　非营利公司

　　public corporation (state-operated corporation)国有公司

　　company　(英)公司，团体，协会

　　insurance company　保险公司

　　limited liability company　(股份)有限公司

(3) good standing　良好信誉

(4) advise　*v.* 劝告，通知，报告；to advise sb. of sth. 建议某人做某事

　　advice　*n.* 忠告，劝告，意见

　　inform　*v.* 通知，告知，报告；inform sb. of sth., inform sb. that…

(5) be interested in sth.　对……感兴趣，欲购

be interested in doing sth. 对做……事感兴趣

(6) on the basis of 在……的基础上

(7) experience in doing sth. 做某件事的经验

(8) enclose *v.* 附寄

enclosure *n.* 附件

We enclose here a catalogue. 我们在此附寄产品目录一份。

Enclosed please find our price list. 我方价格单现附寄于此，请查收。

该句原来的顺序应为 Please find our price list enclosed. 现在"enclosed"过去分词作宾语补足语，放在句首。

(9) in the hope of 希望，"of"后跟动名词

It is our hope that... 我们希望……

It is our hope that we can develop our national economy rapidly. 我们希望迅速发展我国的国民经济。

这是 it 句型的一种。it 为形式主语，hope 为名词，that 后为主语从句，作 it 的逻辑主语。

同类句型：It is our great pleasure that you can attend our party. 您能出席我们的宴会是我们极大的荣幸。

We hope that... 我们希望……

that 后为宾语从句

(10) look forward to，其中 to 为介词，后面跟名词或者动名词，不能将 to 视为动词不定式，不能用 look forward to do sth.。

2. Establishing Compensation Trade Relations

Dear Sirs,

<u>Re: Entering into Compensation Trade Relations</u>

We have noted from your letter of August 15 that you require our Model ×× Butterfly Sewing Machines and wish to pay for them with men's shirts processed under compensation trade arrangements. Subject to satisfactory arrangements as to terms and conditions, we would be pleased to conclude this transaction with you.

We can supply you ×× sets of Butterfly Sewing Machines Model ×× at the price of US $×× per set CIF EMP. The cost of these machines will be advanced by us and be repaid by you on installments, plus freight and interest at ××% per annum.

Would you please let us know your quotation for men's shirts, ×× dozen per month? Upon receipt of your firm offer, we would package these two deals and work out a draft agreement for you to consider.

Awaiting your quotation and your further suggestions.

Yours faithfully,

2. 建立补偿贸易关系

关于：建立补偿贸易关系

我方从你方 8 月 15 日的来函中获悉，你方需购我方××型蝴蝶牌缝纫机，并希望用你方加工的男式衬衫予以补偿货款。如果有关条款方面和条件令人满意，我方乐意与你方达成这笔交易。

我方可以按每台××美元(CIF，欧洲主要口岸到港的价格)，供应你方××型蝴蝶牌缝纫机××台。这些缝纫机的货款将由我方垫付，以后由贵公司以分期付款方式支付，外加运费及××%的年息。

能否请贵方告知男式衬衫每月××打的报价？收到贵方实盘报价后，我方将会把这两笔交易合成一揽，并草拟一份协议书供贵方斟酌。

我方等候你方报价以及进一步的建议。

Words and Expressions

compensation trade	补偿贸易
process	*v.* 加工
produce	*v.* 生产(轻工业产品)
manufacture	*v.* 制造(重工业产品)
install	*v.* 安装
arrangement	*n.* 布置，安排
conclude a transaction	达成交易(同 conclude a deal)
be subject to	以……为条件(The above offer is subject to our final confirmation. 上述报价以我方最后确认为准。)
EMP, European Main Ports	欧洲主要口岸
installment	*n.* 分期付款
quotation	*n.* 报价
repay	*v.* 偿还
upon receipt of	在收到之后
package	*v.* 把……打包，包装；把……作为整体推销
work out	设计出，制定出
draft	*n.* 草案，草图 *vt.* 起草
agreement	*n.* 协定，协议，协议书
contract	*n.* 合同(比 agreement 更完整，更具有法律效力)

Notes

(1) process *v.* 加工
produce *v.* 生产，一般指轻工业产品的生产
manufacture *v.* 制造，一般指重工业产品的制造

(2) EMP，European Main Ports 按照航运工会统一规定，EMP 包括意大利的热那亚(Genoa)，法国的马赛(Marseilles)，比利时的安特卫普(Antwerp)，荷兰的鹿特丹

(Rotterdam)，英国的伦敦(London)，德国的汉堡(Hamburg)，丹麦的哥本哈根 (Copenhagen)等港口。

(3) installment 亦可写为 instalment 分期付款；pay by installments 分期付款；monthly installments 按月分期付款。

buy sth. on installment plan 用分期付款办法购买……

(4) quotation　*n.* 报价，可以连用的动词有 make, send, give, fax

our quotation for… （卖方提出报价）

your quotation of （买方提及卖方报价）

例：

Please let us have your lowest price for computers. 请将你方计算机的最低报价报给我方。

Your quotation of computer is out of line with the prevailing market price. 你方计算机报价和当前市场价格不符。(意指价格偏高)

offer　*v. & n.* 报价，报盘

例：

Please offer us 500 bicycles CIF London. 请报给我方500辆自行车CIF伦敦的价格。

Please quote us your lowest price for 500 bicycles, CIF London. 请报给我方500辆自行车 CIF 伦敦的最低价格。

另外，quotation 指报某一商品的单价。

offer 指报盘，除单价外还要讲明数量、交货期、付款方式、检验方法以及报盘有效期等；成交就是接受对方的报盘，法律上应负有责任。现在一些国家常将这两个词混用。

(5) advance　*v.* 推进，促进，提出；预支，垫款，贷出款项

advance money to sb.　预先付钱给某人，贷款给某人

pay sb. an advance of £30 on his wages　预支给某人30英镑的周工资

pay an advance of 50% of the price　预付50%货款

advance bill　预支票据

advance freight　预付运费

advance deposit　预存款项

advances　预垫款

advances ratio　预支款率(指占银行总存款的比例)

3. Establishing Products Consigning Relations

Dear Sirs,

<u>Re: Establishing Products Consigning Relations</u>

On the recommendation of your Ambassador in Beijing, we have known that you are specialized in foreign product trading and are interested in expanding your business line to more countries and areas.

We are the largest distributor of household electrical appliances in China and we have at the same time enjoyed a wide popularity in the world market. In the hope of broadening our marketing fields with our successful business ability and sound financial standing, we are now venturing to write to you inquiring the possibility of selling our products in your country. We have been informed that your showrooms are well equipped and are situated in the business center of your capital. These showrooms are favorable for exhibiting and demonstrating various products and are as well admirable conditions for the prospective buyers to make quick decision of buying after seeing the appliance's being demonstrated. We wish to know if you agree to put some of our products on consignment in your Company and exhibit our sample appliances in your showroom for the prospective buyers to make trial orders.

As regards to your commission, our usual practice is as follows: 5% on net sales and the extra commission for delcredere is 2.5% as a reward to you. You can as well put some of your products on consignment in our Company.

We look forward to your reply.

Yours faithfully,

3. 建立产品寄售关系

关于：建立产品寄售关系

承蒙贵国驻京大使介绍，我公司获悉贵公司专营进口产品，并有意将业务范围扩展到更多的国家和地区。

我公司是中国最大的家电经销商，同时在世界市场上享有盛誉。我公司希望凭借我们卓有成效的经营能力和良好的财务信誉来扩大经销范围。现冒昧致函贵公司，咨询有无可能在贵国销售我方产品。我公司知道贵公司展览室设备精良，且位于贵国首都的商业中心。展览室极有利于展览陈列及操作表演各种产品，这是预购买主在观看电器展示后，很快作出购买决定的有利条件。我们希望知道贵公司是否能同意寄售一些我方产品，同时在展览室内展示我公司的样机，以便买主订购。

关于佣金，我们习惯的做法是销售净值的 5%，保付货价额外佣金的 2.5%作为回报。如你方愿意，亦可将你方一些产品放在我方寄售。

盼望贵公司回复。

Words and Expressions

ambassador	*n.* 大使
foreign product trade	进口产品贸易
expand	*v.* 扩大
distributor	*n.* 经销人，经销商
household electrical appliance	家用电器
popularity	*n.* 名望，普及，流行
broaden	*v.* 拓宽，扩大
financial	*a.* 金融的，财政的
venture	*v.* 冒险(venture to do sth. 冒险做某事)
enquire	*v.* 咨询
possibility	*n.* 可能性
favorable	*a.* 有利的，顺利的，赞成的

exhibit	v. 展览，陈列
demonstrate	v. 论证，表演，说明
admirable	a. 极妙的，令人钦佩的
prospective	a. 预期的，盼望中的
consign	v. 托运，委托
consign sth. to sb.	把……委托给……零售；寄存，托运
consignor	委托人，发货人，寄售人
consignee	受托人，收货人，承销人
	(同类用法的词有：interview 接见、会见，interviewer 接见者，interviewee 被接见者；employ 雇佣，employer 雇佣者，employee 雇员；以"or"或"er"结尾表示发出动作的人，以"ee"结尾表示收到动作的人。)
commission	n. 佣金
usual practice	习惯做法，惯例
delcredere	n. 保付货价
appliance	n. 应用，适用，用具，装置

Notes

(1) on the recommendation of   承蒙……介绍

(2) be specialized in doing sth.   专门从事……
be specialized in import(ing) and export(ing) business   专门从事进出口业务

(3) foreign product trade   外国产品的生意，即进口生意

(4)
A.   machine   机器(普通用语)
sewing machine   缝纫机
washing machine   洗衣机
machinery   机械(机器的总称，特指机器中的运转部分)
the machinery of a watch   表的运转部分；机械装置(如发动机)

B.   apparatus   器械，仪器(通指物理化学上所用的仪器)
apparatus for electric lighting   电器照明器械
heating apparatus   加热装置
appliance   适用，应用；用具，装置
office appliance   办公用具
medical appliance   医疗器械

(5) after the appliance's being demonstrated
after 后的"being demonstrated"为动名词的被动式，"appliance's"为上述动名词的逻辑主语。

(6) delcredere 保付货价，指寄销受托人按信贷条件售出商品，并担保买主付款，买

主如不付款，由其负责付款，代理人为此得到额外佣金，称为"extra commission for delcredere"或"delcredere commission."。

4. Establishing Sole Agency Relations

The meaning of sole agency: The ×× Corporation of ×× Country entrusts ×× Corporation or ×× Institution with the sole agency for the selling of ×× product in ×× City of ×× Country and sign Sole Agency Agreement. Generally all the purchases and sales in pursuance of this agreement will be on the sole agent's accounts and any loss or gain will be borne by the sole agent.

Dear Sirs，

Re: Sole Agency Agreement

After careful consultations and negotiations between your representative——Mr. ××, the general manager of ×× Corporation and our representative——Mr. ××, the President of our ×× Company, we have decided to entrust you with the sole agency for type ×× electronic computers in Northwest China. We are sending you two originals and two duplicates of the Sole Agency agreement, all with our signature. Please return to us one original and one duplicate with your countersignature for our file.

It is necessary for us to emphasize that all the purchases and sales in pursuance of this agreement will be on your account and any loss or gain will be borne by yourselves. We shall support you with favorable terms in respect of price, discount and payment according to the stipulations of the agreement.

We hope this agreement will make the sale of our products intensified in your market and the cooperation of our two sides developed rapidly.

Sincerely yours，

4. 建立独家代理关系

独家代理权的意义：某国的某公司将其某个产品在某国某个城市的独家经销代理权委托给某公司或机构，并签订独家代理协议。通常独家代理商自行购货、自行销售、自负盈亏。

关于：独家代理协议

经过你方代表——××公司总经理××先生与我方代表——××公司总裁××先生之间的认真协商和洽谈，我方决定将××型电子计算机在中国西北地区的独家经销代理权委托给你方。现将由我方签署的独家经销代理协议书正副本各两份寄上，请会签后将正副本各寄回一份，以供我方存档。

我方有必要强调，根据此协议，你方自行购货、自行销售、自负盈亏。我方将按照协议约定在价格、折扣、支付等方面给予你方一定的优惠。

希望这一协议能够使我方产品在你方市场的销售得以加强，并促进我们双方的合作迅速发展。

Words and Expressions

sole agency	独家代理
negotiation	*n.* 谈判，洽谈
vice president	副总裁
representative	*v.* 代表，代理人
entrust	*v.* 委托，信托
entrust power to sb.	把权利委托给某人
entrust sb. with a task	把一项任务交给某人
electronic computer	*n.* 电子计算机
original	*n.* 正本，原文；*a.* 最初的，原先的
duplicate	*n.* 副本，抄件；*a.* 复制的，完全一样的
	v. 成倍，成双
countersignature	*n.* 会签
file	*n.* 档案
emphasize	*v.* 强调
purchase	*n. & v.* 购买
pursuance	*n.* 追赶，追求；进行，实行，从事
account	*n.* 计算，账，账目
charge sth. on somebody's account	记入……的账
on one's own account	为自己的利益；自己负责，依靠自己
bear	*v.* (bear, bore, born / borne) 负担，承担
bear a heavy burden	重荷
bear the responsibility of	担负……责任
bear the expenses	负担费用
in respect of (to)	关于
stipulation	*n.* 规定
intensify	*v.* 加强，增强，强化
cooperation	*v.* 合作(co+operation 共同+经营=合作；corporation 公司，要注意两者拼写的不同之处)

Notes

(1) consultation　磋商，协商(专家等)会议
negotiation　谈判，洽谈，议妥；negotiate with sb. about sth. 与某人谈判(协商)某事
talk(正式)会谈，谈话，交谈，会议
talk with sb. on sth.　与……会谈……
discussion　讨论

(2) president　校长，院长，社长，主席(企业中，president 一般译为总裁)

(3) agent　代理人
agency　代理，代理权

　　　　sole agent　独家代理人

　　　　sole agency　独家代理权

　　　　sole distributor　独家经销代理人

　　　　sole distributorship　独家经销代理权

　　　　distributor　经销人

　　　　distributorship　经销权

(4)　duplicate　副本

　　　　in duplicate　一式两份

　　　　in triplicate　一式三份

　　　　in quadruplicate　一式四份

　　　　in quintuplicate　一式五份

　　　　in sextuplicate　一式六份

(5)　file　*n*. 文件夹，档案；*v*. 存档，归档；for our file　供我方存档

　　　例：

　　　Please file these letters. 请将这些文件存档。

(6)　pursuance　*n*. 追赶，追求；进行，实行

　　　　in pursuance of a plan (a resolution)　在执行计划(决议)时

　　　　pursuant (to) *a*.　追赶的，追求的；依据的，依照的

　　　　pursuant to the rules　按照规则

　　　　in pursuance of　按照……

(7)　stipulation　规定

　　　　rule　规则

　　　　law　法律

　　　　term　条款

　　　　condition　条件

(8)　countersignature: After one party puts signature on the file, the other party puts countersignature. After many times of negotiations and consultations between the two parties a certain transaction will be concluded and then signing of the agreement will be necessary. After all of the terms have been discussed and determined, the drafting of the contract will be entrusted to one of the two parties. After finalizing the contract drafting, the drafting party will make two copies of the contract and sign its name on both copies. Then these two copies will be sent to the other party and ask the other party to put its signature on them. Such kind of the contract signing is called counter signature. After counter signing, the second signer will send one of the signed contract copies to the drafting party and keep the other copy for its file. The signatures of both parties must be made by hand, then typed with electronic computer in order to make the signatures both clear and right.

　　会签：表示一方先签名(signature)，另一方会同再签。双方经多次协商会谈，确定达成某个交易后要签订协议，双方讨论好条款以后委托一方起草合同，定稿后起草一方将合同一式两份先签上自己一方的名字，然后将两份都寄给对方，让对方也签字，这个过程就是

会签。会签以后，后签名的一方退回一份给对方，自己留下一份存档。双方签名时均须先手签，后用电脑打上名字，使签字清晰无误。

5. Establishing Bartering Relations

Dear Sirs,

Re: Establishing Bartering Relations

We are one of the most famous exporters of Chinese textiles and have enjoyed great popularity in the world market.

As a reliable customer of our Corporation you have imported great quantities of textiles from us for many years. Owing to the growing demand for textiles, we are now involved in the trouble of lacking raw materials. At the same time, we wish to expand the trade between us. So we are writing to you to inquire the possibility of your exporting us a certain quantity of raw materials in the way of bartering against your order for textiles. It is not necessary that your purchase of textiles be equal in value to the raw materials to be supplied to us. The ratio may be settled through negotiations.

In case of your agreeing to do this barter trade with us, our producing ability to export textiles will be increased and, in turn, your financial pressure in importing our textiles will be lightened. So we are confident that our barter trade will contribute to the expanding of the trade between us.

Hoping to be favored with your cooperation.

Yours faithfully,

5. 建立易货关系

关于：建立易货关系

我公司是中国纺织品最有名的出口商之一，并且在世界市场上享有盛誉。

作为我公司一位可靠的顾客，多年来贵公司从我公司进口了大量纺织品。由于对纺织品的需求量不断增大，我方现在陷入缺少原材料的困境之中。同时，我方希望扩大双方的贸易，因此我方致信贵公司，询问贵公司的纺织品订货，能否以易货贸易的方式出口给我公司一定数量的原材料。贵公司购买纺织品的价值不必与供应给我公司的原材料的价值对等，其比率可通过洽谈确定。

如果贵公司同意和我方进行易货贸易，我公司生产出口纺织品的能力将会提高，相应地，贵公司进口我公司纺织品的财政压力也会缓解。因此，我公司相信我们之间的易货贸易将有利于扩大双方的贸易量。

希望贵公司同意合作。

Words and Expressions

barter	v. & n. 易货贸易
reliable	a. 可靠的
textile	n. 纺织品

ratio	*n.* 比率(in the ratio of 5 to 7，比率为 5 比 7)
settle	*v.* 确定，决定，安排
financial	*a.* 财政的，金融的
lighten	*v.* 减轻，减轻负荷，缓解
confident	*a.* 相信的
favorable	*a.* 赞成的，有利的，赢得赞同的
owing to	由于
in case of	如果

Notes

(1) barter 易货 barter trade/ barter deal 易货贸易

barter transaction terms 易货交易条件

(2) owing to 由于

例：

Owing to our joint efforts, we have overfulfilled our task. 由于我们的共同努力，我们超额完成了任务。

(3) be involved in 被卷入，陷入(常用被动语态)

例：

We have been involved in great financial trouble. 我们一直陷入巨大的融资困难中。

Building this highway involves the construction of ten bridges. 铺设这条公路包括建造十座桥梁。

(4) lack *n. & v.* 缺少

例：

His writing shows lack of logic. 他的文章缺少逻辑性。

We must overcome the lack of technical knowledge. 我们必须克服技术知识的不足。

(5) purchase *v.* 购买，买入，获得

例：

They purchased liberty with their blood. 他们以流血为代价获得自由。

purchase 比 buy 更为正式，用在比较重要的场合。buy 比 purchase 普通，意味较广。buy 侧重于消耗金钱，purchase 侧重于物质的获得。

This house was purchased as public property. 这所房子是作为公共财产购得的。

(6) be equal to 相等的，均匀的

例：

One *li* is equal to half a kilometer. 一里等于 500m(半公里)。

equal pay for equal work 同工同酬

例：

He is equal to doing any trial. 他经得起任何考验。

He is equal to doing this task. 他胜任这项任务。

(7) contribute　*v.* 贡献出

例：

Everyone is called on to contribute ideas. 要求人人出主意。

The exchange of goodwill missions greatly contributes to a better understanding between the two countries. 互派友好代表团对两国之间的相互了解大有帮助。

Sentences for Business Relations 业务关系中常用的句子

(1) In doing business with the customers from various parts of the world, we always adhere to the principle of equality, mutual benefits and the exchange of needed goods, thus, by joint efforts, to promote both business and friendship to our mutual advantage.

我们与世界各地顾客进行的贸易都遵循平等互利、互通有无的原则，并通过双方的共同努力促进业务，增进友谊。

(2) We have established ourselves as an exporter for the sale of the goods produced or manufactured in Shanghai.

我公司已成为经销在上海生产和制造的商品的出口商。

(3) Our handicrafts have met with a favorable reception both at home and abroad.

我们的手工产品在国内外广受欢迎。

(4) Thank you in advance for your friendly cooperation and assistance.

对贵公司的友好合作与帮助我方预表谢意。

(5) We enclose here a list of our import and export items for you as a reference.

我方在此随函附寄我方进出口产品的清单一份，供贵方参考。

(6) It will be very much appreciated if you will kindly introduce us to some reliable firms or organizations, with whom we could establish business relationship.

如蒙贵方介绍与可信赖的商号或机构建立业务关系，我方将不胜感激。

(7) Having had your name and address from the U.S. consulate in Guangzhou, as a prospective seller of Chinese bicycles, we avail ourselves of this opportunity to write to you and see if we can establish business relations with you.

从美国驻广州领事馆得知贵公司的名称和地址，作为中国自行车有前途的销售商，我方现借此机会致函贵公司，以与贵公司建立业务关系。

(8) Through the courtesy of the Chamber of Commerce in Beijing, China, we have learned that you are the leading exporter in the line of electronic computers in Europe.

通过中国北京商会的介绍，我们获悉你们是欧洲电子计算机行业的主要出口商。

(9) Thank you for your letter of May 15, expressing interest in establishing business relations. As requested, we are sending you separately our illustrated catalogues and latest price list of our highest quality electronic products.

感谢贵方 5 月 15 日表示希望建立业务关系的来函。应贵方要求，我方将另寄函给贵方带插图的产品目录及质量最高的电子产品的最新价格单。

(10) We are confident that a beneficial and friendly relationship can be established between our two companies.

我们相信双方公司之间将能够建立起互利友好的关系。

(11) The Ambassador of your Embassy in China Mr. ×× has conveyed to us your desire and proposal of establishing business relations with foreign trade corporations of China.

贵方驻中国大使馆大使××先生已经将贵方与中国外贸公司建立业务关系的愿望和提议转达我方。

(12) We shall be greatly obliged if you give us detailed information of the financial status of that corporation and the general reputation they enjoy among your neighbors and correspondents.

请详告该公司的经济状况及其在往来客户中的声誉，非常感谢。

(13) We have reached an agreement on the rights and obligations, mode of doing business and other terms and conditions for appointing you as our sole distributor for ×× (products) in ×× (area).

我们已就委任贵方为我方在××(地区)经销××(产品)的独家代理的权利和义务、具体做法以及其他条款、条件达成了协议。

(14) We shall act as your sole agent for a trial period of 12 months, commencing from April 1st.

我们将成为贵公司的独家代理，代理预期为 12 个月，从 4 月 1 日开始算起。

(15) We can provide you on request first-class references, but for general information concerning our standing in the trade we suggest you refer to the Bank of London.

如果贵方需要，我方可提供第一流的参考资料，如果要了解我方商业信誉的基本情况，我方建议贵方向伦敦银行查询。

Exercises

I. Translate the following sentences from English into Chinese.

1. We wish to establish business relations with you on the basis of equality and mutual benefit.
2. We know that you have already been engaged in the trading of textiles for more than 10 years.
3. We are pleased to know that you require our children bicycles in a large quantity.
4. We are interested in expanding our business relations with you and in concluding more transactions with you.
5. You have been enjoying a wide popularity in the world market.

II. Translate the following sentences from Chinese into English.

1. 我们的合作一定会日益加强。
2. 我们必须认真协商洽谈。
3. 我们已决定委托你方在中国独家代理××产品。
4. 如果你方同意与我方达成补偿贸易协议，我方将十分高兴。
5. 我方希望在贵公司寄售一些我公司的产品。

Chapter 4　Inquiry, Offer and Counter-offer
询盘、报盘及还盘

Learning Objectives:

- Master the ways of making inquiry, offer and counter-offer.
- Identify the difference between a firm offer and a non-firm offer.
- Know the ways of writing letters of inquiry and counter-offer.
- Understand the importance of weighing advantages and disadvantages in business world.

学习目标：

- 掌握询盘、报盘、还盘的方法。
- 区别实盘报盘与虚盘报盘的不同之处。
- 了解写作询盘与还盘信函的方法。
- 理解在商界权衡利弊的重要性。

In business negotiations there are four key links: inquiry, offer, counter-offer and acceptance.

商务谈判中的四个主要环节分别为询盘、报盘、还盘和接受。

Ⅰ. Inquiry

Inquiry is the first step in business negotiations and is the beginning of negotiating the import trade. The inquiry letter is written by the importer to the exporter for grasping the detailed information on specific commodities, especially on prices and the trade terms. The inquiry letters must be written directly and concretely.

一、询盘

询盘是商务谈判的第一步，是商谈进口贸易的开端，是进口商了解具体商品的详细信息，尤其是价格信息以及交易条件，而向出口商发出的书信。询盘信应直接、具体。

1.　The procedures and principles in writing an inquiry letter

(1) Tell your receiver the source of the information you have got for making inquiry at the beginning of the letter.

(2) Introduce your identification and the products you are engaged in.

(3) Tell them concretely the contents you want to know and ask them to send you

catalogue, price list, samples, etc.

(4) Write the inquiring letter politely, briefly and concretely. But there is no need for excessive politeness.

1.　书写询盘信时应遵循的步骤与原则

(1) 信的开头应告诉收信人进行询盘的信息来源，从何处得知对方公司的名称及产品。

(2) 介绍自己的身份及经营的产品。

(3) 具体说明所询问的内容，以及要求对方寄送产品目录、价格单及样品等。

(4) 询盘信必须礼貌、简短、具体，但不必过分客套。

2.　The contents of an inquiry letter

An inquiry letter generally consists of the following contents:

(1) Tell them the name of the commodity which you inquire for and its specifications, quality, available quantity, price, way of delivery, date of shipment, terms of payment, etc.

(2) Request directly for their catalogue, price list and samples.

(3) Introduce briefly your market situation and emphasize your desire for the reasonable and competitive prices which they will offer.

(4) Inquire upon the discount the exporter may offer and inform them your desired terms of payment and the way of delivery.

(5) Inform them of the possibility of your making order for drawing their interest and attention.

2.　询盘信的内容

询盘信通常包括以下内容：

(1) 所询问商品的名称以及规格、质量、可供数量、价格、交货方式、装运日期、付款方式等。

(2) 直接索取所需要商品的目录、价格单和样品。

(3) 简单介绍你方市场情况，强调报价要合理、要有竞争力。

(4) 询问出口人可提供的折扣，说明你方所希望的支付条件及交货方式。

(5) 表明你方订货的可能性，以引起对方的兴趣和重视。

3.　Example

Dear Sirs,

<u>Re: Inquiry About the Price of Cotton Embroidered Dresses</u>

Your Chinese textiles have won great popularity in the world, especially cotton embroidered dresses, for which there has always been active demand in Europe. We are now very glad to inform you that we are as well in the market for these commodities. We would very much appreciate it if you can make us your best offer on CIF London basis for ×× dozen Cotton Embroidered Dresses. It is necessary to emphasize that the cloth you will use for making these dresses must be specially treated to prevent shrinkage and the color of the cloth must not fade.

For your information, if your price is competitive and the quality of the commodities and the delivery date can meet our requirements, we believe that we would place regular orders with you.

We wish to receive your dress samples and your offer as soon as possible.

Sincerely yours,

3. 实例

关于：询问棉制绣花女装的价格

中国产纺织品在世界上甚受欢迎，尤其是棉制绣花女装，欧洲对此的需求量一直很大。我方现在很高兴地通知你方，我方现在想购买这种商品。如果贵公司能给我方报来××打棉制绣花女装 CIF 伦敦到岸的最低价，我公司将十分感谢。另外必须强调，贵公司用来制作女装的布料必须进行特别处理，以防止缩水，而且布料不能褪色。

兹告知贵公司，如果贵公司的价格富有竞争性，供货质量优良，交货日期又能满足我方的要求，我公司将会向贵公司定期订货。

希望尽快收到贵公司的女装样品和报价。

Words and Expressions

inquiry	*n.* 询问，询盘(*v.* inquire)
quotation	*n.* 报盘 (*v.* quote)
counter-offer	*n.* & *v.* 还盘
dress	*n.* 女服，童装；(统指)服装，礼服；evening dress 晚礼服
commodity	*n.* 商品
appreciate	*n.* 欣赏，感谢，意识到
appreciation	*n.* 欣赏，赏识
appreciative	*a.* 有欣赏力的，感谢的(be appreciative of)
treat	*v.* 处理，对待，治疗(*n.* treatment)
shrink	*v.* 缩水(*n.* shrinkage；同类词：*v.* leak 漏水 *n.* leakage)
link	*v.* 联系，连接(*n.* linkage 联动装置，联系)
fade	*v.* 褪色，凋谢
delivery	*n.* 交货
deliver	*v.* 交付，给予(打击)
regular	*a.* 定期的，常规的，规则的
embroider	*v.* 绣花 (*n.* embroidery)
in the market for	欲购

Notes

(1) commodity　商品

　　thing　事物，用品，事情

　　article　物件，物品；文章，论文；项目，条款；冠词

goods　货物

shipment　装载的货物，发运的货物

consignment　寄售、寄存、托运的货物

(2)　dress　*n.* 女服，童装，齐膝女衣

cloth　布 (仅用作单数)

clothe　*v.* 给……穿衣

clothing　衣着(包括帽子、围巾、鞋子等)

suit　一套衣服

(3)　appreciate　*v.* 感谢，感激(可接动名词或不定式)

例：

We highly appreciate your cooperation. 我方十分感谢你方的合作。

We shall appreciate your giving this matter your prompt attention. 我方对你方立即处理此事将十分感激。

We shall appreciate it if you will give your great help in solving this problem. 贵方如能在解决此问题方面给予大力协助，我方将不胜感激。

It will be highly appreciated if you will immediately send us your list of available products for export. 贵方如能立即寄来你方可供出口的产品目录，我方将不胜感激。

We are appreciative of your prompt attention to this matter. 如贵方立即办理此事，我方深表感激。

(4)　delivery　*n.* 交付，交货(delivery date 交货期)

cash on delivery　货到付款(缩写 C.O.D.)

delivery book　交货簿，送货簿

delivery order　交货单，出货单，栈单

delivery port　交货港

delivery receipt　送货(件)回执

deliver　*v.* 交付，投递

deliver a message　送信

deliver a speech　发表讲话

deliver the goods　交货

ship　*v.* 装船，装运，运送(动名词 shipping)

shipment　*n.* 装货，装船，运送；装运的货物

shipment request　装运申请书

shipping advice　装运通知(系出口商发给进口商)

shipping instructions　装运须知，装运指示(系进口商发给出口商)

(5)　for your information　供你方参考

该短语可缩写为 FYI。

Ⅱ. Offer

Offer is the price of making transaction of a certain product offered by the exporter according to some given trading terms. The person making the offer is called "offeror", while the person receiving the offer is called "offeree".

二、报盘

报盘也叫发盘、发价或报价。报盘是出口商将某种产品按一定的交易条件向进口商报出的成交价格。发出报盘的人称为报盘人,接受报盘的人称为受盘人。

1. The contents of an offer letter

(1) Expressing your thankfulness for the letter, fax, mail, etc. you have received.

(2) Informing them of your having sent out the requested catalogue, price list, etc.

(3) Informing them of the detailed conditions about the supplied commodities, and introducing their merits and characteristics.

(4) Emphasizing your desire of the reasonableness and competitiveness of the offered price.

(5) Informing them of the terms of price, discount, commission and payment.

(6) Informing them of your ways of packing and date of delivery.

(7) Informing them of the validity of the offer (i.e. firm offer).

(8) Expressing your sincere expectation of receiving their orders.

1. 报盘信的内容

(1) 提及已收到函件、传真及电子邮件等,并表示感谢。

(2) 通知所索取的商品目录及价格单等已寄出。

(3) 提供所供商品的详细情况,介绍该商品的优点和特性。

(4) 强调所报价格的合理性及具有竞争性。

(5) 说明价格条款、折扣、佣金条件、付款条件等。

(6) 提供包装方式及交货日。

(7) 说明报盘(指实盘报盘)的有效期(如实盘)。

(8) 表达对收到对方订单的热切期望。

The firm offer sent by the offeror has got its stipulation of validity term. The firm offer can not be changed or withdrawn. Once the offeree accepts the firm offer, the transaction will be concluded. When the validity term is overdue, this offer will cease to be effective and the offeror will no longer take the responsibility of carrying out the commitments stipulated in the offer. At this time, even if the offeree wishes to accept the original firm offer, the offeror has the right of declining to close the deal. Moreover, the validity term of the offer is subject to the time when the offeror receives the offeree's answer, not to the time when the offeree sends out his or her reply. For example:

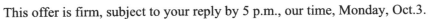

This offer is firm, subject to your reply by 5 p.m., our time, Monday, Oct.3.

In this kind of sentence, the name of the weekday must be mentioned together with the date.

实盘指发盘人所发的规定有效期的盘。在有效期内，实盘不能更改或撤销，受盘人一旦接受，交易即可达成。待有效期一过，此报盘即失效，发盘人不再承担报盘中规定的义务，此时受盘人即使想接受，发盘人也有权拒绝成交。另外，发盘中的有效期是以报盘人收到受盘人答复的时间为准，而不是以受盘人发出接受的时间为准。例如：

该盘为实盘，以 10 月 3 日星期一我方当地时间下午 5 点前收到你方答复为准。

此类句子中提到日期时也应提到星期。

2. Example

Dear Sirs,

<u>Re: Firm Offer for Cotton Embroidered Dresses</u>

Thank you very much for your inquiry dated May 15. We were very glad to receive your inquiry for embroidered dresses and to give you the following reply.

Recently we have received a lot of orders from the customers of various parts of the world. These heavy commitments have made us burdened with production tasks. But since you are a famous reliable corporation in North Europe, we would like very much to deal with you for expanding our trade businesses in the North European areas. As requested, we are airmailing you tomorrow a parcel of dress samples and a sample book of our materials used for making the clothes, from which you will get an understanding of the high quality of our materials and our excellent workmanship. We believe these dress samples and cloth sample book will help you in making both your selection and your decision.

Now we would like to give you our firm offer as follows, subject to your reply reaching us by the end of this month.

Name of Commodity	Style No.	Size	Quantity(Dozen)	Unit Price (per Dozen) CIF London
Cotton Embroidered Dresses	××	Small	××	US $ ×××
		Medium	××	US $ ×××
		Large	××	US $ ×××
	××	Small	××	US $ ×××
		Medium	××	US $ ×××
		Large	××	US $ ×××
	××	Small	××	US $ ×××
		Medium	××	US $ ×××
		Large	××	US $ ×××

Packing: Each piece to a plastic bag, half dozen to a carton and 10 dozen to a wooden case.

Shipment: 2 months after receiving the order.

Payment: By confirmed, irrevocable letter of credit in our favor by draft at sight to reach us one month before shipment and remain valid for negotiation in China till the 15th day after shipment.

Your early order will be appreciated.

Sincerely yours,

2. 实例

<u>关于：棉制绣花女装的实盘报盘</u>

非常感激贵公司5月15日的询盘。我公司非常高兴收到贵公司对绣花女装的询盘，现回复如下。

最近我公司收到许多来自世界各地的订单，数量巨大的订单使我们担负了更多的生产任务。但由于贵公司是北欧信誉可靠的公司，我公司很愿意和贵公司进行交易，以扩展我公司在北欧地区的贸易。按照贵公司的要求，明天我公司将空运一个女装样品邮包以及制衣衣料的样品簿，贵公司从中可以了解我公司衣料的高质量和精良的做工。我们相信这些样品及布样簿会有助于贵公司作出选择和决策。

向贵公司的实盘报盘如下，以贵公司在本月末以前到达我方的回复为准。

商品名称	样式编号	尺　寸	数量(打)	单价(每打) CIF　伦敦
棉制绣花服装	××	小	××	US $ ×××
		中	××	US $ ×××
		大	××	US $ ×××
	××	小	××	US $ ×××
		中	××	US $ ×××
		大	××	US $ ×××
	××	小	××	US $ ×××
		中	××	US $ ×××
		大	××	US $ ×××

包装：每件装一塑料袋，半打装一纸箱，10打装一木箱。

装运：收到订单后的两个月内。

付款：以保兑的、不可取消的、我方为受益人的即期信用证支付。信用证必须在装船一个月前到达我方。装船后15天在中国议付有效。

如蒙早日订货，将不胜感激。

Words and Expressions

as requested	可看成 as you requested 也相当于 as we were requested…
airmail	*v.* 空邮，航寄
parcel	*n.* 邮包，包裹
understanding	*n.* 理解，谅解
excellent	*a.* 卓越的
workmanship	*n.* 工艺
reach	*v.* 到达
select	*v.* 选择
decide	*v.* 决定

carton	*n.* 硬纸板箱
confirmed	*a.* 保兑的
irrevocable	*a.* 不可转让的
draft	*n.* 草图，草案；支取(款项)，汇票
valid	*a.* 有效的
plastic bag	*n.* 塑料袋
wooden case	木箱
letter of credit	信用证，缩写为 L/C
in our favor	以我方为收益人

Notes

(1) firm offer　实盘，确盘(不能还价，而且有时间限制)

non-firm offer　虚盘(可以还价)

an offer without engagement　无约束性报盘，意为虚盘

a combined offer　联合报盘，两种或两种以上的商品同时报盘

a free offer　自由报盘，可随时撤回，意义与 non-firm offer 相同

(2) commit　*v.* 犯(错误，罪行)，干(坏事，傻事)

commit this matter to Board of Directors　把此事提交董事会处理

commitment　*n.* 交托，承担义务；(商业上)约定

heavy commitment　承约很多

(3) burden　*n. & v.* 担子，负担；责任，业务

例：

We are burdened with heavy taxation. 我们被沉重的税收压身。

be burdened with tasks　担负一些工作

(4) deal　*v.* 处理，做生意

deal with　做买卖，处置，安排；deal in　经营

deal properly with all kinds of situations　恰当地应付各种局面

deals　*n.* 买卖，交易

(5) expand　*v.* 扩大，膨胀(*n.* expansion)

expand reproduction　扩大再生产

expand industry　发展工业

(6) sample book　样品簿

cloth sample book　布样簿

布样簿由各种花样、图案、质地、颜色的小块剪样(sample cuttings)装订成本，上面注明商品号码后寄给客户选购。纸张也可装订成纸样簿，但有棱有角的东西不能装成册。

(7) be subject to　以……为条件，可以……的，有待于……的

例：

This plan is subject to your approval. 此计划有待你方批准。

This offer is firm, subject to your reply reaching us here by the end of this month. 此报盘为实盘，以本月末前到达我方的答复为准。

We make you the following offer, subject to the goods being unsold. 我方向你方报盘，以货物未予售出为准。（"being unsold"为动名词的被动结构，"goods"为"being unsold"的逻辑主语，作 subject to 的宾语。）

Our quotation is subject to 5% commission. 我方报价内容包括5%的佣金。

The schedule is subject to change without notice. 本时间表可以随时修改，不另行通知。

(8) remain valid for negotiation 议付有效

III. Non-firm Offer

The non-firm offer is an informal offer made by the offeror, which has got no validity term, but with a clear indication of its confirmation conditions, such as:

subject to our final confirmation

subject to the goods' being unsold.

Therefore, the non-firm offer is actually the same as the offer with no indication of validity term.

Example

Dear Sirs,

<u>Re: Non-firm Offer for Know-how Transferring</u>

In reply to your letter of August 8, we are pleased to know that you are taking great interest in our Preliminary Proposal on the transfer of our know-how for manufacturing cables with an indication price of US $ ×××.

In case of your careful study of the terms and conditions of this proposal, you will find that our charges for engineering design and technical assistance in the supervision of installation, performance test, etc. are rather low, especially lower than the quotations from Japan and America.

On request, a detailed offer with separate prices for the know-how, the training of your technical personnel and as well terms of payment, etc. will be available. This offer is non-firm, without engagement, and price negotiating is still remaining within the bounds of possibility.

We look forward to hearing from you soon.

Truly yours,

三、虚盘

虚盘是发盘人做出的非正式报盘，没有有效期限，但常常注明其确认的条件，如：
subject to our final confirmation   以我方最后确认为准
subject to the goods' being unsold   以货物未售为有效
所以，虚盘和不列明有效期限的报价相同。

实例：

关于：技术转让的虚盘报盘

兹回复贵方 8 月 8 日来函，我们很高兴地了解到贵方对我方以×××美元的参考价格转让生产电缆技术的初步建议甚感兴趣。

如果仔细研究这一建议的条款和条件，贵公司将会发现我们对工程设计及安装指导、性能试验等方面的技术援助的开价还是相当低的，尤其低于日本和美国的报价。

至于技术的各项单列的详细报价、贵方技术人员的培训费用以及其他付款条件等，如果贵方需要，亦可提供。此报盘为虚盘，无约束性，可以进行价格协商。

我方希望尽快听到贵方的消息。

Words and Expressions

know- how	专门技能；(技术、知识)生产经验，体验；技术情报(秘密)
transfer	v. 转移，传输，转让，职务调动，过户(月发票)，汇兑，电汇
cable	n. 电报，电缆 v. 打电报
indication	预示，象征，指示
charge	n. 费用 v. 要价，收费
supervision	n. supervise v. 监督，管理；指导
supervisor	监督人，主管人，督学
performance	n. 履行；行为，行动；演出，表演；性能，特性
personnel	n. 全体人员
payment	n. 支付，付款
engagement	n. 约束，保证
negotiate	v. 协商，谈判
negotiation	n. 协商，谈判
preliminary proposal	初步建议
in reply to	为答复……
transfer from a train to a bus	从乘火车转乘公共汽车
telegraphic transfer	电汇
mail transfer	信汇
indication price	参考价
engineering design	工程设计
technical assistance	技术援助
engineering and technical personnel	工程技术人员

Notes

(1) in case of　假如，万一
in no case of　决不
例：
In no case should erroneous ideas be allowed to spread unchecked. 决不能让错误思想自由泛滥。
In case of fire, sing the alarm bell. 如遇火警，即按警铃。

(2) charge　*v.* 装填，充满
charge a battery　为蓄电池充电
charge oneself with task　承担任务
charge the seller with failure to effect the shipment　指责卖方未能发货
charge the purchases to sb's account　把所购货物记在某人账上，把……记入某人账户
charge　*n.* 费用，价钱　hotel charges 旅馆费用　free of charge 免费

(3) on request　在需要时
例：
The experts came to our college to give lectures at our request. 专家们应我们的邀请来我院讲课。
Catalogues will be mailed on request. 产品目录承索即寄。
References are available on request. 证明人承索即可提供。

(4) detailed offer　详细报价
separate price　单项价格，单列价格
detailed offer with separate price　单列项目的详细报价

IV. Counter-offer

Counter-offer is the response or reply of the offeree to the offeror during negotiations for signing the contract. There are two kinds of replies, one of which is favourable for its showing the offeree's acceptance, and the other is unfavorable for its showing the acceptance of the offeree together with the suggestions of some additions, restrictions or amendments. The latter kind of reply is called counter-offer.

四、还盘

还盘是合同谈判期间，受盘人对报盘人提供的报盘作出的反应或答复。这种答复有两种：一种是有利答复，即表示受盘人接受；另一种是不利答复，即受盘人虽然表示接受，但建议进行添加、限制或更改。后一种答复即构成还盘。

1. The counter-offer letter

Generally a counter-offer letter consists of the following five parts:

(1) Expressing thankfulness to the offeror.

(2) Expressing regretfulness to the offeror for not being able to accept the offer.

(3)　Indicating the reason for not accepting the offer.

(4)　Making counter-offer.

(5)　Urging the offeror to accept your counter-offer.

Once the offeree puts forward some different ideas, requests or suggestions on some terms of the offer, the original offer will lose its effectiveness promptly and the transactions must be begun on the basis of counter-offer. If later on when the fluctuation of the international market or the change of the foreign exchange rate become advantageous to the importer, the importer will be willing to accept the original offer. The exporter may consider his own special situations, weigh the advantages and disadvantages and then come to a decision of whether to accept or not.

1.　还盘信

通常还盘信包括以下五个部分的内容：

(1)　对报盘人表示感谢。

(2)　对不能接受报盘表示遗憾。

(3)　说明不能接受报盘的理由。

(4)　进行还盘。

(5)　敦促报盘人接受还盘。

一旦受盘人对报盘中的某些条款提出不同意见、要求或建议，原报盘即刻失效，交易要在还盘的基础上重新开始。倘若过后进口商因国际市场的行情波动或外汇兑换率对自己有利而又表示愿意接受原报盘，出口商可以根据具体情况权衡利弊，决定接受与否。

2. Example

Dear Sirs,

<u>Re: Counter-offer for 5,000m/t Steel Plates Type ×××</u>

We are in receipt of your letter April 10, offering us 5,000 metric tons of Steel Plates Type ××× at US $ ××× per m/t, CIF EMP.

In reply, we feel regrettable to inform you that our end-users have found your price too high and out of line with the prevailing market level.

Such being the case, it is impossible for us to persuade them to accept your price, as the goods of similar quality is easily obtainable here at a lower price. Some dealers from the European market are lowering their prices to about US $ ××× per m/t. No doubt there is keen competition in the international market.

We do not deny that the quality of your steel plates is slightly higher, but the difference in price should, in no case, be as big as 3%. To develop our trade, we, on behalf of our end-users, make counter-offer as follows:

5,000 metric tons of Steel Plates Type ××× at US $ ××× per metric ton, CIF EMP with other terms as per your letter April 10.

We are anticipating your early acceptance of our counter-offer.

Sincerely yours，

2. 实例

关于：5000 公吨×××型钢板的还盘

贵方 4 月 10 日的来函已收悉，该函对我方 5000 公吨×××型钢板的报盘为 CIF 欧洲主要港口到岸，每公吨×××美元。

兹回复，我方很遗憾地通知贵方，我公司本地用户发现贵方价格太高，并与当前市场水平不一致。

情况既然如此，我方不可能劝说用户接受你方价格，因为相近质量的货物可以在这里以较低的价格买到。来自欧洲市场的一些商家正在降低他们每公吨的价格至×××美元左右。无疑，国际市场上的竞争还是很激烈的。

我方并不否认贵方钢板的质量较高，但无论如何价格差不能达到 3%。为了发展双方的贸易，我方代表本地用户还盘如下：

5000 公吨×××型钢板 CIF 欧洲主要港口到岸每公吨×××美元，其他条件仍依据贵公司 4 月 10 日的来函。

盼望贵公司早日接受我方还盘。

Words and expressions

regrettable	*a.*	令人遗憾的，可惜的，不幸的
end-user	*n.*	用户
persuade	*v.*	劝说(persuade sb. to do sth.)
accept	*v.*	接受(*n.* acceptance)
obtainable	*a.*	可获得的，可买到的
dealer	*n.*	商人
lower	*v.*	降低
keen	*a.*	剧烈的
competition	*n.*	竞争
international market		国际市场
in no case		无论如何
on behalf of		代表
in receipt of		已收到
in reply		兹复，兹回复
steel plate		钢板
out of line		不一致，不符
prevailing market		现有市场
no doubt		无疑

Notes

(1)　out of line (with)　和……不一致(不符)

　　　to be in line with　与……一致，与……相符

　　　to keep in line with　与……保持一致，与……相符

(2) such being the case 情况既然这样

这是含系表倒装的独立分词结构。being 为 be 的现在分词，such 为 being 的表语，此处系表倒装。being such 为分词的正序的系表结构，the case 为 being such 的逻辑主语。由于整个句子的主语是"it"，being such 的逻辑主语不是"it"，有它自己的逻辑主语 the case。带有逻辑主语的分词结构即为独立分词结构。这里把表语"such"提前。类似承上启下的短语还有：under such circumstances 在这种情况下，in this case 在此情况下。

(3) regrettable　*a.* 令人遗憾的

regret　*v.* & *n.* 懊悔，悔恨(regret to do sth.)

例：

I regret not to have ordered this type of machine. 我后悔没订这种机器。

I regret not having ordered this type of machine. 我后悔没订这种机器。

It is much to be regretted that... 使人很遗憾的是……

例：

We are regrettable to say that we can't effect the shipment in time. 我方很遗憾地告知你方，我方不能按时发货。

It is a great regret that... 很遗憾……

Much to our regret... 我方很遗憾……

(4) obtainable　*a.* 可获得的，可取得的

Such machine is obtainable for US $ 100 for each. 这种机器 100 美元可以买到一台。

(5) anticipate　*v.* 预料，预知，期望

例：

We anticipate that we shall hear from you soon. 我们期待很快接到你方来信。

We anticipate hearing from you soon. 我们期待很快听到你方消息。

We anticipate the success of our trading. 我们期待双方的贸易得以成功。

We anticipate your early reply. 我们期望你们早日回复。

expect　*vt.* 期望，预期，盼望　expect sb. to do sth. expect that 期望……

例：

You are expected to effect the shipment in time. 望你们及时发货。

We expect the shipment to arrive next week. 我们盼望所发之货下周到达。

(6) in reply　短语，放在句首

in reply to　放在信首

例：

In reply to your letter dated April 1st. 兹回复贵方 4 月 1 日来函。

(7) with other terms as per your letter April 10.

with +名词+现在分词(短语)/过去分词(短语)/介词(短语)/形容词(短语)

with 短语放在名词后说明名词时作定语，放在动词后说明动词时作状语。

Ⅴ. Declining the Counter-offer

Example

Dear Sirs,

<u>Re: Declining the Counter-offer for 5000 m/t Steel Plates Type ××</u>

We are appreciative of your letter of May 5, which requested a reduction of 3% in the price of 5,000 m/t Steel Plates Type ××, i.e., a price reduction from US $ ××× per m/t to US $××× per m/t.

We are regrettable to say that there is no possibility to cut down our price to the extent you indicated. You know the price of materials has increased substantially to a certain extent and recently we have received a crowd of inquires from buyers in other directions and expected to conclude business with us at something near our level. So, at present, we cannot see our way clear to accept your counter-offer.

But in view of our long lasting and friendly business relations, should you agree to meet each other halfway in prices, we think a price reduction of 2% would make this deal clinched, that is, US $××× per m/t. Looking forward to hearing from you soon.

Sincerely yours，

五、拒绝还盘

实例

<u>关于：拒绝 5000 公吨××型钢板的还盘</u>

我方感谢你方 5 月 5 日的来函，该函要求我方将 5000 公吨××型钢板的价格降低 3%，即将每公吨×××美元降低到每公吨×××美元。

我公司很遗憾地告知贵方，将价格降低至贵方所提的价格是不可能的。贵方知道，材料的价格已大幅上涨，并且最近我方已经收到来自其他地区客户的询盘，且一直希望以接近我方的价格水平成交。因此，现在我公司无法接受你方还盘。

鉴于我们之间长久友好的贸易关系，如果贵公司在价格方面同意各让半步，我们认为降价 2%，即每公吨×××美元，即能使此次交易达成。

盼望尽快听到你方消息。

Words and Expressions

decline	*v.* 拒绝
reduction	*n.* 降低，减少
extent	*n.* 程度，范围
indicate	*v.* 指出，表明
increase	*v.* 增加，提高
substantially	*adv.* 丰富地，大量地
clinch	*v.* 确定，决定(交易)

| a crowd of | 许多 |
| conclude business | 成交 |

Notes

(1) see one's way clear to do sth.   有可能(或有意)做某事

We hope you can see your way clear to settle this dispute. 我方希望你方有可能调解这场纠纷。

We can't see our way clear to reduce our price. 我方不能降低价格。(clear 有时可省略)

(2) in view of   鉴于，考虑到，由于

in view of these facts   考虑到这些事实

(3) meet someone halfway   在半路迎接(迎战某人)，迎合某人，迁就某人

meet each other halfway   彼此半道相见，比喻采取折中办法

Sentences for Inquiry, Offer and Counter-offer

(1) As requested, we shall submit our quotation in triplicate and shall appreciate your placing the order with us as early as possible.

按你方请求，我方将提交我方一式三份的报价，如蒙早日向我方订货，我方将不胜感激。

(2) All quotations, except firm offers, are subject to the sellers' final confirmation and all prices are net, without any discount.

所有报价，除实盘报盘者以外，都以卖方的最后确认为准，所有价格都是净价，没有任何折扣。

(3) Our price has already been very reasonable, but, in order to encourage business between us, we are prepared to allow you a discount of 2%.

我方价格一直是很合理的，但为了鼓励贵我双方之间的贸易，我方准备给予你方 2% 的折扣。

(4) Due to the rising cost of raw materials, we are compelled to raise our price by 2%. 由于原材料价格上涨，我方不得不提价 2%。

(5) This offer will expire on March 30. Your immediate reply by fax will be appreciated.

此报盘 3 月 30 日到期，如蒙贵方传真回复，我方不胜感激。

(6) Especially important are the price per unit, total price, marks and numbers on each package, total quantity of packages and weight and measurements.

特别重要的是单价、总价、唛头、件号、总件数以及重量和尺码。

(7) Your enquiry of June 5 for ×× and ×× has been passed on to us for our attention.

你方 6 月 5 日对××及××的询盘已转交由我方处理。

(8) We think the colors will be just what you want for the fashionable trade, and the beauty and elegance of our designs, coupled with the superb workmanship and reasonable prices should appeal to the discriminating buyers.

我们认为这些色彩恰好是你们时装业所需要的，而且，美丽而优雅的款式配上一流的工艺及合理的价格应该对挑剔的买主具有吸引力。

(9) At your request, we are now making you a firm offer for 2,000 color TV sets of ×× Brand, Type ××.

按你方要求，我方现在给你方 2000 台××牌××型彩电的实盘报价。

(10) Our offer is firm until 15 next month.

我方报盘为实盘，有效期至下月 15 日。

(11) As our buyers are unwilling to make a bid, you'd better make an offer as soon as possible.

因我方买主不愿递盘(出价)，你方最好尽快发盘。

(12) If you can supply goods of the type and quality according to the requirements, please make us a firm offer and quote your lowest unit prices.

如果你方能根据要求的型号及质地供应货物，请给我方报实盘，并报你方最低单价。

(13) To accept the prices you quote would leave us with only a small profit on our sales since this is an area in which the principal demand for articles is to be in the medium price range.

接受你方所报的价格会给我们只留下很小的销售利润，因为此地对商品的主要要求是价格适中。

(14) We would like to suggest that you allow us a discount of , say, 5% on your quoted prices. This would help to introduce your goods to our customers.

我们想建议你们给我们打个折扣，比如说，所报价格的 5%，这将有助于向我们的客户介绍你们的产品。

(15) It is in view of our long-standing business relations that we make you such a counter-offer.

正是考虑到贵我双方的长期贸易关系，我们才给予还盘。

Exercises

I. Translate the following sentences from English into Chinese.

1. Although we would like to help you, we do not think there is room for any further allowance in our quotation, because we have cut our price to the minimum.

2. We would like to ask if you can grant us a discount of 5% for an order of 1,000 dozen.

3. In order to obtain the needed information, the inquirer must make out his inquiry sheet simply and clearly.

4. From the enclosed invoice you will see that our price is well within the maximum figure you stated.

5. We faxed you our offer yesterday and you must have received it by now.

II.　Translate the following sentences from Chinese into English.

　　1.　我方很高兴收到你方 8 月 2 日对我方皮鞋的询价。

　　2.　我们确认已接受你方报盘。

　　3.　如果你方能降价 3%，我们愿意向你方订货。

　　4.　我们将空邮你方一包样衣，收到后请即刻传真告知我方。

　　5.　此报盘为实盘，以我方最后确认为准。

Chapter 5   Placing Orders 订货

Learning Objectives:

- Know the procedures of placing orders with the other foreign companies.
- Learn how to write a letter to express your order placing, order confirmation and order declination.
- Understand the polite way of urging the order delivery.

学习目标：

- 了解向外国公司订货的程序。
- 学会写信订货、确认订货及拒绝订货。
- 了解催促交货的礼貌方式。

Ⅰ. The General Procedures of Transaction Negotiatings

After carrying out some procedures of transaction negotiatings in import and export trade, such as inquiry, offer, counter offer，etc., and after reaching to the acceptance of both sides, the Contract or Sales Confirmation or Purchase Confirmation may be signed.

一、交易洽商的一般程序

进出口贸易中经过询盘、报盘、还盘等多个环节，双方均接受后，就可以签订合同或销售确认书或购货确认书。

Ⅱ. The Writing and the Requirements of the Ordering Letter

1.   The use of the ordering letters

(1) The letter for ordering single commodity is written in letter writing style.

(2) The order for many kinds of commodities is made by the listing style.

(3) If there is any ready-made order sheet, fill it in a rather perfect way.

(4) If there is any ready-made unfilled Purchase Confirmation, fill it as well in a perfect way.

If there is any standard order sheet for ordering general commodities, just as well fill it. But if there are any complex and sophisticated products in need of ordering, the order sheet must be designed and made up specially.

二、订货信的书写与要求

1. 订货信的使用

(1) 订购单一商品用书信式书写。

(2) 订购多种商品用列表方式书写。

(3) 如果有现成的订货单，填写完毕即可。

(4) 如果有现成的未填写的购货确认书，也填写完毕即可。

对一般货物的订货，有标准格式的订货单时填写完毕即可；但对于复杂或尖端产品的订货，则必须专门设计及编制订货单。

2. The writing of the ordering letter

The requirements are stated as follows:

(1) To indicate the number of the catalogue and the type of the commodities.

(2) To indicate precisely the design, specifications, the style and quantity of the commodities.

(3) To indicate clearly the terms of transaction, such as the way of shipment, the date of delivery, insurance, etc.

Once the contract or confirmation has been signed, both sides must take their responsibilities and obligations on their shoulders. Otherwise, some complains or claims will be caused.

2. 订货信的书写要求

书写订货信的具体要求如下：

(1) 指明商品目录的编号及商品型号。

(2) 准确说明商品的花色、规格、式样、数量等。

(3) 清晰指明装运方式、交货期、保险等交易条件。

合同或确认书一经签订，双方都应自觉承担各自的义务与责任，否则会引起不必要的投诉或索赔。

III. Examples

1. Placing an order for men's shirts on the basis of samples

Dear Sirs,

Re: Placing An Order for Men's Shirts

We thank for your quotation of April 15, together with a parcel containing some samples of men's shirts.

On perusal, we find the materials you use for making the shirts are of high quality and the workmanship is excellent, which we believe will make our customers satisfied. So we are pleased to place an order with you according to your terms and conditions for the follows:

Name of Commodity	Style No.	Size	Color	Quantity (Dozen)	Unit Price per Dozen CIF London
Men's Shirts	×××	S, M, L	White, Red,	200	£ ×××
		XL, XXL	Blue, Yellow	50	
		Equally	Green & Grey	50	
		Assorted	Equally	50	
			Assorted	50	
	×××	S, M, L	White, Red,	200	£ ×××
		XL, XXL	Blue, Yellow	100	
		Equally	Green & Grey	100	
		Assorted	Equally	50	
			Assorted	50	
	×××	S, M, L	White, Red,	200	£ ×××
		XL, XXL	Blue, Yellow	100	
		Equally	Green & Grey	100	
		Assorted	Equally	50	
			Assorted	50	
Total quantity: Say ××× Only				1400	
Total Amount: Say Pounds Sterling ××× Thousand ××× Hundred and ××× Only					£×××, ×××

We would like to call on your attention to the following:

(1) The shirts you process should be in exact accordance with the samples. The order sheet with particulars is enclosed in this letter.

(2) Payment should be made in Sterling to your London representative within one month of the goods' arrival at London.

(3) Insurance should be arranged by you with Lloyd's broker through your London representative.

In case of your prompt shipment and your keeping in strict conformity with the samples' workmanship, a regular connection will be established between us.

With best regards.

Faithfully yours，

三、实例

1. 订购男式衬衫

关于：订购男式衬衫

感谢贵方 4 月 15 日的报价以及所寄的装有男式衬衫样衫的邮包。

细察之下，我方发现贵方衬衫质地优良、做工精细，我方相信这会使我方顾客满意。因此我方乐意根据你方条款和条件订货如下：

商品名称	式样号	尺　寸	颜　色	数量(打)	单价(每打) CIF 伦敦
男式衬衫	×××	小、中、大 加大、加加大 号平均搭配	白、红、蓝、黄、灰绿平均搭配	200 50 50 50 50	£ ×××
	×××	小、中、大 加大、加加大 号平均搭配	白、红、蓝、黄、灰绿平均搭配	200 100 100 50 50	£ ×××
男式衬衫	×××	小、中、大 加大、加加大 号平均搭配	白、红、蓝、黄、灰绿平均搭配	200 100 100 50 50	£ ×××
总数量：　×××				1400	
总金额：　×××英镑 (大写)					£ ×××,×××

我方希望你方注意下列几项：

(1)　贵方加工的衬衫应完全按照样品加工，记有具体要求的订单已与此信一同附上。

(2)　货物到达伦敦以后一个月内用英镑向贵方伦敦代表付款。

(3)　保险应由贵方通过贵方伦敦的代表由劳埃德经纪人办理。

如果你方立即发货，并严格按照样品的工艺加工，我们双方之间有望建立固定的业务关系。

Words and Expressions

parcel	*n.* 包裹，邮包
excellent	*a.* 卓越的，极好的
particular	*n.* 详细情节，细目，具体要求
sterling	*n.* 英国货币，英镑(5 Pounds Sterling)
	pound　镑(英镑)；磅(重量)
payment	*n.* 付款，支付
representative	*n.* 代表
arrival	*n.* 到达
insurance	*n.* 保险

Lloyd's	n. 劳埃德保险社，劳合社
broker	n. 经纪人
in case of	如果
keep in conformity with	保持一致
on perusal	仔细查看，细谈，阅读
be satisfied with	对……满意

Notes

(1) 第二段中"excellent"后的"which"指的是上面质量高及工艺好这两个句子，故可将 which 后的句子看作是特殊定语从句。

(2) 信内设计了一个表格，表格最后一项谈到总金额，写信时应该用汉字作为大写形式，后面再写数字作为小写形式。总金额大写时前面加"Say"，后面加"Only"。Say 后要先写币制，如"U.S. Dollars"或"Pounds Sterling"，然后写数字，最后加"Only"。

(3) Lloyd's 劳埃德社，始于 1689 年，1871 年正式成立，是世界上最重要的保险组织。它本身并不承办保险，其业务都是由参加该组织并取得会员资格的承保人办理。Lloyd's broker 劳合社经纪人，是劳埃德公司的成员，作为投保代理人与承保人签署保险合同，商议保险率，把保险单送到客户手中，制备保险单，并由劳埃德保险单签署处签名。经纪人向投保人收取佣金，并转交给承保人。

2. Buying the exhibits at the close of the exhibition

Dear Sirs,

<u>Re: Buying the Exhibits at the Close of the Exhibition</u>

We have been informed by your Commercial Counselor that you offer to sell all of your exhibits at the close of your Industrial Exhibition in our country instead of transporting them back to your States. We are now very pleased to advise you that we are interested in your offer and are intending to buy some of your exhibits for our end-users, for example: Medical Instruments Type ××× and Medical Apparatus Type ×××. We consider your products are all of the three "high"s, that is: "high" quality, "high" precision and "high" technology. In addition, the prices of the exhibits will certainly be much lower than the new ones imported from your country, which is the focal point.

We suggest that the Handing and Taking Over Protocol be drafted by you and be signed by the representatives of our two sides at the exhibition site within 7 days after the close of the exhibition. In addition, we propose that the date of signing be regarded as the date of delivery and your FOB prices be considered as exhibition site prices, which will be further negotiated.

Payment will be made against your presentation of one copy of the Handing and Taking over Protocol, 4 copies of Invoice and two copies of Packing List through your Bank to the Shanghai Branch of the Bank of China.

With best regards.

Sincerely yours，

2. 展览会结束后购买展品

关于：展览会结束后购买展品

贵国商务参赞已通知我方，贵方表示在我国举行的工业展览会结束后不打算把展品运回贵国，而是出售所有展品。我方现在很高兴地通知贵方，我方对贵方的想法甚感兴趣，并计划为我方用户购买贵方某些展品，如×××型医用仪器及×××型医疗设备。我们认为你们的展品具有"三高"特征，即高质量、高精密度和高技术。此外，展品价格要比从贵国进口的新产品要低得多，这一点是至关重要的。

我方建议交接议定书由贵方起草，由我们双方的代表在展览会结束后的 7 天之内在展览会场地签字。此外，我方建议签字日期即作为交货日期，贵方 FOB 价即作为展览会场地交货价，该价有待进一步洽谈。

货款将凭贵方通过贵方银行转交给中国银行上海分行的一份交接议定书、四份发票、两份装箱单支付。

Words and Expressions

offer	v. 提出，出现，提议，意图
exhibit	n. 展览品
transport	v. 运输
intend	v. 想要，打算
flexible	a. 灵活的
operation	n. 操作，运行
draft	v. 起草 n. 草案，汇票
ex	prep. 在……交货
site	n. 地点
propose	v. 提议
presentation	n. 提出，呈递
invoice	n. 发票
packing list	装箱单
commercial counselor	商务参赞
industrial exhibition	工业展览会
focal point	焦点
Handing and Taking over Protocol	交接议定书

Notes

Buying the exhibits at the close of the exhibition

外商到国外举行工业展览会时都选最好的机器运到国外展览，所以其展品都是最精密、最优良的，而且展品在展览会上进行展示操作后还是很新的。他们往往不愿意再包装托运回自己国家，而更愿意在展览地降价销售。展览国的用户往往会看中这个机会，抢先购得，这是十分划算的。

3. Declining An Order Placed for Medical Apparatus Type ×××

Dear Sirs,

Re: Declining the Order for Medical Apparatus Type ×××

We are in receipt of your letter dated May 18, together with your order sheet for Medical Apparatus Type ×××. It is necessary for us to express our great thankfulness for your order.

After careful consideration and explorations of our supplying conditions, we have decided to suggest you to approach to our sister Corporation——Shanghai ××× Corporation Ltd. on your requirement. As you know, the specifications of your required machines are rather complex and the manufacturing of them needs a special area for setting up special equipment and a group of technical workers must be trained to suit the needs of this special manufacturing. At the present period, the commitments from our customers are so heavy that we are unable to throw ourselves into this special production. As to our sister Corporation——Shanghai ××× Corporation Ltd.，it is a corporation specialized in this line of your needed machines and is able to reach the limits of your requirements. Should you agree with our suggestion, we would transfer your order to them.

We are looking forward to your reply.

Faithfully yours，

3. 拒绝XXX型医疗器械的订货

关于：拒绝×××型医疗器械的订货

我方已收到你方 5 月 18 日来函以及你方×××型医疗器械的订单。我方有必要为你方订单向你方致以深切的谢意。

经过我方对供应条件进行认真的考虑和探讨之后，我方建议你方与我方姊妹公司——上海×××有限公司联系。正如你方所知，你方所需机器的规格相当复杂，制造这些机器需要一个专用的区域来安装专用的设备，还要培训一组技术人员来适应这一特殊的生产需要。在当前时期，来自我方用户的承约太多，以致我们不能投身于这种特殊生产。我方姊妹公司——上海×××有限公司是专门从事生产你方所需的这种机器的公司，能够达到你方的要求。如你方同意我方的建议，我方愿将你方订单转至该公司。

盼望你方回复。

Words and Expressions

thankfulness	*n.* 谢意，感谢
consider	*v.* 考虑
approach	*v.* 靠近，接近，与……打交道，临近
explore	*v.* 探索，探讨，探究
suit	*v.* 适应
	n. 套
limit	*v.* 限制

	n. 限度
transfer	*v.* 转移，传递
in receipt of	收到
order sheet	订单
set up	*v.* 开办，创立，装配，安装

Notes

(1)　express one's thankfulness　表达某人谢意

(2)　approach　临近，靠近
　　例：
　　The date of delivery is approaching. 交货日期已经临近。
　　We shall approach to that company on placing orders. 我们将为订货问题与那家公司交涉。

(3)　be unable/ able to do sth. 在某种情况、条件下不能(能)……
　　例：
　　We are able to send you our price list immediately. 我们能立即给你们寄去价格单。
　　He will be able to attend this meeting. 他将能出席这个会议。
　　They have often been able to see him this year. 今年他们时常见到他。
　　Can 也表示"能够"，是情态动词，后面只能跟原形动词，只用于现在时(亦可用于将来时)，过去时为 could，如用"be able to do sth."，则时态比较丰富多彩。
　　can　能……会……，表示能力
　　can　可能，能够，表示可能性

(4)　throw someone into …
　　throw sb. into prison　将某人投入监狱
　　throw sb. into great trouble　使某人陷入极大的麻烦之中

4. Confirming the Order for Steel Pipes Type ×××

Dear Sirs,

Re: Confirming the Order for Steel Pipes Type ×××

Thank you for your order April 20 for 1,000 m/t of Steel Pipes Type ×××

In accordance with the faxes exchanged and as well through our joint efforts, we are now very pleased to confirm the following order with you at your revised price: "1,000 metric tons of Steel Pipes Type ××× at US $ ××× per metric ton FOB Singapore for shipping during October", for which we enclose our Purchase Confirmation No. ××× in duplicate. Please countersign and return one copy for our file at your earliest convenience.

In order to assure you of our best attention to the execution of your order, we are now arranging for immediate shipment as requested. But it's of great importance to remind you that you should open your L/C in our favor through your Bank at once so as to enable us to make early shipment.

Sincerely yours，

4. 确认×××型钢管订单

关于：确认×××型钢管订单

感谢你方 4 月 20 日 1000 公吨×××型钢管的订单。

通过传真交流及共同的努力，现在我方向你方确认你方修改价格的以下订单：

"1000 公吨×××型钢管，新加坡到岸，船上交货价格，每公吨×××美元，10 月发货。"为此，我方附上×××号购货确认单一式两份，请你方尽早会签，并退回我方一份，以供我方存档。

为了使你方确信我方对你方订单的极其重视，我方现在按你方要求安排立即发货，但需要提醒你方的很重要的一点是，你方应通过你方银行立即开立以我方为受益人的信用证，以使我方早日发货。

Words and Expressions

exchange	*v.* 交换，交流
execution	*n.* 执行
importance	*n.* 重要性
in one's favor	以……为受益人
in accordance with	按照，根据
at one's early convenience	(书信用语)尽早

Notes

(1) joint efforts　共同努力；through (by) joint efforts　通过共同努力

(2) confirm　*v.* 进一步证实，进一步确定

　　confirmable　*a.* 可进一步确定的，可批准的

　　confirmation　*n.* 确认，确认书

　　confirm　后也可跟动名词。

　　in confirmation of　以证实……

(3) at revised price　按修正价格，指按通过还盘以后修改的价格

(4) to assure　*v.* assure sb. of sth.　向……确保……，使……确认

(5) attention　除了有"注意"之意，还有"处理，办理"的意思

　　pay immediate attention to your inquiry　立即办理你方询价之事

(6) remind　*v.* 提醒，使想起

　　to remind sb. of sth.　使某人回想起，提醒某人关于某事

　　remind sb. of + that…

　　例：

　　Thank you for your reminding us of what we must do. 感谢贵方提醒我方必须做的事。

(7) execute　*v.* 实行，执行，贯彻

　　execute payment　付款

　　execute shipment　发货

　　execute one's duty　尽职

executive　　*a.* 执行的，行政的，(总)经理，首长

executive committee　　执行委员会

executive authorities　　行政当局

5. Urging Delivery of the Order for Quilting Frame

Dear Sirs，

<u>Re: Urging Delivery of the Order for Quilting Frame</u>

We have the pleasure in concluding the trade with you for the Quilting Frames, measured 2×3 feet and the great convenience in quilting has made your products more and more popular in the customers.

As to the L/C, we have already established and sent you through the Bank of China after signing the Purchase Confirmation.

At present, the busy season is approaching and the brisk demands coming from the customers are pressing us to supply them in time the goods they ordered.

As we are in urgent need of the goods, we feel it necessary to stress the importance of making punctual shipment within the validity of the L/C. Any delay in shipment would be detrimental to our future business. Therefore, we are writing to inform you that in case of your delaying in shipment, we shall cancel our order with you.

We appreciate your cooperation.

Faithfully yours,

5. 催交棉被绗缝架的订货

关于：催交棉被绗缝架的订货

我方有幸就尺寸为 2×3 英尺的棉被绗缝架达成交易，在绗缝棉被时带来的方便使你方产品在客户中越来越受欢迎。

至于信用证，我方已在签署购销确认书后通过中国银行开立，并寄予你方。

眼下旺季已经临近，对棉被绗缝架需求旺盛的用户正在催促我们及时供应他们所订之货。

由于我方对货物的迫切需要，我们感到有必要强调在信用证有效期内准时发货的重要性。任何发货的耽搁都会不利于我们未来的业务。因此，我方写信通知你方，如果你方耽搁发货，我方将撤销与你方所订的合同。

谢谢合作。

Words and Expressions

convenience	*n.* 方便
popular	*a.* 大众喜欢的，流行的
as to	至于，关于
brisk	*a.* 活跃的，旺盛的
stress	*v.* 强调
validity	*n.* 有效期

detrimental	*a*. 有害的，不利的(…to)
delay in shipment	发货耽搁
cancel	*v*. 撤销，取消
urge	*v*. 催促，力劝，怂恿
urge sb. to do sth.	强烈要求
urge sb. into doing sth.	催促某人做某事
conclude the trade	做成生意，达成交易

Notes

(1) have the pleasure in doing   有幸做……事，in 后跟动名词

(2) quilt *n*. 被子

quilting   绗缝被子

quilting frame   被子绗缝架，是一种缝被子用的小机器，一种很容易装配及使用的架子，供生产床上用品的工厂使用。

(3) press sb. to do sth.   催迫某人做某事

(4) be in urgent need of sth.   迫切需要某物

be in bad need of   迫切需要某物

(5) stress the importance of 与 emphasize the importance of 意义相同，"表示强调……的重要性"。

(6) effect shipment 与 make shipment 的意义相同，意思是"进行发货"。

Sentences for Placing Orders

(1) Although the prevailing quotations are slightly higher, we will accept the order on the same terms as before with the view of encouraging business.

虽然当前报价稍高，但为了促进业务发展，我方将按与以前同样的条件接受订单。

(2) We would like to draw your attention to the fact that the stipulations in the relevant credit should strictly conform to our Sales Confirmation for avoiding subsequent amendments.

我方希望你方注意：有关信用证的规定必须严格符合销售确认书，以避免随后的修改。

(3) Judging from the market information, the prices will still go up, so we recommend your immediate acceptance.

根据市场信息判断，价格仍会上涨，所以我方建议你方立即接受。

(4) We confirmed having placed an order with you for ××× tons of walnut meat.

我方确认已向你方订购×××吨核桃仁。

(5) Referring to your enquiry of July 10, we regret that we have no supply in stock and are unable to accept your order. We shall contact you as soon as the supply position improves.

关于你方 7 月 10 日询盘，非常抱歉，我方目前手头无现货，所以不能接受你方订货。当供应状况有所改善时，我方将与你方联系。

(6) With reference to the date of delivery, we suggest to fix it on 15th, May.

关于交货日期，我方建议定于 5 月 15 日。

(7)　We are not in a position to accept your order because of the seismic sea waves' destroying the productive ability in our area.

由于海啸破坏了我地区的生产能力，我方不能接受你方订单。

(8)　If this trial order is smoothly executed, we shall place further orders for your products with you.

如果这次试订货进行顺利，我方将进一步订购你方产品。

(9)　It is our hope that this order will be the first step to the long and friendly business relations between us.

我们希望这次订货将是迈向我们之间长久友好关系的第一步。

(10) It is regrettable to say that we are unable to accept your order at the price requested, since our profit margin is so small that it does not allow us to make any concession by way of discounting prices.

很抱歉，我方不能按你方要求的价格接受订单，因为我方的利润幅度很小，不允许我方在价格上以打折作为让步。

(11) As we are in an urgent need of the commodity for the coming sales season, we would like to receive your fax for acceptance as soon as possible.

由于我方急需此种商品以供给即将到来的销售季节，希望尽快收到你方接受订单的传真。

(12) In case that the goods are not available from stock, we would appreciate it if you could advise us of replacement goods with full particulars of the specifications, which can be supplied from stock.

万一库存无货可供，如蒙推荐库存中可供的替代品，并附全部详细规格，我公司将十分感激。

(13) Should you be interested in any of the items in the list, please let us know your requirements, stating quantity, style and sizes.

贵方如欲购清单中的任何产品，请告知贵方的需要，并请说明数量、式样和尺码。

(14) As to a trial order, we are delighted to give you an order for 100 sets of your Electronic Computers Type ×××. Please note that the goods are to be supplied in accordance with your samples in your showroom.

关于试订，我方希望订购贵公司×××型电子计算机 100 台。请注意，货品必须与你方展览室的样品一致。

(15) We are pleased to receive your prompt reply to our inquiry dated July 15th about the captioned canned food. We want to place our order with you as per our Purchase Order enclosed.

我方 7 月 15 日对你方标题所示项下的罐头食品进行询价，你方的立即回复我方已收到，十分高兴，我方拟按我方所附购货单向你方订货。

Exercises

I. Translate the following sentences from English into Chinese.

1. We hope that you will be satisfied with our selection and that this order of yours will lead to further development of our business.

2. Your Sales Manager faxed us yesterday that our price was acceptable and asked us to secure supplies for you in the next 2 years.

3. CIF is a price term, which means the price includes the cost of goods and the insurance and freight for carrying the goods up to the destination.

4. We are sending you the samples by separate airmail, hoping you will find them satisfactory.

5. If we had been informed in time, we would have reserved these products for you.

II. Translate the following sentences from Chinese into English.

1. 我方有幸将你方来信中所要求的一份最新的目录附寄你方。

2. 我方很遗憾地通知你方，我方库存中没有你方所需的货物。

3. 我们满意地发现你方产品质量高，价格也合理。

4. 请通过劳埃德保险社经纪人为我们安排货物的保险事项。

5. 我方产品的质量肯定能达到你方所要求的程度。

Chapter 6　Letter of Credit 信用证

Learning Objectives:

- Know the procedures of L/C establishment.
- Understand how to urge L/C establishment and how to request L/C extension.
- Master the ways of L/C checking.
- Learn how to request the L/C amendments.

学习目标:

- 了解开立信用证的方法。
- 了解怎样催开信用证，怎样请求展延信用证。
- 掌握审证方法。
- 了解如何请求修改信用证。

Ⅰ. The Function of Letter of Credit

In international trade, if the exporter effects his shipment to the importer before the importer's effecting his payment, he will feel anxious for not being able to receive the money for goods. At the same time the importer will not rest assured of his effecting payment before his receiving the goods, he will be afraid of not receiving the goods. Therefore the importer will apply to the local bank of his country for opening a letter type certificate, i.e. letter of credit, and inform the exporter through the local bank of the exporter. The opening bank will guarantee the importer's payment for goods after the exporter's sending out the shipment documents to the importer according to the stipulations of the L/C for certificating the exporter's shipment having been effected.

一、信用证的功能

在国际贸易中，如果出口商在进口商付款之前发运货物，他会担心将来收不到货款，同时，进口商在收到货物之前也会担心支付货款后将来收不到货物，于是进口商就申请和要求其所在地银行代其向出口商开出一种信函式的凭证(即信用证)，通过出口商所在地银行通知出口商。由开证行担保进口商在出口商将货物发出并按信用证对出口商装货认证的规定将货运单证寄给进口商以后，向出口商支付货款。

Example

Dear Sirs,

Re: Advising the Establishment of L/C

It's a great pleasure to have reached an agreement on Excavator Type ×××　with you two weeks ago. As we have required, you have to effect the shipment of the goods as soon as possible. Therefore we have already established our L/C No. ×××   dated May 28 for Sales Confirmation No. ××× through the Bank of China, Beijing Branch, valid until July 12. Please make the shipment in time.

As to the quality and the performance of your products, we think it is necessary for you to keep them in exact accordance with the samples. Any inconsistency with the required quality and performance of the products will be detrimental to our future business.

Best regards to you.

Yours sincerely,

实例

关于：通知已开立信用证

两周前与你方就×××型挖掘机达成协议，实为荣幸。按我方要求，你方应尽快发货。因此我方已通过中国银行北京分行为×××号销售确认书开立日期为 5 月 28 日的×××号信用证，有效期至 7 月 12 日。请及时发货。

至于你方产品的质量和性能，我方认为你方提供的物品应完全符合你方的样品。任何与产品的质量和性能要求的不符，将有损于我们之间的未来业务。

Words and Expressions

establish	*v.* 建立，开立(*n.* establishment)
valid	*a.* 有效的
performance	*n.* 性能
inconsistency	*n.* 不一致
detrimental	*a.* 有损于，(to)不利于
reach an agreement	达成协议
as to	关于
keep in accordance with	与……保持一致

Notes

与信用证有关的六个当事人如下。

(1) 开证申请人(Applicant)：向银行申请开立信用证的人，即进口人或实际买主，在信用证中又称开证人(Opener)。如果由银行自己开立信用证，则没有开证申请人。

(2) 开证行(Opening Bank or Issuing Bank)：接受开证申请人的委托开立信用证的银行。开证行承担保证付款的责任。开证行一般是进口人所在地的银行。

(3) 通知行(Advising Bank or Notifying Bank)：受开证行的委托，将信用证转交出口人的银行。通知行只证明信用证的真实性，并不承担其他义务。通知行一般是出口人所在地的银行，而且通常是开证行的代理行。

(4) 受益人(Beneficiary)：信用证上所指定的有权使用该证的人，即出口人或实际供货人。

(5) 议付行(Negotiating Bank)：愿意买入受益人交来的跟单汇票的银行。议付行可以是指定的银行，也可以是非指定的银行，由信用证的条款来规定。议付行对受益人有追索权。

(6)　付款行(Paying Bank, or Drawee Bank)：信用证规定的汇票付款人。付款行一般是开证行，也可以是它指定的另一家银行，根据信用证条款的规定来决定。付款行一经付款，对受益人不得追索。

II．The Procedures of Payment Effecting by L/C

(1)　The importer applies to its local bank for opening an L/C.

(2)　The opening bank of the importer opens the L/C.

(3)　The opening bank sends its L/C to the advising bank entrusted by the exporter and the advising bank sends its L/C information to the exporter.

(4)　The exporter checks the L/C. If there are any errors or any terms which the exporter can not accept, then asking the opening bank to amend the L/C is necessary. If the contents of the L/C are in conformity with the requirements, the exporter should effect shipment, get the shipping documents, prepare the draft and send the draft together with all of the shipping documents to the advising bank for negotiating.

(5)　The advising bank sends the draft and the shipping documents to the opening bank for its effecting payment.

(6)　The opening bank sends the draft and the shipping documents to the importer.

(7)　The opening bank remits the money for goods to the advising bank. At this time the opening bank is also called the paying bank.

(8)　The advising bank transmits the money for goods to the exporter.

二、信用证的支付流程

(1)　进口商向其当地银行申请开立信用证。

(2)　进口商开证行开证。

(3)　开证行将信用证寄给出口商委托的通知行，通知行将信用证通知递交出口商。

(4)　出口商对信用证进行审查，如果发现有错误或对信用证内某些条款不能接受，应及时要求开证行修改。如果发现信用证的内容符合要求，出口商应完成装运，取得装运单据，制作汇票，并将汇票及全套装运单据递交通知行要求议付。

(5)　通知行将汇票和装运单据寄给开证行要求支付。

(6)　开证行递交汇票及装运单据给进口商。

(7)　开证行把货款汇给通知行。此时开证行也叫付款行。

(8)　通知行将货款转给出口商。

III．Some Main Contents of L/C

There are no unified styles and forms for the banks' L/C establishing, but the contents of the L/C are fundamentally the same. Here are some main contents which must be included in an L/C.

(1) The name and address of the importer and the name of the opening bank.

(2) The name and address of the exporter and the name of the advising bank.

(3) The name of the commodity, its specifications, quantity, weight, packing and price.

(4) The kind, name and the number of L/C.

(5) L/C opening sentences for illustrating the name of the importer entrusting the opening bank to open the L/C.

(6) The sentences about the draft by which the beneficiary draws the money for goods, with indicating the name of the payer, the amount of money and the kind of draft.

(7) The sentences about documentation with indications of what kinds of documents must be enclosed with the draft and how many copies are in need.

(8) The way of shipment with indications of whether transshipment or partial shipments are allowed.

(9) The term of shipment and the validity term of L/C.

(10) The sentences about the responsibilities of the opening bank, who will take the charge of effecting payment.

(11) The sentences of the opening bank for reminding the negotiating bank of the affairs which should be done in negotiating by the negotiating bank.

(12) The additional terms such as the confirmation terms, and etc.

三、信用证的几个主要内容

各银行开出的信用证无统一格式，但基本内容相同。信用证需要包括的几项主要内容如下。

(1) 进口方名称、地址及开证行名称。

(2) 出口方名称、地址及通知行名称。

(3) 商品名称、规格、数量、重量、包装和价格。

(4) 信用证的性质、种类与号码。

(5) 开证文句，说明受何进口商委托开证行开立信用证。

(6) 汇票文句，受益人应凭汇票取款，说明汇票的付款人、汇票金额及汇票的种类。

(7) 跟单文句，说明汇票应附何种单据及应付几份。

(8) 装运方式，说明是否允许转船或分批装船。

(9) 装船期限及信用证有效期限。

(10) 开证行的责任文句，说明谁将负责开证行的付款任务。

(11) 开证行对议付行的提示文句，说明议付行在议付时应办理的事项。

(12) 附加条款，如保兑条款等。

IV. The Classification and the Kinds of L/Cs

1. Classified according to the payment effecting time

(1) The sight L/C;

(2) The usance L/C.

2. Classified according to the Possibility of Revocating

(1) The revocable L/C;
(2) The irrevocable L/C.

3. Classified according to the necessity of being confirmed by another bank

(1) Confirmed L/C;
(2) Unconfirmed L/C.

4. Classified according to the possibility of transferring the beneficiary's right of the L/C

(1) Transferrable L/C;
(2) Non-transferrable L/C.

5. Classified according to the possibility of revolving

(1) Revolving L/C;
(2) Non-revolving L/C.

6. Classified according to the possibility of automatic revolving

(1) Automatic revolving L/C;
(2) Non-automatic revolving L/C.

7. Classified according to the need of documents' being attached

(1) Clean L/C;
(2) Documentary L/C.

四、信用证的分类和种类

1. 按付款时间分

(1) 即期信用证；
(2) 远期信用证。

2. 按可否撤销分

(1) 可撤销信用证；
(2) 不可撤销信用证。

3. 按需否另一家银行保兑分

(1) 保兑信用证；
(2) 不保兑信用证。

4. 按受益人对信用证的权利能否转让分

(1) 可转让信用证；

(2) 不可转让信用证。

5. 按可否循环分

(1) 循环信用证；

(2) 非循环信用证。

6. 按可否自动循环分

(1) 自动循环信用证；

(2) 非自动循环信用证。

7. 按是否附有单证分

(1) 光票信用证；

(2) 跟单信用证。

Example

Dear Sirs，

<u>Re: Urging the Establishment of L/C</u>

We wrote a letter to you on ×× August to confirm having received your Order for ×× sets of Drilling Machines Type ××× and we, accordingly, enclosed the original of our Sales Confirmation No. ×××, which stipulates the shipment should be made by the end of October and the L/C should reach us one month before the shipment date. Now the shipment date is approaching, but your L/C has not been received by us. We think your immediate attention should be called on to this matter.

Therefore, we have to write to you again for urging your establishment of the above-mentioned L/C in order to enable us to execute your order smoothly.

We thank you for your cooperation.

Truly yours,

实例

关于：催开信用证

我方曾于 8 月××号给你方回信，确认已收到你方××台×××型钻床的订单。我方相应地附寄了我方×××号销售确认书的正本，该确认书规定发货应于 10 月末进行，信用证亦应于发货日期前一个月寄达我方。现在发货日期已经临近，但我方尚未收到你方信用证。我方认为你方应当立即办理此事。

因此，我方不得不再次写信，催促你方开立上述信用证，以便我方顺利执行订单。

感谢你方合作。

Words and Expressions

accordingly	*adv*. 相应地
original	*n*. 原文
stipulate	*v*. 规定
above-mentioned	上述
smoothly	*adv*. 顺利地
call on	呼吁，请求

Notes

(1)   The L/C should reach the Sellers one month before shipment.

信用证应于发货前一个月寄达卖方。(此为一般规定)

(2)   信函和传真中的 SC No. ×××，可以指 Sales Contract 销售合同，也可以指 Sales Confirmation 销售确认书，需视实际情况翻译。

Ⅴ. The L/C Checking

In international trade the opened L/C must be checked according to the contract, confirmation or agreement and the L/C word for word, sentence for sentence, item for item and term for term. If the errors or differences in an L/C can not be checked out or are not amended by importer, the opening bank will refuse to effect payment. The shipment date and the validity date of L/C should not be fixed at the same day. The validity of L/C must be later 10–15 days than the shipment day. If the expirations of the two dates are fixed at the same day, amendment should be requested. If the negotiation place of the L/C is defined outside the boundary of the exporting country, the exporter may request to change the negotiation place of L/C from outside the boundary to inside the boundary of the exporting country.

五、信用证的审核

在国际贸易中对开立的信用证必须根据合同、确认书或协议书以及信用证的条款规定，逐字、逐句、逐条、逐项地进行审核。如果信用证存在差错却没有被审核出来，或者进口商未对其进行修改，开证行将拒付货款。装运日期和信用证有效期要错开，后者应比前者晚 10～15 天。如果两个日期为同一天，应要求修改。如果信用证议付地点被定在出口国境外，出口商可以要求将议付地点改为在出口国境内。

Example

Dear Sirs,

Re: L/C No.   ×××   Issued by Barclays Bank, London

We wish to acknowledge receipt of the above-mentioned L/C, covering your order for ×× sets of Electronic Computers Type ××.

After checking, we have found some discrepancies. Please amend the L/C as follows:

(1)   The amount both in figures and in words should respectively be £ 12,480 and Say

Pounds Sterling Twelve Thousand Four Hundred and Eighty Only.

(2) "Draft to be at sight" should be instead of "at 60 days after sight".

(3) The port of destination should be "London" instead of "Liverpool".

Your early fax amendment to the L/C will be highly appreciated.

Sincerely yours,

实例

关于：伦敦巴克莱银行所开立的××号信用证

我方确认已收到上述支付你方××台××型电子计算机订单的信用证。

审查之后，我方发现一些差错，请对信用证作如下修改：

(1) 金额的数字和文字应分别为 12480 英镑(壹万贰仟肆佰捌拾英镑)。

(2) 汇票应为"即期"，而不是"60 天期"。

(3) 到港应为"伦敦"，不是"利物浦"。

如能早日用传真发来修改后的信用证，将不胜感激。

Words and Expressions

issue	*v.* 开放，开立
cover	*v.* 覆盖，包括，负担(开支)，支付
check	*v.* 审查
discrepancy	*n.* 差异，不一致
respectively	*adv.* 分别地
port	*n.* 港口
amend	*v.* 修改
amendment	*n.* 修改书

Notes

(1) amount in figures　用数字表示的金额(指小写)

(2) amount in words　用文字表示的金额(指大写)。大写时在金额的前面加"Say"，后面加"Only"。如为美金时则写成"Say U.S. Dollars ××× Only"。订单、信用证、发票等的金额均需用文字表示。

(3) draft at sight　即期汇票

(4) at 60 days after sight　见票 60 天支付，即 60 天期期票

(5) port of destination　到港，目的港

VI. Granting Amendment to L/C

Example

Dear Sirs,

Re: Granting Amendment to L/C No. ×××

We are in receipt of your letter dated ××× and have to apologize to you for making mistakes in the captioned L/C, which are made due to the negligence of our new employee.

We now inform that we have already instructed our Bank to amend the relevant L/C and send it to you by fax with the least possible delay. We believe our Bank would certainly pay its prompt attention to this matter when they have received our instructions.

As we are in urgent need of the goods, we hope this amendment of L/C will not affect your punctual shipment of the goods.

Let's express our apology to you again. We are expecting your favorable reply.

Truly yours,

六、同意修改信用证

实例

关于：同意修改×××号信用证

我方已收到贵方×月×日的来信，并且必须为标题项下信用证中的错误致歉，这是我方新来雇员的疏忽所造成的。

我方现在通知你方，我方已指示我方银行尽快修改相关的信用证并尽快传真给你方。我方相信，我方银行接到我方指示后将立即办理此事。

由于我方急需此货，我方希望信用证的这次修改将不致影响你方的准时发货。

我方再次致歉。等候你方佳音。

Words and Expressions

grant	*v.* 批准，同意
apologize	*v.* 道歉，致歉(apology *n.* 道歉)
the captioned	标题项下的
negligence	*n.* 疏忽
employee	*n.* 雇员
relevant	*a.* 有关的
due to	由于，应归于

Notes

(1) with the least possible delay   尽可能少的耽搁，即"尽快"之意。

(2) pay prompt attention to this matter   对某事予以立刻办理，即立即办理此事。

(3) be in urgent need of   处于迫切需要之中，即"急需……"的意思。

(4) affect punctual shipment   影响准时发货

(5) captioned   *adj.* 标题项下的，标题名下的

VII. Requesting Extension of L/C

Example

Dear Sirs,

Re: Requesting Extension of L/C

We thank you very much for your L/C No. ×××　dated ×××, covering your order for Type ××× Children Bicycles. According to our Sales Confirmation, it is our duty to deliver the goods to you next month. But to our great regret, 3 days ago, our No. 2 Workshop was caught on fire. This fire disaster has destroyed our manufacturing equipment in the workshop and made our steel pipes deformed. As a result of this, we have to stop our production to repair our equipment and to buy new materials from the other supplier for manufacturing your bicycles. It is clear that we shall not be able to get our goods ready for shipment next month. Therefore, we request you to extend the shipment date to November 5 and the validity of your L/C to November 20.

Please amend your L/C immediately and accept our apology.

Truly yours,

七、请求展延信用证

实例

关于：请求展延信用证

我方非常感谢你方×月×日支付×××型儿童自行车订单的×××号信用证。根据我方的销售确认书，我方应于下月交货。但极为遗憾的是，三天前我方2号车间失火。这场火灾烧毁了车间的生产设备，并将钢管烧得变形。结果，我方不得不停止生产来修理设备，并从其他供应商处购买材料来生产贵方需要的自行车。显然，我方将不能按时将货备妥，以供下月发运。因此，我方请求贵方将发货日期延至11月5日，我方将贵方信用证的有效期延至11月20日。

请立即修改贵方信用证，并请接受我方致歉。

Words and Expressions

extension	*n.* 展延，延长
workshop	*n.* 车间
disaster	*n.* 灾害
destroy	*v.* 破坏，毁坏，摧毁
deform	*v.* 变形
repair	*v.* 修理
supplier	*n.* 供应商
catch on fire	失火

Notes

(1)　get the goods ready for shipment　将货备妥待运

(2)　as a result of　作为……的结果；in result　结果；without result　毫无结果地

(3)　the shipment date and the validity date of L/C

信用证的有效期一般比装运期晚 10～15 天。如果装运期和有效期是同一时间，通常称作双到期。双到期是不能接受的。装运期应与有效期相隔 10～15 天，即装船后 10～15 天信用证才能到期。

Ⅷ.　L/C Checking and L/C Amending

The ways of checking the letters of credit in English according to the given Chinese Contract terms and the ways of asking the Buyers to amend the letters of credit in English.

八、审证与改证

根据给出的汉语合同条款审查英语信用证以及用英语要求买方修改信用证的方法(这是全国外销员资格考试英语试题的题型，此处有三个例子)。

Example 1

1)　英文信用证

×××　Bank

London, England

Irrevocable Documentary Credit No.　×××

Date and Place of Issue: September 20, 2015, London

Date and Place of Expiry: November 15, 2015, London

Applicant:　×××　Co. London, England

Beneficiary: China National　×××　Import and Export Corporation

Advising Bank: Bank of China, Beijing

Amount: US $ 35,000 (Say US Dollars Thirty Five Thousand Only)

Shipment: From China Port to London, middle October, 2015. Partial shipments and transshipment are prohibited. Credit available by the documents detailed herein and by your draft at sight for full invoice value.

—Signed Commercial Invoice in quadruplicate.

—Full set of clean on Board Ocean Bills of Lading made to order and blank endorsed marked　"Freight Prepaid".

—Insurance Certificate or Policy for full invoice value plus 10%, covering against All Risks and War Risks on 7,000 tins of 500 grams of　×××　Brand canned anchovy at US $ 5 per tin CFRC 2% London.

As per Contract No.　×××

参考译文:

英国伦敦×××银行

不可撤销的跟单信用证×××号

开立日期和地点：2015 年 9 月 20 日，伦敦

到期日期和地点：2015 年 11 月 5 日，伦敦

申请人：英国伦敦×××公司

受益人：中国×××国际进出口公司

通知行：中国银行，北京

金额：35 000 美元(叁万伍仟美元)

装运：2015 年 10 月中旬，从中国港口运至伦敦。不允许分批装运及转运。提呈详述于此的文件及全部发票金额的即期汇票，即可兑付信用证之款项。

- 已签署的商业发票一式四份。
- 洁净已装船的提单，空白抬头且空白背书，并注明"运费付讫"。
- 按发票价值 110%投保一切险和战争险的保险凭证或保险单，投保 7000 听 500 克的×××牌凤尾鱼罐头，每听 5 美元，含佣金 2%，伦敦到岸。

合同号码：×××

Words and Expressions

anchovy	*n.* 凤尾鱼
be made to order, to be issued to order	空白抬头
clean on Board Ocean Bill of Lading	洁净已装运海运提单
blank endorsed	空白背书
Freight Paid	运费付讫

2) 中文合同条款(审证根据)

合同主要条款

卖方：中国×××国际进出口公司

买方：英国伦敦×××公司

商品名称：×××牌凤尾鱼罐头

规格：450 克听装

数量：7000 听

单价：CFR，伦敦，每听 5 美元，含佣金 2%

总值：35 000 美元

装运期：2005 年 10 月中旬，自中国港口至伦敦，在香港转船

付款条件：凭不可撤销即期信用证付款

合同号码：×××

3) The letter asking for amendment of the above L/C 修改上述信用证的英语信函

Dear Sirs,

We are very glad to receive your L/C No. ×××　under Contract No. ×××. But it is a great regret that we have found some discrepancies in the above mentioned L/C. Please make the following amendments:

(1)　The place of expiry should be in Beijing, China, not in London.

(2)　"Partial shipments and transshipment are prohibited" should read " Transshipment in Hongkong is allowed".

(3)　Delete insurance clause.

(4)　The specifications should be tins of "450 grams " instead of "500 grams".

Please amend your L/C as soon as possible and inform us by E-mail after your amending the relevant L/C.

Sincerely yours,

参考译文：

敬启者：

我方很高兴收到你方××号合同下××号信用证。但很遗憾的是，我方在上述信用证中发现了一些差错，请作以下修改。

(1)　到期地点应为中国北京，不是伦敦。

(2)　"不允许分批装运及转运"应改为"允许在香港转船"。

(3)　删除保险条款。

(4)　规格为"450 克"，非"500 克"。

请尽快修改你方信用证，修改相关信用证后请用电子邮件通知我方。

解释修改原因：

(1)　信用证议付地点在卖方，故到期地点应在中国北京。

(2)　汉语合同条款中有"在香港转船"字样，英语信用证中却写成"不允许转船与分批装运"。

(3)　价格为 CFR(成本+运费)，不是 CIF，买方未付保险费，卖方不负责给买方货物投保，故不用写保险条款。

(4)　罐头规格有误，应为 450 克听装，而非 500 克听装。

请尽快修改你方信用证，并在修改相关信用证后用电邮通知我方。

Example 2

1)　英文信用证

×× Bank, Holland

Date: ××, ××, 2015

To: Bank of China, Shanghai Branch

We hereby establish our revocable letter of credit No. L/C ×× in favor of Shanghai Textiles Corporation for account of XX Co. up to an aggregate amount of US $ ×× (Say US $ ×× Only) CIF Rotterdam for 110% of the invoice value relative to the shipment of ×× dozen of Men's Shirts Brand ×× of No. ×× as per Contract No. XX dated ××, 2015.

Shipment from China Port to Rotterdam. Drafts to be drawn at sight on our Bank and accompanied by the following documents:

——Bill of Lading in triplicate made out to order quoting L/C No. ××, and blank endorsed, marked "Freight Paid".

——Signed Commercial Invoice in triplicate.

——One original Marine Insurance Policy or Certificate for 110% full invoice value covering All Risks and War Risks.

——Partial Shipments are allowed.

——Transshipments are prohibited.

——Shipment must be effected no later than August 31, 2015.

Payment should be made by irrevocable L/C by sight.

Draft negotiation is to be effected in China on or before September 15, 2015.

参考译文：

荷兰××银行
日期：2015 年××月××日

致：中国银行上海分行

关于按照 2015 年×月×日第××号合同发运××货号的××打××牌男式衬衫，我方已开立卖方为上海纺织品公司、买方为××公司的第××号可撤销信用证，金额总计为××美元，CIF，鹿特丹到岸，按发票价值 110%投保。

货物从中国港口发往鹿特丹。凭开予我方的即期汇票及下列文件付款。

- 提单一式三份，空白抬头，标示第××号信用证，空白背书，标示"运费已付"。
- 已签署的商业发票一式三份。
- 一份海上保险单或保险凭证原件，按发票价值 110%投保一切险及战争险。
- 允许分批装运。
- 不允许转运。
- 装运不得晚于 2015 年 8 月 31 日。

凭不可撤销的即期信用证支付。

汇票必须于 2015 年 9 月 15 日或 9 月 15 日以前在中国议付。

Words and Expressions

in favor of	以……为受益人；受益方为……(即卖方为……)
for account of	由……支付；支付方为(即买方为……)

2）中文合同条款(作审证根据)

卖方：上海纺织品公司

买方：××公司

商品名称：××牌男式衬衫

规格：第××货号

数量：××打

单价：CIF，每打××美元

总价：××美元

装运期：2015 年 8 月 31 日前自中国港口至鹿特丹，从 6 月份开始按月等量分三批装运不允许转运。

付款条件：凭不可撤销即期信用证付款，于装运前一个月开到卖方，并于最后装运期后 15 天内在中国议付有效。

保险：由卖方根据中国人民保险公司 1981 年 1 月 1 日中国保险条款按发票金额的 110% 投保一切险、战争险以及 TPND 附加险。

合同号码：第××号。

3) 要求修改上述信用证的英语信函

Dear Sirs,

We are in receipt of your L/C No. ×× under Contract No. ××. Please accept our thankfulness. But for your information, after perusal we have found a number of discrepancies. Therefore, we are now writing to you for asking your amendments of the relative L/C as follows:

(1) The L/C should be "irrevocable" instead of "revocable".

(2) Insert "Unit Price is US $ ×× per dozen" after "the aggregate amount of US $ ××".

(3) The insurance terms of "… All Risks and War Risks" should be "… All Risks, War Risk and TPND".

(4) After "…All Risks, War Risks and TPND" insert "as per CIC of January 1st of 1981 of PICC".

(5) "Partial shipments are allowed " should be "Partial shipments should be in 3 equal monthly lots, commencing from June".

Sincerely Yours,

参考译文：

敬启者：

我方已收到你方××号合同下××号信用证，谢谢。但现在通知你方，细审之下，我方发现不少差错。因此，我方现致函你方，请求你方修改信用证如下：

(1) 信用证应为"不可撤销"，非"可以撤销"。

(2) 在"总价××美元"之后加"每打单价××美元"。

(3) 保险条款"……一切险和战争险"应为"一切险、战争险及 TPND 险"。

(4) 在"一切险、战争险及 TPND 险"之后加"根据中国人民保险公司 1981 年 1 月 1 日中国保险条款"。

(5) "允许分批装运"应改为"从六月份开始按月等量分三批装运"。

Example 3

1) 英文信用证

Bank of ××

Irrevocable Credit No. ××

March 15, 2015

To: Beijing ×× Import & Export Corp. Beijing, China

Dear Sirs,

We hereby open an irrevocable credit No. ×× in your favor for account of ×× Co. for a total sum of US $ ×× (US Dollars ××) and available by your draft(s) drawn on us at sight for 100% of the invoice value accompanied by the following documents:

—Signed Commercial Invoice in triplicate indicating Contract No. ××.

—Full set of clean shipped on board Ocean Bills of Lading issued to order and blank endorsed marked "Freight Prepaid".

—Insurance Policy or Certificate for 110% of invoice value, covering WPA and War Risks.

—Inspection Certificate on Quality and Weight issued by the New York Commodity Inspection Bureau in triplicate.

—Certificate of Origin in triplicate.

—Evidencing shipment of ×× metric tons of rice, 1st grade in bulk, at US $ ×× per ton CIF New York, net shipped weight.

—From China to New York not later than April 30, 2015.

—Transshipment is prohibited.

This credit is valid in Beijing until May 15, 2015. All drafts drawn must be marked "Irrevocable L/C No. XX, dated March 15, 2005".

参考译文：

××银行

不可撤销的信用证　第××号

2015 年 3 月 15 日

致：中国北京，北京××进出口公司

敬启者：

我们特此开立以你方为受益人、买方为纽约××公司的不可撤销的信用证，总金额为××美元(大写：××美元)，凭按发票金额 100% 所开的即期汇票及下列单证支付：

- 已签名的商业发票一式三份，写明第××号合同。
- 全套洁净货已装船提单，注明"运费已付"，空白抬头且空白背书。
- 按发票价值 110% 投保的保险单或保险凭证，投保水渍险及战争险。
- 纽约商品检验局颁发的质量与重量检验证，一式三份。
- 原产地证明一式三份。
- 证明发出××公吨散装一级大米，每吨××美元，CIF 纽约，净发运重量。
- 2015 年 4 月 30 日前从中国发往纽约。
- 允许分批装运。
- 不允许转运。

本信用证 2015 年 5 月 15 日于北京到期。所有汇票必须标上"第××号不可撤销信用证，2015 年 3 月 15 日"。

2) 中文合同条款(作审证根据)

××号合同的主要条款

卖方：北京××进出口公司

买方：纽约××公司

××公吨一级大米，装船净重每公吨 CIF 纽约，××美元，散装，卖方可多装或少装 5%，价格仍按单价计算。2015 年 4 月 30 日前从中国运往纽约，不允许转船。允许分批装运。

凭不可撤销的即期信用证付款。

按发票金额 110%投保水渍险和战争险。

3) 要求修改上述信用证的英语信函

Dear Sirs,

Thank you very much for your L/C No. ×× under Contract No. ××. Upon checking we would like to ask you to amend the following discrepancies found in the above-mentioned L/C:

(1) "New York Commodity Inspection Bureau" should read "Beijing Commodity Inspection Bureau".

(2) "US $ ×× per ton CIF New York" should be "US $ ×× per metric ton CIF New York".

(3) Add "The Sellers are allowed to load 5% more or less based on the original unit price" in the shipment clause after "From China to New York not later than April 30, 2015".

(4) The wording of "Partial shipments are permitted" should be inserted.

We hope you will send us your amendment advice without delay in order to enable us to effect shipment in time.

Faithfully yours,

参考译文：

敬启者：

非常感谢××号合同下××号信用证。审查之后，我方请求你方修改上述信用证中的下列差错：

(1) "纽约商品检验局"应为"北京商品检验局"。

(2) "每吨 CIF 纽约××美元"应为"每公吨 CIF 纽约××美元"。

(3) 在"2015 年 4 月 30 日从中国到纽约"这一运输条款中加上"允许卖方在原有单价基础上多装或少装 5%"。

(4) 应加上"允许分批装运"字样。

我方希望你方尽快给我方寄来你方的修改通知单，以便我方及时发运。

Words and Expressions

evidence	*v.* 证明
hereby	*adv.* 特此

inspection certificate	检验证书
Commodity Inspection Bureau	商品检验局
Certificate of Origin	原产地证明

Notes

metric ton　1 公吨=1000 公斤或 2204.6 磅

long ton　1 长吨=1 英吨=1.016 公吨或 2240 磅

short ton　1 短吨=1 美吨=0.907 公吨或 2000 磅

注：要求修改的原因。

(1)　质量与重量检验证应改为由"北京商品检验局"颁发。

(2)　单价"per ton"改成"per metric ton"。

(3)　装船条款中"卖方可多装或少装 5%，价格仍按单价计算"的内容英语信用证中没有，应补全。

(4)　应加上"允许分批装运"字样。

Sentences for Letter of Credit

(1)　In spite of our repeat requests, your L/C has not reached us up to now. Please open the credit by fax immediately to enable us to effect shipment in October.

尽管我方再三要求，至今仍未收到你方信用证。请立即用传真开立信用证，以便我方能在 10 月发货。

(2)　We may accept deferred payment if the quantity is over 10,000.

如果数量超过 10 000，我方可接受延期付款。

(3)　We suggest you to pay by bill of exchange at 30 days' documents against acceptance.

我们建议你们以 30 天期承兑交单支付。(documents against acceptance 可缩写为 D.A. 或 D/A)

(4)　Our draft on you at 60 d/s in favor of ×× Corporation will be presented to you by Bank of China, Shanghai Branch and we would be grateful if you would kindly give it your acceptance.

我方开给你方的以××公司为收益人的 60 天期汇票将由中国银行上海支行提呈你方。如蒙你方承兑，我方将甚为感激。

(5)　In compliance with your request, we exceptionally accept delivery against D/P at sight, but this should not be taken as a precedent.

依从你方要求，我方额外破例，同意根据即期付款交单交货，但下不为例。

(6)　The relevant L/C should be issued through a third bank acceptable to the seller.

有关信用证应通过卖方能接受的第三家银行开出。

(7)　Much to our regret, our draft on you dated 2 August and due on 1 October was returned dishonored yesterday by our Bank.

很遗憾，我方开给你方的日期为 8 月 2 日并于 10 月 1 日到期的汇票昨天已被我方银行拒收退回。

(8)　It is a great regret for us to find that there are certain clauses which don't confirm to those of the Contract.

我方很遗憾地发现有些条款与合同条款不一致。

(9)　It is possible that the above mistakes are clerical. We hope that you will make the necessary amendments immediately by fax, so that we can ship the goods in time.

上述错误可能为笔误，我方希望你方立刻发传真作必要的修改，以便我方及时装运货物。

(10)　Enclosed please find advice of amendment to L/C No. ××.

××号信用证的修改通知书已附寄，请查收。

(11)　Greatly satisfied with your cooperation in the past, we shall extend the relevant L/C in compliance with your request for two weeks.

由于与你方过去的合作甚为满意，我方将根据你方请求，展延相关信用证两周。

(12)　Please amend L/C No. ×× to read "The extra freight is to be on buyer's account".

请将××号信用证改为"额外运费由买方负担"。

(13)　We have found that the amount of your L/C is insufficient. Please increase the unit price from US $ ×× to US $ ×× and the total amount from US $ ×× to US $ ××.

我方发现你方信用证中的金额不足，请将单价从××美元增至××美元，将总金额从××美元增至××美元。

(14)　Please delete the clause "by direct shipment" and insert the wording "Partial shipments and transshipment are allowed".

请取消"用直达轮"条款，加上"允许分批装运及转船"字样。

(15)　The amendment advice should reach us by November 15, failing which you must extend the validity of the L/C to the end of this year.

修改通知书当于 11 月 15 日之前到达我方，否则你方须将信用证的有效期延至今年年底。

Exercises

Ⅰ．Translate the following sentences from English into Chinese.

1.　Before accepting the draft, the bank will require you to produce documents such as Bills of Lading, Commercial Invoice, Packing List, etc.

2.　Provided you fulfill the terms of the L/C, we will accept the drafts drawn under this credit.

3.　After receiving our L/C, you must effect the shipment of the goods as soon as possible.

4.　The performance of your products must keep in exact accordance with our samples.

5. It is necessary to call your attention to the establishing of your L/C, because the date of our shipment is approaching.

Ⅱ. Translate the following sentences from Chinese into English.

1. 买方信用证应于发货日期前一个月寄达卖方。

2. 运输公司已经通知我方,胜利轮将于本月 20 日或 20 日左右离开我港驶往伦敦。

3. 我方有幸通知你方,我方已将你方所订货物全部备妥待运,请速开信用证。

4. 我们可以立即发出手头所有的货物,而不用等到所有货物备齐。

5. 今天早晨我方发传真给你方,请你方修改×××号信用证。

Chapter 7　Shipment 装运

Learning Objectives:

- Identify the difference between shipping instructions and shipping advice.
- Understand the necessity of booking shipping space in advance.
- Know the correct treatment of the non-delivery of the goods.
- Master certain procedures of shipment effecting.
- Transshipment and Partial shipments.

学习目标：

- 区别装船指示和装船通知之间的不同。
- 懂得预订舱位的必要性。
- 知道如何正确处理货物的提货不着。
- 掌握发货的一定程序。
- 转船与分批装运。

Ⅰ. International Goods Transportation and Goods Shipment

In international trade, the international goods transportation and goods shipment are two of the important component parts of the international trade. Only through transporting can the goods be transported from the seller's country to the buyer's country. After signing the selling and buying contract, the seller should ship the goods to the buyer according to the time, place and way of shipment stipulated in the contract. In carrying out the procedures of foreign trade, the concept of time should be paid great attention to. The fields in which foreign trade is involved are extensive, the transportation lines are long. The links and procedures are numerous, so the foreign traders must be equipped with fundamental knowledge of the international cargo transportation and shipment. Only by this way can the deliberate consideration be offered to the problems of the cargo transportation and the terms of transportation may be worked out integratedly, definitely and reasonably, thus making sure of the successful effecting of the contract.

一、国际货物运输和装运

在国际贸易中，国际货物运输和装运是国际贸易的两个重要组成部分，只有通过运输才能将货物从卖方国家转移到买方国家。在买卖合同签订之后，卖方必须按照合同中规定的时间、地点和运输方式将货物运交买方。外贸流程的时间概念很强，涉及面广，路线长，环节程序多，所以外贸人员一定要具备国际货物运输及装运方面的基本知识，只有这样，才能在商洽贸易及签订合同时充分考虑运输方面的问题，然后完整、明确、合理地制定出装运条款，确保合同顺利地履行。

II. Kinds of Transportation in International Trade

There are ocean marine transportation, rail transportation, air transportation, highway transportation, river transportation, postal transportation, etc. The ocean marine transportation has won its advantages of large holding capacity and low freight, so in spite of its disadvantages of slow navigation speed and strong risks, it still makes up over two-thirds of the total freight volume of the transportation in international trade.

二、国际贸易运输的方式

国际贸易运输的方式有海洋运输、铁路运输、航空运输、公路运输、江河运输、邮政运输，等等。其中，海洋运输因运输量大、运费低的优势，尽管存在航速低、风险大的不足，仍在国际贸易运输中占总运输量的 2/3 以上。

The Transshipment and Partial Shipments

The transshipment and partial shipments also belong to the kinds of shipments. It is necessary to instruct in the contract and in the L/C whether transshipment or partial shipments are permitted and to observe these stipulations strictly. In L/C checking these stipulations should be checked carefully and the checking of how many partial shipments need to be effected and the dates of these partial shipments should not be left.

转船与分批装运

转船与分批装运也属于运输方式，必须在合同上及信用证上写明是否允许转船与分运，并严格遵守约定。审证时对这些规定必须认真审阅，对分批装运的次数、分批装运的日期等的审阅不能遗漏。

(1) Partial shipments: When a large quantity of goods is dealt with, the transport conditions, the source of the goods and the goods' marketing sometimes may affect the conclusion of the deals, so it will be necessary to make partial shipments. At this time, the buyer and the seller should stipulate the time and the frequency of the partial shipments. If the shipment needs to be effected only once in single lot, the limited term of prohibiting the partial shipments must be written in the contract and in the L/C.

(1) 分批装运：进行大宗货物交易时，运输条件、货源及货物营销市场，有时会影响交易的完成，因此需要对货物进行分批装运。此时，买卖双方应规定分批装运的时间及次数。如果需要一次装运完毕，则须在合同及信用证中写明不允许分批装运的限制性条款。

For example:

The shipment is to be effected/made in 3 equal monthly instalments beginning from March 2006.

例：

从 2006 年 3 月开始，货物将分 3 批按月等量装运。

(2)   Transshipment: If the goods should be reloaded and transshipped at the intermediate ports, the increase of the expenses and the losses of the goods should be caused. So the buyer is always unwilling to accept the transshipment term. But sometimes there are no direct ships or no appropriate ships sailing to the destination port or the conditions of the port are rather poor, then the seller and the buyer have to stipulate the term of "allowing transshipments".

(2)   转船：货物通过中途港口重新装载和转运，会导致费用增加及货物损失，因此买方往往不愿意接受转船条款。但有时没有直达船或没有合适的船舶驶往目的港，或者港口条件太差时，买卖双方不得不在合同及信用证中规定"允许转船"的条款。

III. Urging the Delivery of the Goods

Dear Sirs,

Re: Urging the Delivery of the Goods

We have sent you a fax dated Nov. 7, asking about the delivery of the order No. ×× for 800 woolen sheetings originally scheduled for 15, Nov. It's a pity that up till now we haven't received any news of delivery of these goods. Now the cold season is approaching and our customers are in urgent need of them. Your deferring in delivery will cause us great inconvenience. If you have got any difficulty in fulfilling this order, you must inform us the reason of your not being able to supply the goods in time.

We hope that you will do your utmost to deliver the goods as soon as possible.

We are waiting for your reply.

Sincerely yours,

三、催交货物

关于：催交货物

我方曾于 11 月 7 日给你方发去一份传真，询问关于××号订单 800 条羊毛毯的交货问题，该批货物原定于 11 月 15 日交货。很遗憾，迄今为止我方尚未收到这批货物的交货消息。现在寒季已快来临，我方用户迫切需要这批货物。你方推迟交货将给我方带来极大的不便。如果你方完成订单有困难，应该将你方不能按时供货的理由通知我方。

希望你方尽最大努力尽快交货。

等候你方回复。

Words and Expressions

schedule	v. 将……列入计划表，排定，安排
approach	v. 临近，来临；走近某人，和联系事
deliver	v. 交货
defer	v. 推迟，延期
inconvenience	n. 不方便
do one's utmost	尽最大努力
as soon as possible	尽快

woolen sheeting　　　　　　　　　　羊毛毯

Notes

"offer us the reason of your not being able to supply the goods in time" 一句中，your 为动名词否定结构 "not being able to" 的逻辑主语。

Ⅳ. Shipping Advice

In international trade buyers sometimes send shipping instructions (including shipping requirements) to sellers. Sometimes buyers will write to sellers for informing the sellers of effecting shipment in time in case of shipment delay.

After the shipment of the goods, sellers will send buyers the Shipping Advice to inform the buyers the relevant shipment details, the contents of which are as follows:

(1) The date of shipment;

(2) The shipped goods;

(3) The way of shipment.

四、装船通知

在国际贸易中，买方有时会给卖方发出装船指示(包括装船要求)，或因为装船延误写信通知卖方及时装运。

卖方在货物装运后，会给买方发装船通知，告知买方有关装运的细节，内容包括：

(1) 装运日期；

(2) 装运货物；

(3) 装运方法。

Example

Dear Sirs,

Re: Shipping Advice

We take the great pleasure in informing you that the machines you ordered August this year under Contract No. ×× have now been dispatched per SS "East Wind" sailing tomorrow from New York to Shanghai.

In order to assure you of the goods' reaching you in good condition, all of them were packed in special container. We wish you to unpack and examine them immediately on arrival. Any complaints as to damage should be notified to us and the shipping company within ten days.

Enclosed please find one set of Shipping Documents covering this consignment which comprises:

(1) One copy of non-negotiable Bill of Lading;

(2) Commercial Invoice in duplicate;

(3) A copy of Certificate of Origin;

(4) Certificate of Quality in duplicate;

(5)　Packing List in duplicate;

(6)　Insurance Policy in duplicate;

(7)　One copy of Survey Report.

We hope this shipment will reach you in time and in good order to meet with your full satisfaction.

Yours faithfully,

实例

关于：装船通知

我方非常荣幸地通知你方，你方今年八月在××号合同中所订的机器现在已由"东风"号轮船装运，该船明日从纽约起航驶往上海。

为了确保货物完好无缺地到达你方，所有货物都被打包装在专用集装箱内。我方希望货到后你方能立刻开箱检查,关于损伤的任何投诉均须在10天之内通知我方及运输公司。

有关这笔托运货物的一套装运单证现附于此，请查收。单据中包括：

(1)　不可转让的提单一份；

(2)　商业发票一式二份；

(3)　原产地证明一份；

(4)　质量证书一式二份；

(5)　装箱单一式二份；

(6)　保险单一式二份；

(7)　检验报告一份。

我方希望这笔货物及时、完好地到达你方，使你方充分满意。

Words and Expressions

dispatch	*n.* 发送，装运
per	*prep.* 经，由；按照，根据
container	*n.* 容器，集装箱
unpack	*v.* 拆包，启封
complaint	*v.* 投诉，抱怨
damage	*v.* 破坏，损坏
notify	*v.* 通知
non-negotiable	*a.* 不可转让的
certificate	*n.* 证明书，证书
certificate of origin	原产地证明书
certificate of quality	质量证明书
insurance policy	保险单
survey report	检验报告
shipping company	运输公司
Bill of Lading	提单
commercial invoice	*n.* 商业发票

Notes

(1)   shipping advice   装船通知(卖方在货物装船后发给买方的通知)

(2)   shipment (ship 的名词)   装货；所装运的货，所运输的货

(3)   take great pleasure in doing sth.   极为荣幸地做某事，做某事极为荣幸

(4)   reach in good condition   在完好情况下到达

(5)   contain   包括，装有

　　　container   容器，储存器，集装箱

　　　container ship   集装箱运货船

　　　containerize   用集装箱运，集装箱化

(6)   insurance certificate   保险凭证，保险凭据

　　　正式保险单制成以前发给被保险人的保险凭据，不属于正式保险单。但在正式保险单发下以前，如果被保险人发生事故，依此凭证也可向保险公司索赔。

　　　insurance policy   保险单(正式的保险凭据)

(7)   notify   *v.* 通知

　　　notify sb. to do sth.   通知某人做某事

　　　notify sb. of sth.   将某事通知某人

　　　notify sb. of doing sth.   通知某人做某事

　　　notify sb. that   通知某人……

Ⅴ．Booking Necessary Shipping Space in Advance

1. The Ways of Managing the Ocean Marine Transport

1)   Liner transport

The ships sail along the regular routs from port to port according to the sailing schedules. The freights are collected in accordance with the rates published beforehand. Shipping space of the ships in liner transport should be booked in advance. The liner transport has got its regular routs, regular ports regular sailing schedules and relatively regular rates. The liner transport is especially suitable for transporting the groceries of various sizes and the goods in penny trade.

五、预订必需的舱位

1. 海洋运输的经营方式

1)   班轮运输

船舶在固定的航线上和港口间按船期表(sailing schedule)航行，按事先公布的费率收取运费。班轮运输中船舶的货物舱位需预订。班轮运输有固定航线、固定港口、固定船期以及相对固定的费率。班轮运输尤其适合一般杂货和小额贸易货物的运输。

2)   Shipping by chartering or shipping by tramp

The shipping by chartering has got irregular sailing routes, irregular ports, irregular schedules and irregular freights. This kind of shipping suits for transporting the goods of large amount and of small worth.

2)　租船运输或不定期船舶运输

租船运输不定航线、不定港口、不定船期、不定货价，适合运输货值较低的大宗货物。

2. The Ways of Shiping by Chartering

1)　Voyage or Trip Chartering

It is based upon the voyages. The chartering can be carried out in accordance with the different kinds of voyages, for example: one-way voyage, round-trip voyage, and successive voyage. Voyage chartering is also available on the basis of Chartering contract.

2)　Time Chartering

It is based upon the time limit. In the stipulated time the charterer does his controllings, operating and managing work by himself. The rent for the ship is counted monthly per deadweight tonnage.

3)　Bareboat chartering

The ship owner rents his ship only, with no crew provided. The charterer must allocate the crew by himself and take the responsibility of doing all self-operating and self-managing work.

2. 租船运输的方式

1)　定程租船

以航程为基础，如按单程、往返航程、连续航次。定程租船也可在租船合同的基础上进行。

2)　定期租船

以期限为基础。在规定期限内租船人自行调度及经营管理。租金每月按每载重吨计算。

3)　光船租船

船主只出租船只，不提供船员，租方必须自行配备船员，自行负责经营和管理一切事项。

Example

Dear Sirs,

<u>Re：Booking Shipping Space in Advance</u>

We are in urgent need of dispatching ×××　m/t of ×××　from Shanghai to Sydney by the end of May. We know that as a rule, the direct vessels, whether liners or tramps, sailing for your port are few and far between, so we feel very anxious that the shipping space will be fully booked up. In such circumstances, we are approaching you to get your support and your assistance. We shall be highly appreciated if you can allow us to ship our goods of ×××　m/t of ×××　in one lot per SS "Queen" sailing from Shanghai for your port Sydney on/about 15 May. If you are not in a position to offer us the shipping space for the whole lot of ×××　m/t of ×××, we would like very much to ask you to favor us a chance of making partial shipments of all the goods per your liner.

Please take good consideration of our urgent request and let us have your favorable reply.

Yours faithfully

实例

关于：预订舱位

我方迫切需要在 5 月底以前从上海至悉尼发出×××公吨的×××。我方知道，通常来说，驶往你港的直达班轮，无论是定期班轮还是不定期货轮，都是很少的，且班期相隔甚远，故我方十分焦急，担心舱位将被全部订出。在此情况下，我方现与你方联系，寻求你方的支持和协助。如果你方能允许我方通过将于 5 月 15 日或 5 月 15 日左右从上海驶往你方港口悉尼的"皇后"轮一次运出我方×××公吨的货物，我方将不胜感激。如果你方不能为我方×××公吨的整批货物提供舱位，我方十分希望你方能给我方一个机会，通过你方班轮分批发出全部货物。

请你方对我方的迫切要求予以照顾，并给予我方以可喜的回复。

Words and Expressions

book	*v.*	预订(book up)
liner	*n.*	定期班轮
tramp	*n.*	不定期货轮
anxious	*a.*	焦急
approach	*v.*	向……靠近
assistance	*n.*	协助
queen	*n.*	皇后
favor sb. with a chance		给予……一个机会
partial shipment(s)		分批装运
shipping space		舱位
in advance		预先
direct vessel		直达班轮
as a rule		通常，一般说来
in such circumstances		在此情况下
approach sb. on (about) sth.		为某事和某人打交道

Notes

(1) be in a position to do sth.   能做……

be not in a position to do sth.   不能做……

(2) favor sb. a chance of making partial shipments of …   赐予一个分批装运的机会。此处的"机会"，即使能得到，还需征得买方同意。

(3) take good consideration of   很好地考虑，还有"优惠"的意思，故直译为"照顾"。

VI. Shipment Packing and Shipping Marking

It is generally listed in four lines. Figures and marks in each line should not be exceeded by seven words.

(1) The first line: The code names, initials or abbreviations of the consignee and consignor.

(2) The second line: Numbers of the contract and the L/C.

(3) The third line: Port of destination.

(4) The fourth line: Package number and order number.

These four lines can be designated into the marks of triangle, or lozenge, or hexagon in order to make the goods easier to be recognized, to be transported or to be stored.

In addition, some eye-catching graphs and simple words can be used to remind the transport workers, such as:"Fragile" "Easy to Be Damaged" "Easy to Be Deteriorated (Degenerated)". Painting the warning marks on the packages is also available to show "Inflammable" "Explosive" "Poisonous", etc.

六、运输包装及运输唛头

运输唛头一般包括 4 行，每行包括数字和符号在内不超过 7 个字母。

第一行：收货人或发货人的代号、首字母或简称。

第二行：合同号码或信用证号码。

第三行：目的港。

第四行：件号、序号。

这四行可设计在三角形、菱形或六角形内，从而易于识别货物，方便运输、储存等。

此外，也可用一些醒目的图形和简单的文字提醒运输人员注意，如"易碎""易损""易变质"等；或用警告性标志刷在包装上，表示"易燃""易爆""有毒"等。

Example

Dear Sirs,

Re: Shipment Packing and Shipping Marking

We are writing to you to invite your attention to our order No. ×××　covering 2,000 sets of chinaware for dinner service made in Jingdezhen. According to the Contract No. ×××, this order should be due on 15 December. To our surprise, up till now we still have not heard from you any news of delivery of these goods. Please pay attention to the delivery date and arrange the shipment as early as possible.

In addition, the chinaware are easily to be broken and are, especially, not capable of withstanding the rough handling. Therefore taking good care of well packing is of great importance for reducing the losses in transporting. It is necessary for you to pack the goods in strong wooden cases bedded with foamed plastics for protection from being broken.

As to the shipping marking, we wish you to do it according to our requirements as follows:

(1) Correctly and distinctly mark the cases with our initials in a triangle, under which

comes the destination port with Contract number.

(2) Conspicuously stencil on both sides of the wooden cases with the words "FRAGILE, HANDLE WITH CARE" with indelible paint which will not run off or blur because of dampness or rubbing.

Your full cooperation will be expected.

Sincerely yours,

实例

关于：运输包装装船及运输唛头

我方给你方写信的目的是希望你方能关注我方 2000 套景德镇制造的瓷餐具的×××号订单。根据×××号合同，这一订单应于 12 月 15 日到期。使我方惊讶的是，我方迄今尚未得到任何关于这些货物的交货消息。请你方注意交货期，并尽早安排发货。

此外，瓷器易碎，尤其不能经受粗暴装卸。因此，妥善包装对减少运输途中所产生的损耗而言是至关重要的。你方必须用坚固的木箱包装货物，并垫以泡沫塑料以防止破损。

至于运输唛头，希望你方根据我方如下要求进行标示：

(1) 正确、清楚地将我方单位首字母标在三角形内，下面标示目的港及合同号。

(2) 在木箱两侧醒目地用模板印刷上"易碎，小心轻放"字样，要用不会因受潮或受摩擦而脱落或模糊的油漆印刷。

盼望你方充分合作。

Words and Expressions

mark	v. 作标志，标明，打印
	n. 标记，唛头
chinaware	n. 瓷器
due	a. 到期
withstand	v. 经受，忍受
transport	v. & n. 运输
bed	n. & v. 铺垫
distinctly	adv. 清楚地
triangle	n. 三角形
conspicuously	adv. 醒目地，明显地
stencil	v. 用模板印刷
fragile	a. 易碎的
indelible	a. 去不掉的，擦不掉的
blur	v. 弄得模糊不清，弄脏
dampness	n. 潮湿
rub	v. 摩擦
be capable of	能够……的
rough handling	粗暴装卸

take care of	照顾，照料
foamed plastics	泡沫塑料
HANDLE WITH CARE	小心轻放

Notes

(1) invite one's attention to sth.

call on one's attention to sth.

pay one's attention to sth.

均为同义词组，表示"引起某人注意某事"，也可用被动语态表示，如"attention will be invited to …"。

(2) the packing of the chinaware 瓷器的包装

瓷器为易碎货物，高档瓷器的包装特别讲究，高昂的包装费用也提高了瓷器的成本。

(3) Shipping Mark 运输唛头

买方如对运输唛头有所要求，一般在合同内即需表明。如不作要求，则由卖方决定。此时，在"Shipping Mark"这一项之后一般打上"At Sellers' Option"字样，或"Up to the Sellers' Option"。

VII. Non-delivery of the Metal Box Containing Tool Kit and Accessories

Dear Sirs，

<u>Re: Non-delivery of the Metal Box Containing Tool Kit and Accessories</u>

We felt very regrettable to hear the bad news from your fax this morning, informing us that the metal box containing tool kit and accessories didn't reach your port of destination. Since the number of this metal box is mentioned on the Packing List and the whole consignment was examined and checked by the Chief Supervisor of the Transport Company before shipment in the storehouse of the dock, the non-delivery of this box does not fall within our responsibility. As requested, we have insured the goods against the TPND risks, so you may lodge your claim against this TPND with the Insurance Company.

It has been said in your fax that all the machines of the complete production line have already arrived at your production site and some of them are being installed there. It is a great regret that the non-delivery of the box containing tool kit and the necessary accessories has made the installation work broken down and brought it to a standstill. With the view of helping you to complete the construction of the whole production line and to bring your production line into an early operation, we have decided to deliver you by air another metal box with tool kit and accessories on Flight No. ×× flying from our ×× Airport to your ×× Airport the day after tomorrow. The cost of the tool kit and accessories, as well as the air freight, will be borne by you or by the Insurance Company later. We are now faxing you the relevant documents in order that you can take delivery of the goods at the airport.

With regards.

Faithfully yours，

七、装有全套工具及配套附件的金属箱提货不着

关于：装有全套工具及配套附件的金属箱提货不着

今晨从你方传真中得悉装有全套工具及配套附件的金属箱未运抵你方目的港的坏消息，我方甚感遗憾。因为金属箱的编号列于装箱单内，整批货物发送前在码头仓库由运输公司的主管人员检查核对，所以此箱的提货不着不属于我方的责任范围。按你方请求，我方曾将货物投保盗窃与提货不着险，故你方可向保险公司就所投保的盗窃与提货不着险提出索赔。

你方传真中曾经提到，全套生产线的所有机器都已运抵生产现场，其中有些正在那里安装。很遗憾全套工具及配套附件的金属箱的提货不着使安装工作受阻并陷入停顿状态。为帮助你方完成整个生产线的建设，并使生产线早日投入运行，我方决定通过后天从我方××机场飞往你方××机场的××航班将另一装有全套工具及配套附件的金属箱空运给你方。全套工具及配套附件的成本以及空运费今后将由你方或保险公司承担。我方现在将有关单证传真给你方，以使你方能够在机场提货。

谨致问候。

Words and Expressions

non-delivery	*n.*	提货不着
kit	*n.*	成套工具
fax	*v. & n.*	传真
check	*v.*	检查，核对
supervisor	*n.*	管理人，主管人
insure	*v.*	投保，保险
site	*n.*	现场
install	*v.*	安装
standstill	*n.*	停止，停顿
airport	*n.*	机场
fall within the…responsibility of		属于……的责任
lodge a claim		提出索赔
insurance company		保险公司
break down	*v.*	崩溃，破损，垮塌
bring … into operation		使……投入运行

Notes

(1) TPND (Theft, Pilferage and Non-Delivery)是一种保险险种，theft 表示整体被偷，pilferage 表示部分被盗。

TPND risks   偷窃与提货不着险

(2) Metal box containing tool kit and accessories 装有全套工具及配套附件的金属箱

这是一个很重要的箱子，没有工具箱和附件，非常影响安装，所以卖方在摆脱责任后立即配齐工具及附件，进行空运，以免影响买方整条生产线的安装。

Sentences for Shipment

(1)　Since there is no direct steamer sailing from here to your port prior to May 15, we are extremely sorry for our inability to advance the shipment as requested.

由于 5 月 15 日前没有从这里驶往你方目的港的直达班轮，我方十分抱歉，不能按你方要求提前发货。

(2)　If you require earlier delivery, we can only make a partial shipment of 50 tons of ×× in June, and the balance of 50 tons of ×× in July.

如果你方要求提前交货，我方只能分批发货，在 6 月发出 50 吨××，其余 50 吨则在 7 月发出。

(3)　For the goods under our Contract No. ××× we have booked space on SS "Victory" which is due to arrive in EMP on/about 10 April. For loading arrangements, please communicate with our shipping agent Singapore ××× Corporation.

我方已在"胜利"轮上订妥舱位，以装载×××号合同项下货物，该轮定于 4 月 10 日或 4 月 10 日左右到达欧洲主要港口。至于装船事项，请与我方运输代理新加坡×××公司接洽。

(4)　We have been informed that your Company is now operating a shipping container service of the Indian Ocean and the Mediterranean route. We are writing to you for asking some particulars of this service. Charges for using the service are also expected to be offered.

我方获悉贵公司正在营运印度洋及地中海的船运集装箱服务。我方现咨询该项服务的详细情况，并望提供使用该项服务的费用。

(5)　The shipping containers are of two sizes, namely 10ft and 20ft long and built to take loads up to 2，4 tons respectively.

船运集装箱有两种尺寸，10 英尺、20 英尺，装载量分别为 2 吨、4 吨。

(6)　The shipping containers can be opened at both sides for loading and unloading at the same time. They are watertight and airtight and can be loaded and locked at the factory.

船运集装箱能从两侧开启，供同时装货及卸货。船运集装箱是防水和密封的，在厂内可以装货并上锁。

(7)　Your shipment should be effected in two equal monthly lots during November and December.

你方的货物应在 11 月份及 12 月份分两次等量装运。

(8)　We are pleased to inform you that the goods under S/C No. ××× went forward per SS "Washington" of the Pacific line on 8 March, and the relevant samples had been dispatched to you by air before the steamer sailed.

我方很高兴地通知你方，×××号销售确认书项下货物已于 3 月 8 日装太平洋航运公司"华盛顿"号轮，有关货样已于该轮起程前空邮你方。

(9)　We are now notifying you that we have shipped you today by SS "President" ××× cases of ×××, which are to be transhipped at Hongkong and are expected to reach your port early next month.

现通知你方：我方今日已由"总统"轮将×××箱×××运往你方，该货将于香港转船，预计下月初到达你方港口。

(10) We are sorry to notify you that owing to your delay in opening the relative L/C for two weeks, the shipment of your Order No. ××× cannot be effected in February as contracted and should be postponed until March.

兹通知你方：由于你方推迟开证两周，我方无法依合同要求于 2 月份发出你方×××号订单的货物，将延至 3 月份，甚歉。

(11) After contacting the shipping company in Port Rotterdam, we were informed by the agents that your missing cases had been discharged at that Port by mistake.

在和鹿特丹港运输公司联系以后，该方代理商通知我方，你方丢失的箱子错卸于该港。

(12) We are very pleased to inform you that we have arranged for the cases discharged at Rotterdam by mistake to be returned by the first available ship for discharging at London.

我方很高兴地通知你方，我方已安排将错卸于鹿特丹的箱子通过第一艘可以装运的船只运回，在伦敦卸港。

(13) We trust you will see to it that the order is shipped within the stipulated time, as any delay would cause us no little inconvenience and financial loss.

我方相信你方会注意订单需在规定时间内发运一事，因为任何耽搁都会引起我方许多不便和经济损失。

(14) Your long delay in delivery our goods under S/C No. ××× has thrown us into considerable inconvenience. We are now insisting on your immediate delivery, otherwise we would be compelled to cancel the order in accordance with the stipulations of the contract.

你方长久耽误我方第×××号销售项下货物的交付，已导致我方相当大的不便。我方现在坚持请你方立即交货，否则我方定会根据合同规定撤销订单。

(15) We feel rather regrettable for our being unable to ship the goods within the time limit of the L/C owing to the unforeseen difficulties on the part of our manufacturer. We shall get the goods ready in 15 days. Please accept our apologies.

十分抱歉，由于我方生产厂家方面意料之外的一些困难，我方不能在信用证限制的时间内发货。我方将在 15 天内备好货。请接受我方道歉。

Exercises

Ⅰ. Translate the following sentences from English into Chinese.

1. Special instructions have been given to our dispatch department to send your orders on August 15 and September 15 separately, as specified in your letter of July 15.

2. We wish to stress that shipment must be made within the prescribed time limit, as a further extension will not be considered by our endusers.

3. It is not necessary to indicate the name and address of the consignee on each package, since shipping marks comprise the initials of the buyer's name.

4. In order to assure you of the goods reaching you in good condition, all of them

were packed in special container.

5.　The non-delivery of this package falls within the responsibility of the insurance company, so you may lodge a claim with the insurance company.

Ⅱ.　Translate the following sentences from Chinese into English.

1.　有时允许转船及分批装运。视具体货物的不同而定。

2.　你们所要求的货，我们有库存，一旦收到你们的订单，我们将立即交货。

3.　包装费用包括在价格内，不管你们什么时候需要，我们都可以交货。

4.　我方很抱歉，短发了 50 吨货。

5.　我们必须提醒你方注意我方××号订单的交货日期，希望你们尽早作出安排。

Chapter 8　Payment Effecting 付款

Learning Objectives:

- Learn how to advise L/C establishment.
- Know how to ask for cash payment.
- Master the way of effecting installment payments.
- Understand the formalities of negotiating payments and the expressions of asking for deferring payments.
- Learn the tools and ways of payments and deformation of CIF and FOB terms.

学习目标：

- 了解如何通知信用证的开立。
- 知道如何请求现金付款。
- 掌握进行分期付款的方法。
- 懂得议付手续及请求延迟付款的表达方式。
- 了解支付工具、支付方法，以及 CIF、FOB 的术语变形。

Ⅰ. The Ways of Payments

In international trade the tools for payments are Draft, Promissory Note and Check. There are three ways of payments: Remittance, Collection and Letter of Credit.

1. The Ways of Remittance

There are four ways of remittance.

(1) Payment in Advance;

(2) Cash with Order (CWO);

(3) Cash on Delivery (COD);

(4) Open Account Trade.

The open account trade is also called buying or selling on credit, or account charging. In (1) and (2) the exporter receives money first, and then delivers goods. The funds will not lie idle and these two kinds of remittances are based upon sufficient trust of the importer in the exporter. In (3) and (4), the exporter delivers goods first and then receives money. The funds will lie idle and these two kinds of remittances are based upon sufficient trust of the exporter in the importer.

一、支付方法

在国际贸易中，支付的工具有汇款单、本票和支票。支付的方法有三种：汇付、托收和信用证。

1. 汇付方式

汇付有四种方式。

(1)　预付货款；

(2)　随订单付现；

(3)　交货付现；

(4)　记账交易。

记账交易也叫赊账，指赊销或挂账。(1)(2)两种为出口商先收款后交货，资金不积压，其基础为进口商对出口商的充分信任；(3)(4)两种为出口商先交货后收款，资金会积压，其基础为出口商对进口商的充分信任。

2.　The Kinds of Collection

1)　Documentary Collection

After effecting shipment, the exporter establishes the draft, attaches shipping documents to the draft and sends them to the bank for entrusting it the collection of goods payment from the importer. In international trade the documentary collection is mostly used in foreign trade.

According to the different conditions of paying the shipping documents, the documentary documents are classified into the following two kinds.

(1)　Documents against Payment(D/P).

The payment of the importer is effected on the condition of the exporter's delivering the draft and the whole set of shipping documents. That is to say, if the exporter does not deliver the shipping documents, the importer will not effect his payment.

(2)　Documents against Acceptance(D/A).

The exporter delivers his documents on the condition of the importer's accepting the draft. That is to say, the exporter will deliver his shipping documents only after the importer has effected the acceptance by the draft in order to ensure the exporter's receiving the goods payment.

2)　Clean Collection

The drawer delivers only the draft, but does not attach the shipping documents to it. This kind of collection is generally used to collect the balance of the goods payments, the sample fees, the commissions, the advanced payment for something and for other subordinate expenses used in the trade. Generally, the collection of this kind uses the draft attached with the receipt, detailed list, etc.

2. 托收的种类

1)　跟单托收

出口商装运货物后开具汇票，连同全套货运单据委托银行向进口商收取货款。国际贸易中大都采用跟单托收。

根据进口商交付货运单据的条件不同，跟单托收分为以下两种。

(1) 付款交单(简称 D/P)。

进口商的付款是以出口商出具汇票和全套货运单据为条件的，即出口商如果不出具货运单据，则进口商不付货款。

(2) 承兑交单(简称 D/A)。

出口商的交单是以进口商在汇票上的承兑为条件的，即进口商在汇票上承兑后，出口商才交出货运单证，以保证收到货款。

2) 光票托收

出票人仅出具汇票，不随附货运单据。这种托收通常用于托收货款尾数、样品费、佣金、代垫费用及其他贸易从属费用。一般附有收据、清单等。

II. Urging Shipment

In order to execute the contract and to do the foreign trade well, the first task we must fulfill is to ask your opposite party to effect shipment, then the following procedures such as payment effecting, delivery taking, etc. can be carried out. So the letter for urging the shipment is one of the foreign trading letters we often see.

二、催促发货

要完成贸易合同，做好外贸交易，首先是要对方发货，然后才能进行下列步骤，如付款、提货等，所以催促发货的信件往往是最常见的外贸书信之一。

Example

Dear Sirs,

Re: Urging Shipment

We have pleasure to inform you that the Letter of Credit No. ××× for the order No. ××× was established in your favor through the Bank of China, Shanghai Branch on the 10th of this month and we trust that by now you would have received the advice from the Bank at your end.

As you know, our clients need the goods badly at the present time owing to the approaching of the busy season and we would be very grateful in case of your arranging to effect the shipment as soon as possible. Your prompt shipment of the goods would certainly attract our prospective buyers and lead to a prosperous development of the trading between us.

Yours faithfully,

实例

关于：催促发货

我方有幸通知你方，以你方为受益人的支付×××号订单的×××号信用证已于本月10日通过中国银行上海分行开立。我方相信现在你方一定已收到你方银行的通知。

正如你方所知，由于忙季来临，目前我方用户正迫切需要这些货物。如果你方能尽快安排发货，我方将十分感激。你方的立即发货肯定会吸引我方未来的买主，并且导致双方贸易的繁荣发展。

Words and Expressions

client	*n.* 委托人，(律师的)当事人；(商店等的)顾客
customer	*n.* 顾客，主顾，消费者(end customer 最终消费者；end-user 最终用户)
attract	*v.* 吸引，引起兴趣，引起注意
prospective	*a.* 预期的，盼望中的，未来的
prosperous	*a.* 繁荣的，顺利的

Notes

信用证有很多种，如：

commercial L/C　商业信用证

documentary L/C　跟单信用证

irrevocable L/C　不可撤销信用证

revocable L/C　可撤销信用证

confirmed L/C　保兑信用证

unconfirmed L/C　非保兑信用证

circular L/C　流通信用证

blank L/C　空白信用证

III. Asking for Cash Payment

Example

Dear Sirs,

<u>Re: Asking for Cash Payment</u>

We are in receipt of your letters dated 25 May and 2 June and now we are very glad to advise you that 100 pieces of art crafts you ordered last month have been shipped to you per SS "Queen" due at Rotterdam on 12th, next month.

It is necessary to tell you that all the goods we shipped were selected by us with great care in order to meet with your requirements.

We have enclosed a copy of invoice with the price of US $ ××× and have drawn on you for this amount at sight through the Bank of ××, who will hand over documents against payment of the draft.

It is necessary to inform you that as our usual practice, we place order with new customers only on a cash basis and it is a pity that your urgent need of the goods gave us no sufficient time to make usual enquiry.

In case that you would like to deal with us regularly in future, we would be prepared to consider open account terms with quarterly settlements. We think this term of transaction will be welcomed by you. As to the above mentioned order, we wish you expedite your cash payment.

Truly yours,

三、请求以现金付款

实例

关于：请求以现金付款

我方已收到你方 5 月 25 日及 6 月 2 日的来信，现在很高兴地通知你方上月所订的 100 件工艺品已经由"皇后"轮发运你方，该轮预定于下月 12 日抵达鹿特丹。

必须告知你方的是，我方发出的所有货物都经由我方仔细选择以满足你方要求。

我方已附上一份价目为×××美元的发票，并已将上述金额通过××银行开出即期汇票，该银行在你方兑付汇票时递交单证。

必须通知你方的是，按照我方惯例，我们同新客户只在现金基础上进行交易，但你方对货物的迫切需要未给我方提供足够的时间来按常规征询意见。

如果你方希望将来与我方定期进行交易，我方准备考虑实行赊账交易，每季度结算一次。我方认为这种交易条款会受到你方的欢迎。至于上述订单，希望你方尽快以现金付款。

Words and Expressions

due	*a.* 预定应到的，预期的
Rotterdam	*n.* 鹿特丹港(荷兰港口)
select	*v.* 选择
invoice	*n.* 发票
draw	*v.* 开汇票，开立票据
pity	*n.* 遗憾的事，可惜的事
sufficient	*a.* 充分的，充足的
quarterly	*a.* 按季度的
settlement	*n.* 结算，支付
hand over	递交
usual practice	惯例，习惯做法
open account	赊账

Notes

(1) invoice 发票，发票有很多种，如：

commercial invoice 商业发票

consignment invoice 寄售发票

purchases invoice 售货发票

incoming invoice 进库发票

outgoing invoice 销货发票

proforma invoice 形式发票

customs invoice 海关发票

consular invoice 领事发票

(2) 付款方式也有许多种，如：

remittance 汇款，寄款

mail transfer (M/T) 信汇

telegraphic transfers (T/T) 电汇

postal remittance 邮政汇款

demand draft (D/D) 票汇

collection 托收

applicant for collection 托收人

collection on clean bill 光票托收

collection on documents 跟单托收

Ⅳ. Accepting the Installment Payments

Example

Dear Sirs,

<u>Re: Accepting the Installment Payments</u>

Our Vice President Mr. ××× has already come back from your States, from whom we have known that with respect to our production line of manufacturing ××× you have given your serious consideration. In order to develop the future business between our two corporations, you are intending to offer us an installment payments terms for the transaction of our importing the machinery Type ××× and equipment Type ××× of our production line, for which we would like to express our great thankfulness. We suggest to effect our installment payments by L/C according to the following schedule:

(1) The 1st payment: 25% payable within 10 days against your clean draft after the signing of the contract.

(2) The 2nd payment: 50% payable within 15 days after receiving your full set of shipping documents of the machinery and equipment.

(3) The 3rd payment: 25% payable within 20 days after the performance acceptance testing and normal operating of the machinery and equipment. Thank you for your friendly cooperation.

Truly yours,

四、同意以分期付款方式支付

实例

关于：同意以分期付款方式支付

我公司副总裁 XXX 先生已经从美国返回，他告诉我们贵方对制造×××的生产线十分重视。为了贵我双方两个公司之间未来业务的发展，贵公司正拟对我方进口生产线的×××型机械以及×××型设备的这笔交易提供分期付款。为此我方甚为感谢。我方建议按照下列计划凭信用证进行分期付款：

(1) 第一次付款：合同签订后 10 天内凭贵方光票支付 25%。

(2) 第二次付款：收到你方全套机械及设备的装运单据后 15 天内支付 50%。

(3) 第三次付款：机械及设备性能验收试验及正常运行后 20 天内支付 25%。

感谢贵方的友好合作。

Words and Expressions

accept	*v.* 接受
States	*n.* 此处指美国，美国的全称为 "The United States of America"
state	国家，合众国，州
schedule	*n.* 计划表，程序表；一览表，细目单；议事日程
payable	*a.* 可支付的
installment payment	分期付款
vice president	副总裁
with respect to	关于
clean draft	光票
performance acceptance testing	性能验收试验
normal operation	正常运行

Notes

(1) serious consideration　认真考虑，十分重视

　　considerable　*a.* 值得重视的

(2) 文中三次分期付款对双方都有利。

第一次付款：一般付款在装运期前一个月开立信用证，但现在是合同签订后就付 25%，对出口方有利。

第二次付款：一般设备到货后就应付清全部货款，这里先付 50%，对进口方有利，收到装运单据后 10～15 天内议付是合乎常规做法的。

第三次付款：性能试验及正常运行后 20 天内支付 25%，更有利于进口方，万一设备机械出现问题，对方可马上派人检修或更换零件等。

Ⅴ. Negotiating Payment Documents

Example

Dears Sirs,

<u>Re: Negotiating Payment Documents</u>

We are in receipt of your letter dated 15 July. Referring to your question of the required documents for negotiating payment, we are pleased to give you our prompt reply. The documents required for negotiating payment are as follows:

(1) Draft made out according to the provisions in the L/C.

(2)　Full set of negotiable clean shipped on board Ocean Bill of Lading marked "Freight prepaid" (for CIF transaction) and "Freight to collect" (for FOB transaction) and made out to order and endorsed in blank.

(3)　Invoice in＿＿＿ copy (copies), indicating contract number and shipping marks.

(4)　Packing List in＿＿＿ copy (copies), indicating gross and net weights and measurements.

(5)　Certificates of Quality and Quantity/Weight and Inspection Report, each in＿＿＿ copies.

(6)　Copy of Fax Shipping Advice in＿＿＿ copies.

　　　Best regards.

Truly yours,

五、议付单证

实例

关于：议付单证

贵公司 7 月 15 日来函我公司已收悉。关于贵公司咨询议付所需单证的问题，我公司很高兴给予你方立即回复。议付所需单证如下：

(1)　根据信用证条款所开的汇票。

(2)　全套可以议付的、洁净的、已装运的海运提单。空白抬头，空白背书，注明"运费已付"(CIF 交易者)，或注明"运费待收"(FOB 交易者)。

(3)　发票＿＿＿份，注明合同号、唛头等。

(4)　装箱单＿＿＿份，注明毛重、净重及尺寸。

(5)　质量证书、数量/重量证书及检验报告各＿＿＿份。

(6)　装运通知传真副本＿＿＿份。

顺颂商祺。

Words and Expressions

negotiate	协商，议定；议付，兑现
provision	*n*. 规定，条款
CIF (Cost, Insurance & Freight)	CIF=成本+保险+运费，以前习惯上都把 CIF 译作"到岸价"，目前一般都译作"CIF 价"，因为到岸价可以不包括保险
FOB (Free on Board)	船上交货价，离岸价
indicate	*v*. 说明，表明
measurement	尺寸
certificate	证明书
inspection report	检验报告
make out	书写，填写，开列
shipped on Board	已装船
freight prepaid	运费已付

freight to collect	运费待付
make out to order	做成空白抬头
endorse in blank	空白背书
gross weight	毛重
net weight	净重

Notes

(1) make out   书写，填写，开列

　　make out a cheque   开支票

　　make out a document in duplicate   缮写文件，一式两份

(2) blank endorsed/endorsement in blank   空白背书

　　bill endorsed in blank   空白背书汇票

　　blank receipt   空白收据(未经签字的收据)

　　blank bill of lading   空白提单

　　endorse   在支票汇票等背面签名，背书；indorse(美)

　　endorser   背书人，转让人；indorser(美)

　　endorsee   被背书人；indorsee(美)

(3) order bill of lading 记名提单，指提单收货人栏内填有"to order"，可凭托运人、收货人或银行的背书将提单的货物转让他人。

(4) on board   在船上，在车上，在飞机上

　　free on board   船上交货，离岸价格

Ⅵ. Asking for Deferring Payment

Payment deferring is, in fact, an action of contract breading. So don't defer any payment unless it is absolutely necessary. If you want to put forward your requirement for deferring payment, you must be very polite and tactful and as well state the reason and express your apology to him. If the contract deferring is caused by Force Majeure, the party who breaks the contract will not be responsible for the compensation, but it is still necessary for him to inform them the reason politely in time for getting pardon from his partner and to inform him the estimated deferred time of effecting the contract.

六、请求延期付款

延期付款实际上是一种违约的行为，因此除非不得已绝不能延期付款。如果请求对方同意延期付款，一定要十分委婉客气，还必须说明原因并致歉。如果是因不可抗力的因素而造成的违约，违约方不负责赔偿，但仍应及时地将延期原因告知对方，以求得对方谅解，并确定推迟履约的大概时间。

Example

Dear Sirs,

<u>Re: Asking for Deferring Payment</u>

As you know rather well, we have been an enterprise with high financial prestige. We have been persisting in meeting our commitments and in prompt settling our accounts with our trading partners.

But owing to the Force Majeure cause, to the great tsunami happening in Indian Ocean, our industry and agriculture have been destroyed, our communications and transportations have been collapsed, and the national economy and most fields of our constructions have been put into standstill. It will take us a long time to restore our economy and our production. Under such circumstances, we are now unable to effect our payment for the goods under Contract No. ×××　in time and have to ask your favor of allowing us to defer our payment of your present accounts for 3 months.

It is because that the above-mentioned payment deferring is caused by the Force Majeure, we would be very grateful if you would excuse us from the penalty resulted from the deferred payment.

Please accept our apologies again.

Truly yours,

实例

<u>关于：请求延期付款</u>

你方十分了解，我方一直是金融信誉很高的企业。我方一直能够坚持完成承担的义务，并且迅速结清与贸易伙伴之间的账款。

由于不可抗力的原因，印度洋发生的大海啸使我们的工业和农业都遭到了破坏，通信和交通崩溃了，国民经济和大部分建设领域也都瘫痪了。恢复经济和生产需要很长时间。在此情况下，我方现在无法按时交付×××号合同项下的货物，并且不得不恳请贵方同意我方推迟三个月支付贵方目前的账款。

由于上述推迟付款是不可抗力所造成，如果贵方能免去我方由于推迟付款而引起的罚款，我方将不胜感激。

再次致歉。

Words and Expressions

defer	*v.* 延迟，延期	
enterprise	*n.* 企业	
prestige	*n.* 信誉	
persist	*v.* (in)坚持	
commitment	*n.* 承担的义务，承约	
settle	*v.* 解决	
account	*n.* 账目，报表，计划，说明	

Force Majeure [ma:za:]	(使无法履行契约的)不可抗力(如天灾，战争)
tsunami [tsu'na:mi]	n. 海啸，海震，地震海浪
Indian Ocean	印度洋
industry	n. 工业
agriculture	n. 农业
destroy	v. 破坏
communication	n. 通信
transportation	n. 运输
collapse	v. 崩溃
field	n. 领域
standstill	n. 停顿
restore	v. 恢复
circumstance	n. 环境，情况，(有关)事项
excuse	v. 给……免去……(excuse sb. from …)
penalty	n. 罚款
result	v. 由于……引起，由于……造成(result from)

Notes

Force Majeure (法)　意为"不可抗力，不可抗拒的压力"，指人类无法控制的意外事件，包括天灾、人祸，如闪电、飓风、战争、封锁、罢工等。因不可抗力的因素而造成合同不能履行时，违约方可以不负赔偿责任。旅游时因不可抗力而取消几个旅游点或改变旅游线路，旅行社也不负责赔偿责任。

VII. Some Deformations of FOB and CIF Terms

As per the stipulations of INCOTERMS 2000, the seller of the FOB contract should timely ship the goods to the shipping port and make the delivery on board the ship or load on board the ship. The delivery point is at the side of the ship. After being crossed the side of the ship, the risks of the goods' being damaged or being lost have been transferred to the buyer. If the buyer asks the seller to hand " the clean on board bill of lading", the delivery point of that contract has already been extended from the hold of the ship to the side of the ship. The seller should bear the charges for loading the goods on board the ship and should take the responsibility of all the risks on his shoulder until the goods' being loaded into the hold. As to this respect, there are no definite stipulations and no usual practices in the international trade. So it is necessary for the both two parties to add additional conditions to the term of "FOB" and to form a deformation of FOB term. For example:

(1)　FOB Liner Terms: It means that the seller will not bear the charges of loading the goods on board the ship as per liner terms.

(2)　FOB Under Tackle: It means that the seller only takes the responsibility of delivering the goods to the place of ship as far as the tackle can reach. The seller will not be responsible for the charges for lifting off the goods into the hold and for other charges.

(3)　FOB Stowed (FOB S)(FOB+stowed): It means that the seller is responsible for the charges for loading the cargo into the hold, including the charges for stowing the hold.

(4)　FOB Trimmed (FOB T)(FOB+Trimmed): It means that the seller will bear the charges for loading the cargo into the hold, including the charges for trimming the cargo in the hold, which can keep the ship balanced and enables the ship to sail smoothly and stably .

(5)　FOB Trimmed and Stowed (FOB ST)(FOB+Stowed + Trimmed): It means that the charges paid by the seller for loading the cargo on board the ship,　including the charges for stowing and trimming the cargo in the hold.

In signing the contract, the additional commitments caused by the terms deformation should be stipulated definitely in order to avoid disputes.

七、FOB 及 CIF 的术语变形

按照 INCOTERMS 2000(2000 年国际贸易术语解释通则)的规定，FOB 合同的卖方必须及时将货在装运港"交至船上"(Deliver on Board)或装上船(Load on Board)，其交货地点(Point of Delivery)为船舷，越过船舷时货物损坏丢失等风险已由卖方转至买方。如果买方要求卖方提交"已装船清洁提单"，那么该合同的交货点已从船舷延伸到船舱，卖方就需要负担装船费用，并承担直至货物装入船舱为止的一切风险。对于这一点，国际贸易中没有明确的规定，也没有贸易惯例。所以，买卖双方需要在 FOB 术语后附加条件，形成 FOB 术语变形。例如：

(1)　FOB 班轮条件(FOB Liner Terms)：指卖方不负担装船费用，按班轮条款办理。

(2)　FOB 吊钩下交货(FOB Under Tackle)：指卖方仅负责将货交到指定船只的吊钩所及之处。卖方不负担将货吊入船舱的费用及其他费用。

(3)　FOB S——船上交货并理舱(FOB Stowed)：卖方负责货物装入船舱的装船费用，包括整理船舱的理舱费。

(4)　FOB T——船上交货并平舱(FOB Trimmed)：卖方负责货物装入船舱的装船费用，包括整理垫平船舱货物以使船只保持平衡航行，并且不损伤船舶结构的平舱费。

(5)　FOB ST——船上交货及理舱平舱(FOB Stowed and Trimmed)：卖方支付的装船费用中既要包括理舱费，还包括平舱费。

签订合同时，对术语变形所产生的额外义务要作具体明确的规定，以免产生纠纷。

1. CIF transaction

CIF is a trade term. "C" means Cost, "I" means Insurance and "F" means Freight. It is necessary to add the name of the destination port after CIF. For example: CIF London. This term means that the seller takes the responsibility of chartering the ship or booking the shipping space, loading the goods onto the ship sailing to the destination port and arranging the goods' insurance. The seller also holds himself responsibilities for paying the shipment and the insurance premium. The seller also charges himself with all the expenditures and of the risks before loading the goods onto the ship. The freight here refers to the normal freight of sailing along the usual sailing line, not including any extra charges happening in the transportation.

Since the goods' being crossed the side of the ship, the risks have already been transferred from the seller to the buyer, so the delivery point of the seller is on board the ship at the shipping port. As per the implication of CIF, the unloading charges after arriving at the destination port are not included in the price of CIF, and the problem of who will bear the expenses from the barge and from the wharf are still not stipulated, so after CIF it is necessary to indicate certain additional conditions, such as:

(1) CIF Liner Terms: The unloading charges will not be borne by the buyer as per liner terms.

(2) CIF Landed: It means unloading on land. That is to say the seller bears the unloading charges.

(3) CIF EX Ships Hold (CIF delivery is at the hold): It means that the seller will not take the responsibility of the unloading charges. The delivery is on board the ship at the destination port. The buyer takes the responsibility of opening the hold and unloading the cargo. The unloading charges from the bilge hold to the wharf will be borne by the buyer.

So the old name of CIF (in Chinese translation "到岸价") is not suitable for the practical business of the present time. It is necessary to add the above-mentioned additional conditions after CIF. This kind of " CIF+ additional conditions" forms the deformation of the CIF terms.

1. CIF交易

CIF (Cost, Insurance and Freight)是贸易术语，即成本、保险费和运费。CIF 后面必须加指定的目的港名称，例如：CIF 伦敦。这一术语指卖方负责租船或订船，在合同规定期限内将货物装上驶往目的港的船只，办理货物运输保险，负责支付运费及保险费，负担货物装上船以前的一切费用和风险。这里的运费仅指惯常航行的正常运费，不包括运输途中任何额外的费用。

自货物在装运港越过船舷时起，风险即由卖方转为由买方负担，因此卖方的交货地点是在装运港的船上。按 CIF 的含义，未包含货物到达目的港后的卸货费用，对驳船费用和码头费用都由谁负担的问题也未加以规定。所以有必要在 CIF 后添加一定的附加条件，如：

(1) CIF 班轮条件(CIF Liner Terms)：买方不负担卸货费用。

(2) CIF 卸到岸上(CIF Landed)：买方负责卸货费用。

(3) CIF 舱底交货(CIF EX Ship's Hold)：卖方不负责卸货费用，在目的港船上交货，买方负责起舱卸货费用并支付由舱底至码头的卸货费用。

所以，CIF 的旧称"到岸价"已不适合现在的实际业务，需在 CIF 后加上上述各种附加条件，这种 CIF 加附加条件的说明形成了 CIF 术语变形。

2. FOB transaction

FOB is also a trade term. It means "Free on Board" — the delivery is on board the ship. After FOB it is necessary to add the designated loading port, for example: "FOB Shanghai".

This term indicates that in the stipulated term of the contract, the seller should load the goods on to the buyer's designated ship at the designated shipping port and bear all the charges of loading the goods on board the ship.

2. FOB交易

FOB 也是贸易术语。FOB (Free on Board)即"船上交货(装上船)"。FOB 后面要加指定的装货港，例如："FOB 上海"。

这一术语指卖方在合同规定的期限内，在指定的装运港将货物装到买方指定的船上，并承担货物装上船为止的一切费用与风险。

Sentences for Payment Effecting

(1) In international trade, there are three major modes of payment that the buyers may accept: namely remittance, collection and letter of credit.

国际贸易中买方可以接受的支付方式主要有三种，即汇付、托收和信用证。

(2) The payer (usually the buyer) remits a certain sum of money in accordance with the parties agreement to the payee (usually the seller) through a bank.

付款人(通常为买方)根据双方的协议，通过银行向收款人(通常为卖方)汇付一定数量的款项。

(3) Where the paying agreement is D/A, the collecting bank will only give the buyer the shipping documents after buyer's acceptance of the bill drawn on him, i.e. the buyer signs his name on the bill promising to pay the sum when it matures.

(Documents against acceptance (D/A)，译为"承兑交单")

在承兑交单时，只有在买方承兑向他开出的汇票，即在汇票上签名承诺到期时付款的情况下，代收行方把运输单据交给买方。

(4) Documents against payments, as the term suggests, is that the collecting bank will only give the shipping documents representing the title to the goods on condition that the buyer effects payment.

(Documents against payment (D/P)，译为"付款交单")

付款交单，顾名思义，就是代收行只有在买方进行付款的前提下才交付代表货物所有权的运输单据。

(5) In view of the amount of this transaction being very small, we are prepared to accept payment by D/P at sight for the value of the goods shipped.

鉴于此笔交易金额很小，我们同意以即期付款交单方式支付所发运的货物。

(6) We hope that D/P payment will result in a considerable increase of your orders and assure you that we shall always endeavor to execute them to your complete satisfaction.

我方希望以付款交单方式支付货款能大量增加你方的订货，同时向你方保证我方将尽力履行交货，以使你方完全满意。

(7) The banker's transfer is a simple transference of money from the bank account of a buyer in his own country to the bank account of the seller in the seller's country.

银行划拨是从买方自己国家的银行账户将钱划拨到卖方国家的卖方银行账户的一种简单程序。

(8) We have remitted ×× Corp. US $ ××× in payment for the sample sent us last week.

我方已给×××公司汇去×××美元，用于支付上周寄给我方的样品。

(9) We have charged your account with the account of money.

我们已将这笔钱记在你们的账上。

(10) The bill of exchange (also called a draft) is an order in writing from a debtor to a creditor to pay on demand or on a named date a certain sum of money to a person named on the bill.

汇票是债权人写给债务人的一份书面命令，命令其在被要求时或在某一固定时间向汇票上列名的人支付一笔金额。

(11) We shall thank you very much for handing us your check for US $ ××× in settlement at your earliest convenience.

如果你方能尽早递交我方一张×××美元的支票，以便结账，我们将十分感谢。

(12) Our draft on you at 60 D/S in your favor will be presented to you by the ××× Bank. Please give it your acceptance.

我方开给你方的以你方为受益人的60天期汇票将由×××银行呈递你方，请予以承兑。

(13) Much to our regret, our draft on you dated 1 August, and due on 1 September was returned dishonored two days ago by our Bank.

我方甚感遗憾，8月1日开给你方的9月1日到期的汇票两天前已被我方银行拒付退回。

(14) We propose to effect payments by bill of exchange at 30 days' documents against acceptance. Please confirm if it is acceptable to you.

我方打算以30天期承兑交单的汇票进行付款，如果你方可以接受，则请确认。

(15) Deferred payment is acceptable if the order is under the amount of US $ ×××.

如果订单金额不足×××美元，可以接受延期付款。

Exercises

Ⅰ. Translate the following sentences from English into Chinese.

1. The delayed payment interest commencing from May 15 to the date of payment December 15 at the interest of 10% per annum amounting to US $ ××× should be for your account.

2. We would like to inform you that you will be invoiced for all the samples if they are not returned to us within 120 days.

3. We expect certain orders to be paid within the next two months and ask if we may defer payment of your account from June 2 to July 15.

4. For future transactions D/P will be accepted if the amount involved for each transaction is below Stg. 5,000.

5. Please see to it that all the payments under the Contracts No. ××× and No. ×× must be effected in time.

Ⅱ. Translate the following sentences from Chinese into English.

1. 我们认为必须通过挂号信寄出发运单证。

2. 一旦有货，我们将传真你方。

3. 这类商品通常按承兑交单出售。

4. 我方很高兴地通知你方，我方已按××号信用证规定，完成 100 台电子计算机的付款。

5. 我方已开立以你方为收益人的、金额为×××美元的、不可撤销的第××号信用证。

Chapter 9　Insurance 保险

Learning Objectives:

- Know how to enquire about the insurance information.
- Master the main types of insurance.
- Learn how to write letters for offering insurance coverage and for claiming on poor quality.
- Understand the necessities of prompt settlement of the customer's claim and of sincere apologizing to the customers for causing troubles.

学习目标：

- 知道如何咨询保险信息。
- 掌握保险的主要类型。
- 学会如何写提供保险服务及提出质量索赔的信。
- 理解为何必须迅速地对顾客的索赔进行理赔，并且必须为造成的麻烦向顾客诚挚致歉。

In international trade, the goods are transported for a long distance from one country to the other. They need to be loaded and unloaded, to be stored, etc. So the goods often run various risks and suffer great losses. In order to get economic compensation after suffering losses, the buyer and the seller have to insure their goods to be shipped against the cargo transportation risks.

The insurance clauses drawn up by People's Insurance Company of China are called "China Insurance Clause" in short, and its abbreviation is CIC. The revised edition was made up on January 1, 1981 and is used at the present time. These clauses are classified according to the different transportation terms into the following kinds:

(1) Cargo Insurance Clause for Ocean Marine Transportation;

(2) Cargo Insurance Clause for Overland Transportation;

(3) Cargo Insurance Clause for Air Transportation;

(4) Cargo Insurance Clause for Parcel Transportation.

The capacity of Ocean Marine transportation is the largest of those of the other transportations, the origin of which is the earliest. Its history is the longest and the range it involves is the widest, so in this Chapter "Cargo Insurance for Ocean Marine Transportation" is taken as the main content.

在国际贸易中，货物从一国运往另一国，需要经过长途运输、装卸、储存等环节，因此常会遇到各种风险而遭受损失。为了在遭受损失后得到经济补偿，买方和卖方有必要为运输的货物投保货物运输险。

中国人民保险公司保险条款简称"中国保险条款"(China Insurance Clause，CIC)，目前使用的是 1987 年 1 月 1 日的修订本。该条款按不同的运输条款分为以下四种：

(1)　海洋运输货物保险条款；

(2)　陆上运输货物保险条款；

(3)　航空运输货物保险条款；

(4)　邮包保险条款。

因海洋运输业务量最大，起源最早，历史最久，涉及面也最广，故本章主要介绍海洋运输货物保险。

Ⅰ. Cargo Insurance for Ocean Marine Transportation

The fundamental insurances of the Cargo Insurance for Ocean Marine Transportation are classified into the following three kinds.

1) Free from Particular Average (FPA)

This insurance covers the total loss or constructive total loss caused by natural disasters, the total loss or partial loss caused by the ship's being stranded, hitting a rock, sinking, ships' crashing, fire, explosion and any other accidents

2) With Particular Average (WA or WPA)

This insurance covers the partial loss caused by natural disasters, such as: the bad weather, except for various duties of FPA.

3) All Risks (AR)

Except for various duties of FPA and WPA, this insurance takes the responsibilities for the total or partial loss caused by general extraneous risks in transit, but it is not responsible for the losses caused by all risks.

一、海洋运输货物保险

海洋运输货物保险的基本险有以下三种。

1)　平安险(FPA)

责任范围为因自然灾害造成的全部损失或推定全损，船只搁浅、触礁、沉没、互撞、失火、爆炸等意外事故造成的全部或部分损失。

2)　水渍险(WA 或 WPA)

责任范围除平安险的各项责任外，还负责由于恶劣气候等自然灾害造成的部分损失。

3)　一切险(AR)

责任范围为除平安险、水渍险的各种责任外，还负责运输途中因一般外来原因所造成的全部或部分损失，但不是对一切风险造成的损失都赔偿。

Ⅱ. General Additional Insurance

There are several additional insurances as follows:

(1) Theft, Pilferage and Non-Delivery(TPND);

(2) Fresh Water and Rain Damage;

(3) Risk of Shortage;

(4) Risk of Intermixture and Contamination;

(5) Risk of Leakage;

(6) Risk of Crash and Breakage;

(7) Risk of Odor;

(8) Hook Damage;

(9) Damage Caused by Sweating and Heating;

(10) Breakage of Packing;

(11) Risk of Rust.

In case of having insured the goods against All Risks, the goods owner needn't insure any other additional risks. The kinds of some Special Risks are as follows.

二、一般附加险

一般附加险包括下列几类：

(1) 偷窃提货不着险；

(2) 淡水雨淋险；

(3) 短量险；

(4) 沾污险；

(5) 渗漏险；

(6) 碰撞、破碎险；

(7) 串味险；

(8) 钩损险；

(9) 受潮、受热险；

(10) 包装破裂险；

(11) 锈损险。

凡已投保一切险者就不需加保任何一种一般附加险。几种特殊附加险如下。

III. Special Additional Insurance

Both the general additional insurances and special additional insurances should not be covered individually.

(1) Failure to Delivery;

(2) Import Duty Risk;

(3) On Deck Risk;

(4) Rejection Risk;

(5) Aflatoxin Risk;

(6) Fire Risk Extension Clause for Storage of Cargo at Destination Hongkong (including Kowloon or Macao);

(7) Strikes Risks;

(8) Ocean Marine Cargo War Risk.

三、特殊附加险

特殊附加险和一般附加险都不能单独投保。

(1)　交货不到险；

(2)　进口关税险；

(3)　舱面险；

(4)　拒收险；

(5)　黄曲霉素险；

(6)　出口货物到香港(包括九龙或澳门)存仓火险责任扩展条款；

(7)　罢工险(罢工、暴动和民变险)；

(8)　海运战争险。

IV．Inquiring about Insurance Information

Example

Dear Sirs,

Re: Inquiring about Insurance Information

We shall have a consignment of 5,000 Stereo Sets assembled here in Shanghai Electronic Factory with components and auxiliary materials supplied by Adlar Electronics Inc. Hongkong, valued at US $×××, to be shipped from Shanghai China to ××× (Rotterdam) and wish to have this consignment to be insured by your Company. Therefore we are writing to enquire about the terms and conditions of different kinds of insurance.

We would appreciate your sending us all of your information and quoting us your present insurance rates for different kinds of insurance at your earliest convenience.

Truly yours,

四、咨询保险信息

实例

关于：咨询保险信息

我方有一批 5000 台价值×××美元的立体声收音机，是在上海电子厂用香港 Adlar 电子公司供应的组件及辅助材料装配而成的，将从中国上海运往鹿特丹。我方希望向贵公司投保。因此我们现在写信咨询各类保险的条款和条件。

若蒙贵公司尽早寄予我方一切信息以及告知各类保险目前的保险费率，我方将不胜感激。

Words and Expressions

component　　　　　　　　　　*n.* 组件，元件

Adlar Electronics Inc.　　　　　Adlar 电子公司

assemble	v. 组装
insurance rate	保险费率
Shanghai Electronic Factory	上海电子厂
auxiliary materials	辅助材料

Notes

1) insurance 表示"投保，办理保险"时搭配的动词或动词词组如下。

arrange insurance

cover insurance

effect insurance

provide insurance

take out insurance

2) insurance 的用法

(1) 表示所保货物，后跟 on，例如：insurance on 100m/t of rice   投保 100 公吨大米。

(2) 表示投保的险别，后跟 against，例如：insurance against All Risks   投保一切险。

(3) 表示"保额"，后跟 for，例如：insurance for 120% of the invoice value   按发票金额 120%投保。

(4) 表示"保险费"或"保险费率"，后跟 at。

insurance at the rate of 5% 按 5%的保险费率投保。表示"向保险公司投保"，用 with。

insurance with the People's Insurance Company of China   向中国人民保险公司投保

Ⅴ. Answering to the Inquiry about Insurance Information

Example

Dear Sirs,

Re: Information Concerning Insurance

In reply to your letter dated ××× enquiring about the insurance information, we wish to inform you of the following:

All Risks: Generally we cover insurance W.P.A. & War Risks in the absence of definite instructions from the clients. If you wish to cover All Risks, we can provide such coverage at a slightly higher premium.

Breakage: Breakage is a special risk, for which an extra premium will have to be charged. The present rate is about ×%. Claims are payable only for that of the loss, that is over 5%.

We would advise you that the rate now being charged by us for the proposed shipment against All Risks including War Risks is 0.50%, subject to our own Ocean Marine Cargo Clauses and Ocean Marine War Risks clauses, copies of which are enclosed herewith for your reference.

We believe the above information will meet your purpose and hope to hear from you soon.

Faithfully yours,

五、对保险信息的咨询进行回复

实例

<u>关于：保险信息</u>

兹回复你方×月×日咨询保险信息的来函如下。

一切险：在客户不作明确指示的情况下，我方将按一般惯例保水渍险和战争险。如贵方拟报一切险，我方可以提供这种保险服务，但保险费用稍高。

破损险：破损险是一种特别险，必须支付额外保险费用。现有保险费率约为×%，我方仅对超过 5%部分的损失进行赔偿。

现奉告，根据我公司海洋运输货物保险条款和海洋运输货物战争险条款的规定，承保上述货物一切险，包括战争险的现行费率是 0.5%。现附上述条款，请参阅。

我方相信上述信息将会满足贵方的需要，希望不久收到回音。

Words and Expressions

concern	v. 涉及，与……有关
All Risks	一切险(编号 A.R.)
in the absence of	在缺乏……的情况下
coverage	保险(范围)，保险(服务)
premium	保险费
Breakage	破损险
Special Risk	特别险
Ocean Marine Cargo Clauses	海洋运输货物保险条款
Ocean Marine War Risks Clauses	海洋运输货物战争险条款
meet one's purpose	满足……需要

Notes

1) 三大基本险

(1) 平安险(Free from Particular Average, FPA)，单独海损不赔。

(2) 水渍险(With Particular Average, WPA)包括部分海损险，或"单独海损赔偿"。

(3) 一切险(或称"综合险"；All Risks, AR)，不能包括一些特殊附加险。

2) 风险种类

(1) 海上风险：如恶劣气候、风暴、海啸、洪水，不包括一般的刮风下雨及海浪打击所造成的风险。

(2) 意外交通事故风险：包括船舟搁浅、触礁、沉没、互撞、失火、爆炸等。

(3) 其他风险：如盗窃、雨淋、短量、渗漏、破损、受潮、战争、罢工、交货不到及拒绝收货等。

VI. Offering Insurance Coverage

Example

Dear Sirs,

<u>Re: Offering Insurance Coverage</u>

After receiving your letter dated ×××, we have known that with reference to your S/C No. ××× for ××× cases of ×××, in addition to F.P.A. and War Risks, you require insurance to cover T.P.N.D. and S.R.C.C. which were not under agreement of both of our two Parties.

According to our usual practice, we cover F.P.A. for the kind of your commodities. In case you require to have your shipment insured against T.P.N.D., we can arrange such insurance coverage for you, but the extra premium will be on your account.

In addition, we have to inform you that S.R.C.C. is as well a kind of special risk, the coverage of which is accepted by the People's Insurance Company of China from now on and will be provided in accordance with the international practice.

In such circumstances, it is necessary for you to send us your amendment to your L/C to increase the amount in order to cover the extra premium.

As soon as your L/C amendment reaches us, we would get the necessary insurance coverage and shipment ready for you.

Sincerely yours,

六、提供保险服务

实例

<u>关于：提供保险服务</u>

收到你方×月×日来函后我方知悉，关于你方×××号销售合同×××箱×××货物，除了平安险及战争险外，你方还要求投保盗窃和提货不着险及罢工、暴动、民变险，这一点过去未经双方协议。

根据常规做法，我方对你方这种货物投保平安险。如果你方要求将你方所发货物投保盗窃和提货不着险，我方可以为你方安排此项保险(服务)，但额外保险费将由你方负担。

此外，我方必须通知你方，罢工、暴动、民变险也是一种特别险，中国人民保险公司从现在起也承办这种保险，并根据国际惯例提供这项保险服务。

在此情况下，你方必须寄给我方你方信用证的修改通知书，以增加金额，支付额外保险费。

一旦你方信用证修改后寄达我方，我方一定将为你方所需的保险及装船事项准备妥善。

Words and Expressions

commodity	*n.* 商品
international practice	国际惯例

business practice	商业惯例
the People's Insurance Company of China	中国人民保险公司
in addition	另外
War Risks	战争险
T.P.N.D.(TPND)	盗窃和提货不着险(Theft Pilferage and Non-Delivery)
S.R.C.C.(SRCC)	罢工、暴动和民变险(Strikes, Risks and Civil Commotions)
under agreement	达成协议
usual practice	一般惯例，习惯做法

Notes

(1)　in such circumstances　在此情况下

(2)　in case　假使

　　　in case of　如果发生……，万一

　　　in no case　绝不

　　　in this case　既然这样，假使这样的话

(3)　Special Risk　特别险

　　　Shortage Risk　短量险

　　　Inter-mixture & Contamination Risks　混杂沾污险

　　　Leakage Risk　渗漏险

　　　Breakage Risk　破损险

　　　Taint of Odor Risk　串味险

　　　Breakage of Packing Risk　包装破裂险

　　　Hook Damage Risk　钩损险

　　　Sweating & Heating Risk　受潮受热险

　　　Rust Risk　锈损险

　　　Aflatoxin Risk　黄曲霉素险

(4)　与 insurance 搭配的词组：

　　　insurance agent　保险代理人

　　　insurance amount　保(险)额

　　　insurance policy　保险单(正式)

　　　insurance certificate　保险凭证，保险收据

　　　insurance coverage　保险范围

　　　insurance declaration　保险声明书

　　　insurance claim　保险索赔

VII. Claiming on Poor Quality

Example

Dear Sirs,

<u>Re: Claiming on Poor Quality</u>

With reference to your S/C No. ××× for ××× m/t's of wheat, shipped per SS "Queen Victoria" and discharged at the Destination Port ×××, we feel regrettable to inform you that after inspection, we found about ×× of the wheat bags were affected with damp, and ×× of them even went moldy, we, therefore, are compelled to lodge our claims with you as follows:

Claim No.	Claim for	Quantity (bag)	Weight (m/t)	Amount (US $)
×××	Quality	×××	×××	×××
Total Amount: Say US $ ××× Only (in words)			US $ ××× (in figure)	

In order to support our claims, we enclose herein one copy of Inspection Certificate No. XXX together with our Statement of Claims amounting to US$ XXX.

We are confident that you would give our claim your most favorable consideration and make your prompt settlement as early as possible.

Truly yours,

七、提出质量索赔

实例

关于：提出质量索赔

你方第×××号销售合同×××公吨小麦已由"维多利亚女王"号轮船运来，并在目的港卸货。我方很遗憾地告知你方，经检查，我方发现约有××袋的小麦受潮，甚至有××袋小麦发生霉变。因此，我们不得不向你方提出索赔如下：

索赔号	索赔原因	数量(袋)	重量(公吨)	金额(美元)
×××	质量	×××	×××	×××
总金额： ×××美元(用文字，大写)			×××美元 (用数字，小写)	

为了支持我方的索赔，在此附上第×××号检验证明书复印件及索赔报表各一份，索赔总额计×××美元。

相信你方对于我方的索赔一定会给予优先的考虑并尽早理赔。

Words and Expressions

claim   *vt.* 索赔

discharge   *v.* 卸货

inspection	*n.* 检查
lodge a claim with sb. for damage	向谁提出索赔损失
Inspection Certificate	检验证明书
Statement of Claims	索赔报告(报表，声明书)
with reference to	关于
one fourth	四分之一
be affected with damp	受潮

Notes

1) claim 的用法:

(1) 表示索赔的原因，后跟"for"，例如：claim for damage 因损坏提出索赔。

(2) 表示索赔的金额，后跟"for"，例如：claim for US $ ××× 索赔×××美元。

(3) 表示对货物索赔，后跟"on"，例如：claim on the goods 对货物提出索赔。

(4) 表示向某人索赔，后跟"against"，例如：claim against the underwriters 向保险商索赔。

2) 和 claim 连用的词组:

(1) 和 claim 连用表示"提出索赔"的词组有：lodge a claim, register a claim, file a claim, raise a claim。

(2) 和 claim 连用表示"提出索赔"的常用动词有：put in，make，issue，lay，render，enter，bring up，set up 等。

(3) 动词和 claim 组成的动词词组:

accept a claim	同意索赔	admit a claim	同意索赔
entertain a claim	受理索赔	dismiss a claim	驳回索赔
reject a claim	拒绝索赔	relinquish a claim	撤回索赔
settle a claim	解决索赔	waive a claim	放弃索赔

例如：claim for US $×××	索赔×××美元
claim a compensation of US $×××	要求索赔美元×××
claim US $××× for damage	因损坏索赔美元×××
claim US $××× on the goods	对货物索赔美元×××
claim US $××× from the underwriters	向保险商提出索赔×××美元

VIII. Settling the Claim

Example

Dear Sirs,

<u>Re: Settling the Claim</u>

After receiving your letter dated ××× lodging claim with us for the quality of the wheat under S/C No. ×××, we have carried out our own investigations and have found the following causes of the wheat's being moldy:

(1) The continual rains of the rainy season initiated the dampness of the warehouse.

(2) The warehouse has long been out of repair, and there appeared leaks in the roof and drove the rains into the warehouse.

(3) The wheat had been stored in this warehouse for two weeks before it was shipped.

Owing to your having covered the insurance against Fresh and/or Rain Water Damage Risks, we now therefore, enclose our Check No. ×××　for US $ ×××　in full and final settlement of your claim No. ×××.

We apologize for the trouble caused to you and please acknowledge your receipt of our Check.

Sincerely yours,

八、理赔

实例

关于：理赔

收到你方×月×日关于×××号销售合同项下因小麦质量而提出索赔的来函以后，我方经自查发现，小麦发生霉变有如下几个原因：

(1) 雨季的连绵雨水使得仓库潮湿。

(2) 仓库年久失修，而且库顶漏雨，以致雨水漏入仓库。

(3) 小麦装船前曾在此仓库储放两周。

由于你方已投保淡水雨淋险，故我方现附寄×××美元的×××号支票一张，作为对你方×××号索赔的全部、最终的解决。

我方为给你方带来的麻烦致歉，收到支票后请来信告知。

Words and Expressions

initiate	*v.* 引发，发动
dampness	*n.* 潮湿
warehouse	*n.* 仓库
appear	*v.* 出现
leak	*v.* 渗漏
roof	*n.* 屋顶
Fresh and /or Rain Water Damage Risks	淡水雨淋险
check	*n.* 支票
acknowledge	*v.* 确认

Notes

与 claim 一起常用的词组：

claim against a person   向某人索赔

claim arising from a breach of the contract   违约引起的索赔

claim arising on a bill of lading   有关提单引起的索赔

claim based on lack of conformity of the goods   货物不符产生的索赔

claim for compensation of damages   损害赔偿的索赔

claim for contribution in general average   要求分摊共同海损

claim for financial loss   关于经济损失的索赔

claim for general average   共同海损分担的索赔

claim for inferior quality   由于品质低劣的索赔

claim for payment   要求付款的诉权

Sentences for Insurance

(1) For CIF transactions, we usually effect insurance for 110% of the invoice value against risks.

对于 CIF 交易，我们一般按发票金额的 110%投保风险。

(2) We have covered the above shipment against All Risks.

我们已为上述货物投保了一切险。

(3) If a higher percentage is required, we may do accordingly, but you have to bear the extra premium as well.

如果要求更高的百分率，我们也能照办，但你们必须承担额外的保险费。

(4) For transactions concluded on CIF basis, we usually effect insurance with PICC against All Risks, as per *Ocean Marine Cargo Clauses of PICC* dated 1 January,1981.

对于按 CIF 达成的交易，我们通常按 1981 年 1 月 1 日中国人民保险公司制定的《海洋运输货物保险条款》向中国人民保险公司投保一切险。

(5) We have insured at (for) 110% of the invoice value.

我们已按发票金额的 110%投保。

(6) Insurance is to be effected (to be covered，to be taken up) by the seller on the subject article against All Risks for 110% (115%, 120%) of the invoice value.

标题商品将由卖方按发票金额 110% (115%, 120%) 投保一切险。

(7) The extra premium for additional coverage, if required, shall be borne by the buyer.

如果需要，投保额外险别的额外保险费需由买方承担。

(8) Should any damage occur, you may put in a claim within 30 days after the arrival of the consignment.

如果出现任何损坏，贵方可在货到 30 天内提出索赔。

(9) Insurance validity expires on the 60th day after the insured goods are unloaded at the final port of loading.

保险有效期在被保货物于最后的卸货港卸货以后的第 60 天到期。

(10) Our insurance company is enjoying high prestige in settling claims promptly and equitably, you are advised to do business with us on CIF basis and leave the insurance to be

affected by us.

我保险公司在及时公平理赔方面享有极高的声誉，建议你方在 CIF 基础上和我们进行保险业务，由我们代为保险。

(11) We have just received the Survey Report from the Shanghai Commodity Inspection Bureau evidencing the short weight of ×× lbs.

我们刚收到上海商检局的检验报告，证明短重××磅。

(12) Please see to it that the above-mentioned goods are to be shipped before the 15th May and the goods are to be covered for 130% of invoice value against All Risks. We know that according to your usual practice, you insure the goods only for 10% above invoice value, therefore the extra premium will be on your account.

请注意上述货物将在 5 月 15 日前装出，保险将按发票价格的 130%投保一切险。我们知道按照你方的一般惯例，你方只按发票价格加价 10%投保，因此额外保费由我方负担。

(13) We regret to inform you that the goods shipped per SS "××" arrived in such an unsatisfactory condition that we cannot but lodge a claim against you.

我方很遗憾地告知你方，由"××"轮运来的货物的状况令人十分不满，以致我方不得不向你方提出索赔。

(14) The claim should be supported by sufficient evidence. The Survey Report issued by the China Inspection Bureau will be taken as final and binding upon both parties.

你方索赔须有充分的证据，由中国商品检验局出具的检验报告将作为对双方都有约束力的最终依据。

(15) It has been agreed that we have the right to reject the goods if they are unqualified. Now we regret to inform you that we have to return the goods to you at your expenses.

双方曾经同意，如货物质量不合格，我方有权拒收。现在我方很遗憾地告知你方，我方不得不将货物退回你方，费用由你方承担。

Exercises

Ⅰ. Translate the following sentences from English into Chinese.

1. We are ready to compensate your loss and will send you the claimed amount, US $ ×× by T/T. We hope this oversight on our part will not undermine our good relations.

2. Regarding our order No. ×××, we are sending you the official document that shows the quantity delivered to us is less than ordered.

3. We are not responsible for any damage which happened during transit from the warehouse to the destination.

4. It was found upon examination that nearly 20% of the packages had been broken, which was obviously attributed to improper packing.

5. Since the premium varies with the extent of insurance, extra premium is for buyer's account.

II. Translate the following sentences from Chinese into English.

1.　保险费将与运费一起加在发票中。

2.　如果买方国家阻止合同的执行，这种风险就叫国家风险。

3.　如果你方想保破损险，你方必须支付额外保险费。

4.　现附去上述保险条款，请参阅。

5.　我方能按照国际惯例为你方提供这种保险服务。

Chapter 10　International Tendering 国际招标

Learning Objectives:

- Know the kinds and procedures of international tendering.
- Learn the letter writing of the bidding application and tendering accepting.
- Master the ways of writing the guarantee for bid bond and qualification documents.

学习目标：

- 知道国际招标的种类和程序。
- 学会写投标申请书及通知中标信。
- 掌握书写银行保函及资格文件的方法。

The international tendering is generally used in international trading activities. It is mainly used in contracting the international projects and is always used by the national governmental institutions, the state-owned enterprises and the public utility unit in the procurement trading of goods, materials and equipment. Nowadays the credit items of international governments and international financial institutions must be stipulated in loan agreements. Loanees must adopt international public tendering to procure item goods and materials and contract a project out to the others.

国际招标是国际经济贸易活动中一种通行的交易方式，主要用于国际承包工程，也常用于国家政府机构、国有企业或公用事业单位采购物资、器材或设备的交易中。目前国际政府贷款项目和国际金融机构的贷款项目必须在贷款协议中加以规定，接受贷款方必须采用国际公开招标方式采购项目物资或发包工程。

Ⅰ. The Processes of Tendering

1. Invitation for Bids

The buyer (that is the procuring or the constructing unit), as a tenderer, must do the following work in his tendering:

(1) Issuing the Notice of Invitation for Bids or releasing "Bid Form".

(2) Putting forward detailed specifications and quantity of the project to be bought or to be constructed and state conditions of concluding the business.

(3) Inviting the seller (this is the supplier or the project contractor) to fill the form.

(4) Sending the firm offer to participate in the bidding in a certain period of time.

一、招标的流程

1. 招标

作为招标人，买方(采购商或建筑商)在招标时必须做下列工作。

(1)　发出招标公告或招标单。

(2)　提出准备买进或兴建工程的详细规格、数量及成交条件。

(3)　邀请卖方(供货商或承包商)在一定期限内填制表单。

(4)　递出实盘，参加投标。

2. Bidding

The seller, as the bidder, according to the conditions of the "Notice of Invitation for Bids" and the "Bid form" carries out careful study and preparation to work out and fill up the Form, then sends out his offer to the tenderer.

2. 投标

卖方作为投标人，根据招标公告或招标单的条件进行认真研究和准备，编制填写投标书后，在规定的时间内，应邀向招标人发盘。

3. Bids Opening and Bid Winning

In order to win the Bids, the Bidder's offer is often the lowest. The tenderer makes public bids opening at the stipulated time, stipulated place and according to the stipulated requirements. After the bids' opening and comparing with different offers of the bidders, their qualifications and operating capacities, the bids winner will be chosen. Then the notice of the bids winner will be issued.

3. 开标与中标

投标人为争取中标，发盘往往是最低的，招标人按规定的时间、地点及要求，当众开标。开标后比较各投标人的发盘、资质及经营能力进行筛选，选出中标者后发出中标通知书。

II. The Ways of Tendering

There are two methods to distingwish the ways of Tendering.

1. According to the extent of tendering competition

According to the extent of tendering competition, the ways of tendering are classified into the following two ways.

(1)　Public Tendering (also called unlimited competitive tendering): The tenderer issues the "Notice of Invitation for Bids". In the light of the address showed in the notice, the companies willing to join in the tendering may approach to the responsible person to get relevant recommendation documents and "Preliminary Qualification Investigation Form". After passing the preliminary investigation, the companies may join in the tendering, with the number of joining bidders unlimited.

(2) Selective Tendering (also called limited competitive tendering): In accordance with his own concrete business relations and with relative information, the tenderer may choose certain number of suppliers in the limited scope and invite them to join in the bidding.

二、招标方式

有两种方法对招标进行分类。

1. 按招标引起的投标竞争程度分

按招标引起的投标竞争程度，可分为以下两类。

(1) 公开招标(又称无限竞争性招标)：招标人发出招标通告后，凡愿参加投标的公司按通告中地址领取有关介绍资料及资格预审表格，通过资格预审者均可参加投标，不限数量。

(2) 选择性招标(又称有限竞争性招标)：招标人根据自己具体的业务关系及情报资料，在有限范围内选择一定数量的供货商，邀请其参加投标。

2. According to the conditions of awarding the contract in tendering

According to the conditions of awarding the contract in tendering, the ways of tendering are classified into the following two ways.

(1) The Tendering's Automatic Condition: The tenderer takes the lowest offer as prerequisite condition. The contract will be automatically awarded to a certain bidder. Such kind of tendering is suitable for the tendered commodities with unanimous specifications and qualities.

(2) The tendering's ad libitum conditions: The tenderer does not take prices as the basis of judging the bidders. His judging may be made by performances of new-typed products, by "After Sale Service", etc.

(3) Negotiation Tendering: The tenderer may freely negotiate with any bidders over the contract conditions after the tendering's opening and then define the bid's winner.

2. 按招标授予合同的条件分

按招标授予合同的条件，可分为以下三类。

(1) 自动条件招标：招标人以最低报价为先决条件，自动将合同授予某个投标人。这种招标适用于规格统一、质量一致的招标商品。

(2) 随意条件招标：招标人授予合同的条件可以不以价格作为评判投标人的依据，也可以其他条件为评判的主要依据，如按新型产品的性能、售后服务等条件来评判。

(3) 谈判招标(又称议标)：招标人在开标后可以自由地和任何一个投标人就合同条件进行洽商，然后确定中标人。

III．Calling for Tenders

Example

Dear Sirs,

<u>Re: Calling for Tenders</u>

We are pleased to inform you that the China International Tendering Corporation on behalf of our government has invited tenders for carrying out the engineering designing of a hydraulic power station in Hunan Province, together with the designing and manufacturing of the project equipment in whole set and the whole engineering construction work. We think that a lot of eligible suppliers would be very interested in this tender and you, as a famous giant enterprise, would be undoubtedly willing to participate in it as well.

If you wish to participate in this tender, please send us the information on the hydraulic engineering projects which you have designed and constructed, including the following data as cost and period of the construction project, etc.

Upon receiving your information, we shall register you as the participant of this tender and send you a complete set of tender documents needed for accepting prequalification, but the expense shall be borne by you.

Please note that the bidding deadline is set for ×× 2015. Your offer and documents must be available for us before the closing time.

Waiting for your sincere cooperation.

Sincerely yours,

三、招标

实例

关于：招标

我们很高兴地通知贵方，中国国际招标公司代表我国政府宣布就湖南省水力发电站的工程设计、全套项目设备的设计和制造，以及整个工程的建设工作进行公开招标。我们认为很多合格的供应商对此都会有兴趣，贵公司作为一家有名的大企业肯定也会愿意参加。

如果贵方愿意参加投标，请将贵方设计及建设过的水力工程项目的资料寄予我方，包括建设工程的成本、时期等数据。

在收到贵方资料后，我方将把贵方作为投标参加者进行登记，并寄给贵方一整套接受资格预审所需的招标文件，但费用将由贵方承担。

请注意，投标截止日期为 2015 年×月×日，贵方的报价及文件必须在该期限前送达我方。

期待你方的真诚合作。

Words and Expressions

engineering	*n.* 工程
project	*n.* 计划，方案规划；工程，工程项目
construction	*n.* 建设
eligible	*a.* 合格的
supplier	*n.* 供货商，供货者
enterprise	*n.* 企业
undoubtedly	*adv.* 无疑地，肯定地
register	*v.* 登记
participant	*n.* 参加者
prequalification	*n.* 资格预审
deadline	*n.* 最后期限
set for	*v.* 安排，设定(日期、限度、价格等)
to invite tender	招标
hydraulic power station	水力发电站
Hunan Province	湖南省
be willing to do sth.	愿意做某事
participate in	参加
bear the expense	承担费用

Notes

(1) Tender *v. & n.* (英) 投标

Bid *v. & n.* (美) 投标(拍卖中)，出价，递价，出价(购买人出的价)竞买

上面两个词在美国通用，无差别。但在英国，tender 指对标购招标的卖方的投标，bid 指对标售招标买方的投标。

(2) call for tender (bid)   招标

invite to tender (bid)   招标

put in a tender for sth.   投标承办某事物

make a tender for sth.   投保承办某事物

invitation to (for) tender (bid)   招标

常和 bid 这一名词连用的动词有：open, reject, send in, submit，put in, accept, invite, get, entertain, make, withdraw, write, win, receive 等。

(3) bid against each other on (for) a new project

投标相互竞争以取得一项新工程的营造权

make a bid for   投标争取……的营造权，出价竞卖

enter a bid   投标

bid in sth.   拍卖人故意出最高价使拍卖物落入己手

bid up sth.   哄抬拍卖物的价钱

international bid (tender)   国际性投标

closed bid　(一定范围内邀请参加)不公开招标

public bid　(不限范围邀请参加)公开招标

sealed bid　密封投标，保密投标

open bid　不保密投标

tenderer=bidder　投标人

successful tenderer　中标人

winning tenderer (bidder)　中标人

Ⅳ. Sending the Application for Bidding

Example

Dear Sirs,

<u>Re: Application for Bidding</u>

We thank you very much for your letter of September 19 and for your invitation for bidding. After perusing your terms and conditions concerning the engineering design, the project equipment design and manufacture, as well the engineering construction work, we deeply believe that we are in a position to fulfill all these tasks well and we are sufficiently confident that we shall win in this competition bidding.

Now we are pleased to send you the following documents:

(1)　Schedule of Prices;

(2)　Schedule of Requirements;

(3)　Specifications Compliance Form;

(4)　Qualification Documents;

(5)　Bid Security in the amount of＿＿ issued by ＿＿Bank;

(6)　All documents required in response to clauses No. ×× and No. ×× of the Instructions to Bidders.

We are looking forward to your opening the tenders and to hearing from you that we are awarded the contract.

Yours Truly,

四、投标申请书

实例

<u>关于：投标申请书</u>

我方十分感谢贵方 9 月 19 日的来信，感谢邀请我方参加投标。在细读贵方有关工程设计、工程设备设计及制造以及工程建设工作的条款条件之后，我方深信我方能很好地完成所有这些任务，并且我方也深信在此次竞争性投标中我方是能获胜的。

现在我方很高兴地给贵方寄去如下文件：

(1)　投标价格表；

(2) 货物要求一览表；

(3) 规格差异表；

(4) 资格证书文件；

(5) 由____银行开具的金额为____的投标保证金保函；

(6) 投标须知第××条和第××条要求投标人提交的所有文件。

我方盼望贵方开标及我方中标的消息。

Words and Expressions

application	*n.* 申请书
peruse	*v.* 细谈，细读
concern	*v.* 涉及，对……有关系，*n.* 关怀，担心
fulfill	*v.* 完成
sufficiently	*adv.* 足够地
competition	*n.* 竞争
schedule	*n.* 一览表，细目单；计划表，日程表，议事日程
specification	*n.* 规格
compliance	*n.* 依从，屈从
security	*n.* 保证人，担保人；抵押品，保证金
instructions	*n.* 教育，指导；说明书
award	*v.* 授予，判给；奖，奖品
in response to	响应，反应

Notes

(1) win the bidding   赢得投标，即中标

(2) bid security   投标保证金(投标时需交保证金，由银行出具保函担保)

(3) be awarded the contract   意即中标后可以签订合同，并承建工程项目

(4) in compliance with   依从，按照

Ⅴ. Accepting the Tender

Example

Dear Sirs,

Re: Informing the Acceptation of the Tender

We have the honour to inform you that your tender dated ×× No. ×× for the supply of ×× has been accepted. Here we express our great thankfulness to you.

Commodity: ××

Unit Price: US $ ××, CIF EMP

Total Price: US $ ××, CIF EMP

Shipment: in ×××, 2015

Shipping Marks: up to the Seller's option

We here send you by registered express mail our Contract No. ×× in duplicate, both of which have been signed by us and please return us one copy after your countersigning at your earlier convenience. It is necessary to emphasize that both of the designing schedule and the shipment of the equipment in set must be strictly carried out according to the stipulations of the Contract and any delay in executing the Contract will affect the fulfilling of the economic construction plan of our country. Therefore, any delay in shipment or poor quality of the equipment would make you suffer from penalty.

We wish a good beginning of our trading cooperation would certainly bring us a fruitful end.

五、通知中标

实例

关于：通知中标

我方甚感荣幸地通知贵方，日期为××的第××号供应××设备的标单已经中标。我方向贵方致以深深的谢意。

商品：××

单价：××美元 CIF, EMP

总价：××美元 CIF, EMP

装货期：2015 年×月

装船唛头：由卖方选定

我方现用挂号快件寄予贵方××号合同一式两份，此两份均已由我方签字，会签以后请贵方尽快寄回我方一份。必须强调的是，设计计划及设备装运均须严格按照合同规定执行，任何执行合同的耽误都将影响我国经济建设计划的完成。因此，任何发运的耽搁及质量的差劣均会使贵方遭受罚款。

我方希望双方贸易合作的良好开端将会带来一个丰硕的结果。

Words and Expressions

thankfulness	*n.* 谢意
register	*v.* 登记，挂号
execute	*v.* 执行
penalty	*n.* 处罚，罚款
fruitful	*a.* 富有成效的，富饶的
accept a tender	中标

VI. Letter of Guarantee for Bid Bond

Example

Issuing date:_____

To:_____

Bid bond for Bid No. _____ for supply of _____

This Bond is hereby issued to service as a bid bond of (hereinafter called the Bidder) for Bid No._____ for supply of _____ (description of goods) to _____.

The _____ (name of the Issuing Bank) hereby unconditionally and irrevocably guarantees and binds itself, its successors and assigns to pay you immediately without recourse, the sum of ($ / £ / ¥)_____ upon receipt of your written notification stating any of the following:

(1) The Bidder has withdrawn its Bid after the time and date of the bid opening and before the expiration of its validity period;

(2) The Bidder has failed to enter into contract with you within thirty (30) calendar days after notification of contract award;

(3) The Bidder has failed to establish acceptable Performance Bond within fourteen (14) calendar days after the effective date of the contract.

It is fully understood that this guarantee takes effect from the issuing date and shall remain valid for a period of sixty days after the opening date of the bid, and during the period of any extension thereof that may be agreed upon between you and the Bidder with notice to us, unless sooner terminated and/or released by you.

_____ (Name of Issuing Bank)

By_____ (Printed name and signature of official authorized to sign on behalf of issuing bank)

(OFFICIAL SEAL)

(Date)

六、银行保函

实例

合同号：_____

致：

关于为提供____的第____号招标通告的投标保函

本保函作为_____(投标人名称)(以下简称投标人)对_____(招标单位)第____号招标, 关于提供____(货物名称)的投标保函。

____银行无条件地、不可撤销地保证并约束本行或其后继者和其受让者，一旦受到贵方提出下列任何一种情况的通知后，立即无追索权地向贵方支付总额____(美元、英镑、人民币等，须写明币制)：

(1) 投标人在开标后或投标有效期满前撤回其投标。

(2) 中标通知书发出后 30 个日历天内，投标人未能和贵方签订合同。

(3) 在投标人签订合同后 14 个日历天内，未能提交可接受的履约保证金。

本保函自开标之日起 60 天内有效，除贵方提前终止或解除本保函外，凡贵方和投标人同意延长的任何期限，投标人均须通知本行。

出证行名称：＿＿＿＿＿＿

正式授权代表的印刷体姓名和职务：＿＿＿＿＿＿

公章：＿＿＿＿＿

出具日期：＿＿＿＿＿

Words and Expressions

bond	*n.* (付款)保证书，保证人
unconditionally	*adv.* 无条件地
irrevocably	*adv.* 不可撤销地
bind	*v.* 约束
successor	*n.* 后继者
assign	*n.* 受让者，接受转让的人
recourse	*n.* 追索权
notification	*n.* 通知
withdraw	*v.* 撤回
fail	*v.* 失败，不合格；不，不能
calendar	*n.* 历法，日历
extension	*n.* 延长期限
official	*a.* 公务的，官方的，正式的
	n. 官员，行政人员；代表；高级职员
authorize	*v.* 授权，委任
Letter of Guarantee	保函，保证信
enter into contract	签订合同
calendar days	日历天(日历上的日期，意思就是一周按 7 天算，与"工作日"相对应)
performance bond	履约保证书
take effect	(法规)生效，(药)见效

VII. Qualification Document

Example

Gentlemen:

Re: Statement Concerning Qualification

In connection with your invitation for Bid No. ＿＿＿ (Bid Document No. ＿＿＿, dated ××× ,

2015), the undersigned would like to participate in the bid for the supply of _____, Item No._____ which is specified in Technical Specifications, and submits the Qualification Documents as required.

I hereby certify that the statements made in the Qualification Documents are true and correct. Our bank is the ××× Bank, London, England. A letter of reference from our bank is attached.

Sincerely yours,

七、资格文件

实例

关于：资格声明书

关于贵公司第××号招标(标书号：××；日期：2015 年×月×日)，本函签字人愿意参加投标，供应××项号 ×× 设备(详见技术规格)，现将所需资格证书附呈。

兹保证资格证书的内容真实无误。我方银行为×××银行，英国，伦敦。随函送上该行所开证明信。

Words and Expressions

qualification	*n.* 资格
statement	*n.* 声明书
in connection with	关于
undersigned	*a.* 在下面(或文件末尾)签名的
specify	*v.* 指定，详细说明
submit	*v.* 呈送，提交
certify	*v.* 证明
attach	*v.* 附加，隶属
the undersigned	(下面的或文件末尾的)签名人，签名者
letter of reference	证明信，保证信

Sentences for International Tendering

(1) We have heard from our Ambassador that you have put your … on the market for 3 years and so would be grateful for full details. We think the information about this will be helpful for our tender invitation.

从我国大使处了解到你方××已投放市场 3 年，所以很想了解详情，我方认为有关这方面的信息将有助于我方招标。

(2) We need liberal samples previous to approaching the suppliers. It is necessary for our tendering participating.

在同供应商联系之前，我们需要大量样品，这也是我们参加投标所必需的。

(3) The last date for receipt of bids is 6:00 p.m. October 7, 2015 (local time).

投标文件接受的最后截止日期为 2015 年 10 月 7 日，下午 6:00(当地时间)。

(4)   Bids received after that date and time or which are not accompanied by a bid bond, as provided for in the bidding conditions will not be accepted.

逾期到达的投标文件或未按招标条件要求提交投标保证金的投标文件，恕不接受。

(5)   The Bidder will take the responsibility and obligation for accomplishment of the Contract in accordance with all provisions of the Bidding Documents.

投标人根据招标文件的规定承担执行合同的责任和义务。

(6)   In the event that the bid is withdrawn after the time and date set for bid opening, within the period of validity his bid security shall be forfeited by the Buyer.

如果开标后，在投标的有效期内撤回投标，则投标保证金将由买方没收。

(7)   The bid is valid for a period of 60 calendar days from the day of bid opening.

投标自开标之日起 60 个日历天内有效。

(8)   The contract is made by and between the Buyers and the Sellers in accordance with the Bid No. ××× whereby the Buyers agree to buy and the Sellers agree to sell the undermentioned commodity according to the following terms and conditions.

本合同由买卖双方根据第×××号投标签订，按照合同，买方同意购买，卖方同意出售下列商品，条款如下。

(9)   The technical specifications of the goods to be supplied and delivered shall be in conformity with those specified in the technical specifications of this Bidding Document as well as in the Specification Compliance Form attached.

提供和交付的货物技术规范应与招标文件规定的技术规范以及所附的规范合规表一致。

(10) A set of bidding documents may be purchased in the 10th floor at the address below between 9:00 a.m. and 6:00 p.m. (Saturdays, Sundays and holidays excepted) from 1 May 2015, or be promptly dispatched by express mail upon receipt of the nonrefundable payment of RMB ×× (or US $ ××) plus RMB XX (or US $ ××) postage fee.

2015 年 5 月 1 日起(周六、周日及节假日除外)从上午 9:00 至下午 6:00 可以在下列地址的第 10 层买到招标文件。在收到人民币××元(或美金××元)的付款之后(售款不退)，将会立即用快件发出招标文件，但需加邮费人民币××元(或美金××元)。

(11) We confirm we intend to submit a bona fide Tender in accordance with all your requirements by the date and time stated in your letter of Invitation to Tender.

我公司确认打算在贵方招标信上所说明的日期和时间前根据贵方的全部要求进行诚意投标。

(12) Tenders shall be submitted in accordance with the Instructions to Tenderers and Form of Tender. Any deviation from the requirements of these Instructions may render your Tender invalid.

投标人应根据投标人须知及投标单提交标书，不符合这些要求的投标者投标无效。

(13) Your tender must be received no later than 12:00 on Friday, 1 June, 2015 (closing date) at the office of the Purchaser in Beijing, PRC.

贵方的标书必须于 2015 年 6 月 1 日，星期五 12 时前(截止日期)送达中华人民共和国北京购方办事处。

(14) Uninvited visits to our offices to discuss the Invitation to Tender are not acceptable and that all contact shall be in writing (by letter or fax) as set out in the Instructions to Tenderers.

未经邀请来我办事处讨论招标事项者恕不接待，一切联系均按招标说明中的规定以书面形式(通过书信或传真)进行。

(15) The tenderers shall consider this enclosed Invitation to Tender to be confidential, and the contents shall not be divulged to any person or persons not directly concerned with the preparation of the Tender.

投标人应将此所附招标信看成是保密的，其内容不得泄露给与招标无直接关系的人员。

Exercises

Ⅰ. Translate the following sentences from English into Chinese.

1. The total bid price for the supply and delivery of the goods specified in the Bidding Document is RMB ×× (in words) or US $ ××.

2. The Bidder will take the responsibility and obligation for accomplishment of the Contract in accordance with all provisions of the Bidding Documents.

3. The technical specifications of the goods to be supplied and delivered shall be in conformity with those specified in the Technical Specifications of this Bidding Documents.

4. Delivery of the goods and performance of Services shall be by the Seller in accordance with the time schedule specified by the Buyer in its schedule of Requirements.

5. All bids from foreign manufacturers must be submitted by their representations registered in Beijing.

Ⅱ. Translate the following sentences from Chinese into English.

1. 投标自开标之日起 60 天内有效。

2. 我公司拟通过公开招标购买电站设备。

3. 我公司欢迎国内外企业投标扩建××港口集装箱码头。

4. 各项投标文件均须为经正式签署的正文，并经封签后寄出。

5. 此次投标结果为：由××公司以次低标中标。

Chapter 11　Invitation　邀请函

Learning Objectives:

● Learn how to inform the others of your visiting intention.

● Master the writing of invitation cards and reply cards.

● Know the designing of the itineraries and programmer list.

学习目标：

● 学会如何将访问意向通知他人。

● 掌握请柬及回帖的写法。

● 知道预定日程及活动安排表的设计。

In international trading course it is always necessary for the foreign economic and trade cadres and for the business personnel to organize the trade delegations, investigating delegations, marketing and purchasing groups to go abroad for visiting and to meet various foreign organizations coming to China for paying visits. In this way, a series of preparation work must be carried out. A lot of communication tasks must be fulfilled, such as: writing letters or faxing or E-mailing to each other for concrete arranging of the work according to the aims of visitings.

在国际贸易过程中，外经贸干部和业务人员经常需要组织贸易代表团、考察团、推销小组、购货小组等出国访问或接待外国来华访问的各种组织。这样就需要进行一系列的准备工作，就访问目的及具体安排等方面通过信件、传真或电邮联系。

According to the contents of the letters, faxes and E-mails, there are four contents of invitations to be classified.

根据信件的内容，邀请函可分为四种。

1)　Visiting suggestions

Before paying visits, the units or individuals going abroad must firstly write letters to the other party to state the intention and the purpose of your visit, the composition of your visiting members, the time of your visit, the place to be visited, etc. It is necessary to ask the opposite party to offer invitation to you for your visit and to help you to make arrangements and to go the necessary procedures. If you get the information through the third party and you wish to pay through visit, state the source of the relevant information. The letter must be written precisely and politely.

1)　访问建议

出访的单位或个人在准备出访前，必须先写信通知对方，说明出访的意图、目的、出访的人员、时间、地点等，请对方提出邀请，作出安排并协助办理必要的手续。如果是通过第三方得到信息并希望出访，还要说明消息的来源。信要写得简明扼要、谦逊有礼。

2)　Invitation letters

After receiving the letter asking for paying visit from the opposite party and in case of your enabling to receive them, an invitation letter must be sent out. In order to arrange accommodation for visitors and to get visas for them, in the invitation letter, the receiving party should request the opposite party to acknowledge them the visiting members' identifications, positions, sexes, ages, etc. Definite answers for date of their visiting and the days of their staying must be obtained.

The invitation letter may as well be initiatively sent out to you by your opposite party. The purpose of inviting you to pay the visit, the time and the contents of your visit are necessary to be definitely stated in order to attract your interest and to inspire your decision making.

2)　邀请信

接到对方要求来访的信件以后，如果认为可以接待，就发出邀请信。在邀请信中要求对方确认来访人员的身份、职位、性别、年龄等，以便安排食宿及办理签证。来访的日期、停留的天数等需要对方给出明确答复。

邀请信也可由对方主动发给你方，同样需要明确说明邀请你方出访的目的、时间、内容等，以引起你方出访的兴趣及决心。

3)　Particular arrangements of the itinerary and programs of the visit

After sending out the invitation letter, the reception country should arrange the visiting itinerary according to the information and requirements offered by the visiting country and make clear about their flight number in order to do well the arranging work of receiving the guests, confirming the flight number, the itinerary of the guests, the time of receiving the guests, and their accommodations. After making up the itinerary and programs of the visit, send it to the opposite country and wait for the reply. In foreign affairs, the person in charge of receiving, interviewing, negotiating and entertaining must be ascertained according to, the positions of the visitors. The position of the person in charge of reception should be equal to that of the delegation head's. Otherwise, it will be impolite and explanation and apology must be made to the delegation.

3)　具体安排访问日程

接待国发出邀请后根据出访国提供的信息及要求，安排访问日程，确认航班，以便做好接机、入宿等接待安排，然后将日程表寄给对方，等待对方回复。在外交上负责接待工作的人员的职务高低要和来访人员的团长的职务相当，否则不礼貌。负责接待、会晤、谈判、娱乐活动的人员必须依来访人员的身份来确定。如果做不到这样，一般接待方必须向代表团说明并致歉。

4)　Letter for expressing thankfulness

After finishing the visit, the relevant leader or a certain individual of the delegation should write a simple and sincere letter to the receipting side to express thankfulness.

4)　感谢信

访问结束后，访问团的有关领导人或个人应该写一封简单、诚恳的信给接待方表达谢意。

Ⅰ. Informing the Visiting Intention

Dear Sirs,

<u>Re: Informing the Visiting Intention</u>

It's a great pleasure to announce you that our President Mr. ××× intends to visit Xi'an, China with some of our technical and commercial directors in order to hold business negotiations with you about the San Men Xia Water Conservancy Project and of course to carry out the on-the-spot investigation with your technical and commercial directors and concerned personnel.

We would like to visit Xi'an in October this year. We should very appreciate it if you would furnish us with your invitation letter, with which we can apply for the entry visas at the Chinese Embassy or Chinese Consulate.

Faithfully yours,

一、通知访问意向

关于：通知访问意向

我方非常高兴地通知贵方我方总裁×××先生意欲与公司的几位技术经理及商务经理出访中国西安，以便和贵方就三门峡水利工程项目举行业务洽谈，当然也打算和贵方的技术及商务经理，以及贵方有关人员一起进行实地考察。

我方打算今年10月到西安访问，如贵方能发给我方一封邀请函，我方将不胜感激。借此我方可向中国大使馆或中国领事馆申请入境签证。

Words and Expressions

announce	v. 宣布，宣告；预告，通知
intend	v. 企图，打算；intend to do sth. 打算做某事
director	n. 指导者，处长，署长，主任，总监，理事，董事
investigation	n. 调查，考察
concerned	a. 有关的
personnel	n. 全体人员(集合名词)，人事(部门)
furnish	v. 供应，提供，装备
invitation letter	邀请信
entry visa	入境签证
Chinese Embassy	中国大使馆
Chinese Consulate	中国领事馆
apply for	申请
commercial director	商务总监，商务经理
technical director	技术总监，技术经理
water conservancy project	水利工程项目
on-the-spot	当场，立即，在现场

Notes

(1) on-the-spot investigation　实地考察

(2) invitation letter　一般一方接到另一方邀请函后才可以申请签证。邀请信可以由邀请方主动发给受邀方，邀请对方来参观访问。但想访问他国的国家也可以自己提出访问要求，并要求对方发出邀请信。

II．Sending the Invitation Letter

Dear Sirs,

<u>Re: Sending the Invitation Letter</u>

We have the great pleasure to learn your intention to visit Xi'an in October this year. It will be a great honor for us to negotiate face to face with you about the San Men Xia Water Conservancy Project. We believe that the cooperation of our two Companies would be developed rapidly in the near future. We enclose herewith our invitation letter. We would be very much obliged if you would send us a list of the composition of your delegation and inform us your view on the timing of the visit, together with indication of what you would like to see and to do in Xi'an in order that we can make specific arrangement for your delegation.

We are expecting your arrival.

Truly yours,

二、寄送邀请函

关于：寄送邀请函

喜获贵方欲在今年10月访问西安。和贵方面对面地洽谈三门峡水利工程项目对我们来说是十分荣幸的。相信我们之间的合作不久将得到迅速发展。在此附寄我方的邀请函。望贵方能给我们寄来贵方代表团成员的名单，并告知关于来访时间等方面的意见。在西安期间贵方想参观的地方及所需办理的事项亦请一并告知，以便我方能为贵方代表团进行具体的安排。

恭候光临。

Words and Expressions

composition	*n.* 组成，成分(文中为成员)
indication	*n.* 表明，说明
arrival	*n.* 到达
specific arrangement	具体安排
face to face	面对面

III．Sending the Delegation Composition List

Dear Sirs,

<u>Re: Sending the Delegation Composition List</u>

We shall be leaving Tokyo on 10th October, subject to the issuing of the visa. We propose to stay in Xi'an for four days, and send you here a list of our delegation composition in order you can arrange the accommodation for us.

Should time be sufficient, we would like to visit the Museum of Terra-cotta Warriors and Horses of Qin Dynasty in Lintong and the Famen Temple in Baoji.

In addition, we would like to mention that all the members of our delegation have not any special dietary requirements.

Thank you for your cooperation.

No.	Name	Sex	Age	Position

三、寄送代表团成员名单

关于：寄送代表团成员名单

我方将于 10 月 10 日离开东京，以签证的签发为准。我方计划在西安访问 4 天。在此给贵方寄去我方代表团成员的名单，以便贵方能为我方安排食宿。

如果时间充裕，我方还想参观临潼的秦朝兵马俑及宝鸡的法门寺。

顺便再提一下，我方代表团全体成员对饮食都没有任何特殊要求。

感谢合作。

序号	姓名	性别	年龄	职务

Words and Expressions

issue	v. 发布，发行，签发
propose	v. 提议，提出；建议；打算，计划
accommodation	v. 供应膳宿
sufficient	a. 足够的
terra	n. 土，地；白土；石膏粉
terra-cotta	n. 赤土，赤陶

warrior	*n.* 武士，勇士，原始部落的斗士
dietary	*a.* 饮食的
Qin Dynasty	*n.* 秦朝
Famen Temple	法门寺

Notes

Terra-cotta Warriors and Horses of Qin Dynasty   秦朝兵马俑

Ⅳ. Itineraries and Programs 行程表及项目

Itineraries and Programs For Water Conservation Project Negotiations
October 10—October 14, Xi'an

水利项目洽谈行程表
10 月 10 日—10 月 14 日，西安

Oct.9.	21:00 p.m.	Arrive at Xianyang Airport by Flight No. ×× 乘 ××号航班飞机到达咸阳机场	Met by Mr. ×× 迎候者：××先生
	22:00 p.m.	Arrive at Bell Tower Hotel 到达钟楼饭店	
Oct.10.	9:00—11:30 a.m.	Negotiate at ×× Corp. 在××公司洽谈	Reception Given by Mr. ×× 由 Mr. ××举行招待会
	12:00 Noon	Luncheon at ×× Corp. 在××公司午餐	
	2:00—4:00 p.m.	Visit the workshops of XX Corp. 参观 XX 公司车间	
	4:00—5:30 p.m.	Continue the negotiations 继续洽谈	
	6:00—8:00 p.m.	Dinner Party 晚餐会	
Oct.11.	9:00—11:30 a.m.	On-the-Spot Investigations 现场考察	
	12:00 Noon	Luncheon at ×× Restaurant 在××餐厅午餐	
	1:30—5:30 p.m.	On-the-Spot Investigations and Discussions 现场考察与讨论	
	6:00—8:00 p.m.	Dinner at Tang Cheng Hotel 在唐城酒店晚餐	
	8:00 p.m.	Watch the Performances of the Tang Dynasty Music and Dance 观看仿唐乐舞	
Oct.12.	9:00—11:30 a.m.	Negotiate at ××× Corp. 在××公司洽谈	
	12:00 Noon	Luncheon at ××× Restaurant 在××餐厅午餐	
	1:30p.m.	Sightseeing to Lintong 参观临潼	
Oct.13	9:00—11:30	Sightseeing to Famen Temple 法门寺参观	Sent off by Mr. ××× 送行者：×××先生
	12:00 Noon	Luncheon at ××× Restaurant 在××餐厅午餐	
	2:00—5:30 p.m.	Sightseeing in Xi'an 西安参观	
	6:00p.m.	Farewell Banquet 告别宴会	
	9:00p.m.	Leave for Tokyo by Flight No. ×× 乘××号班机离西安返回东京	

Ⅴ．Invitation Card

> **Formal Invitation Card**
> **To Commemorate the 20th Anniversary**
> **Mr. ×××, President**
> **of**
> **××× Corp.**
>
> ## Requests the pleasure of your Company
>
> <u>At a Cocktail Party</u>
> **On Saturday, May ××**
> **At 6:00 to 8:00 p.m.**
> **At the Bell Tower Hotel**
> **To express sincere appreciation**
> **R.S.V.P.**
> **Enclosed Reply Card**

Accepting with Pleasure:

> **××× Corp.**
>
> **Accepts with pleasure**
> **Mr. ×××'s**
> **Invitation to Cocktail Party**
>
> ## On Saturday, May × ×
>
> **At 6:00 p.m.**
> **At the Bell Tower Hotel**

五、请柬

> 为庆祝 20 周年纪念，谨定于
> 5 月××日星期六晚 6:00—8:00 于
> 钟楼饭店举行鸡尾酒会，敬请
> 贵公司同仁光临
> ×××公司总裁×××先生
>
> 谨请回复
> 附答复卡

愉快地接受邀请：

> 我公司很愉快地接受×××先生的邀请
> 参加 5 月××日（星期六）
> 晚 6:00 在钟楼饭店举行的鸡尾酒会
> ×××公司谨复

Words and Expressions

cocktail	鸡尾酒，西餐中头道进食的开胃品(如茄汁)
R.S.V.P. = RSVP	(法)re pondez s' l vous plait=(英) Please reply (请帖等用语) 请答复
Cocktail Party	鸡尾酒会，酒会
reply card	答复卡

Sentences for Invitation

(1) Allow me to propose a toast on behalf of my Corporation. It's really a great pleasure having you as our guests.

请允许我代表我公司举杯祝酒，能请贵方前来做客使我们无比高兴。

(2) It can be anticipated that through our joint efforts, new contracts can be signed to further our business relation.

可以预见，通过我们的共同努力，新合同的签订一定能促进我们之间的业务关系。

(3) Let's drink to the greater trade and economic exchanges in the future.

让我们为将来取得更大的贸易和经济交流干杯。

(4) We are back now in New York. We wish to express, for myself and for the entire delegation, our heartfelt thanks to you and through you to other officials of your Corporation for the kind hospitality tended to us during our visit in Xi'an.

我们现已返回纽约。在此我代表本人及整个代表团在西安访问期间贵方给予我们的款待向您及贵公司的其他领导致以衷心的感谢。

(5)

On the occasion of the National Day

the Ambassador of Indonesia

requests the honor of your presence

at a Reception

On Friday, ×××, 2015

From 6:00 p.m. to 8:00 p.m.

The Beijing Hotel

R.S.V.P.

谨订于 2015 年×月×日(周五)下午 6:00—8:00

北京饭店举行印度尼西亚国庆日招待会
恭请光临
印度尼西亚大使
(签名)

请赐复

(6)　　　　　　　　　Mr. Smith

Accepts with pleasure

Mr. and Mrs. Zhang's

Kind invitation to dinner

On Friday, May the 4th

At 7:00p.m.

承张先生夫妇 5 月 4 日下午 7 点(周五)盛邀晚餐，谨知。史密斯先生谨复。

(7)　　　　　　　　　Mr. Smith

regrets that a previous engagement

prevents him from accepting

Mr. and Mrs. Zhang's

Kind invitation to dinner

On Friday, May the 4th

承 5 月 4 日(星期五)张先生夫妇盛邀晚餐，因事先有约不能前往，谨谢。史密斯先生谨复。

(8)　I have to thank you for your kind invitation to dinner at ×× Restaurant at 6:00 p.m. next Saturday, but regret that owing to previous engagement I shall not be able to accompany you.

非常感谢你下周六下午 6:00 在××饭店晚餐的邀请，但因有他约在先，本人无法参加，甚为抱歉。

(9)　Our heartiest congratulations for your promotion.

衷心祝贺您得到晋升。

(10) I hope you are feeling better and these flowers will help to cheer you.

祝您康复，愿这些鲜花使您愉快。

(11) The purpose of our general manager's visit to Stockholm is to collect the information about the latest development in industry and to explore the possibilities of our cooperating in manufacturing and trading our ×× equipment.

我们总经理这次出访斯德哥尔摩的目的是收集工业方面最新发展的情况，并探索生产与经营××设备方面双方进行合作的可能性。

(12) You are kindly expected by the Committee of 2015 International Fair for the business negotiations and conclusion of transactions.

2015 年国际博览会组委会特邀贵公司到会洽谈贸易，并达成交易。

(13) If you are interested in pursuing the possibilities of developing exchange programs

with our Corporation or referring visiting scholars to us for collaborative research and study , we would welcome your visit.

如贵公司愿与我公司就发展交换计划的可能进行探讨，并向我公司推荐访问学者在学术研究方面进行合作，我公司将欢迎贵公司来访。

(14) We feel honored to have begun a trading program with you and look forward to our continuing relationship with high hopes and great expectations.

我公司与贵公司在贸易计划方面有了开端，深感荣幸，我公司热切盼望继续加强这种关系。

(15) We would deeply appreciate any help you may be able to extend to our President Mr. ××× in his visit and in the discussion concerning the possibilities of trading programs.

如蒙贵公司在我公司总裁×××先生访问期间以及在有关贸易计划的商讨中给予协助，我方将不胜感激。

Exercises

Ⅰ. Design an invitation card and an invitation accepting card.

Ⅱ. Make up a visiting schedule.

Ⅲ. Choose the correct answers.

1. We hope you will be pleased with our selection and _____ order of yours will lead to further business with us.
   A. that this　　　B. that those　　　C. a　　　D. it

2. Mr. John Brown, your Import Manager, wrote us last week that our price was_____ and asked us to secure supplies the earliest possible.
   A. fortunate　　　　　　　　B. impossible
   C. acceptable　　　　　　　D. managerial

3. CIF is a price term, meaning the price includes the cost of goods and the insurance and____ for carrying the goods up to the destination.
   A. freight　　　　　　　　　B. foreign
   C. friendly　　　　　　　　D. forwarding

4. An agreement is ____ as a result of the process of offer and acceptance.
   A. included　　　B. resulted　　　C. reached　　　D. had

5. We have pleasure in enclosing a copy of our latest catalogue_____ for in your letter.
   A. asked　　　B. asks　　　C. ask　　　D. asking

6. We regret to inform you that we do not have in stock the goods in the ____ quantity.
   A. desiring　　　B. desired　　　C. desires　　　D. desire

7. We regret having received your offer too late, because we＿＿＿ our needs elsewhere.

   A. have already cover   B. already covered

   C. already covered   D. had already covered

8. As said on the telephone this morning, we are sending you by separate airmail the samples, ＿＿＿ you will find them satisfactory.

   A. to hope   B. hopefully   C. hoping   D. hope

9. If we had been informed in time, we ＿＿＿ these products for you.

   A. would have reserved   B. had reserved

   C. would reserve   D. will reserve

10. Naturally, a successful and attractive company profile sheet can elicit direct orders ＿＿＿ requests for more detailed information.

   A. as well   B. good

   C. as well as   D. as good as

Chapter 12 Resume and Job-application Form
简历与求职表

Learning Objectives:

- Learn how to perfectly and all-roundly design an English-Chinese bilingual job-application form.
- Know how to fill-in the English-Chinese bilingual job-application form in the different chronological orders of English and Chinese languages.
- Master the ways of writing application letters and resumes.
- Get familiar with the English expressions in job-hunting.

学习目标：

- 学会如何完美、全面地设计英汉求职表。
- 知道如何按英语和汉语不同的时间顺序填制英汉求职表。
- 掌握写求职信及简历的方法。
- 熟悉求职中英语应用的表达方法。

The aim of learning designing and writing an English-Chinese bilingual resume and an English-Chinese bilingual Job-application letter is in fact to learn how to sell yourself as a kind of commodity to the relative organization. So you must learn how to use your words and sentences to introduce yourself and to boast a little of your good qualities and your special abilities in order to attract the interest of the prospective employer to yourself and to get the opportunity of being interviewed, even get the chance of filling the post you want. This is the same kind of job as you look for the buyers for the products you sell through your introducing of their performances, characteristics and advantages.

学会设计和书写中英文简历及中英文求职信的目的，事实上就是学会如何把自己作为一种商品推销给有关组织。所以必须学会如何使用句子和词汇来推销自己，介绍自己的良好素质及专业技能来吸引潜在的雇主以获得面试的机会，甚至获得你想得到的职位。这与通过对产品的性质、特点和优点的介绍来寻找买主一样。

Designing and making out a listing type of your English-Chinese bilingual resume and as well an English-Chinese bilingual job application letter will make your prospective employer get a rather comprehensive understanding of you from your clear and smart resume among piles of resumes of the interviewees. The employer's good impressions on you will perhaps make him pay attention to you, and perhaps you will get your opportunity of being interviewed.

设计和制作一份表格式的中英文简历以及一份中英文求职信，将使你的未来雇主在成堆的应聘者简历中通过你清楚和美观的简历对你有相当全面的了解。雇主对你的良好印象可能会使他注意到你，使你得到面试的机会。

I . Resumes and Job-application Letters

1. A blank job-application form designed perfectly and all- roundly

Resume of Position Sought

Name						(Photo)
Birth Date		**Birthplace**				
Height		**Weight**		**Health**		
Nationality		**Male** ☐	**Female** ☐	**Married** ☐	**Single** ☐	
ID Card No.						

Address	**Present**		**Tel** **E-mail**	**Fax** **Post Code**
	Permanent		**Tel** **E-mail**	**Fax** **Post Code**
English Proficiency			**Speciality**	

Work Experience

From		To		Job Title	Name & Address of Work Unit	Reason for Leaving
Mo.	Yr.	Mo.	Yr.			

Educational Background

Grade	From		To		Name of School	Degree
	Mo.	Yr.	Mo.	Yr.		
College						
High						
Secondary						
Others						
Technical Qualifications						
Special Skill						
Interests			References			
Rewards						
Career Objective						

一、简历与求职信

1. 一份设计完美、完整的求职简历表

求职简历

姓名						贴
出生日期		出生地				照
身高		体重		健康状况		片
国籍		男□	女 □	已婚 □	未婚 □	
身份证号码						

通信地址	现在		电话 电子邮箱		传真 邮编	
	永久		电话 电子邮箱		传真 邮编	

英语水平			专业		

工作经历

自		至		职位	工作单位名称与地址	离职原因
年	月	年	月			

教育程度

等级	自		至		学校名称	学位
	年	月	年	月		
初中						
高中						
大学						
其他						

技术资格证			
特殊技能			
爱好		证明人	
奖励			
应聘职位			

2.   A filled-out job-application form

Resume of Position Sought

Name	Li Ming-hong					(Photo)
Birth Date	1 July,1980	**Birthplace**	Xi'an Shanxi			
Height	××cm	**Weight**	×× kg	**Health**	Good	
Nationality	Chinese	Male ■	Female □	Married □	Single ■	

ID Card No.					
Address	**Present**	115 Da-Xing Road, Xi'an	**Tel**	**Fax**	
			E-mail	**Post Code**	
	Permanent	33 Chang-An Bei Road,Xi'an	**Tel**	**Fax**	
			E-mail	**Post Code**	
English Proficiency		CET Band Four	**Speciality**	International Trade	

Work Experience

From		To		Job Title	Name & Address of Work Unit	Reason for Leaving
Mo.	**Yr.**	**Mo.**	**Yr.**			
Sept.	2014	July	2015	Salesman	Sales Dept. of ×× Co., Beijing	Better Job Hunting
July	2013	August	2014	Part time Tutor		

Educational Background

Grade	From		To		Name of School	Degree
	Mo.	**Yr.**	**Mo.**	**Yr.**		
College	Sept.	2010	July	2014	Northwest University	
High	Sept.	2007	July	2010	Xi'an Senior Middle School	
Secondary	Sept.	2004	July	2007	Xi'an No.2 Middle School	
Others						

Technical Qualifications	
Special Skill	Computer Operating; Car Driving; English Teaching
Interests	Basketball Playing **References** Available on Request
Rewards	"Excellent Student Leader" in 2003; "Three Goods Student" in 2001, 2002
Career Objective	Department Manager

2. 一份填好的求职简历表

求职简历

姓名	李铭宏					
出生日期	1980 年 7 月 1 日	出生地	陕西西安			贴照片
身高	×× 厘米	体重	×× 公斤	健康状况	佳	
国籍	中国	男 ■	女 □	已婚 □	未婚 ■	

身份证号码				
通信地址	现在	西安市大兴路 115 号	电话 电子邮箱	传真 邮编
	永久	西安市长安北路 33 号	电话 电子邮箱	传真 邮编
英语水平	CET 四级		专业	国际贸易

工作经历

自		至		职位	工作单位名称与地址	离职原因
年	月	年	月			
2013	7	2014	8	兼职家庭教师		
2014	9	2015	7	销售员	北京××公司销售部	寻求较好工作

教育程度

等级	自		至		学校名称	学位
	年	月	年	月		
初中	2004	9	2007	7	西安市第二中学	
高中	2007	9	2010	7	西安高级中学	
大学	2010	9	2014	7	西北大学	
其他						

技术资格证	
特殊技能	计算机操作；汽车驾驶；讲授英语
爱好	打篮球 证明人 承索即寄
奖励	2003 年获"优秀学生干部"奖；2001 年、2002 年获"三好学生"奖
应聘职位	部门经理

Words and Expressions

Main college courses and marks	大学主要课程及分数
Marketing Strategies	营销策略
Marketing Research and Forecast	市场调整与预测
Sales Force Management	营销队伍管理
Business Law	商业法

Notes

(1) 大中专院校毕业生及毕业后还在待业的求职者写简历时应突出学历，写英文简历时从最高学历开始写，以突出最高学历，写到中学为止，小学一般不写。

(2) 英文简历中写个人经历时采用倒叙，离现在最近的写在最前面，以突出求职者最近的工作经历。

(3) 以上两点的中文写法则刚好相反，中文学历是按照从低学历到高学历的顺序书写，个人经历也是从最早的经历写到最近的经历。

(4) 简历要精心设计，既要清晰、完善，又要美观、大方，从而给人一种赏心悦目的良好印象。语句要精练，语法要准确，同一类项目的用词要统一。主语"I"可省略；可以用缩略语，如月份、国名、学位等。

(5) 简历要用电脑打印，中英文对照准确整齐，反复校对后随求职信一起发出。

(6) 当前外资企业、合资企业、独资企业、外事机构等高层高薪单位招聘时往往要求中英文简历，所以准确地设计一份高水平的英文简历不仅可以显示自己的英语水平和综合能力，还可以增加自己的受聘机会。

(7) 简历不宜太长，不宜超过一页，如需要可加上"大学所学课程及分数"等内容，以示自己的知识面及能力，可单列一栏。

Main College Courses & Marks	Marketing Strategies	80
	Marketing Research & Forecast	90
	Sales Force Management	85
	Business Law	88

(8) 写简历时要实事求是，如上栏内的分数，不可随意写；否则，会造成恶劣影响。

(9) 简历也可以分项书写，不设计表格(但以表格形式出现更整齐、醒目)。

(10) 自行设计简历时，如果没有学位或没有奖励等内容填写，就把这些项目删掉，不予设置。

Ⅱ. A Resume Written in Items

Resume of Liu Xinxin

Address: Shanghai ××× Co., Ltd., No. 100 Zhongshan Bei Road

Post Code: ××××××   Tel: ××××××   Fax: ××××××   E-mail: ××××××

Position Sought: Computer engineer with ××× Data Engineering Co., Ltd.

Qualification: Four years' work experiences in operating computers and in computer programming.

Professional Experiences:

1. Computer engineer at Shanghai ××× Co., Ltd., from 2012 to date.

2. Being adept at operating flow-charts and collecting business information for management.

3. Being skillful at operating IBM-PC and Compact Computer.

Education:

Graduated from Fudan University, B.S. in Computer Science, July 2012

Shanghai Yucai Middle School, 2004—2008

Courses included:

1. Computer Science

2. PASCAL Programming

3. COBOL Programming

4. FORTRAN Programming

5. D-BASE Programming

6. Operating System

7. System Design and Analysis

8. Systems Management, etc.

English Proficiency: Fluent in speaking and writing

Hobbies: Bridge, Stamp Collecting

Personal Data:

Born: March 18, 19×× in Shanghai   Health: Excellent

Marital Status: Single   Height: ××× cm

Weight: ××× kg

References: Available on Request

二、分项书写的简历

刘欣欣简历

地址：上海×××股份有限公司，上海中山北路 100 号

邮编：××××× 电话：×××××× 传真：×××××× E-mail: ××××××

谋求职位：×××数据工程有限公司 计算机工程师

任职资格：4 年电脑操作及计算机编程的经验

专业经历：

1. 2012 年至今，上海×××股份有限公司。

2. 比较熟练地操作管理流程，收集商务管理信息。

3. 熟练操作 IBM-PC 及 Compact 电脑。

学历：

2004—2008 年上海育才中学

2012 年 7 月毕业于复旦大学计算机学专业，并获计算机学士学位

所学主要课程：

1.　计算机科学
2.　PASCAL 编程
3.　COBOL 编程
4.　FORTRAN 编程
5.　D-BASE 编程
6.　操作系统
7.　系统设计与分析
8.　系统管理

英语水平：说写流利

业余爱好：桥牌、集邮

个人资料：

出生：19××年 3 月 18 日，上海

健康状况：极佳

婚姻状况：未婚

身高：×××厘米

体重：×××公斤

证明人：承索即寄

Words and Expressions

program(me)	*v.* 编程
analysis	*n.* 分析
bridge	*n.* 桥牌(桥)
stamp collecting	集邮
BS, B. S.= Bachelor of Science	理学学士
Data Engineering Co., Ltd.	数据工程股份有限公司

Ⅲ．Hunting for a Provisional Job

Dear Sirs,

Having noticed your advertisement in this morning's "China Daily", I learned that you are seeking some provisional English interpreters for the forthcoming Export Commodities Fair. I would like very much to apply for this job.

I am a boy of 22 years old and shall be graduated from Shanghai ×× University next year. My major is International Trade. The courses which I have taken in my University are International Marketing, International Business Law, Foreign Trade English, Negotiation Technique, English Interpreting, etc., and my marks in all these courses examinations have all been excellent. Last year I got an opportunity to work as a part-time English interpreter in a foreign trade company and got some favorable experiences in doing this work which has greatly increased not only my English language skills, but also my self-confidence in selecting this job as my lifework. I happen to have some spare time in this spring, the period of which is suitable for your Spring Fair. So I send you my application for this provisional work. If necessary, I would like to visit you at your appointed time. My telephone number is ××××××.

Sincerely yours,

×××

三、寻找临时工作

敬启:

我从今晨贵公司在《中国日报》上所登的广告获悉,贵公司正在为即将到来的出口交易会招聘几名临时英语口语翻译,我非常愿意申请这项工作。

我是一名 22 岁的男孩,明年将从上海××大学毕业。我的专业是国际贸易。在大学里我所修的课程有国际市场营销学、国际商业法、外贸英语、谈判技巧以及英语口译等,而且成绩优异。去年我曾在一家外贸公司担任兼职英语口译,并且在这项工作中获得了一些非常珍贵的经验,不但大大提高了我的英语语言技巧,而且增强了我将这个职业作为自己终生事业的自信。这个春季我正好有一些空闲,与贵方春交会的时间相吻合。在此寄上我申请这一临时工作的申请书。需要时我非常愿意在约定的时间里拜访贵方。我的电话号码是××××××。

Words and Expressions

advertisement	*n.* 广告
seek	*v.* 寻找(招聘)
interpreter	*n.* 口译工作者
provisional	*a.* 临时的,暂时的
forthcoming	*a.* 即将来临的
graduate	*v.* 毕业
major	*n.* 专业
self-confidence	*n.* 自信
lifework	*n.* 终身事业
be suitable for	适合于
China Daily	中国日报
apply for	*v.* 申请
international marketing	国际市场营销
international business law	国际商业法
negotiation technique	谈判技巧

IV. Hunting for a New Job

Dear Mr. ×××,

I feel very excited on hearing that you are in your in-house posting for the position of Associate Project Manager with your Corporation. So I am writing to you to apply for this job.

Your Embassy in China Mr. ××× alerted me to this opening and suggested me to contact you directly.

I majored in Computer Science and was graduated from Tsinghua University in 2009. After graduation from University, I have got 6 years' experiences in collecting business information for management during my service in a Sino-America ××× Joint Venture Corp. and have mastered the update methods of operating IBM-PC and Compact Computers.

In addition, I am adept in various kinds of programmings, such as PASCAL, COBOL, FORTRAN and D-BASE programmings. Since you are updating your computer network and application software, I think you will be in urgent need of expertises in every import and export business department. Should you like to meet me, please arrange a time for interview and telephone me. My telephone No. is ××××××. Waiting for your favorable news.

Truly yours,

×××

四、寻找新工作

×××先生：

本人得悉贵公司内部招聘项目副经理后十分兴奋，特写信应聘。贵国驻中国大使×××先生告诉我贵公司有此空缺，并提醒我直接和您联系。

我主修计算机科学，2009 年毕业于清华大学。大学毕业后，我在×××中美合资企业工作期间，在收集商务管理信息方面积累了 6 年经验，并掌握了操纵 IBM-PC 及 Compact 计算机最先进的方法。

此外，我还精通各种程序语言，如 PACAL、COBOL、FORTRAN 及 D-BASE 程序语言。由于贵公司正在更新计算机网络系统及应用软件，我想贵公司每个进出口部门都将迫切需要专业人员。如果您愿意和我见面，请安排一个面试时间，并请电话告知，电话号码是××××××。等候您的佳音。

Words and Expressions

in-house	机构内部的
post	v. 任命，派任
alert	v. 使……处于待命状态，提醒……注意……
major	v. 主修，专门研究
opening	n. (职位)空缺，机会
service	n. 服务
update	v. 使……现代化，更新，不断改进
adept	a. 善于……的，精通……的，擅长……的
expertise	n. 内行，专家
in respond to	根据；为响应……，应……而
application software	应用软件
Sino-America Joint Venture Co.	中美合资公司

Sentences for Resume and Job-application Form

(1) I am 22 years of age, get along exceedingly well with people.

今年 22 岁，善于与人相处。

(2) I have an inquisitive and analytical mind— I enjoy finding out about things. I have tact and good humor— and the ability to draw people out.

我头脑清晰，善于分析——喜欢将事情搞个水落石出；性格幽默，很有魅力——有让人说真话的能力。

(3) Perhaps you will agree that these qualities, plus enthusiasm, persistence, and the willingness to work hard and long, make me acceptable for the job you offer as a beginner on your research department.

这些品质加上热情，恒心和吃苦耐劳的精神，使我能够胜任研究部门新手的工作。

(4) I specialized in advertising and merchandising at New York University, from which I graduated in June. I have unusual letters of recommendation from my instructors in these subjects. I should like the opportunity of showing them to you.

今年 6 月我毕业于纽约大学，主修广告业务和广告推销。我的老师们给我写了评价很高的推荐信，希望有机会把信给您看看。

(5) I believe I am just the kind of person you are looking for. I was very interested in the insurance topics we studied in our Applied Economics course here at Metropolitan High, and I did well in all my business subjects. I also received a certificate for my service to the school and a perfect attendance award.

我相信我正是您在寻找的那种人。我在麦特鲍雷顿高中学习应用经济学课程时，就对保险产生了浓厚的兴趣，我的各门商业课程都学得很好，因为在学校表现突出，还荣获了出勤奖励。

(6) As a recent graduate of a foreign trade institute, I've had up-to-date training in marketing. Additionally, several of my class research projects were done on consumer goods and consumer demands, so I have good knowledge which is related to your business line.

我一直在接受市场营销方面的现代化培训，最近才从外贸学院毕业。另外，我还进行过几个消费品与消费者需求方面的课题研究，因而具备了您的行业所需要的扎实知识。

(7) I learned to communicate well with English speaking customers, often having returning customers asking for me to be their server. This ability to relate well to customers is a valued trait for your sales representative. I've also learned how to use database software. This will help me to work more efficiently.

我能够与讲英语的顾客进行良好的沟通，经常有老顾客要求我再次为他们提供服务。这种与顾客建立密切联系的能力是您所需要的销售代表应具有的一个重要特点。我还能够使用数据库软件，这将会使我的工作效率更高。

(8) As you can see on the attached resume, my education and experience have been well rounded. This should make me a successful sales representative for your Corp.

正如您在随信所附的个人简历中看到的那样，我的学历和工作经历丰富而全面，这足以使我胜任贵公司的销售代表。

(9) I am an ambitious, hardworking person who enjoys the challenges of product development and marketing, challenges which I know "Deka Chemicals" has met so well for so many years.

我对工作有热情、努力，勇于面对产品开发及市场上遇到的各种挑战，而且据我所知"德科化学公司"多年来也经历了无数次挑战。

(10) Your advertisement offers a most tempting job to a young man just out of college. I can't think of any job I'd like better than consumer research for a famous organization like yours, and I look upon it as a wonderful opportunity.

您的招聘广告为一个刚走出校门的年轻人提供了一个诱人的工作机会。为您这样赫赫有名的机构进行消费者研究方面的工作是我最向往的。下面我谈谈自己的情况。

(11) Please consider me an applicant for the position which you advertised in "China Daily" of December 5.

我想应聘贵公司 12 月 5 日在《中国日报》上刊登的招聘广告中提到的职位，请予以考虑。

(12) Having noticed the advertisement in this morning's "China Daily", I wish to apply for the position referred to.

从今天的《中国日报》上得知贵公司正在招聘人才，我愿意申请此职位。

(13) Your advertisement for a computer operator in the "Times" of March 8 has interested me. I believe I can fill that position.

贵公司 3 月 8 日在《时报》上刊登广告，招聘一名电脑操作员，我很感兴趣，而且相信能胜任此职。

(14) As it is nearing the Christmas season, it occurs to me that you may need additional assistance in selling gifts in your shop. I have a whole week before Christmas, from 18 to 24, when I might assist you. I could also work evenings from six o'clock before December 18.

圣诞节将至，贵店可能需要圣诞礼物的临时售货员。我在圣诞节前一周(12 月 18 日至 24 日)均有空闲，可以帮忙。18 日以前每晚 6 时以后也可以帮忙。

(15) You will find enclosed an outline of my education and business training and copies of two letters of recommendation.

有关本人学历、业务培训的概述，连同两封推荐信一同呈上。

(16) Enclosed please find my resumes, together with my photo and autobiography.

随函寄上本人履历表、照片及自传各一份，请查收。

(17) I would welcome the opportunity to discuss with you my qualifications for the position of assistant product manager for your Corp.

我期望着与您见面，以讨论我能否胜任贵公司生产部副经理这一职位。

(18) I understand from your ad. that an interview can be arranged in the Milwaukee area in late July. Please write or call me to arrange an interview at your convenience. My telephone number is ××××××.

从您的广告中得知面试将于 7 月下旬在密尔沃基地区进行。请在您方便的时候为我安排一次面试，并请写信或电话告知。我的电话号码是××××××。

(19) May I have the opportunity to talk further about the job? You can reach me by telephone at 576-2000. Thank you for your time and consideration.

我能有机会与您进一步谈一下这一工作吗? 我的电话号码是 576-2000。谢谢您花费时间予以考虑。

(20) The enclosed resume shows some of the reasons why I believe I am qualified to assume the position of assistant product manager, listed in the July issue of "American Marketing" magazine. Would you please consider me an applicant for that position?

7 月份的《美国市场》杂志上刊登了您想招聘一位生产部副经理的广告, 我认为自己有能力担任此职务, 随信寄来的个人简历可以说明原因。请您考虑将这个机会赐予本人。

Exercises

Ⅰ. Design a job-application form and write a resume for yourself carefully, then smartly type them neatly and correctly. If possible, ask your teacher to correct them for you.

Ⅱ. Choose the correct answers.

1. We are ready to ____ your loss and will send you the claimed amount, US $ ×× by T/T. We hope this ____ on our part will not undermine our good relations.

    A. take, lost duty   B. make, overbook
    C. compensate, oversight   D. compensating, negligence

2. Regarding our order No. ×××, we are sending you the official document that shows the quantity delivered to us is ____ ordered.

    A. smaller   B. less than   C. less   D. smaller than

3. Insurance ____ will be added in invoice amount together with the freight charges.

    A. changes   B. money   C. premiums   D. policies

4. If the buyer's country prevents performance of the contract, this kind of risk is called____.

    A. customer risk   B. contingency risk
    C. assert risk   D. country risk

5. Warranty clause is suitable to certain products such as ____.

    A. mushrooms   B. native products
    C. machines   D. canned food

6. We are not ___ for any damage which happened during transit from the warehouse to the destination.

    A. responding   B. responsible   C. response   D. respond

7. It was found upon examination that nearly 20% of the packages___, which was obviously attributed to improper packing.

    A. had been broken   B. broken
    C. was   D. been already broken

8. Complaints _____ if the contract is not fulfilled in some way, amounting to a breach of conditions.

    A. will make   B. were made

    C. make   D. will be made

9. Since the premium varies with the extent of insurance, extra premium is for buyer's account, _____ additional risks be covered.

    A. if   B. should   C. must   D. as

10. Your L/C calls for an insurance account for 130% of the invoice value._____ we would request you to amend the insurance clause.

    A. Such being the case   B. Such is the case

    C. The case being it   D. The case is like this

Chapter 13　E-mail, Fax, E-commerce and EDI
电子邮件、传真、电子商务及电子数据交换

Learning Objectives:

- Learn how to write and send an E-mail.
- Master the way of writing and sending a fax.
- Know what is E-commerce and what is EDI and know their future development.

学习目标：

- 学会如何书写及发送电子邮件。
- 掌握书写和发送传真的方法。
- 了解电子商务、电子数据交换以及它们的未来发展。

Ⅰ. E-mail

1. The advantages of E-mail

(1) The price of E-mail is cheap, which enables the enterprises to reduce their cost to about two thirds.

(2) The speed of transmitting an E-mail is incomparably fast, which increases the efficiency of office working of the governments and enterprises. Nowadays in many countries there is computer linked with E-mail network in almost every family. The governments and enterprises mostly handle official business by internet, impelling the development of E-mailing.

一、电子邮件

1. 电子邮件的优点

(1) 电子邮件价格低廉，大大减少了企业成本，可达 2/3 左右。

(2) 电子邮件发送的速度相当快，提高了政府和企业的办公效率。当今许多国家几乎每个家庭都使用电脑并通过电子邮件进行联系。政府和企业也大多在网上通过电子邮件办公，从而更促进了电子邮件的发展。

2. The concept of an E-mail

The full name of E-mail is "Electronic mail". The Chinese translation of it is "电子邮件" or "电邮" for short, commonly known as "伊妹儿"(E sister). The coming out of the internet since 1990s has brought people into the increasing usage of the E-mail system to transmit information, resulting in the gradual formation of a no paper society. E-mail has been promoting the development of E-commerce, and the developments of E-commerce and internet have thus been impelling the leaps and bounds of the E-mails. E-mail has changed the models of business operating and office work of the enterprises, and as well has transformed the financial activities and purchasing models. The communicating pattern of E-mail is both fast and cheap and is now obtaining its globalization and popularization to an increasingly widened extent.

2. E-mail的概念

"E-mail" 全名 "Electronic mail"，中文译作 "电子邮件"，简称 "电邮"，俗称 "伊妹儿"。自 20 世纪 90 年代互联网问世以来，人们越来越多地利用电子邮件系统传递信息，逐步进入无纸社会。E-mail 促进了电子商务的发展，而电子商务和互联网的发展又促进了 E-mail 的飞跃。E-mail 改变了企业的经营模式和办公模式，改变了人们的金融活动和购买方式。E-mail 这一通信方式快捷且便宜，正在逐渐广泛地普及。

3. E-mail Address

- From (The sender's E-mail address)
- To (The receiver's E-mail address)
- CC (the receiver's E-mail address)
- BCC (Blind Carbon Copy) (The receiver's E-mail address)
- Date (The hour, day and month automatically showed on the E-mail)

The E-mail address of the receiver is to be written in the column of "To" or to be selected from the E-mail Address Book.

The receiver's address is composed of three parts:

The receiver's name + @ (at sign) + the host name connected with the internet

The parts of the receiver's name are composed of the first name (with all of the letters or some of the letters) + the last name (with the first two letters or only the first letter).

For example:

mingzh@xianelectric.com: This is composed of 3 parts, from the right to the left are the following parts:

. com: one-level domain name.

xianelectric: the company's name (Xi'an Electric Co.). It is the two-level domain name.

ming: the name of the individual person. (It is the Chinese phonetic alphabet of "明").

zh: The first and second letter of the name "zheng".

Sometimes all the letters are written out according to the Chinese phonetic alphabet, for example, "zhengming" is used as the receiver's name. But sometimes both of the first letter of the two phonemes in the first name and last name are all written out as "zheng+mm". For example, in English "robertb" is written out to show Robert Brown.

3. E-mail地址

- From：寄(发件人电子邮件地址)
- To：送、转(收件人电子邮件地址)

- CC：抄送，副本(收件人电子邮件地址)
- BCC(Blind Carbon Copy)：密件抄送，隐蔽副本(收件人电子邮件地址)
- Date：日期(电子邮件上自动出现年月日和钟点)

收件人电子邮件地址在 To 栏填写，也可从通讯录中选取。

收件人电子邮件地址由三部分组成：

收件人账号 ＋@(at 标记) ＋ 与因特网连接的主机名

收件人账号的构成：名(名的全拼或其中的部分字母)+姓(拼音的头两个字母或头一个字母)

例如：

mingzh @ xianelectric.com 由三部分组成，从右向左依次是：

. com：一级域名

xianelectric：公司名(Xi'an Electric Co.)，为二级域名

ming：人名("明"的全拼)

zh：姓的第一个和第二个字母(郑，全拼为 zheng)

有时用中文姓名的全拼作为收件人的账号，如"zhengming"(郑明)，但有时用名中两个音的头一个字母和姓的全拼作为账号，如："zheng+mm"是"郑明明"中"郑"的全拼和"明明"的拼音首字母的组合。

英语也一样，如：robertb (Robert Brown)。

4. E-mail Subject

Subject (heading or title)

Re. (used in formal documents)

Attachment (the relevant documents or materials attached)

Urgent (it is added only in case of necessity)

4. E-mail标题

标记(题目或主题)

回复(用于正式文件)

附件(附上有关的文件或资料)

急件(需要时添加)

5. The formal signature of an E-mail

It must be combined with the personal name, title, the name of the unit, telephone number, E-mail address, and company's Website (with five lines at most).

5. E-mail正式署名

正式署名包括本人的姓名、职位、单位名称、电话号码、电子邮件地址和公司网址(不超过 5 行)。

6. E-mail body

The language used in E-mail is not only rather simple and clear, but even gets close to the colloquial form as well.

In order to know clearer about the language characteristics and principles of the E-mail writing and master better ways of choosing the words and phrases in working out a standard E-mail with high language cultivation, it is necessary to remember some characteristics and principles of drafting, amending and editing the E-mails:

In writing E-mail, drafting is necessary to do at first, then give your E-mail your revision and checking. Put E-mail editing and E-mail sending into the last processes. You should check the E-mail address again and again to make it free of errors. Should you be able to write English letters, there would be no doubt about your being able to draft your E-mails. The colloquial form is adoptable in the E-mail body, with less strictness in writing E-mail than in writing letters. Attention should be paid to the English language and English grammar. Writing arbitrarily with lots of mistakes will reveal your insufficiency in language cultivation and as well your lacking in politeness and respect for the others.

6. E-mail正文

在 E-mail 中使用的语言不但要简单、清晰，并且类似于口语。

为了更清楚地了解电子邮件的语言特点及写作原则，掌握选择单词和词组的方法，写出标准、得当的电子邮件，必须牢记起草、修改和编排电子邮件的几个原则。

写 E-mail 时首先要起草，然后进行修改、审校，最后编排并发出邮件。要再三校对电子邮件地址，不能有任何错误。只要会写英文书信，起草 E-mail 就不成问题，而且 E-mail 正文也可以采用口语形式，不像写书信那样严谨。要注意英语的语言及语法。写得太随意，错误也很多，不但会暴露自己运用语言的功底不足，而且显得对对方不够礼貌和尊重。

7. E-mail Samples

1)   Enquiry

From:
To:
CC:
BCC:
Date:

Subject: (or Re.) Enquiry
Attachment: Enquiry Sheet

Dear Sirs:
We know that you are an exclusive agent of ××× Brand ×× (product) made in Japan.

We are planning to purchase 50 sets of these products for our employees, but we are not quite clear about the current marketing situation about the products available on the market. Please send us your detailed information on the products of ××× you can supply now and as well your price list.

    Best Regards，

Friendly yours

(Signature)
Title and Unit Name
Ph:
E-mail:
Website:

7. E-mail实例

1)   询价

发自：

送至：

抄送：

密件抄送：

日期：

标题：询价

附件：询价单

获悉贵方是日本产×××牌××(产品)的独家代理商。我方计划为雇员购买50套该产品，但不十分清楚当前该产品的市场行情。请给我方寄来贵方现在能供应的×××产品的详细信息以及价格单。

结束语
(签名)
职务及单位名
电话：
电子邮件：
网址：

2)   A Reply to the E-mail Enquiry

Thank you very much for your E-mail enquiry and now we feel pleased in attaching you our price list of the products for this year，as well a catalogue of our products. The prices shown on the list are negotiable and our Representative in China Mr. ××× would like to visit you in a few days for demonstrating you the products and for establishing business relationship with you.

2)   回复询价

非常感谢贵方的 E-mail 询价，我方很乐意给贵方附寄去我方今年的产品价格表以及一份产品目录。表上所列的价格是可以协商的，而且我方驻中国代表×××先生愿意几天后拜访贵方，以便展示产品并与贵方建立业务关系。

3)　Assessment Sheet

Please ensure all of your Assessment sheets are completed accurately and legibly before the last day of the course and handed to the relevant Student Record Office for authorization.

3)　学生成绩单

请本课程结束前一天将所有成绩单正确无误、字迹清晰地填写完毕后交学生档案办公室供核准。

Words and Expressions

legibly	清楚地
authorization	核准，批准，认可
Student Record Office	学生档案办公室
assessment sheet	成绩单

8. Some Characteristics and Principles of E-mail Language

1)　Four "More"s and four "Less"s

(1)　Use more verbs and less verbal nouns.

Chinese Meaning (中文意义)	More Using of Verbs (多用动词)	Less Using of Verbal Nouns (少用动词性名词)
到达	Arrive	Arrival
协助	Assist	Assistance
碰撞	Collide	Collision
依靠	Depend	Dependence
发展	Develop	Development
履行	Perform	Performance
翻译	Translate	Translation
传送	Transmit	Transmittance

The verbal nouns are formed by verbs + suffixes and are usually the abstract nouns indicating the qualities, states, processes, extents, results, etc. So it's better to use more verbc.

8. E-mail语言的特点和原则

1)　四"多"和四"少"

(1)　多用动词，少用动词性名词。(表略)

动词性名词由"动词+后缀"构成，通常都是抽象名词，表示性质、状态、过程、程度、结果等，因此最好多用动词。

(2)　Use more active voices and less passive voices, as well as the sentence patterns of "it is" and "there is".

Because, firstly, the words used in passive voices are more than those used in active voices, so it is easier to make evitable mistakes in writing E-mails. Secondly, the sentence of passive voice without the prepositional phrase of "by" will always make the person who makes the action not clear to the readers. So in E-mail writing the active voices are more popular in use. But if only stating what happens is necessary and there is no need to make the action receiver clear, the passive voices may as well be put into use.

In addition, the sentences of "It is (was)" and "There is (was)" are not to be used often.

For example:

It has been decided that…

There is not only an "it" form in this sentence but as well with a passive voice coming behind, you will feel a little "heavy" in reading. If we change it into the following expression:

We have decided that …

Obviously, you will feel more relaxed.

(2) 多用主动语态，少用被动语态和"It is (was)""There is (are)"句型。

因为，首先被动语态中所用的词与词组比主动语态中用得要多，因此在书写电子邮件时容易犯本来可以避免的错误。其二，被动语态句中不带"by"的介词短语的句子，经常使读者弄不清谁是施动者，所以在书写电子邮件时，用主动语态更为普遍。但如果仅仅需要说明发生了什么事，也没有必要弄清楚谁是受动者时，被动语态仍可使用。

另外，"It is (was)"及"There is (are)"句型也不宜常用。

例如：

It has been decided that …

此句中不但使用了 it，而且使用了被动与 that，显得有些笨重，如果我们将 it 省略，且改用被动语态，如：We have decided that…则显得轻松舒服得多。

(3) Use more short sentences and less long sentences.

The long sentences are superfluous and are difficult to be organized, to be understood and to be remembered. At the same time it is easy to make mistakes and the work will be held up. So try your best to use short sentences and simple sentences to express yourself.

(3) 多用短句，少用长句。

长句累赘，不容易组织、理解和记忆，而且容易出错，耽误工作，所以要尽量用短句和简单句来表达意思。

(4) Use more English colloquial form, less written form.

Chinese Meaning (中文意义)	Less using of Written English (少用书面语)	More using of Colloquial English (多用口语)
帮助	assistance	help
估计	estimate	guess
联系	contact	get in touch
机会	opportunity	chance
改善	improve	get better
请求	request	ask
满意，好	satisfactory	Ok/all right

In modern E-mail correspondence the colloquial English form is used widely. Even the word of "OK" may be used in business E-mails. Of course, it is better not to use the colloquial from abusively in writing rather official correspondence.

(4)　多用口语，少用书面语。(表略)

在现代电子邮件通信中，人们广泛地使用口语。甚至"OK"一词也常用于商务电子邮件中。当然非常正式的商务电子邮件中还是最好不要用口语。

2)　Four "No"s

(1)　No using of major terms, use common words.

Chinese Meaning(中文意思)	No Major Words (不使用太正式的词)	Use Common Words (使用常用词组)
减轻	alleviate	reduce
确定	ascertain	make sure
开始	commence/initiate	start/begin
终止	discontinue/terminate	stop
如果	in the event of	if
使用	utilize	use

(2)　No using of superfluous words, use common words or delete them:

Chinese Meaning (中文意思)	No Superfluous Words (不使用赘语)	Use Common Words (使用常用词组)
那时	at that point of time	then
借助	by means of	by
因为	by reason of	because of
为了	in order to	to
收讫	in receipt of	receive
方面	in respect of	about/for

(3)　No using of discriminate words, use polite words or delete them.

(4)　No using of the drastic words or delete them.

Even if your opposite side use caustic unreasonable words in their letters, you must resist the temptation of replying them in the similar tone and terms, you must reply then politely with your self-restraint, but not with servility and bumptiousness.

Four "More"s and four "Less"s of E-mails can also be applied to fax.

2)　四"不"

(1)　不使用大词，使用常用词。(表略)

(2)　不使用赘语，使用普通词或省略。(表略)

(3)　不使用歧视性语言，使用礼貌用语或删除歧视性语言。

(4)　不使用过激语言，或者删除过激语言。

即使对方来信语言尖刻、无礼，也不能以这种语调回信，必须克制情绪，不卑不亢、客客气气地回信。

E-mail 语言的特点和原则中"四多四少"和"四不"同样也适用于 Fax 的语言使用。

II. Fax

1. The concept of Fax

The original word of "fax" is "facsimile", which means "copy", "imitate" or "reproduce". The Chinese translation of it is "传真". Any letter, document, manuscript, drawing, graph and chart can be transmitted to the opposite party by facsimile machine with great reality and vividness which is incomparable with any previous communicating instruments and appliances of letters, cables and telexes. Faxing is fast and cheap, with great reality in conveying the drawings, charts, etc., facilitating the business operations and at the same time saving time to reproduce them. Faxing is one of the newest communicating means and method developed recently in communicating business.

The facsimile machine can be installed through the telephone line of any family. So long as exists the line, there is possibility of receiving end sending faxes at any place and any time. After dispatching a fax, the facsimile machine will tell you "Transmission is "OK" or "No answer" or "Try again". With this kind of safety and reliability your work will be done without any delay.

二、传真

1. Fax的概念

Fax 的原词为 facsimile，意为"摹传、摹真本"或"复制"之意，中文译为"传真"。通过传真机可以将书信、文件、手稿、图纸、图形、表格等按照原样传给对方，其保真性和清晰性是以往书信、电报、电传等都无法企及的。传真不仅快，而且便宜，能够真实地传递图纸、表格等，在方便业务的同时可以节省重新制作的时间，所以它是电信业务中最新发展起来的其中一种通信工具与方法。

传真机可以装在家用电话线上，只要有线路，任何地点、任何时间都可以收发。传真发出以后，传真机会告诉你"发送成功"，或发出"没有回应"或"再试一次"的信息，安全可靠，绝不会耽误工作。

2. Some contents of a fax

To: 发至：

 Name: (receiver)   姓名：(收件人)

 Title: 头衔：

 Unit Name: 单位名称：

 Tel: 电话：

 Fax: 传真：

 E-mail: 电子邮件：

From: 发自：
    Name: (sender)   姓名：(发件人)
    Title: 头衔：
    Unit Name: 单位名称：
    Tel: 电话：
    Fax: 传真：
    E-mail: 电子邮件：

Date：   日期：
Attention: 经办：
CC: 抄送：
Subject: 标题：
Dear Sirs，   称呼，主题
(Fax Body)   (正文)

Some regular companies and units will add the following items:

(1)   CC (or Copies to);

(2)   Ref No.;

(3)   Total pages.

The items and the arranging order may be set by the individual person or by the unit itself.

2.　传真的内容

有些正规公司及单位还要加上以下内容：

(1)　抄至；

(2)　文编号；

(3)　总页数。

设置项目及排列次序也可以按各人及各单位的情形制订。

3.　Fax Samples

1)   Payment terms

    We are very pleased to know that you have the goods we want to order in stock and can make shipment in two weeks' time. But you demand that the payment be effected by sight L/C, which made us quite disappointed.

    Since we have established business relations for more than 10 years and have already concluded many transactions between your cooperation and ours, we wish you would entitle us to effect the payment by 60 days' at sight.

    Looking forward to your favorable news.

Yours friendly,

×××

General Manager, ×× Co., Ltd.

2) Shipment of the Goods

We have the pleasure of informing you that the confirmed, irrevocable L/C No. ××××, amounting to US $ ××× has been opened this morning through the Bank of ××× and we have been informed by the ××× Shipping Company that SS " Victory" is due to sail from your city to our port on/or about 15th next month. We hope that you will try your best to ship our goods by that steamer.

We await your shipping advice.

Yours faithfully,

×××

Sales Manager, ×× Co., Ltd.

3. 传真实例

1) 支付条款

很高兴获悉我方想要订购的货物你方有库存，并且两周内就能发运。但你方要求凭即期信用证付款，这一点很使我方失望。

由于双方建立业务关系已有十多年之久，并且成交了不少生意，希望你方允许我方以60天期汇票支付。

盼望你方可喜的消息。

×××

××有限公司　总经理

2) 货物发运

我方十分高兴地通知你方，保兑的、不可撤销的××××号信用证，金额为×××美元，今天上午已在×××银行开立。×××运输公司已通知我方，"胜利"轮定于下月15号或15号前后从你市开来我港，希望你方尽最大努力通过该轮发运我方货物。

等候你方装船通知。

×××

××有限公司　销售经理

III. E-commerce and EDI

1. The concepts of E-commerce and EDI and the relationship between each other

E-commerce can be translated into Chinese as "电子商务". To exchange the information by internet is the base of E-commerce development. E-commerce is to carry on the purchase dealing on internet and on the base of the computer network for exchanging the commodities, services and information. E-commerce is to effect the information transmission, the dealing and payment of the commodities or services through the telephone line, computer network and other electronic means. E-commerce has reduced the service cost and simultaneously raised the service speed, resulting in the increasing of the products' quality. E-commerce can be used in the family banking, on line market purchasing, stock exchanging, job hunting, network auction, cooperative researching and developing of the projects. For instance, buying a set of software from a certain network station to effect the goods' delivering, payment and agency business fully by numeralization. In this way the so-called E-commerce is realized. Buying food from the automatic vending machine by Intelligent Card is also a kind of E-commerce.

E-commerce includes not only the online transactions, but also the market investigation, business hunting, keeping in contact with the business institutions and the suppliers, cooperative designing of the products. The activities carried out are flexible, extensive and all-rounded. As to EDI (Electronic Data Interchange), it is to interchange the electronic data among the computers of the trading partners and to handle the trading business automatically. Therefore, EDI is only a part of E-commerce.

三、电子商务与电子数据交换

1. E-commerce与EDI的概念及两者之间的关系

E-commerce 可译为"电子商务"，在因特网上的信息交换是电子商务发展的基础。电子商务是指在因特网上及在计算机网络上进行买卖交易，进行商品、服务及信息的交换。电子商务通过电话线路、计算机网络及其他电子手段实现信息传递、商品或服务的买卖与支付。电子商务在降低服务成本的同时提高了服务速度，使产品质量得以提高。电子商务可用于家庭银行、网上商场购物、股票交易、求职、网上拍卖、合作研发项目等。例如，从某个网站购买一套软件，递送、支付和代理则都是数字化进行，这就是电子商务。用智能卡从自动售货机购买食品也是电子商务的一种。

电子商务不仅包括在线交易，还包括进行市场调研，寻找商机并和商务伙伴、商务机构及供应商保持交往，共同设计产品等，可以进行的活动灵活、广泛全面。而 EDI(Electronic Data Interchange，电子数据交换)只是在贸易各方的计算机之间进行传输和自动处理贸易业务，所以 EDI 只是电子商务的一部分。

2. The character of E-commerce and its trading partners

It is divided into the following six categories:

(1) Business institution ◄──► business institution

The direct information exchanges carried on between two institutions or among several institutions.

(2) Business institution ◄──► consumer

Retail E-commerce activities carried on between the enterprise institutions and the personal individual.

(3) Consumer ◄──► consumer

The trade made between the consumers themselves through classifying advertising, their selling articles, offering technical services, selling technical knowledge, etc.

(4) Consumer ◄──► commercial institutions

The consumer's selling their articles, services, technical knowledge, etc. to the commercial institutions.

(5) noncommercial institutions ←→ noncommercial institutions

This is the E-commerce carried on between or among the noncommercial institutions of the governmental, the academic and the social organizations. It can help to increase the working efficiency and raise the service level.

(6) Inside Institutions

This is the institution's supplying its employees products, trainings, etc. inside itself.

2. 电子商务的特征及交易对象

电子商务可以分为以下六类。

(1) 商业机构 ←→ 商业机构：两个或多个机构之间信息的直接交易。

(2) 商业机构 ←→ 消费者：商业机构与消费者之间的零售电子商务活动。

(3) 消费者 ←→ 消费者：消费者之间通过分类广告、出售物品或提供技术服务、出售技术知识等方式进行交易。

(4) 消费者 ←→ 商业机构：消费者向商业机构出售商品、服务、技术知识等。

(5) 非商业机构 ←→ 非商业机构：政府机构、学术机构、社会组织等非商业机构之间进行的电子商务，有助于提高工作效率与服务水平。

(6) 机构内部

通过机构内部向雇员提供产品及培训等。

3. The development of EDI and Customs Electronic Declaration

With the fast development of the international trade, the traditional tabulating and settlement of exchange can no more meet with the requirements of this development because of the variety of the documents and the complexity of the programs. The necessity of spending a lot of time doing this work and the result of slow circulation have forced the computerization of the documents tabulation and management to be realized with the telecommunication of the information transmitting following behind. The EDI has thus emerged as the times require and gradually abrogated the paper documents with "no-paper trading" coming forward.

At present, EDI has been quickly developed in North America, Western Europe, Japan, Singapore, etc. As far back as 1980s, America announced that any applicant using EDI in Customs declaration may get preferential treatment. Singapore has done away with all the paper trading documents and EDI must be used in Customs declaration without exception.

3. EDI的发展与电子报关

随着国际贸易的迅速发展，传统的制单结汇已不再适应发展的需要，因为单证种类多，程序复杂，费时，流通也不快，所以对单证的制作与管理要实现计算机化，信息传递要电信化。EDI 就应运而生，并逐步淘汰纸面单证，实现"无纸贸易"。

目前，在北美、西欧、日本、新加坡等 EDI 已迅速发展。早在 20 世纪 80 年代末美国就宣布对使用 EDI 方式报关者给予优先办理。新加坡已废除了所有纸面贸易文件，报关一律使用 EDI 方式。

4. The applying of EDI

The applying of EDI is to transmit, interchange and process the data of the Order Sheet, Invoice, Bill of Lading, Customs Application Form, Import and Export License, etc. in standardized forms through the computer and internet, finishing the whole trading process with "trading" taken as its core.

In the whole process of taking "trade" as its core, all the links are not necessary to be processed manually and they are in no need of posting the interchanged documents, thus the transactions will be effected faster and in great quantity with great efficiency and accuracy. The brilliant prospects of EDI is immeasurable and will inevitably lead the foreign trade personnel into a business revolution on a global scale.

4. EDI 的应用

EDI 的应用指的是将贸易过程中的订货单、发票、提货单、海关申报单、进出口许可证等数据以标准化格式，通过计算机和网络进行传递、交换、处理，完成以贸易为中心的全部过程。

在以贸易为核心的过程中各环节都不使用人工处理信息，也不用邮递互换单证，从而使交易加快，高效、巨量、精确，前途不可估量。因此外贸人员必然要投入到这场全球性的商业革命中。

Exercises

Ⅰ. Draft an E-mail to apply for a part-time job.

Ⅱ. Draft a fax to invite your foreign trading partners to visit the Museum of Terra-cotta Warriors and Horses of Qin Dynasty.

Ⅲ. Choose the correct answers.

1. The delayed payment interest commencing from Dec. 31 to the date of payment February 25 at the interest rate of 10%____ amounting to US $ ××× should be for your____.
   A. per annum, amount
   B. annual, money
   C. per annum, account
   D. annually, sake

2. In most cases, 80%—85% of the contract value can be provided by a buyer's ___ , while the remaining part is paid by the ____ in cash.
   A. debt, debtor
   B. credit card, buyer
   C. credibility, debtor
   D. credit, buyer

3. If the goods are placed in the foreign market before collection of money, this type of payment term or the mode of trade is _____.
   A. consignment account
   B. compensation trade
   C. installment payment
   D. open account

4. We have___ your account with the amount of US $ ××× for extra costs.

    A. credited   B. remitted   C. debited   D. deducted

5. Your statement has been checked and found correct and we have instructed our bank to make remittance_____.

    A. according to   B. according   C. as according   D. accordingly

6. We would like to inform you that you _____ for all the samples if they are not returned to us within 120 days.

    A. will invoice   B. invoice   C. will be invoiced   D. invoiced

7. We would ask that we ___ to pay your account by four monthly remittances of US $ ×××, with a final adjustment in the fifth month.

    A. allowing   B. be allowed

    C. allowed   D. having to allow

8. We expect certain sizeable orders_____ for within the next two months and ask if we may defer payment of your account from June 2 to July 15.

    A. paying   B. to be paid

    C. for being paid   D. to be paying

9. We _____ to allow you a special discount if you increase your order to 1,000 pairs.

    A. are prepared   B. were prepared

    C. do prepare   D. have prepared

10. With an application form enclosed, we shall be glad if you _____ an irrevocable letter of credit.

    A. arrange for open   B. arrange to open

    C. be arranged to open   D. will arrange to open

Chapter 14 Specimens of Documents in International Trade
外贸单证范例

Learning Objectives:

- Learn how to read various English documents in international trade.
- Master the ways of making them up by yourselves.

学习目标：

- 学会阅读外贸英语中的各种单证。
- 掌握自行制作这些单证的方法。

International trade is international selling and buying of Commodities, but in practical business the main manifestation of international trade is selling and buying carried out by documents.

在国际贸易中，国际贸易是国际商品买卖，但在实际业务中主要表现为单证的买卖。

Ⅰ. The Kinds of Foreign Trade Documents

Foreign trade documents are classified into the following two categories.

1. Internal Documents

Customs Declaration Documents submitted to the Customs by exporters for going through the export formalities are called internal documents, such as Customs Declaration of the Exported Goods, Export Licence, Insurance Policy, Shipment Documents, the Inspection Documents required by the Commercial Inspection Bureau, etc. These documents are all internal documents and are all in need of being submitted to the relevant departments.

一、外贸单证的分类

外贸单证主要分为以下两大类。

1. 对内单证范例

出口商为办理出口手续向海关提交的报关单据，称作对内单证。如出口货物报关单、出口许可证、向保险公司申请投保的保险单、托运单据及商验局所需的报检单据。都是需要向国内有关部门提交的对内单证。

2. External Documents

The documents required for negotiating in negotiating banks and for collecting payments from buyers are called Exchange Settlement Documents. All these documents must be submitted to opening banks abroad and buyers, so they are also called external documents.

The external documents are classified into the following:

1) Commercial Documents

Commercial Invoice, Packing List, Inspection Certificate, etc.

2) Shipping Documents

Ocean Marine Transportation Bill of Lading, etc.

(1) Air Transportation Documents: Receipt of Cargo Acceptance, etc.

(2) Insurance Documents: Insurance Policy and Insurance Certificate.

(3) Financial Documents: Draft, Promissory Note and Cheque.

(4) Other Documents: Certificate of Origin, Shipping Advice, and the other relevant certificate documents.

2. 对外单证

向议付行议付或向买方收款所需的单证，称为结汇单证。这些单证都要提交给国外的开证行及买方，所以称为对外单证。对外单证又分为以下几种。

1) 商业单证

商业发票、装箱单、检验证等。

2) 运输单证

海运提单等。

(1) 航空运单：货物承运收据等。

(2) 保险单证：保险单和保险凭证两种。

(3) 金融单证：汇票、本票和支票三种。

(4) 其他单证：产地证、装船通知以及其他相关的证件等。

II. The Document Making

1. The basis of document making and its requirements

The documents are made on the basis of sales contract, letter of credit, delivery order and original materials offered by the supplying departments. The documents should be done correctly, completely, promptly, concisely and cleanly.

二、制单

1. 制单的基础及要求

单据是根据买卖合同、信用证、货物出库单、供货部门提供的原始资料来制作的，制作时应做到正确、完整、及时、简明、整洁。

2. The procedures of making documents

(1) Before making documents, check Delivery Order with letter of credit or contract.

(2) Before making documents, count the size, weight, unit price, total price, and etc. of the

goods.

(3)　Dispose necessary copies.

(4)　Make documents.

The document making should be started with contract, L/C, Invoice, Packing List, etc. and ended with the examining work of the document making.

The various document published in this book can help the students to understand the styles and phraseology of the documents. The styles of electronic documents are not completely the same as those of the former documents, but the sentence patterns and phraseology are the same. (In the documents the terms and sentences are published bilingually, so the word list is omitted.)

2. 制单流程

(1)　制单前须核实交货单与信用证或合同是否一致。

(2)　制单前计算货物的尺码、重量、单价、总价等。

(3)　制作所需的份数。

(4)　制单。

制单应从合同、信用证、发票、装箱单开始，以制单的检查工作结束。

本书所列各种单证可供学生了解一些单证的格式及用语。电子单证的格式和以前的单证格式不完全一样，但使用的句型和词汇是一样的(此章所列各表均为中英文对照，故单词释义省略。)

III．Bill of Lading 提单

托运人		中国		
收货人 Consignee To Order Bank of ***	或让受人 or Assigns	远洋运输公司 CHINA OCEAN SHIPPING COMPANY 总公司　HEAD OFFICE:　　北京　Beijing 分公司　BRANCH OFFICE:　　Guangzhou Shanghai Tianjin		
船名 Vessel****	航次 Voy.	Notify: 提单　　　　　　　　　　　正本 BILL OF LADING　　　　　ORIGINAL 直运或转运　　　DIRECT OR WITH TRANSSHIPMENT 装货单号　　S/O No.　　提单号　　B/L No.		
装货港 Port of Loading		卸货港 Port of Discharge		
国籍 Nationality		运费支付地 Freight Payable at		支付
托运人所提供的详细情况 Particulars Furnished by the Shipper				
标志和号数 Marks and Numbers	件数 No. of Packages	货名 Description of Goods	毛重 Gross Weight	尺码 Measurement
***	***	***运费付讫 Freight Prepaid		
合计件数　（大写） Total Packages (in words)		SAY ×××　PACKAGES ONLY		

Shipped on board the vessel named above in apparent good order and condition (unless otherwise indicated) the goods or packages specified herein and to be discharged at the above mentioned port of discharge or as near thereto as the vessel may safely get and be always afloat.

上述外表情况良好的货物(另有说明者除外)已装在上列船上并应在上列卸货港或该船所能安全到达并保持浮泊的附近地点卸货。

The weight, measure, marks, numbers, quality, contents and value, being particulars furnished by the Shipper, are not checked by the Carrier on loading.

重量、尺码、标志、号数、品质、内容和价值是托运人所提供的，承运人在装船时并未核对。

The Shipper, Consignee and the Holder of this Bill of Lading hereby expressly accept and agree to all printed, written or stamped provisions, exceptions and conditions of this Bill of Lading, including those on the back hereof.

托运人、收货人和本提单的持有人明白表示接受并同意本提单及其背面所载的一切印刷、书写或打印的规定、免责事项和条件。

运费和其他费用 Freight and Charges:	

为证明以上各节,承运人或其代理人已签署提单一式三份,其中一份经完成提货手续后,其余各份失效。

In witness whereof, the Carrier or his Agents has signed THREE Bills of Lading all of this tenor and date, one of which being accomplished, the others to stand void.

请托运人特别注意本提单内与该货保险效力有关的免责事项和条件。

签单日期　　　　　　在

Date .... 　　　　at ....

船长

.............For the Master

Shippers are requested to note　particularly the exceptions and conditions of this Bill of Lading with reference to the validity of the insurance upon their goods.

IV．Insurance Policy (Certificate) 保险单(凭证)

中国人民保险公司
THE PEOPLE'S INSURANCE COMPANY OF CHINA

总公司设于北京　　　　　1949 年创立
Head Office: Beijing　　　Established in 1949

发票号码 Invoice No.	保险单 INSURANCE POLICY	保险单号次 Policy No.

　　中国人民保险公司(以下简称本公司)根据＿＿＿＿＿＿＿＿中国×××进出口公司广州分公司(以下简称被保险人)的要求，由被保险人向本公司缴付约定的保险费，按照本保险单承保险别和背面所载条款与下列特款承保下述货物运输保险，特立本保险单。

　　This Policy of Insurance witnesses that The People's Insurance Company of China (hereinafter called "The Company"), at the request of × × × × I & E Corp. Guangzhou (hereinafter called the "Insured") and in consideration of the agreed premium paying to the Company by the Insured, undertakes to insure the undermentioned goods in transportation subject to the conditions of this Policy as per the Clauses printed overleaf and other special clauses attached hereon.

标记及号码 Mark & No.	包装及数量 Quantity	保险货物项目 Description of Goods	保险金额 Amount Insured
****			****

总保险金额：****美元

Total Amount Insured: U.S. $ ****

保费　　　　　　　费率　　　　　　　　装载运输工具：S.S. ****

Premium: As arranged 　 Rate: As arranged 　 Per conveyance S.S. ****

开航日期：****当天或左右　　　自****　　　　　　　　至***

Slg. on or abt. **** 　　　　From **** 　　　　　　to ***

承保险别

Conditions

根据 1981 年 1 月 1 日版中国人民保险公司远洋海运货物条款和海洋海上货物战争险条款，承保一切险和战争险(包括仓至仓条款)。

　　　　Covering All Risks and War Risks as per Ocean Marine Cargo Clauses
　　　　and ocean Marine cargo War Risks Clauses (1/1/1981) of The People's
　　　　Insurance Company of China (abbreviated as I.C.C. – All Risks & War
　　　　Risks)(Warehouse to Warehouse Clause is included).

　　如所保货物遇出险，本公司凭本保险单及其他有关证件给付赔款。

　　Claims: If any, payable on surrender of this Policy together with other relevant documents.

　　所保货物，如发生本保险单项下负责赔偿的损失或事故，应立即通知本公司下述代理人查勘。

　　In the event of accident whereby loss or damage may result in a claim under this Policy immediate notice applying for survey must be given to the Company's Agent.

　　下述

　　as mentioned hereunder:

　　赔款偿付地点　　　　中国人民保险公司广州分公司

　　　　　　　　　　THE PEOPLE'S INSURANCE CO. OF CHINA, GUANGZHOU BRANCH

　　Claim Payable at

　　日期×××××

　　Date×××××

V. Draft (Bill of Exchange) 汇票

凭 中国银行(香港)
Drawn under Bank of China , Hongkong
信用证或购买证第　　　号
L/C or A/P No. ****
日期 ****
Date ****

1

按息　　　　付款
Payable with interest @　　　　% per annum
号码　　　汇票金额　　　中国，广州　　　年　月　日
No.　　　Exchange for　　　Guangzhou, China
见票　　　日后(本汇票之副本未付)付
　　At　　　　sight of this FIRST of Exchange (Second of exchange being unpaid)
pay to the order of ****或其指定人
金额 ****
the sum of ****

此致
To　　　　　　　　　　　　　　China National ＿＿＿＿＿＿
　　　　　　　　　　　　　　　　I & E Corp.

凭　中国银行(香港)
Drawn under Bank of China , Hongkong
信用证或购买证第　　　号
L/C or A/P No. ****
日期 ****
Date ****

2

按息　　　　付款
Payable with interest @　　　　% per annum
号码　　　汇票金额　　　中国，广州　　　年　月　日
No.　　　Exchange for　　　Guangzhou, China
见票　　　日后(本汇票之副本未付)付
At　　　　sight of this FIRST of Exchange (Second of exchange being unpaid)
pay to the order of ****或其指定人
金额 ****
the sum of ****

此致　　　　　　　　　　　　　中国进出口公司
To　　　　　　　　　　　　　　China National ＿＿＿＿＿＿
　　　　　　　　　　　　　　　　I & E Corp.

VI. Certificate of Origin 产地证明书

中国国际贸易促进委员会

THE CHINA COUNCIL FOR THE PROMOTION OF INTERNATIONAL TRADE

产地证明书

(CERTIFICATE OF ORIGIN)

年　　月　　日

(Date:　　　　)

发货人(Consignor) _____

收货人(Consignee) _____

起运地点(Port of Shipment)_____

运往地点(Destination)_____

标记及号码 (Mark & No.)	品名 (Commodity)	产地 (Place of origin)	数量 (Quantity)	重量 (Weight)
		中华人民共和国 The People's. Republic of China		

兹证明上列商品确系中华人民共和国出产或制造。

(This is to certify that the above mentioned commodities were produced or manufactured in the People's Republic of China.)

中国国际贸易促进委员会

The China Council for the Promotion

of International Trade

VII. Shipper Note 托运单

海运出口货物托运单(一)

托运人 Consignor		编号 No.		船名 Ship Name	
合同号: Contract No.			目的港 Destination Port		
标记及号码 Mark & No.	件数 Quantity		货名 Goods Description	重量(公斤) Weight in Kilos	
				净 Net	毛 Gross
共计件数(大写) Total Number of Packages in Writing SAY: ×× ××× CARTONS				运费付款方式 Way of Freight payment	
运费计数 (大写) Freight in Writing			尺码 Measurement		
备注 Note					
抬头 TO ORDER OF	With Transshipment□ 可转船□ No Transshipment□ 不可转船□		With Partial Shipment□ 可分批装船□ No Partial Shipment□ 不可分批装船□		
通 知 NOTIFY	装期 Shipment Date		效期 Validity Shipment	提单 张数 NO of B/L Pages	
	金额 Sum				
收货人 Consignee	银行 编号 Bank No.		信用 证号 LC No.		

制单日期
Made on

Shipper Name: （船名）				D/R No.(编号)		
Address:						
Consignee (收货人) TO ORDER OF				Equipment Interchange Receipt 配舱回单		
Notify Party (通知人) Name：（姓名） Address：（地址）						
Pre-carriage by （前程运输）	Place of Receipt(收货地点)					
Vessel Voy. No. (船名) （航次）	Port of Loading （装货港）					
Port of Discharge (卸货港)	Place of Delivery （交货地点）		Final Destination for the Consignee (收货人地址) Address of consignee			
Container No. (集装箱号)	Seal No.(封号) Mark & No. (标号与号码)	No. of Containers or p' kgs (箱数或件数)	Kind of Packages; Goods Description (包装种类与货名)	Gross Weight 毛重(公斤)	Measurement 尺码(立方米)	
TOTAL NUMBER OF CONTAINERS 集装箱总数 OR PACKAGES (IN WORDS) 集装箱数或件数合计(大写)						
FREIGHT & CHARGES (运费与附加费)	Revenue Tons (运费吨)	RATE (运费率)	Per (每)	Prepaid (预付)	Collect (到付)	
Ex. Rate: (兑换率)	Prepaid at (预付地点)		Payable at (到付地点)		Place of Issuing (签发地点)	
	Total Prepaid (预付总额)		No. of Original B/L (正本提单份数)			
With Transshipment□可转船 No Transshipment□不可转船	With Partial Shipment□可分批装运 No Partial Shipment□不可分批装运		提单签发 Issuing of B/L			
装期 Shipment Date	效期 Shipment Validity					
金额 Sum						

海运出口货物托运单(二)				
托运人 Shipper 编号　　　　　　　船名 No.　　　　　　　　S/S 目的港 To				
标记及号码 Mark & No.	件数 Quantity	货名 Description of Goods	重量(公斤) Weight in Kilos	
			净 Net	毛 Gross
			尺　码 Measurement	
共计件数 (大写) Total Number of Packages (in Writing)			运费付款方式 Way of Freight Payment	
运费计算 Freight in Writing				
备注 Note				

转船□ With Transshipment	不可转船□ No Transshipment	分批□ With Partial Shipment	不可分批□ No Partial Shipment	装期 Shipment Date	效期 Shipment Validity	
备注 Note						

配船回单　第一联

Shipper (发货人)		D/R		外代货号	第
Consignee (收货人)					二
Notify Party (通知人)		集装箱货物托运单			联

船代留底

Pre-carriage by (前程运输)	Place of Receipt (收货地点)	
Vessel (船名) Voy. No. (航次)	Port of Loading (装货港)	
Port of Discharge (卸货港)	Place of Delivery (交货地点)	Final Destination for the Merchant's Reference (目的地)

Container No. (集装箱号)	Seal No. (封号) Mark & No. (标号与号码)	No. of Containers or p's kgs (箱数或件数)	Kind of Packages; Description of Goods (包装种类与货名)	Gross Weight 毛重(公斤)	Measurement 尺码(立方米)

TOTAL NUMBER OF CONTAINERS OR PACKAGES (IN WORDS)
集装箱数或件数合计(大写)

FREIGHT &CHARGES (运费与附加费)	Revenue Tons (运费吨)	RATE (运费率)	Per (每)	Prepaid (预付)	Collect (到付)
Ex. Rate (兑换率)	Payable at (预付地点)	Place of Issue (到付地点)	Place of Issue (签发地点)		
	Total Prepaid (预付总额)	No. of Original B(s)/L (正本提单份数)			

With Transshipment □可转船 No Transshipment □不可转船	With Partial Shipment 可分批装运 No Partial Shipment 不可分批装运	Reefer Temperature Required (冷藏温度)	℉	℃

TYPE OF GOODS (种类)	□Ordinary □Reefer □Dangerous □Auto (普通) (冷藏) (危险品) (裸装车辆) □Liquid □Living Animal □Bulk □_____ (液体) (活动物) (散货)	危险品	Class 等级 Property 属性 IMDG Code Page 国际海运危险货物规则的页码 UN No. 联合国危险品编码

装期 Time of Shipment	有效期 Shipment Validity
金额 Sum in Words	
制单日期 Date of Document Making	

VIII. Invoice 发票

××××进出口公司

××× IMPORT & EXPORT CORPORATION

INVOICE
发票

发票号码
Invoice Number
订单或合约号码
Sales Confirmation No.
发票日期
Date of Invoice

装船口岸　　　　　　　　　目的地
From　　　　　　　　　　　 To
信用证号码　　　　　　　　 开证银行
Letter of Credit No.　　　　 Issued by

标记及号码 Marks & Numbers	数量与货品名称 Quantities and Descriptions	总值 Amount

××××进出口公司
××× IMPORT & EXPORT CORPORATION

IX. Packing List 装箱单

<table>
<tr><td colspan="8" align="center">XXXX 进出口公司
XXX IMPORT & EXPORT CORPORATION</td></tr>
<tr><td colspan="3">标记及号码
MARK & No.
****</td><td colspan="3" align="center">装箱单
PACKING LIST</td><td colspan="2"></td></tr>
<tr><td colspan="5">目的港
To:
品名
Name of Article</td><td colspan="3">总重量　　　净重
　　　　　　毛重
　Total　　N.W.
　　　　　　G.W.</td></tr>
<tr>
<td>件号
PACKAGE
No.</td>
<td>规格
型号
STYLE
SIZE</td>
<td>颜色
COLOUR</td>
<td>货品描述
DESCRIPTION</td>
<td>件数
QUANTITY
(PCS)</td>
<td colspan="2">重量(公斤)
WEIGHT IN KILOS
净　｜　毛
NET ｜ GROSS</td>
<td>尺码
MEASU-
REMENT</td>
</tr>
<tr>
<td></td><td></td><td></td><td>TTL:</td><td></td><td></td><td></td><td></td>
</tr>
<tr>
<td colspan="8">
Banykok Modern Terminals　旁注
B.M.T.　　　　SIDE MARKS:
　　　　　　　品名号　　　　　　品名号
　　　　　　　ARTICLE NO:　　　ARTICLE NO.:
　　　　　　　物品　　　　　　　物品
　　　　　　　ART:　　　　　　ART:
箱号　　　　　规格　　　　　　规格
C/T NO.　　　SIZE:　　　　　　SIZE:
　　　　　　　颜色　　　　　　　颜色
　　　　　　　COLOUR:　　　　COLOUR:
　　　　　　　件数　　　　　　　件数
　　　　　　　QUANTITY:　　　QUANTITY:
　　　　　　　　　　　　　　　××进出口公司
　　　　　　　　　　　　××× IMPORT & EXPORT CORPORATION

　　　　　　依据销售合同号
　　　　　　AS PER S/C NO.
　　　　　　信用证号
　　　　　　L/C NO.
</td>
</tr>
</table>

X．Commercial Invoice 商业发票

对美国出口的纺织品出口许可证/商业发票 纺织品出口许可证/商业发票 TEXTILE EXPORT LICENCE / COMMERCIAL INVOICE 正本 ORIGINAL			
1.出口人(名称和地址) Exporter (Name & Address)	2．许可证号码 LICENCE NO.		
	3．协议年度 Agreement Year		4．类别号 Category No.
	5．发票号码 Invoice No.		
6．收货人(名称和地址) Consignee (Name & Address)	7．装运港、装运期及目的地 Place & Time of Shipment Destination		
	8．中国港口离岸价值 Value of FOB Chinese US		
9．唛头-包装件数-商品名称 Marks & Numbers -Number of Packages -Description of Goods	10．数量 Quantity	11．单价 Unit Price	12．总值 Amount
13．出口人签章 Exporter's Stamp and Signature 日期 Date	14．发证当局签章 Issuing Authorities' Stamp and Signature		

Exercises

Choose the correct answer.

1. You are_____ to draw-on us at 60 days against this credit for the amount of your invoice upon shipment of the consignment to the consignee.
   A. able   B. authorized   C. right   D. powerful

2. Aldar Company wants to purchase ×××from XYZ Company. _____ will apply for

the letter of credit.

    A.   opening bank   B.   XYZ Company

    C.   both   D.   Aldar Company

3.   The shipper named on the B/C should be ＿＿.

    A.   the shipping company   B.   the shipping agent

    C.   the account party of the L/C   D.   the beneficiary of the L/C

4.   The draft is only drawn by ＿＿.

    A.   buyer   B.   seller   C.   agent   D.   bank

5.   The time of waiting for payment agreed upon by both sides is the period of ＿＿.

    A.   credit   B.   shipment

    C.   draft   D.   letter of credit

6.   A L/C requests all the following documents except＿＿.

    A.   packing list   B.   sales letters

    C.   bills of lading   D.   commercial invoice

7.   The bank on the buyer's side in collection arrangement is＿＿.

    A.   notifying bank   B.   remitting bank

    C.   opening bank   D.   collecting bank

8.   The letter of credit authorized you to draw at 60 days on our Bank for the amount of your invoice ＿＿ shipment is made.

    A.   after   B.   before   C. as   D.   follows

9.   ＿＿ accepting the draft, the bank will require you to produce documents such as Bills of Lading, Commercial Invoice, Packing List, etc.

    A.   After   B.   Before   C.   As   D.   Follows

10.   ＿＿ you fulfill the terms of the L/C, we will accept the drafts drawn under this credit.

    A.   Supplied   B.   To provide   C.   Provided   D.   Furnished

Chapter 15　Contract　合同

Learning Objectives:

● Learn and study the strict style and language characteristics of the English contracts.
● Master the skills of making up some simple English contracts.

学习目标：

● 学习研究英语合同的严谨风格及语言特点。
● 掌握编制一些简单的英语合同的技巧。

Ⅰ. The Concept of Contract

A contract is an agreement established between equal main bodies (for example: natural persons, legal persons or organizations) for defining, revising or terminating civil rights and civil duties.

Some dictionaries give the definition of contract as follows: A contract is a kind of promises. Violating the promise may obtain legal compensation. The law will consider the executing of the said promise as a kind of duties. That is to say, "A contract is an agreement with legal binding force".

一、合同的概念

合同是平等主体(如自然人、法人或组织)之间设立的确定、修改或终止民事权利和义务的协议。

有的词典上将合同定义为：合同是一种承诺，违反承诺可以得到法律补偿，法律将履行该承诺看成一种义务。也就是说"合同是有法律约束力的协议"。

Ⅱ. The Contents of Contract

The contents of contract are as follows:

(1)　Titles.

(2)　Preamble.

The date and place of contract signing; the names and positions of the persons concerned; the reason of signing the contract; the principles of reaching the agreement or of signing the contract and the scope of the authorized rights, etc.

(3)　Essential Clause.

The name of the commodity; the terms of quality, price, payment, shipment, insurance, delivery, inspection, import and export license and taxation, etc.

(4)　Special Clause.

The terms of installation and adjustment, loading and unloading, training, etc.

(5)　General Clause.

The terms of force Majeure, claims, arbitration, breaching , releasing, applicable laws, etc.

(6)　The Other Clauses.

The terms of contract amendments, the bribes declining and the other items which have not been defined in the Contract.

(7)　Witness Clause.

The validity of the contract, the language of the contract, the signature of the legal representatives of two parties of the contract, their positions, etc.

二、合同的内容

合同内容包括如下几方面。

(1)　合同名称。

(2)　合同总则。

签订合同的日期和地点；当事人的姓名和职务；签约原因；达成协议或签订合同的原则；授权的范围等。

(3)　基本条款。

商品名称；质量条款；价格条款；付款条款；装运条款；保险条款；交付条款；检验条款；进出口许可证条款；税收条款等。

(4)　特别条款。

安装调试条款；装卸货条款；培训条款等。

(5)　通用条款。

不可抗力条款；索赔条款；仲裁条款；违约条款；解约条款；适用法律条款等。

(6)　其他条款。

合同修改条款；拒绝受贿条款；其他在合同中未曾明确的条款。

(7)　结尾条款。

合同有效期；合同使用的文字；合同双方法人代表的签名；合同双方法人代表的职务等。

Ⅲ. The Requirements of Working out Contracts and the Styles and Characteristics of Contract Language

The literary form of contract language is the most formal and strictest one in English, so in drafting or translating the contract the following requirements should be fulfilled:

(1)　All the parts and articles should be arranged clearly, definitely and orderly.

(2)　The items and articles must be numbered correctly and clearly.

(3)　The items and articles should be drafted and edited concisely and smoothly, and be kept in accordance with the international practices.

(4)　The sentences and phrases, the technical terms and punctuations should be written clearly and correctly. Special attention should be paid to the English Grammar. The English sentences and phrases should be written out grammatically in order to make them understandable.

(5) The typing of the contract should be checked once and again. The spelling, the capital letters, the numbers, the amounts, the types of the commodities and so on should be paid great attention to in order to avoid the evitable mistakes in your contract.

(6) The contract is the kind of official documents and some of the sentences may be too long and too difficult for the first learners of Business English to understand, to imitate or to write. Therefore mastering business English is rather important in your future work of trading with the foreign businessmen.

三、拟订合同的要求以及合同语言的风格及特点

合同语言的文体格式是英语中最正式、最严谨的格式之一，因此在起草与翻译合同时应达到下列要求。

(1) 所有部分及条款必须安排得清楚、明确而有条理。

(2) 所有事项和条款必须正确、清楚地编号。

(3) 所有事项和条款的起草和编制必须简明、通顺，符合国际惯例。

(4) 句子、短语、技术用语及标点必须清楚、正确地书写。应特别注意英语语法。英语句子和短语的书写必须符合语法规则，以使人能够读懂。

(5) 合同打印后应再三核对。拼写、大写字母、号码、金额、商品的型号等应特别注意，以避免出现本可避免的错误。

(6) 合同是一种正式文件，有些句子可能太长、太难，商务英语的初学者可能难以理解、模仿和书写。因此掌握商务英语对于将来工作以及与外商做生意是相当重要的。

Words and Expressions

content	*n.*	内容
preamble	*n.*	总则
license	*n.*	许可证
installation	*n.*	安装
adjustment	*n.*	调试
loading	*v. + ing*	装货
unloading	*v. + ing.*	卸货
training	*v. + ing*	培训
arbitration	*n.*	仲裁
breaching		违约
releasing	*n.*	解约
bribe	*n.*	受贿
orderly	*adv.*	有条理地
number	*n.*	数字，号码
	v.	编号
edit	*v.*	编制

concisely	*adv*. 简明地
smoothly	*adv*. 流畅地
understandable	*a*. 可以理解的
evitable	*a*. 可避免的
imitate	*v*. 模拟
businessman	*n*. 生意人，商人
authorized right	授权范围
essential clause	基本条款
general clause	通用条款
Force Majeure	*n*. 不可抗力
applicable law	适用法律
witness clause	结尾条款
literary form	文字形式
international practice	国际惯例
official document	正式文件

Notes

1)　Characteristics of contract

The contract language has been provided itself with serious and dignified style and as well with the following characteristics.

(1)　Strong specialization.

(2)　Long and complex sentences.

(3)　The obscurity in wording and the difficulty in understanding.

(4)　The usage of many foreign words in the contracts.

1)　合同的特点

合同语言具有严肃、凝重的风格，以及下列特点。

(1)　专业性强。

(2)　句子长而复杂。

(3)　用词晦涩难懂。

(4)　使用很多外来语。

2)　Some examples in wording

(1)　The seriousness and strictness in the wording.

Meaning　意义	In Use　使用	Not in Use　不使用
因为	by virtue of	because
开始	Commence(ment)	start, begin
事实上	in effect	in fact
在……之前	prior to	before
愿意做某事	intend to do st.	want to do st.
希望做某事	desire to do st.	wish to do st.

(2) The strong specialized character in wording of the contract.

remedy　救济

Force Majeure　不可抗力

defect　瑕疵

jurisdiction　管辖

(3) The using of some words with special function.

Some particles of special function are always necessary to be put into use:

hereby　特此

thereof　由此，因此

where as　有鉴于

hereinafter referred to as…　在下文中简称

2) 用词举例

(1) 用词严肃和严谨。(表略)

(2) 合同用语专业性强。(例略)

(3) 需要使用具有特殊含义的虚词。(例略)

3) Four legal words

There are four legal words which the readers must pay attention to and must use in the correct way. They are：shall, may, must and may not (shall not).

(1) In expressing the right of the party concerned:

Use " may do" , not " can do".

(2) In expressing the duty of the party concerned:

Use " shall do", not "should do" or " ought to do".

(3) In expressing the mandatory duty:

Use " must do" not "can do".

(4) In expressing the prohibited duty:

Use " may not do" or " shall not do", not "can not do" or "must not do".

3) 四个法律上使用的词语

有四个法律上使用的词语，读者必须予以重视并正确使用：shall, may, must, may not (or shall not)。

(1) 表达当事人的权利：可以做什么，用"may do"，不用"can do"。

(2) 表达当事人的义务：应当做什么，用"shall do"，不用"should do"或"ought to do"。

(3) 表达强制性义务：必须做什么，用"must do"，不用"can do"。

(4) 表达禁止性义务：不可做什么，用"may not do"或"shall not do"，不用"can not do"或"must not do"。

4) The differences between the words of " Contract" and " Agreement"

The founding of a contract needs some specified essential conditions, such as:

(1) The offer and acceptance.

(2) The consideration.

(3)　The intention to create legal relations.

(4)　The capacity of setting up a contract.

But the agreement is free of these limits. Contract is an important component of an agreement. Therefore, a contract is certainly an agreement, but an agreement is not certainly qualified to be a contract. So the contract and the agreement are not exchangeable in use.

　　4)　合同与协议的区别

合同的成立必须有几个要件：

(1)　要约和承诺。

(2)　约定。

(3)　建立法律关系的愿望。

(4)　缔约能力。

合同的成立一定有必备条款的限制。合同是协议的重要组成部分，所以合同一定是协议，而协议不一定都是合同，因而合同和协议在使用时不能互换。

Ⅳ．The Main Kinds of Contracts 主要的合同类型

(1)　Sales Contract　买卖合同或销售合同

(2)　Contract for Supply of Power, Water, Gas, Heat　电、水、气、热力供应合同

(3)　Gift Contract　赠予合同

(4)　Contract for Loan of Money　借款合同

(5)　Leasing Contract　租赁合同

(6)　Financial Leasing Contract　融资租赁合同

(7)　Work-for-Hire Contract　承揽合同

(8)　Contract for Construction Projects　建设工程合同

(9)　Carriage Contract　运输合同

(10) Technology Contract　技术合同

(11) Safe- keeping Contract　保管合同

(12) Ware housing Contract　仓储保管合同

(13) Agency Appointment Contract　委托代理合同

(14) Commercial Contract　商业合同

(15) Purchase Contract　购货合同

(16) Commercial Agency Contract　商业代理合同

(17) Joint Venture Contract　合资经营合同

(18) Contract for Joint-Operating Enterprises　合作经营企业合同

(19) Labour Contract　劳动合同

(20) Insurance Contract　保险合同

(21) Chartering Contract　租船合同

(22) Purchase and Sales Contract　购销合同

(23) Contract for Transfer of Technical Know-how　技术诀窍转让合同

(24) Counter purchase Contract　回购合同

(25) Contract for Processing with Supplied Materials and Assembling with Supplied Parts　来料加工和来件装配合同

(26) Non-Governmental Trade Contract　非政府贸易合同

(27) Sales Agency Agreement　销售代理协议

(28) General Agency　总代理协议

(29) Assignment Agency　委派协议

(30) Agreement for Setting-up a Repair and Maintenance Service Center　成立维修服务中心协议

(31) Sole-Agency Agreement　独家代理协议

(32) Sales Confirmation　售货确认书

(33) Compensation Trade　补偿贸易合同

Ⅴ. Kinds of Standard Contracts

1. Standard Contract

Contract No. ×××

Date: April 1, 2015

The Seller: ××× Industrial Co., Ltd.

The Buyer: ××× Development Corp.

The Seller and the Buyer have agreed to the following transactions according to the terms and conditions stipulated below:

(1) Name of Commodity: ××× Brand Electronic Computer

(2) Specifications: Type ×××

(3) Quantity: 200

(4) Unit Price: US $ ×××

(5) Total Price: US $ ×××

(6) Packing: In wooden case

(7) Time of Shipment: Seven days after receipt of letter of credit

(8) Loading Port: ×××

(9) Destination: ×××

(10) Insurance: To be effected by the Buyer

(11) Terms of Payment:

①　The Buyer shall send a confirmed, irrevocable, transferable and divisible letter of credit to be drawn by sight draft to the Seller before May 2, 2015. The Letter of Credit remains Valid until 15 days after the delivery of the goods and will expire on June, 7, 2015.

②　A deposit of 10% of the total price should be paid by the Buyer immediately after the signing of the Contract.

(12) Shipping mark and clearance: Shipping mark to be at the Seller's option

(13) Remarks:

The Seller: ×××　Industrial Co., Ltd.　　The Buyer: ×××　Development Co.

　　　　　(Signature)　　　　　　　　　　　　　(Signature)

Words and Expressions

transaction	*n.* 买卖，交易，会计事项
transferable	*a.* 可转让的
divisible	*a.* 可分割的
deposit	*n.* 定金，押金，保证金
clearance	*n.* 出港许可证，出港手续，结关放行
standard contract	标准合同

五、标准合同的种类

1.　标准合同

合同号码：No. ×××

合同签订日期：2015 年 4 月 1 日

卖方：×××产业股份有限公司

买方：×××发展公司

买卖双方同意成交下列商品，订立条款如下：

(1)　商品：×××牌电子计算机

(2)　规格：×××型

(3)　数量：200 台

(4)　单价：×××美元

(5)　总价：×××美元

(6)　包装：用木箱包装

(7)　装运期：收到信用证后 7 天装运

(8)　装运口岸：×××

(9)　目的地：×××

(10) 保险：由卖方投保

(11) 付款条件：

①　买方于 2015 年 5 月 2 日前将保兑的、不可撤销的、可转让、可分割的即期信用证开到卖方。信用证议付有效期为交货后 15 天，至 2015 年 6 月 17 日到期。

②　买方需在签约后，立即支付合同金额的 10%作为定金。

(12) 装运唛头及结关手续：

装运唛头由买方选择。

(13) 备注：

卖方：×××产业股份有限公司(签名)　　　　买方：×××发展公司(签名)

2. Sales Contract

Date: 7 November, 2014

Contract No.: ×××

Signed at: Beijing

Sellers: China National Textiles Imp.&Exp. Corp.

Buyers: London Textiles Co., Ltd.

This Sales Contract is made by and between the Sellers and Buyers where the sellers agree to sell and the buyers agree to buy the under-mentioned goods according to the terms and conditions stipulated below.

Name of Commodity	Pattern No.	Quantity(Yard)	Unit Price per Yard, CIF London	Amount
Printed Linen Cloth	50	5,000	×××	×××
	60	6,000	×××	×××
	70	7,000	×××	×××
Total Amount: Say Pounds Sterling ××× Only				£ ×××

Shipping Mark: CT

Packing: In wooden cases

Insurance: To be covered by the Sellers for 110% of the invoice value against All Risks and War Risks. Should the Buyers desire to cover for any other extra risks besides the aforementioned, the Sellers' approval must be obtained beforehand. All the additional premiums thus incurred shall be for the Buyers' account.

Time of Shipment: To be effected not later than 31 December, 2014, allowing transshipment with partial shipments prohibited.

Port of Shipment: Tianjin

Port of Destination: London

Terms of Payment: By irrevocable L/C available by draft at sight to reach the Sellers a month prior to the time of shipment and remain valid for negotiation in China until the 15th day after the final date of shipment.

Words and Expressions

pattern	*n.*	花式
aforementioned	*a.*	前面提到的
beforehand	*n.*	事先预先
approval	*n.*	同意，批准
transshipment	*n.*	转船
available	*a.*	得到的，可以达到的
prior	*a.*	在先的，在前的，居先的
negotiation	*n.*	议付

printed linen cloth	印花亚麻布
additional premium	附加保险费
for the buyers' account	由买方负担
partial shipment	分批装运

2. 销售合同

签订日期：2014 年 11 月 7 日

合同号：第××号

签订地点：北京

卖方：中国纺织进出口公司

买方：伦敦纺织品股份有限公司

买卖双方签订合同，根据下列所规定之条款、条件，卖方同意销售、买方同意购买下列货物。

商品	花式	数量(码)	单价(每码)CIF 伦敦	金额
印花亚麻布	50	5000	×××	×××
	60	6000	×××	×××
	70	7000	×××	×××
总价金额：××× 英镑　（大写）				×××英镑

运输唛头：CT

包装：木箱

保险：由卖方按发票价值 110%投保一切险和战争险。如买方欲增加其他险种，须事先征得卖方同意，其增保费由买方承担。

装运期限：不晚于 2014 年 12 月 31 日，允许转船，不允许分批装运。

装运港：天津

到港：伦敦

付款条件：凭不可撤销的即期信用证付款，于装运期前一个月开到卖方，并在最后装运期后 15 天内在中国议付有效。

3. Sales Confirmation 销售确认书

字第　×××　号

No. ×××

销售确认书
SALES CONFIRMATION

卖方：中国×××进出口公司　　　　　　　　　　　日期：

Sellers: China National ××× Import & Export Corporation　　Date:

签约地点：

Signed At:

地址：   传真：

Address: Fax:

电邮：

E-mail:

买方：

Buyers: Smith & Co., Ltd.

地址：   电邮：

Address: E-mail:

兹经买卖双方同意成交下列商品订立条款如下：

The Undersigned Sellers and Buyers have agreed to close the following transaction according to the terms and conditions stipulated below:

(1) 商品：

Name of Commodity:

(2) 规格：

Specifications:

(3) 数量：

Quantity:

数量及总值均得有 5%的增减，由卖方决定。

With 5% more or less both in amount and quantity allowed at the Sellers'option.

(4) 单价：每公吨×××美元，CIF

Unit Price: US $ ××× per metric ton CIF

(5) 总值：×××美元

Total Value: US $ ×××

(6) 包装：散装

Packing: All in bulk

(7) 装运期：×××期间

Time of Shipment: During ×××

(8) 装运口岸和目的地：从×××至×××，可转运和分装。

Loading Port & Destination: From ××× to ×××, transshipment & partial shipments allowed.

(9) 保险：由卖方按发票价值的 110%投保一切险和战争险。

Insurance: To be covered by the Sellers for 110% of the invoice value against ALL RISKS and WAR RISKS.

(10) 付款条件：买方须于×××前将保兑的、不可撤销的、可转让、可分割的即期信用证开到卖方。信用证议付有效期至上列装运期后 15 天在中国到期。

Terms of Payment: By Confirmed, Irrevocable, Transferable, and Divisible Letter of Credit to be available by sight draft to reach the Sellers before ×××, and to remain valid for negotiation in China until the 15th day after the aforesaid Time of Shipment.

(11) 装船标记：由卖方决定。

Shipping Mark: At the Sellers'option.

(12) 开立信用证时，请注明我方成交确认书号码。

When opening L/C, please mention our Sales Confirmation number.

(13) 其他条款：

Other terms:

<table>
<tr><td>卖方</td><td>买方</td></tr>
<tr><td>THE SELLERS</td><td>THE BUYERS</td></tr>
<tr><td>签名</td><td>签名</td></tr>
<tr><td>(Signature)</td><td>(Signature)</td></tr>
</table>

VI.　Preparing and Filling out Sales Contracts in English

1.　Use the information you have got from the following Chinese letter, work out an unfilled-in Sales Contract in English and then fill in various terms and conditions as necessary

六、编制英文销售合同

1.　根据下列汉语信函中的信息，编制一份英语合同，然后按照需要填入各种条件、条款

(此合同实际上是供学习填制用的。填制合同是考外销员资格证的一项英语考试内容。此处安排三个合同，第一个合同是从汉语信函中取得信息，读者自行编制合同。)

1)　示例

汉堡服装公司总经理史密斯先生：

很高兴从×月×日来信得悉你方已接受我方×月×日的报盘。作为答复，我方确认向贵公司出售 3000 打×××型号天坛牌男衬衫，颜色蓝、黄、白平均搭配，每打尺码搭配为 S/3、M/6、L/3，价格每打××英镑，CIF 汉堡，半打装一纸盒，一打装一大纸盒。由卖方按发票金额的 110%投保一切险和战争险，2015 年×月×日由中国港口运往汉堡，允许转船和分批装运。唛头由我方选定，以不可撤销的即期信用证付款。信用证必须在装运前 30 天到达我方。按照惯例，信用证有效期为最后装运期第 15 天在中国到期。

附寄售货合同××号，2015 年×月×日签订于北京。

中国服装出口公司经理

×××谨上

2)　Filled-in Contract　已填制合同

Contract No.　×××

Sellers: China National Garment Export Corporation

Buyers: Hamburg Garment Company

This Contract is made by and between the Buyers and the Sellers, whereby the Buyers agree

227

to buy and the Sellers agree to sell the under-mentioned commodity according to the terms and commodity stipulated below:

Commodity: Tiantan Brand Men's Shirts

Specifications: Pattern No. ××, Blue, Yellow, White equally assorted, S/3, M/6 and L/3 per dozen

Quantity: 3,000 dozen

Unit Price: US $ ×× per dozen CIF Hamburg

Total Value: US $ ×××

Packing: Half a dozen to a paper box, 10 dozen to a carton

Insurance: To be covered by the Sellers against all Risks and War Risks for 110% of the invoice value.

Time of Shipment: September 2015, with transshipment and partial shipments allowed.

Port of Shipment: China Port

Port of Destination: Hamburg

Shipping Mark: At the Sellers' option

Terms of Payment: By irrevocable L/C payable by draft at sight to reach the Sellers 30 days before shipment and remain valid for negotiation in China till the 15th day after the final date of shipment.

Done and signed in Beijing on this ×× day of ××, 2015.

Words and Expressions

garment	*n.* 服装
assorted	*a.* 各式各样的，分类的
payable	*a.* 可支付的

2. Use the information you have got from the English E-mails below to work out an unfilled English contract, then fill-in it in English

2. 从下列英语电子邮件中寻找信息，拟制一份未填制的英语合同，然后用英语填制

Example 1

1) E-mail 1

Subj.: Offer for Cotton Bed sheets

Dear Mr. ××,

Many thanks for your enquiry for 1,200 dozen of Pacific Ocean Brand Cotton Bed sheets pattern No. ×× and No. ×× CIF, New York. We are now very pleased to inform you that the firm-offer for 1,200 dozen of the above mentioned articles is US $ ××××, CIF, New York. If you are able to accept this offer, please E-mail us your other requirements.

Best regards.

Zhang Rong

Sales Manager

China National Light Industrial Products

Imp. & Exp. Corp.

2)   E-mail 2

Subj.: Order for Cotton Bed sheets

Dear Mr. ××,

In replying to your offer for 1,200 dozen of Pacific Brand Bed sheets we would like to inform you and we think your offer is acceptable. Now we want to place an order with you as follows:

(1)   The ordered goods should be packed in boxes of half dozen each and 20 boxes in a carton.

(2)   Please ship our order in 3 equal shipments of 400 dozen each month commencing from June, 2015.

(3)   We shall open an irrevocable L/C by sight draft in your favor after receipt of your Sales Confirmation. We hope the goods will be insured against all Risks and War Risks for 120% of the invoice value.

(4)   We are sending you two copies of our Sales Contract No. ××× signed in Beijing on ×× May 2015. Please return one copy countersigned at your earliest convenience.

Bill Walker

Sales Manager

New York Trading Co. Ltd.

3)   The filled-in contract (已填制合同)

Contract No. ×××

Sellers: China National Light Industrial Products Imp. & Exp. Corp.

Buyers: New York Trading Co., Ltd.

The undersigned Sellers and Buyers have agreed to close the following transactions according to the terms and conditions stipulated below:

Commodity: Pacific Ocean Brand Cotton Bed sheets

Specifications: Pattern No. ×× and No. ××

Quantity: 1,200 dozen

Unit Price: US $ ×× dozen, CIF, New York

Total Price: US $ ××××

Packing: Half dozen in a box, 20 boxes in a carton

Shipping Mark: at the Sellers' Option

Insurance: To be covered by the Sellers against all Risks and War Risks for 120% of the Invoice Value.

Time of Shipment: In 3 equal monthly lots, 400 dozen for each month, commencing from June, 2015.

Port of Shipment: China Port

Port of Destination: New York

Terms of Payment: To be effected by confirmed, irrevocable L/C payable by draft at sight upon presentation of shipping documents.

Done and Signed in Beijing on ××, 2015

Example 2

1) E-mail 1

Subj.: Intending to place order for Woolen Sweaters

Dear Sirs,

We are pleased to inform you that we are satisfied with both your quality and your prices, and are ready to place the following order with you according to your terms and conditions.

Commodity	Style No.	Unit Price per Dozen (US $) CIF Rotterdam	Size	Quantity (Dozen)
Woolen Sweaters	××	××	S	16
	××	××	M	24
	××	××	L	20

The above is subject to your goods' arriving at Rotterdam before December 15, with transshipment and partial shipments prohibited.

As to the insurance, we wish to cover all Risks and War Risks as per the relevant Ocean Marine Cargo Clauses of PICC and to effect the payment by D/P 60 days.

Please kindly give us your confirmation.

S. W. Easton

Director

Holland Textiles Trading Co. Ltd

2) E-mail 2

Subj.: Confirming order for Woolen Sweaters

Dear Sirs,

We are glad to know that you intend to place an order with us on the Woolen Sweaters and now we inform you that we have booked your order on the following terms and conditions.

Commodity	Style No.	Unit Price per Dozen (US $) CIF Rotterdam	Size	Quantity (Dozen)
Woolen Sweaters	××	××	S	16
	××	××	M	24
	××	××	L	20
Total Value: Say U.S. Dollars Seven Thousand Five Hundred and Eighty-four Only				

These goods will be packed in boxes of half dozen each and 10 dozen to a carton, to be shipped from China Port to Rotterdam in November 2015, with no transshipment and partial shipments. Insurance is to be covered by us against All Risks and War Risks for 110% of the invoice value.

As to payment terms, we usually require Letter of Credit. This time, in view of our long and pleasant relations, we agree to accept D/P 60 days, with no precedent established.

Enclosed is our Sales Contract No. ×× signed in Beijing on ×× September, 2015 in duplicate, a copy of which please return us after counter signing for our file.

Li Ming

Sales Manager

Beijing Garments Corp.

3) The filled-in contract (已填制合同)

Sales Contract No. ×××　　　　　　Date: ×××

Sellers: Beijing Garments Corp.

Buyers: Holland Textiles Trading Co., Ltd.

This Sales Contract is made and between the Sellers and the Buyers, where by the Buyers agree to buy and the Sellers agree to sell the undermentioned commodity according to the terms and conditions stipulated below:

Commodity	Style No.	Unit Price per Dozen (US $) CIF Rotterdam	Size	Quantity (Dozen)
Woolen Sweaters	××	××	S	16
	××	××	M	24
	××	××	L	20
Total Value: Say U.S. Dollars Seven Thousand Five Hundred and Eighty-four Only				US $ 7,584

Packing: In boxes of half dozen each, 10 dozen to a carton

Shipping Mark: At the Sellers' option

Insurance: To be covered by the Sellers against All Risks and War Risks as per the relevant *Ocean Marine Cargo Clauses of PICC*. If other coverage or an additional insurance amount is required, the Buyers must have the consent of the Sellers before shipment, and the additional premium is to be borne by the Buyers.

Port of Shipment: Xingang of Tianjin, China

Port of Destination: Rotterdam

Time of Shipment: December, 2015. Transshipment and partial shipments are prohibited.

Terms of Payment: D/P 60 days

Done and signed in Beijing, ×××, November, 2015.

VII. Contract for Processing with Supplied Materials and Assembling with Supplied Parts

×× Co., Ltd. (hereinafter referred to as Party A) and China ×× Co., Ltd. (hereinafter referred to as Party B) have succeeded in reaching an agreement on the contract for processing with supplied materials and assembling Colour TV sets with supplied components and parts in China under the following terms and conditions:

(1) Party B shall process with the materials supplied by Party A and assemble Colour TV sets with components and parts supplied by Party A in total of ×× sets within a period of ×× years.

(2) All necessary materials and parts listed in the Contract shall either be supplied by Party A, or purchased in international market by Party B in accordance with the technical requirements stipulated by Party A.

(3) The processing charge for each set is US $ ××, not including insurance premium.

(4) The materials, parts and components requiring for processing and assembling shall be sent from ×× to ×× by Party A. If there is any shortage or damage, Party A shall take the responsibility for supplying replacements.

(5) Payment for the processing charges and costs of parts, consumables and materials purchased in the international market by Party B and shipping expenses shall be made by sight L/C to be opened by Party A one month before shipment of the finished products.

(6) Party B shall complete the processing and assembling of all types of Colour TV sets, and effect shipment within the agreed date without delay except in the occurrence of uncontrollable and unforeseeable events.

(7) Insurance for the parts and components and auxiliary materials, etc. during their storage in Party B's storehouse and the finished products during transit from the shipment port to the destination is to be taken care of by Party A on behalf of Party B.

(8) The allowance for damage to parts, components and auxiliary materials during processing and assembling is 2.5%. Party A shall take the responsibility of supplying the damaged parts, components and materials free of charge within the damage rate of 2.5%. Should the damage rate exceed 2.5%, Party B shall supply additional necessary parts, components and materials.

(9) All parts and materials supplied by Party A for all types of ×× shall be processed by Party B strictly in accordance with the designing drawings without any modification.

(10) Should Party A fail to supply the components, parts and materials or Party B fail to deliver the finished products in time as contracted, as a result of which loss is incurred, the responsible party shall compensate the Party affected for the entire loss thus sustained.

(11) Shipment of the finished products shall be effected according to the shipping instructions given by Party A one month in advance. Should shipment of parts, components and materials sent by Party A be wrong or in excess, Party B shall return the excessive portion at the

expense of Party A; in case of short shipment, Party A shall make up the shortage.

(12) Packing:

×× sets to a wooden case suitable for export. Packing charges are for Party A's account, on cost basis.

(13) After signing the contract, Party A shall send at its own expenses 10—12 technicians and 5 administrative staff members to Party B's factory to render technical assistance during assembly and inspection and to inspect the finished products before delivery. Party A shall allow its technicians to remain with Party B for inspection of the finished products. In such case, Party B agrees to pay a monthly salary of US $ ×× for each person and all other expenses including round trip tickets shall be borne by Party A.

(14) Other terms and conditions:

A. The trademark of the finished products shall be supplied by Party A.

B. Party B shall prepare samples of all types of the processed products at any time and send them to foreign buyers appointed by Party A.

(15) This contract is signed by both Parties in two original copies in English. Each Party holds one copy.

Party   A

Boston ×× Co., Ltd.

Signed _____

×××, 2015

Party   B

China ××× Co., Ltd.

Signed_____

×××, 2015

七、来料加工及来件装配合同

××_____股份有限公司(以下简称"甲方")及中国_____股份有限公司(以下简称"乙方")成功地就在中国进行来料加工及来件装配彩色电视机的合同达成协议，条件、条款如下：

(1) 乙方将用甲方供应的材料加工，以及用甲方供应的组件及零件在中国装配总数为××台的彩色电视机，为期××年。

(2) 合同中所列的所有必需的材料应由甲方供应，或由乙方在国际市场上购买，材料必须符合甲方提供的技术要求。

(3) 每套的加工费用为××美元，不包括保险费。

(4) 加工及装配所需材料、零件及组件应由甲方由××运至××。如有缺少或损坏，甲方应负责补充供应。

(5) 加工费用，乙方在国际市场上购买的零件、消耗品及材料的成本费用，以及运输费用应由甲方在成品交货前一个月开立即期信用证支付。

(6) 乙方应在双方同意的日期内完成各种型号的彩色电视机的加工及装配，不得延迟，除非发生不可控制及不可预见的情况。

(7) 零件、组件及辅助材料等在乙方仓库储存期间的保险，以及成品从装船港运至目的港的保险由甲方代表乙方办理。

(8) 零件、组件及辅助材料在加工及装配过程中的损耗津贴为 2.5%。甲方应负责免费供应 2.5%损耗率之内的损坏的零件、组件及材料，如果损耗率超过 2.5%，应由乙方供应添加部分必需的零件、组件及材料。

(9) 甲方提供加工各种型号××的所有零件及材料应由乙方严格按照设计图纸加工，不得更改。

(10) 甲方未能按合同规定及时供应组件、零件及材料，或乙方未能按合同规定及时交付成品，因此造成损失时，违约方应赔偿受损方由此造成的所有损失。

(11) 成品应根据甲方提前一个月所给的装运须知装运。如果甲方误运零件、组件及材料，或超运，乙方应退还超运部分，费用由甲方承担；若短运，甲方应补充短缺部分。

(12) 包装：××套装适合出口用之木箱，包装费用由甲方按成本支付。

(13) 在签订合同以后，甲方应自费派出10～12名技术工人及5名行政管理人员至乙方工厂，在安装及检验期间提供技术援助，并在交货前检验成品。甲方应允许其技术人员留在乙方检验成品。为此，乙方同意支付每人月工资××美元。其他一切费用，包括往返旅费应由甲方承担。

(14) 其他条款条件：

① 成品的商标应由甲方提供。

② 乙方应随时准备所有加工产品的型号的样品，并且按甲方的指定寄给国外的买主。

(15) 本合同由双方签署，英文正本两份，双方各执一份。

甲方	乙方
波士顿××股份公司	中国××股份有限公司
签名_____	签名_____
2015 年×月×日	2015 年×月×日

Words and Expressions

process	v. 加工
assembly	v. 组件，装配
part	n. 零件
component	n. 组件，元件
hereinafter	v. 下文
succeed	v. 成功
list	v. 列表
replacement	n. 替换物，补充物
consumable	n. 消耗品
finished product	成品
occurrence	n. 发生
uncontrollable	a. 不可控制的
unforeseeable	a. 不可预见的
storehouse	n. 仓库
transit	n. 运输，运送

allowance	*n.* 津贴
additional	*a.* 额外的，添加的
modification	*n.* 更改，修改
incur	*v.* 招致，遭受
affect	*v.* 影响
sustain	*v.* 蒙受，遭受
technician	*n.* 技术人员
render	*v.* 提供
inspection	*n.* 检验
salary	*n.* 工资(月工资；发给干部、工人的工资为周工资(wages))
trademark	*n.* 商标
appoint	*v.* 指定
reach an agreement	达成一份协议
processing charge	加工费用
take the responsibility for (of) doing	对做……事负责任
on behalf of	代表
take care of	照顾，照料
administrative staff member	行政管理人员
round trip ticket	往返旅费(车票)

VIII.　Compensation Trade Contract

This Contract is made on August 1, 2013, in Xi'an, China, between Xi'an ×× Power Cable Co., Ltd. with its principal office at Xi'an, China (hereinafter called Party A), and Nokia ×× Investment Co., Ltd. with its principal office at Helsinki, Finland (hereinafter called Party B). The two Parties agree to conclude the following compensation trade under the terms and conditions set forth below:

Whereas Party B has machines and equipment, which are now used in Party B's manufacturing of power cables, and is willing to sell to Party A the machines and equipment;

Whereas Party B agrees to buy the products—the cables, made by Party A using the machines and equipment Party B supplies, in compensation of the price of the machines and equipment;

Whereas Party A agrees to purchase from Party B the machines and equipment;

Whereas Party A agrees to sell to Party B the products—the cables, in compensation of the price of Party B's machines and equipment.

Now therefore, in consideration of the premises and convenances described hereinafter, Party A and Party B agree as follows:

1.　Purchase Arrangement

Party A agrees to purchase from Party B the following commodity under the terms and conditions set out below:

 1.1 Commodity, Specifications and Its Capability:

   Commodity:

   Specifications:

   Capability:

 1.2 Quantity:

 1.3 Price:

   On FOB basic:

   Unit Price: US $ ××

   Total Price: US $ ××

 1.4 Payment:

   The price of the machines and equipment shall be compensated with the products, the cables, manufactured by Party A using the machines and equipment supplied by Party B. The payment of the total price shall be effected three times equally in 3 successive years, beginning in_____.

 1.5 Shipment:

   Time of shipment:

   Port of loading:

   Port of destination:

   Shipping marks:

 1.6 Insurance:

   To be effected by Party A.

 1.7 Inspection:

 1.8 Guarantee:

   Party B guarantees that the machines and equipment are unused, sophisticated and of best quality, and that the machines and equipment are capable of manufacturing the cables of ×× specifications with a production of ×× meters per hour.

2. Sales Arrangement

Party A sells to Party B the cables in compensation of the price of the machines and equipment Party B sells to Party A.

 2.1 Commodity and Specifications:

   Commodity: Cables

   Specifications:

 2.2 Quantity:

   ×× meters of cables per year, of which the price shall be US $ ×× per annum.

 2.3 Price:

   The Price of the cables shall be set on the basis of the prevailing price in the world market at the time when shipment is made. The price shall be based on CIF basis.

2.4　Shipment:

Shipment shall be made twice a year, in March and in September, each for the value of US $ ××.

Port of loading:

Port of destination:

Shipping marks:

2.5　Packing:

2.6　Payment:

Payment shall be effected by confirmed and irrevocable letter of credit in favor of Party A, payable at sight, allowing transshipment. The letter of credit shall reach Party A 30 days before the month of shipment and shall be valid for not less than 60 days.

The letter of credit shall be in strict accordance with terms and conditions of the Contract, otherwise Party B shall hold the responsibility for the delay in shipment and Party A may lodge claims against Party B for the losses arising therefrom. All the expenses arising from the amendments shall be for Party B's account.

2.7　Insurance:

To be covered by Party A for 110% of the invoice value, covering W. P. A. and War Risks.

2.8　Inspection:

The quality certificate issued by Party A shall be regarded as final. If, on arrival of the goods at the port of destination, Party B finds the quality not up to the specifications mentioned above, Party B shall notify Party A within 45 days after arrival of the goods at the port of destination. Both Parties shall have consultations for a settlement of the matter in dispute.

3.　Force Majeure

Party A or Party B shall not be responsible for any failure or delay in delivery of the entire lot or a portion of the goods under the contract as a result of any force majeure accident(s).

4.　Arbitration

All disputes arising in connection with this contract or in the execution thereof, should be settled amicably through negotiations. In case no settlement can be reached, the case in dispute shall then be submitted for arbitration in ××. The decision of the arbitration shall be accepted as final and binding upon both Parties.

5.　Governing Law

The formation, interpretation and performance of the contract shall be governed by the laws of the People's Republic of China.

6.　Original Text

The contract is made, in English, in two originals, one for each party.

7.　Duration

Party A: _____　　　　**Party B:** _____

　　　　(signature)　　　　　　　　　　　　(signature)

八、补偿贸易合同

本合同由西安××电力电缆股份有限公司，主营业所在地中国西安(以下称"甲方")，与诺基亚××投资股份有限公司，主营业所在地芬兰赫尔辛基(以下称"乙方")于2013年8月1日在中国西安签订。双方同意就下列所订条款达成补偿贸易如下：

鉴于乙方拥有现用于制造电缆的机器设备，并愿意将机器设备卖给甲方；

鉴于乙方同意购买甲方用乙方提供的机器设备生产的电缆，以补偿其机器设备的价款；

鉴于甲方同意从乙方购买该项机器设备；

鉴于甲方同意向乙方出售电缆，以偿还乙方的机器设备价款。

因此，考虑到本协议所述的前提和约定，甲、乙双方特此立约：

1. 购买协议

甲方同意从乙方按下列条款购买下述商品：

1.1 商品、规格及其生产能力：

商品：

规格：

生产能力：

1.2 数量：

1.3 价格：

××港 FOB 价：

单价：××美元

总价：××美元

1.4 支付：

机器设备价款以甲方用乙方所供机器设备生产的产品电缆偿还，全部价款在连续的三年内平均三次付清，自××日开始支付。

1.5 装运：

装运期：　　　　　　　　　　　　　装运港：

目的港：　　　　　　　　　　　　　装运唛头：

1.6 保险：

由甲方保险。

1.7 检验：

1.8 保证：

乙方保证其机器设备从未用过，性能先进，质量好，并保证该机器能生产××规格电缆，产量每小时××米。

2. 销售协议

甲方以电缆偿还购买乙方机器设备的价款。

2.1 商品及规格：

商品：电缆

规格：

2.2　数量：

电缆每年××米，每年价格××美元。

2.3　价格：

电缆的价格按交货时国际市场 CIF 价确定。

2.4　装运：

每年两次装运，一次在三月，另一次在九月，每次货价为××美元。

装运港：

目的港：

装运唛头：

2.5　包装：

2.6　支付：

凭以甲方为受益人的保兑的、不可撤销的即期信用证支付，允许转船。信用证必须于装运日期前 30 天到达甲方，有效期不少于 60 天。

信用证要与本合同条款完全一致，否则，乙方对迟装负责；而且，甲方有权就因此引起的损失向乙方提出索赔，修改信用证的费用由乙方承担。

2.7　保险：

由甲方保险，投保水渍险和战争险，投保金额为发票金额的 110%。

2.8　检验：

甲方出具的品质检验证书为最后依据。若货到后乙方发现质量与上述规定不符，乙方在货到目的港后 45 天内通知甲方，由双方协商解决有争议的问题。

3.　不可抗力

若因不可抗力事故，甲方或乙方对未交或迟交本合同项下的部分或全部货物不负责任。

4.　仲裁

有关或执行本合同的一切争议应友好协商解决。若达不成协议，有关争议案应在××提交仲裁。仲裁决定是终局的，并对双方均具有约束力。

5.　适用法律

本合同的签订、解释和履行以中华人民共和国法律为准。

6.　正本条款

本合同以英文书写，正本两份，每方各持一份。

7.　有效期

甲方：_____　　　　　　　乙方：_____

　　　　（签字）　　　　　　　　　　　　　　（签字）

Words and Expressions

Helsinki	*n*. 赫尔辛基
Finland	*n*. 芬兰
hereafter	*adv*. 以下
cable	*n*. 电缆，电报

premise	*n.* 前提
convenance	*n.* 惯例，约定
describe	*v.* 描写，叙述
hereinafter	*adv.* 下文
capability	*n.* 生产能力
FOB	离岸价
successive	*a.* 连续的
guarantee	*v.* 保证
prevailing	*a.* 流行的，通行的
therefrom	*adv.* 从那一点，从那里
consultation	*n.* 协商
dispute	*n.* 争议
as a result of	作为……的结果
execution	*n.* 执行
there of	*adv.* 由此，因此
amicably	*adv.* 友好地
submit	*v.* 提交
binding	*a.* 有约束力的
formation	*n.* 形成，签订
interpretation	*n.* 解释
performance	*n.* 履行
govern	*v.* 统治，管理
duration	*n.* 有效期
conclude the compensation trade	达成补偿贸易
in compensation of	以补偿……
in connection with	与……有关
governing law	适用法律(经济、管理)

IX. Exclusive Agency Agreement

This agreement is made and entered into by and between the two parties concerned on ×× (date) in ×× (area), China on the basis of equality and mutual benefit to develop business on terms and conditions mutually agreed upon as follows:

Article 1　The Parties Concerned

(1)　Party A:

Registered office address:

Tel:　　　　　　　　Fax:　　　　　　　E-mail:

(Hereinafter called the Manufacturer)

(2)　Party B:

Registered office address:

Tel: Fax: E-mail:

(Hereinafter called the Agent)

Article 2 Appointment

Party A hereby shall appoint Party B as its Exclusive Agent to solicit orders for the Commodity stipulated in Article 3 from customers in the territory stipulated in Article 4, and Party B shall accept and assume such appointment.

Article 3 Commodity

Commodity: ×××

Article 4 Territory

Territory: ×××

In the territory of ＿＿＿ only.

Article 5 Duties of the Agent

The Agent shall:

5.1 Solicit customers in the territory.

5.2 Transmit to the manufacturer enquiry and orders received by him.

5.3 Bring to the notice of the customers the terms and conditions of sales prescribed by the Manufacturer.

5.4 Perform informative work and carry out to his utmost sales work to obtain orders.

5.5 Acquire a technical knowledge of the products and cover any expenditure for necessary promotion from his commission.

5.6 Take measures to get informed of the solvency of the customers having ordered the commodity mentioned in Article 3.

5.7 Assist the Manufacturer in recovering debts due.

5.8 Be entitled to receive observations and complaints made by the customers with respect to the products delivered, inform the Manufacturer of such case and act in the Manufacturer's best interests.

5.9 Keep the Manufacturer informed of the market condition and the state of competition.

5.10 Supply the Manufacturer and send a report on his activities every four month to the Manufacturer with quotations and advertising materials on similar products of other suppliers.

Article 6 Duties of the Manufacturer

The Manufacturer shall:

6.1 Provide the Agent all information and documents necessary for the exercise of the Agents activities including conditions of sales, price lists, technical documents, advertising materials and as well immediately notice the Agent of any change in his prices, his sales conditions and payment terms.

6.2 Notify the Agent of any orders reaching him directly from the customers in the territory and shall entitle the Agent to the commission provided for in Article 10 on such orders.

6.3 Assist the employees of the Agent to acquire the technical knowledge of the Products and provide them board and lodging during their training.

Article 7　Minimum Turnover

The Agent shall undertake to solicit orders for the Commodity in Article 3 from the customers in the Territory in Article 4 during the effective period of this Agreement for not less than US $ ×××.

Article 8　Price and Payment

8.1　The price for each individual transaction shall be fixed through negotiations between the Agent and the buyer and shall be subject to the Manufacturer's final confirmation.

8.2　Payment shall be effected by confirmed, irrevocable L/C established by the buyer in favor of the Manufacturer, which shall reach the Manufacturer 30 days before the date of shipment.

Article 9　Exclusive Right

In consideration of the exclusive rights granted herein, the Manufacturer shall not grant to any other person or undertake the right to represent or to sell the commodity in the Territory. The Manufacturer shall notify the Agent of any orders reaching him directly from the customers situated in the Territory. The Agent shall be entitled to the commission provided for in Article 10 on such orders.

Article 10　Commission

10.1　The Manufacturer shall pay the Agent a commission of 5% on the net invoiced selling price on all orders directly obtained by the Agent and accepted by the Manufacturer. Commission shall be paid only after the Manufacturer's receiving the full payment for each order.

10.2　Commission shall be calculated on the net invoiced price, any additional charges, such as charges for packing, transport and insurance, dues and taxes levied by the customers or in the country into which the goods are imported shall be excluded if they are invoiced separately.

10.3　The Manufacturer shall pay the Agent the commission not later than 30 days after he has received the payment of the commodity from the customer.

10.4　Commission shall be payable after it has been calculated and transferred in the currency of the transaction.

Article 11　Term of the Agreement

This agreement when duly signed by the both Parties concerned, shall remain in force for 12 months from ×× to ××, and it shall be extended for another 12 months upon expiration unless notice in writing is given to the contrary.

Article 12　Termination

During the validity of this agreement, if either of the two Parties is found to have violated the stipulations herein, the other party has the right to terminate this agreement.

Article 13　Force Majeure

Either Party will not be held responsible for failure or delay to perform all or any part of this agreement due to flood, fire, earthquake, draught, war or any other events which could not be predicted, controlled, avoided or overcome by the relative Party. The affected Party shall inform the other Party of its occurrence in writing as soon as possible and send a certificate issued by the relevant authorities to the other Party within 15 days after its occurrence.

Article 14　Arbitration

All disputes arising from the performance of this agreement shall be settled through friendly negotiations. Should no settlement be reached through negotiation, the case shall be submitted for arbitration to the China International Economic and Trade Arbitration Commission (Beijing) and the rules of this Commission shall be applied. The award of the arbitration shall be final and binding upon both Parties.

Party　A	Party　B
Name:_____	Name:_____
Legal Representative:_____	Legal Representative:_____
(Signature)	(Signature)

九、独家代理协议

为发展业务关系，有关双方在平等互利基础上，于××年××月××日在中国××订立本协议，双方同意并约定如下：

第一条　协议双方

(1)　甲方：

注册地点：

电话：　　　　　　　传真：　　　　　　　电子邮件：

(以下简称"制造商")

(2)　乙方：

注册地点：

电话：　　　　　　　传真：　　　　　　　电子邮件：

(以下简称"代理商")

第二条　委任

制造商(甲方)委任代理商(乙方)为其独家代理，就第三条项下的商品从第四条规定的区域中拓展顾客，代理商接受上述委任。

第三条　代理商品

代理商品：×××

第四条　代理区域

代理区域：仅限于 ×××

第五条　代理商的职责

代理商应该：

5.1　在代理区域内拓展用户。

5.2　将收到的询价和订单转送制造商。

5.3　使顾客注意制造商所规定的销售条款条件。

5.4　开展情报工作，尽力做好销售工作，以获得订单。

5.5　精通产品的技术知识，从佣金中支付促销产品所需的费用。

5.6 采取适当方式了解第三条中所提商品的订货人的支付能力。

5.7 协助制造商收回应付货款。

5.8 有权接受用户对所发出商品的意见与投诉，及时将情况通知制造商并维护制造商的最大利益。

5.9 向制造商提供商品的市场信息及竞争情况。

5.10 将同类产品其他供应商的报价及广告资料报与制造商，每 4 个月向制造商递送工作报告。

第六条　制造商的职责

制造商应该：

6.1 提供代理商进行活动所需的一切信息与文件，包括销售情况、价格表、技术文件和广告资料，并将产品价格、销售情况、付款条件的任何变化及时通知代理商。

6.2 将直接来自该地区用户的订单通知代理商，并按第十条所提将该订单的佣金付与代理商。

6.3 协助代理商的雇员了解产品的技术知识，并提供他们在培训期间的食宿。

第七条　最低营业额

乙方同意，在本协议有效期内从第四条的代理区域内拓展顾客，购买第三条中的产品，订单金额不低于×××美元。

第八条　价格与支付

8.1 每笔交易的价格应通过代理商与买主之间的协商确定，并由制造商最后确认。

8.2 由买方开出以制造商为受益人的保兑的、不可撤销的信用证付款，信用证应在装运日期以前 30 天到达甲方。

第九条　独家代理权

考虑到本协议中所授予的独家代理权，制造商不得同意他人在该地区取得代表或销售代理商品的权力。制造商应将其直接从该地区顾客处获得的订单通知代理商，并应按第十条的规定向代理商支付每笔订单的佣金。

第十条　佣金

10.1 对代理商直接取得及由制造商接受的所有订单，按净发票售价由制造商向代理商支付每笔交易 5%的佣金。佣金在制造商收到每笔订单的全部货款后予以支付。

10.2 佣金以净发票金额计算，任何附加费用，如包装费、运输费、保险费、海关税或由进口国家征收的关税等应另开发票。

10.3 制造商在收到用户对商品的付款后 30 天之内支付代理商佣金。

10.4 佣金按成交的货币计算、汇兑和支付。

第十一条　协议期限

本协议经有关双方如期签署后生效，有效期为一年，从××年××月××日至××年××月××日。除非有内容相反的通知，本协议期满后将延长 12 个月。

第十二条　协议的终止

在本协议有效期内如果发现有一方违背协议条款，另一方有权终止协议。

第十三条　不可抗力

由于水灾、火灾、地震、干旱、战争或其他无法预见、无法控制、无法避免或无法克服的其他事件导致有关一方不能或不能全部或部分履行本协议的，该方不负责任。但受不可抗力事件影响的一方须尽快将发生的事件书面通知另一方，并在不可抗力事件发生后 15 天内将有关当局出具的证明寄交另一方。

第十四条　仲裁

本协议履行中所发生的一切争议应通过友好协商解决。如协商不能解决，应将此争议提交中国国际贸易仲裁委员会(北京)，按仲裁规则进行仲裁。仲裁是终局的，对双方均具有约束力。

甲方　　　　　　　　　　　　　　　　乙方
名称：　　　　　　　　　　　　　　　名称：
法人代表：　　　　　　　　　　　　　法人代表：
(签名)　　　　　　　　　　　　　　　(签名)

Words and Expressions

solicit	*v.* 拓展，招揽
territory	*n.* 领土，地区
transmit	*v.* 转送
prescribe	*v.* 规定，开处方，嘱咐
acquire	*v.* 获得
expenditure	*n.* 花费，支出
promotion	*n.* 提高，促进
solvency	*n.* 支付能力
recover	*v.* 收回
observation	观测，注意，意见，言论
complain	*v.* 申诉，投诉，抱怨
lodge	*v.* 供给住宿
minimum	*n.* 最低量，最小量
turnover	*n.* 营业量
commission	*n.* 佣金
invoice	*v.* 开发票
	n. 发票
exclude	*v.* 除外
due(s)	*n.* (复)应付款
levy	*v.* 征收，强索(征集)
award	*n.* 裁决书，判决
award	*v.* 授予，判给
exclusive agency	独家代理权
exclusive agent	独家代理人
bring sb. to the notice of	引起某人对……的注意
take measures	采取措施

with respect to	关于
keep sb. informed of	向某人报告，通知某事
advertising	广告
entitle sb. to do sth.	给某人权利做某事，给某人资格做某事
board in	在住宿处搭伙
board and lodging	膳宿
exclusive right	专卖权，独家代理权

Ⅹ. Joint Venture Contract

Article 1　General Provisions

In accordance with *The Law of the People's Republic of China on Sino-Foreign Equity Joint Ventures* and other relevant laws and legislations of the People's Republic of China, the ×× Electric Power Corp. of Xi'an and ×× Electric Machinery Corp. of Japan have agreed to establish a joint venture Company "×× Electric Power Products Manufacturing Co., Ltd."on the basis of equality and mutual benefit. And herein have signed this Contract.

十、合资企业合同

第1条　总则

根据《中华人民共和国中外合资经营企业法》及中华人民共和国其他的有关法律、法规，西安××电力公司及日本××电力机械公司双方同意在平等互利的基础上成立合资经营公司"××电力产品制造股份有限公司"，并签订本合同。

Article 2　Two Parties of the Joint Venture Company

2.1　Party A:

2.1.1　Name: ×× Electric Power of Xi'an (a Chinese registered enterprise)

2.1.2　Registered Address: Xi'an Economic and Technological Development Zone, Xi'an City, Shanxi Province, People's Republic of China

2.1.3　Legal representative of Party A:

(A) Name: ××

(B) Position: General Manager

(C) Nationality: Chinese

2.2　Party B:

2.2.1　Name: ×× Electric Machinery Corp. of Japan

2.2.2　Registered Address: ××, ×× Tokyo, Japan

2.2.3　Legal Representative of Party B:

(A) Name: ××

(B) Position: General Manager

(C) Nationality: Japanese

第 2 条　合营双方

2.1　甲方：

2.1.1　名称：西安 XX 电力公司(一家中国的注册企业)

2.1.2　注册地址：中华人民共和国陕西省西安市西安经济技术开发区

2.1.3　甲方法定代表：

①　姓名：××

②　职务：总经理

③　国籍：中国

2.2　乙方：

2.2.1　名称：日本××电力机械公司

2.2.2　注册地址：日本，东京××

2.2.3　乙方法定代表：

①　姓名：××

②　职务：总经理

③　国籍：日本

Article 3　Name and Address of the Joint Venture Company

3.1　Name

Chinese Name of the Joint Venture Company shall be "××　电力产品制造股份有限公司".

English Name of the Joint Venture Company shall be "×× Electric Power Products Manufacturing Co. ,Ltd."

Japanese Name of the Joint Venture Company shall be "××".

3.2　Registered Address

Legal Address of the Joint Venture Company: Xi'an Economic and Technological Development Zone, Xi'an City, Shanxi Province, People's Republic of China

第 3 条　合营公司的名称和地址

3.1　名称

①　合营公司的中文名称为：××电力产品制造股份有限公司。

②　合营公司的英文名称为：×× Electric Power Products Manufacturing Co., Ltd.。

③　合营公司的日文名称为：日本×××株式会社。

3.2　注册地址

中华人民共和国陕西省西安市经济技术开发区

Article 4　Purpose of the Parties to the Joint Venture Company

4.1　To strengthen economic cooperation and technological exchanges between the Parties through the adoption of advanced international management methods based upon market economic conditions, and to utilize advanced technology in the manufacture, marketing and selling of the Products, in order to enhance the market competitiveness of the Parties and to expand their markets in and outside China.

4.2　To obtain good economic results and beneficial profits for both Parties.

第 4 条　合营公司的宗旨

4.1　加强合资双方的经济合作和技术交流,采用以市场经济条件为基础的先进的国际化管理方式,利用先进的技术,生产、营销产品,加强合资双方的市场竞争力,扩大双方的国内外市场。

4.2　为双方带来良好的经济成果和实际利益。

Article 5　Scale of the Joint Venture Company

5.1　The headquarters of the Joint Venture Company shall be situated in the Xi'an Economic and Technological Development Zone.

5.2　In accordance with business requirements, the Joint Venture Company may establish branches in Beijing or other cities within or outside China after 2015, subject to relevant department's approvals.

5.3　In accordance with the Feasibility Study, the annual production capacity of the Joint Venture Company is estimated to be US $ ×××.

第 5 条　合营公司的规模

5.1　合营公司的总部设在西安经济技术开发区。

5.2　根据业务需要,经有关部门批准,合营公司可以在 2015 年以后在北京或中国国内及国外的其他城市设立分支机构。

5.3　根据可行性研究报告,合营公司的生产经营规模达年产值×××美元。

Article 6　Scope of Business of the Joint Venture Company

The scope of business of the Joint Venture Company is to manufacture, market and sell the operating mechanism (including parts) and ××× equipment.

第 6 条　合营公司的生产经营范围

制造、经营和销售×××操作装置(包括部件)和×××设备。

Article 7　Total Investment

The total amount of investment required by the Joint Venture Company is US Dollars Nine Million Six Hundred Thousand (US $ 9,600,000).

第 7 条　总投资

合营公司的投资总额为玖佰陆拾万美元(US $ 9,600,000)。

Article 8　Registered Capital

The total amount of the Joint Venture Company's registered capital shall be US Dollars Five Million Two Hundred Thousand (US$ 5,200,000).

第 8 条　注册资本

合营公司的注册资本总额为伍佰贰拾万美元(US $ 5,200,000)。

Article 9　Contributions to Registered Capital

9.1　Party A's contribution to the registered capital of the Joint Venture Company shall be the equivalent of US Dollars Two Million Six Hundred Thousand (US $ 2,600,000) in cash representing 50% of the registered capital.

9.2　Party B's contribution to the registered capital of the Joint Venture Company shall be the equivalent of US Dollars Two Million Six Hundred Thousand (US $ 2,600,000) in cash representing 50% of the registered capital.

9.3　The Parties shall begin to make their contributions to the registered capital of the Joint Venture Company in installments in accordance with the Chinese laws and regulations 2 months after issuing their Bussiness License. The first installment shall be made in USD XXX of 2 months after issuing of the Bussiness Licence and the second and the last installments in USD XXX shall be made no later than 2017.

9.4　Party A shall make its contribution in cash in RMB or US Dollars, and Party B shall make its contribution in cash in US dollars. Where Party A makes its contribution in cash in RMB, the calculation for conversion of RMB into US Dollars shall be the average of the opening buying rate for US Dollars and the opening selling rate for US Dollars published by the Bank of China, Xi'an Branch on the day of the contribution.

第 9 条　注册资本的出资

9.1　甲方对合营公司注册资本出资二百六十万美元现金(US $ 2,600,000)，占注册资本的 50%。

9.2　乙方对合营公司注册资本出资二百六十万美元现金(US $ 2,600,000)，占注册资本的 50%。

9.3　根据中国法律规定，贵公司甲乙双方于营业执照颁发后 2 个月内向合资公司支付注册资本，第一期分期付款为颁发营业执照后 2 个月内支付 ×××美元，第二期及最后一期应于 2017 年前支付×××美元。

9.4　甲方应以人民币或美元现金出资，乙方应以美元现金出资。甲方若以人民币现金出资，应将人民币换算成美元，换算价格以出资日中国银行西安分行公布的美元买价和卖价的平均值为准。

Article 10　Investment Certificate

After each installment of each Party's contribution to the registered capital has been made, an accountant registered in China shall, at the expense of the Joint Venture Company, verify the contribution and issue a contribution verification report. Thereupon, the Joint Venture Company shall issue, within sixty (60) days after receiving the verification report, an investment certificate to each Party signed by the Chairman and the Vice Chairman of the Board.

第 10 条　出资证明

甲乙双方对注册资本出资金额的每笔分期付款都交齐以后，中国的注册会计师证明出资金额及签发出资证明书。费用由合营公司支付。合营公司在收到证明书后 60 天内签发由董事会董事长和副董事长签署的投资证明书给每一方。

Article 11　Responsibilities of the Parties

11.1　Responsibilities of Party A

11.1.1　To obtain the necessary approvals, permits and licenses for the establishment and operation of the Joint Venture Company in a timely manner and then assist the Joint Venture Company in applying for and obtaining tax and customs duty reductions and exemptions and the benefit of other investment incentives available to the Joint Venture Company under China's national and local laws, regulations and practices.

11.1.2　To assist the Joint Venture Company to apply to the land authority in Xi'an to enter into the Land Use Rights Grant Contract with the Joint Venture Company.

11.1.3　To assist the Joint Venture Company to procure within China raw materials, equipment and supplies of suitable quality and at a reasonable and fair market price.

11.1.4　At the Joint Venture Company's request, to assist the Joint Venture Company in procuring qualified Chinese management personnel and working personnel.

11.1.5　To assist the Joint Venture Company with the procedures for the import of machinery, equipment, supplies and materials and arrange inland transportation.

11.1.6　To assist the employees of the Joint Venture Company recruited outside China and other personnel dispatched by Party B to obtain all necessary entry visas and work permits.

11.1.7　To assist the Joint Venture Company in opening RMB and foreign exchange bank accounts in China.

11.1.8　To handle other matters entrusted by the Joint Venture Company.

11.2　Responsibilities of Party B

11.2.1　To assist the Joint Venture Company to recruit suitably qualified Management Personnel.

11.2.2　To assist the Joint Venture Company in the purchase or lease of equipment and machinery and the purchase of supplies manufactured outside China at a reasonable and fair price and in their delivery to a convenient port in China.

11.2.3　To assist the Chinese personnel (the Joint Venture Company's directors, managers, technicians, workers and others engaged on a full or Part-time basis in the operation of the Joint Venture Company), to obtain visas necessary in order to enable them to participate in technical training in Japan.

11.2.4　To assist in the formulation and implementation of accounting policies in accordance with the Accounting System of the People's Republic of China for Foreign-invested Enterprises and other relevant Chinese laws and regulations.

11.2.5　To assist the Joint Venture Company in opening bank accounts outside China.

11.2.6　To handle other matters which may be entrusted by the Joint Venture Company.

第 11 条　双方责任

11.1　甲方责任

11.1.1　为合营公司的成立和经营及时获得必需的核准、许可及营业执照，协助合营公司申请及获得税务及关税减免，以及在中国国家和地区的法律、法规、规章及惯例下合营公司可以得到的其他投资鼓励方面的利益。

11.1.2　协助合营公司向西安的土地局申请，以便与合营公司签订土地使用权使用许可合同。

11.1.3　协助合营公司在中国境内获得质量合格、市场价格合理而优惠的材料、设备及供应物资。

11.1.4　按合营公司请求，协助合营公司招聘称职的中国管理人员及工作人员。

11.1.5　协助合营公司办理机械设备、供应物资和材料的进口手续，以及协助安排内陆运输事宜。

11.1.6　协助中国境外合营公司的受聘雇员及受乙方派遣的人员获得所需要的入境签证及工作许可证。

11.1.7　协助合营公司在中国境内开立人民币和外币的银行账户。

11.1.8　办理合营公司委托的其他事宜。

11.2　乙方责任

11.2.1　协助合营公司征聘合适称职的管理人员。

11.2.2　协助合营公司购买或租借设备和机械，并以合理、优惠的价格购买中国境外制造的供应物资，并将其运到中国的方便港口。

11.2.3　协助中方人员(合营公司的董事、经理、技术人员、工人及其他参与合营公司经营的专职或兼职的人员)办理签证，使他们能参加在日本的培训。

11.2.4　根据中华人民共和国外商投资企业会计制度及其他有关的中国的法规，制定及执行会计制度。

11.2.5　协助合营公司在中国境外开立银行账户。

11.2.6　办理合营公司可能委托的其他事宜。

Article 12　Sale of Products

12.1　The Products shall be sold only to Party A, Party B and a company wholly-owned by Party B.

12.2　The Products may only be sold to the other countries upon approval of the Board and with the prior written consent of both Parties.

12.3　The sale price of the Products shall be set by the General Manager in accordance with guidelines established by the Board.

12.4　The Parties shall purchase the Products made by the Joint Venture Company provided that the Products meet the relevant standards and specifications.

12.5　The Joint Venture Company shall appoint Party B and its Affiliates to handle sales of Products outside the PRC. Prices of such exports are to be agreed between the Joint Venture Company and Party B and its Affiliates.

第12条　产品的销售

12.1　产品只能销售给甲方、乙方及乙方全权拥有的公司。

12.2　产品在经过董事会批准及有双方事先的书面同意才能销售给其他国家。

12.3　产品价格由总经理根据董事会所定指标确定。

12.4　如果产品符合有关的标准及规格，双方均应购买合营公司所制造的产品。

12.5　合营公司委派乙方及其分支机构经营产品在中国境外的销售。这些出口品的价格须取得合营公司、乙方及其分支机构的同意。

Article 13　Board of Directors

13.1　The Board shall consist of six (6) directors, three (3) of whom shall be appointed by Party B and three (3) of whom shall be appointed by Party A. At the time this Contract is executed and each time directors are appointed, each Party shall notify the other Party of the names of its appointees.

13.2   Each director shall be appointed for a term of four (4) years and may serve consecutive terms if reappointed by the Party which originally appointed him. The term of appointment of the members of the initial Board shall commence on the date of issuance of the Joint Venture Company's Business License. If a seat on the Board is vacated by the retirement, resignation, illness, disability or death of a director, the Party which originally appointed such director shall appoint a successor to serve out such director's term.

13.3   During the first four (4) years, a director appointed by Party B shall serve as the Chairman of the Board and a director appointed by Party A shall serve as the Vice Chairman of the Board. For the succeeding four (4) years, a director appointed by Party A shall serve as the Chairman and a director appointed by Party B shall serve as the Vice Chairman of the Board.

13.4   The Chairman shall be the legal representative of the Joint Venture Company and shall exercise his authority within the scope authorized by the Board. Whenever the Chairman is unable to perform his responsibilities, the Vice Chairman is authorized to represent him.

第 13 条　董事会

13.1   董事会由 6 名董事组成。甲方委派 3 名，乙方委派 3 名。甲乙双方应于合营合同签订时和每届董事会换届时将委派的董事名单通知对方。

13.2   董事任期 4 年。届满时，经委派方继续委派可以连任。首届董事的任期始于合营公司营业执照签发之日。董事在任期内因退休、辞职、患病、伤残、死亡等造成缺额时，原委派方可另派人出任当届董事。

13.3   首届(头 4 年)董事长由乙方委派的董事担任，甲方委派的董事担任副董事长。第二届(第二个 4 年)董事长由甲方委派的董事担任，乙方委派的董事则担任副董事长。

13.4   董事长是合营公司的法定代表人，在董事会授予的权限内行使职权。董事长因故不能履行职责时，可授权副董事长代理。

Article 14   Senior Managements Structure

14.1   The business management structure of the Joint Venture Company shall comprise one (1) General manager and one (1) Deputy General Manager.

14.2   The General manager and the Deputy General Manager shall be appointed and dismissed by the Board. The terms of the offices of the General Manager and the Deputy General Manager shall be four (4) years.

14.3   During the first four (4) years the Board shall appoint a General Manager nominated by Party A and a Deputy General Manager nominated by Party B. For the succeeding four (4) years, the Board shall appoint a General Manager nominated by Party B and a Deputy General Manager nominated by Party A.

14.4   Powers of the General Manager

14.4.1   To prepare for approval by the Board the annual budgets, final financial statements, annual operating plans and work reports of the Joint Venture Company.

14.4.2   To formulate for approval by the Board strategies, operating targets, policies, procedures and development plans of the Joint Venture Company.

14.4.3   To formulate for approval by the Board the rules and regulations of the Joint

Venture Company.

14.4.4   To formulate for approval by the Board the annual production and marketing plans on the basis of the medium term and long term plans approved by the Board.

14.4.5   To purchase assets required for the Joint Venture Company's production and business operations of not more than (US $ 100,000) or its equivalent value on each occasion.

14.4.6   To manage the Joint Venture Company's cash in the ordinary course of business, including short-term and long-term bank deposits in RMB and foreign exchange.

14.4.7   To sign any agreement in the ordinary course of business concerning the purchase of office supplies, or the sale of Products of not more than (US $ 100,000) or its equivalent value on each occasion.

14.4.8   To determine the particulars of remuneration, bonuses and other relevant subsidies for the management personnel and the working personnel within the guidelines determined by the Board.

14.4.9   To appoint and dismiss all working personnel and management personnel (with the exception of the Deputy General Manager, the Administration Department Manager and the Manufacturing Department Manager.

14.4.10   To borrow any loans or take other credits so far as this relates to the ordinary course of business of the Joint Venture Company and so far as this does not exceed US $ 100,000 or its equivalent value on each occasion.

14.4.11   To handle other matters entrusted to the General Manager by the Board from time to time; and other matters not expressly required to be decided by the Board.

14.5   Powers of the Deputy General Managers

The Deputy General Manager shall assist the General Manager in his work and shall report to the General Manager. The General Manager shall appoint the Deputy General Manager, in writing, to act on his behalf in his absence. The Deputy General Manager may concurrently be a manager of a department.

第 14 条   高级经营管理机构

14.1   合营公司的经营管理机构应包括 1 名总经理、1 名副经理。

14.2   合营公司的总经理、副总经理由董事会聘用和解聘。总经理和副总经理的任期均为 4 年。

14.3   首届(头 4 年)董事会聘用的总经理由甲方提名推荐，副总经理由乙方提名推荐。第二届(第二个 4 年)总经理由乙方提名推荐，副总经理由甲方提名推荐。以此类推。

14.4   总经理的权力

14.4.1   制定合营公司的年度预算及决算表、年度经营计划及工作报告并报董事会批准。

14.4.2   制定合营公司的战略方针、经营目标、政策、程序及发展计划并报董事会批准。

14.4.3   制定合营公司的各种规章，并报董事会批准。

14.4.4   在经董事会批准的中期与长期计划基础上制订年生产与销售计划，并报董事会批准。

14.4.5   购买合营公司生产及业务经营所需的资产，每次不超过 10 万美元或相当于 10

万美元。

14.4.6　管理合营公司业务常规进程中的现金，包括短期和长期的人民币和外汇的银行存款。

14.4.7　签订业务常规进程中有关购买办公用品或产品销售的协议，每次不超过 10 万美元或相当于 10 万美元。

14.4.8　根据董事会所规定的指标决定管理人员及工作人员的酬劳、红利及有关津贴方面的细节。

14.4.9　聘用和解雇所有工作人员和管理人员(副总经理、行政部门经理及生产部门经理除外)。

14.4.10　借贷或放贷。只要此项贷款涉及合营公司常规业务进程，只要不超过 10 万美元或相当于 10 万美元。

14.4.11　其他由董事会不时委托总经理办理的事项，以及其他未特别要求由董事会决定的事项。

14.5　副总经理的权力

副总经理协助总经理工作，向总经理禀报工作。总经理因故不在时，由总经理书面指定副总经理代行总经理职务。副总经理可以兼任一个部门的经理。

Article 15　Department Managers

The Board shall establish a departmental management structure under the General Manager including one departmental manager in charge of administration (" Administration Department Manager") and one in charge of manufacturing (" Manufacturing Department Manager"). The administration Department Manager shall be concurrently the chief accountant and the Manufacturing Department Manager shall be concurrently the chief engineer. The Administration Department Manager and the Manufacturing Department Manager shall be appointed and dismissed by the Board. The Administration Department Manager shall initially be nominated by Party A and the Manufacturing Department Manager shall initially be nominated by Party B, but the right to nominate these two Department Managers may be changed as agreed by the Parties from time to time. The other departmental managers shall be appointed by the General Manager, and shall be responsible for the work of their respective departments, handle the matters delegated to them by the General Manager and shall report to him from time to time.

第 15 条　部门经理

董事会设立总经理领导下的部门管理机构，包括一名负责行政的部门经理(行政部门经理)及一名负责生产的经理(生产部门经理)。行政部门经理兼任总会计师，生产部门经理兼任总工程师。行政部门经理及生产部门经理由董事会聘任及解聘。行政部门经理最初由甲方提名，生产部门经理最初由乙方提名。但提名这两位部门经理的权利根据双方同意，可以不时变换。其他部门经理由总经理委任，负责有关部门的工作，处理总经理授权给他们的工作，并不时向总经理禀报。

Article 16　Taxation, Financial affairs and Auditing

16.1　Taxation

16.1.1　The Joint Venture Company shall pay applicable taxes under the relevant national and local laws of China.

16.1.2　The Parties shall use best endeavors to apply for and obtain preferential tax treatment, reductions and exemptions, as provided by relevant laws and regulations. Specifically, prior to the Effective Date, the Parties shall submit the Tax Memorandum to the relevant tax and customs authorities to obtain confirmation of the tax and customs treatment set forth therein.

16.2　Accounting System

16.2.1　The Joint Venture Company shall adopt the internationally used accrual basis and debit and credit accounting system in the preparation of its accounts.

16.2.2　The Joint Venture Company shall maintain accounting systems and procedures in accordance with the *Accounting System of the People's Republic of China for Foreign-invested Enterprises*, the supplementary stipulations promulgated by the Ministry of Finance of China.

16.2.3　The Joint Venture Company shall adopt RMB as its standard bookkeeping base currency, but may also use US dollars or other foreign currencies as supplementary bookkeeping currencies. The calculation for conversion of RMB into US dollars or other currencies shall be the average of the opening buying rate for US dollars and opening selling rate for US dollars published by the Bank of China, Xi'an Branch.

16.2.4　Routine accounting records, vouchers, books and statements of the Joint Venture Company shall be made and kept in Chinese. At Party B's request, a Japanese version shall be provided.

16.3　Auditing

16.3.1　For accounting and auditing, the Joint Venture should hire accountants and auditors registered in the People's Republic of China, and report these results to the Board of Directors and the General Manager. If Party B is willing to hire auditors of another country for auditing the annual finance, Party A should agree, but all charges shall be paid by Party B.

16.3.2　In the first three months of the business year, the Debit/Credit accounts of the last business year, documents of profit/loss accounts and profit sharing plan should be initiated by the General Manager and submitted to the Board of Directors for review and approval.

第 16 条　税务、财务和审计

16.1　税务

16.1.1　合营公司应按照有关的中国国家的和当地的法律，缴纳适当的税金。

16.1.2　双方应尽最大努力申请和获得有关法规所提供的优惠的税务待遇、免税及减税。特别是双方应在有效日期以前向有关税金和关税当局递交税金备忘录，以便获得其中设定的税金及关税待遇的确认书。

16.2　财务

16.2.1　合营公司记账时应采用国际上通用的权责发生制和借贷记账法。

16.2.2　合营公司应根据中国财政部颁布的辅助规定——《中华人民共和国外商投资会计制度》坚守财务制度和程序。

16.2.3　合营公司记账的本位币为人民币。也可用美元或其他外币作为辅助记账货币。人民币同其他货币换算时，按中国银行西安分行公布的当日买价和卖价的平均价计算。

16.2.4　合营公司的一切财务记录、凭证、账簿和报表用中文书写。乙方要求时，应提供日文的译本。

16.3　审计

16.3.1　合营公司的财务、审计应聘请在中国注册的会计师或审计师，并将结果报告董事会和总经理。如乙方需聘请其他国家的审计师对年度财务予以审查，甲方应予以同意，但一切费用由乙方支付。

16.3.2　每一营业年度的前三个月，由总经理编制上一年度的资产负债、损益表和利润分配方案提交董事会审查通过。

Article 17　Foreign Exchange Control

17.1　The Joint Venture Company shall open RMB bank accounts and foreign exchange accounts within or outside China in currencies used by the Joint Venture Company.

17.2　The Joint Venture Company's foreign exchange transactions shall be handled in accordance with the regulations of China relating to foreign exchange control.

17.3　Liquid funds in the Joint Venture Company's foreign exchange account shall be used in the following order of priority.

(1)　Payments of principal and interest on foreign exchange loans taken out by the Joint Venture Company from third parties.

(2)　Payments for imported equipment and materials.

(3)　Payment of salaries of expatriate personnel of the Joint Venture Company which are payable in foreign exchange.

(4)　Payments of principal and interest on loans taken out by the Joint Venture Company from the Parties or their Affiliates.

(5)　Payment of dividends to Party B.

(6)　Other payments which the Board decides should be made in foreign exchange.

第 17 条　外汇管理

17.1　合营公司应在中国境内外将合营公司使用的货币开立人民币银行账户或外汇账户。

17.2　合营公司的外汇交易应根据与外汇管理有关的中国规章进行。

17.3　合营公司外汇账户内的流动资金应按下列顺序使用：

(1)　支付合营公司从第三方借入的外汇贷款的本金和利息。

(2)　支付进口的设备和材料的款项。

(3)　支付合营公司用外汇支付的外籍雇员的工资。

(4)　支付从双方及其关联公司借入的外汇贷款的本金和利息。

(5)　支付给乙方的红利。

(6)　支付董事会决定的其他外汇款项。

Article 18　Profit Distribution

18.1　After payment of taxes in accordance with the pertinent laws and regulations of the PRC and after accumulated losses of previous years have been fully made up, the Joint Venture Company shall allocate a percentage of its annual after tax profit for contribution towards the

Reserve Fund, Enterprise Expansion Fund and Bonus and Welfare Fund for Staff and Workers.

18.2　Unless otherwise decided by the Board in any particular year, the percentages of the Joint Venture Company's annual after tax profit to be contributed to the abovementioned funds shall be as follows:

Reserve Fund	(　　)%
Enterprise Expansion Fund	(　　)%
Bonus and Welfare Fund for Staff and Workers	(　　)%

18.3　After making the payments referred to in Articles 17.1 and 17.2, the remaining profit of the Joint Venture Company will be available for distribution and shall be distributed to the Parties according to the profit distribution plan (as approved by the Board) in proportion to each Party's contribution to the registered capital.

18.4　The profit distribution plan shall be prepared by the General Manager and presented to the Board for approval.

18.5　The Joint Venture Company shall not distribute profits unless the losses of previous fiscal year(s) have been fully made up. Remaining undistributed profit from previous years can be distributed together with that of the current year.

18.6　The Joint Venture Company shall pay profits due to Party B in foreign exchange, and Party A shall assist in this respect. If in any fiscal year, the Joint Venture Company does not have sufficient foreign exchange funds to pay to Party B in full its share of profits, Party B at its option may take its profit for that fiscal year in RMB in China or determine that the balance of any dividend unpaid in that year shall be paid when foreign currency becomes available (calculated at the exchange rate of the day the dividend is declared) together with an amount of interest on such balance in the foreign currency for the period from the date of declaration up to the date of payment calculated at the average rate of interest charged by the Bank of China for loans of such currency in the same amount for the same period.

18.7　The Board shall be entitled to declare and pay interim dividends during the course of a year.

18.8　All payments to be distributed under this Article shall at the request of the receiving Party be transmitted electronically to an account at a bank specified in advance by such Party or may be paid by other means agreed to by the Parties.

第 18 条　利润分配

18.1　根据中华人民共和国相应的法律法规缴税及对以前年度的积累损失全部予以补偿之后，合营公司将划拨一定比例的年税后利润用于缴纳储备基金、企业发展基金、职员和工人的奖金和福利基金。

18.2　合营公司分配给上述基金的年税后利润的百分比如下(在特定某年中由董事会决定者除外)：

储备基金	(　　)%
企业发展基金	(　　)%
职工及工人的奖励	(　　)%

18.3　根据 17.1 和 17.2 两款所述，支付利润以后，合营公司的其余利润就可以进行分配，可以根据利润分配计划(按董事会所批准)按各方对注册资本的出资比例分配给对方。

18.4　利润分配计划由总经理准备，并由董事会批准。

18.5　如果未完全补偿前一个(或前几个)会计年度的亏损，合营公司不应分配利润。前几年留下的未分配利润可与当年的利润一起分配。

18.6　合营公司用外汇支付应给予乙方的利润，甲方在这方面应给予协助。如果任何会计年度中合营公司没有足够的外汇资金支付乙方全部利润份额，乙方应选择在中国用人民币领取该会计年度的利润或决定该会计年度未付红利的余额在有外汇时(按宣布红利当天的兑换率计算)与这一余额的外币利息一起领取。利息自宣布之日计算到支付日(按中国银行对这种货币同额、同期贷款的平均利率计算利息)。

18.7　董事会有权宣布及支付一年过程中的期中股利。

18.8　在此条款下分配的任何支付都应按接受方的请求用电子输送的办法输送到预先由这一方所指定的银行账户来进行，或用双方所同意的其他方法来进行支付。

Article 19　Insurance

19.1　The Joint Venture Company shall, insure against the fire risks and other risks during the operation of the Joint Venture Company. Each engineering project of the Joint Venture Company should be insured by an insurance company. The procedures should be handled by the General Manager.

19.2　The types, amounts and currencies of insurance coverage shall be determined by the General Manager.

19.3　All items of the Joint Venture Company shall be insured with an insurance company registered in China or (to the extent permitted under Chinese law) overseas.

第 19 条　保险

19.1　合营公司在经营期间应投保火险及其他险。合营公司的每一工程项目均应由一家保险公司保险。保险程序由总经理掌握。

19.2　保险的种类金额及币种由总经理决定。

19.3　合营公司的一切项目都应向在中国注册的一家保险公司或在中国法律允许的范围内向海外的一家保险公司投保。

Article 20　Preparation and Construction Office

20.1　The Board shall establish a preparation and construction office ("Construction Office") for the period of preparation and construction of the plant of the Joint Venture Company. The Construction Office shall be comprised of (　) persons nominated by Party A and (　) persons nominated by Party B. The Board shall appoint a member designated by Party (A) as the chief and a member designated by Party (B) as the deputy chief of the Construction Office. The chief and deputy chief may (may not) serve concurrently as General Manager or Deputy General Manager of the Joint Venture Company.

20.2　The Construction Office shall, pursuant to the decision of the Board, review the specific designs and enter into the contracts for the construction work, as well as procure and inspect/accept all related commodities such as equipment, materials, etc. The Construction Office shall also establish the progress schedule for construction work for the Joint Venture Company's plant, formulate the spending plan for such construction work, pay the costs of such construction, settle the accounts, implement the relevant control methods, and maintain all documents, drawings, and data relating to the construction work.

20.3　At the request of the Construction Office, Party A and Party B shall, during the period of preparation and construction of the plant of the Joint Venture Company, dispatch engineers under conditions agreed with the Construction Office, and have such engineers perform, in cooperation with the Construction Office, supervision, inspection, check/acceptance, and performance tests, in relation to the design, quality, equipment, materials, and technologies introduced.

20.4　All costs of the Construction Office (including salaries of its members and costs of the engineers dispatched in accordance with Article 20.3 shall be borne by the Joint Venture Company and shall be incorporated into the budget for the construction work agreed by the Board.

20.5　The Construction Office shall, upon confirming that the construction work for the Joint Venture Company's plant has been executed according to the design (and that the Products have passed the tests), apply to the relevant Chinese government department to issue the necessary certificates for completion of construction and occupation (and commencement of production), and submit a completion report to the Board. Such report shall include a final accounting for construction costs.

20.6　The Construction Office shall be dissolved upon approval by the Board of the completion report and finalization of all turning-over procedures.

第 20 条　筹建处

20.1　董事会在筹建合营公司工厂期间应设立筹建处。筹建处应包括甲方提名者(　)人，乙方提名者(　)人。董事会应任命甲方选派的一名成员为筹建处主任，乙方选派的一名成员为筹建处副主任。主任和副主任可同时为合资公司总经理和副总经理。

20.2　筹建处应按照董事会的决定，检查具体的设计，订立筹建工作合同采购，检验(验收)所有有关商品，如设备、材料等。筹建处也应为合营工厂的筹建工作设立进展程序表，制订筹建工作的经费计划，支付这一工作的成本，结算账目，执行有关的管理工作，保管有关筹建工作的所有文件、图纸和资料。

20.3　按筹建办公室的请求，在合营公司工厂筹建期间，在筹建办公室同意的条件下甲乙双方派遣工程师。由这些工程师与筹建处合作，对所采用的设计质量、设备、材料及技术进行监督、检验、验收及性能测试。

20.4　所有筹建工作的成本(包括其成员的工资，以及根据 20.3 条派遣的工程师的成本)由合营公司支付，并纳入董事会筹建工作预算。

20.5　在确认合营公司工厂筹建工作已根据设计加以完成(产品也通过测试)之后，筹建处应向中国政府有关部门申请发放筹建完工及开工(开始生产)的必需证明书，并向董事会呈交完工报告。这一报告应包括建设成本的决算在内。

20.6　董事会批准完工报告及所有移交程序结束后，筹建办公室将予以解散。

Article 21　Joint Venture Term

21.1　The Joint Venture Term shall commence on the date of the issue of the Business License and shall expire on the Date thirty (30) years after the issue of the Business License.

21.2　Any Party to this Contract may propose an extension of the Joint Venture Term not later than twelve (12) months before expiry of the Joint Venture Term. If such proposal is accepted by the other Party and approved unanimously by the Board, then an application for approval to extend the Joint Venture Term shall be submitted to the department in charge 180 days prior to the expiry date of the Joint Venture Term. Upon such approval being granted, the Joint Venture Company shall proceed with registration formalities to extend the Joint Venture Term.

21.3　In accordance with the laws, the Joint Venture should be liquidated upon the expiration of the Joint Venture or termination of the business in advance. The liquidated proportion should be distributed according to the ratio of investment made by Party A and Party B.

第 21 条　合营期限

21.1　合营期间应自营业执照发放之日起算至发放营业执照之日后的 30 年止。

21.2　本合同的任何一方在合营期满 12 个月前均可提议延长合营期限。此提议如为另一方所采纳，并经董事会一致通过，可在合营期满前 180 天向有关部门提出延长合营期限的申请。在获得审批后，合营公司应进行登记手续，以延长合营期限。

21.3　合营期满或提前终止，合营公司应依法进行清算，清算后的财产根据甲乙方投资的比例予以分配。

Article 22　Amendment, Termination and Release of the Contract

22.1　When amendment is made to the contract and its appendixes it shall not be valid unless a written agreement is signed by both Parties and submitted to and approved by the original inspection authorities.

22.2　With the unanimous agreement of the Board of Directors and approval of the original inspection department, the Joint Venture can be terminated prior to the original term or the contract be terminated in advance if the Joint Venture suffers losses in consecutive years and is incapable of going on with the business for certain reasons.

第 22 条　合同修改、终止与解散

22.1　本合同及附件予以修改时，必须经甲乙双方签署书面协议，并报原审批部门批准，方能生效。

22.2　合营公司由于某些原因出现连年亏损，无力继续经营，经董事会一致通过，并报原审批部门批准，可提前终止合营期限或解除合同。

Article 23　Obligation of the Party Breaching the Contract

23.1　If either Party fails to contribute the amount of the investment committed by the time stipulated in Article 9 of the contract, the Party breaching the contract shall pay the Party observing the contract ____% of the total amount of investment overdue each day counting from the 30th bank date overdue. Should the Party breaching the contract fail to contribute the amount of capital it committed for 90 days, apart from total sum of ____% of the above-mentioned fines, the Party observing the contract has the right to terminate the contract according to Article 22 of the Contract and demand the Party breaching the contract to compensate for its losses.

23.2　Obligation should go to the Party if it is that Party's fault that effects the implementation or complete implementation of the contract and its appendixes. Both Parties shall be liable for the breach of the contract, if the fault is due to both Parties.

23.3　In order to guarantee the implementation of this contract and its appendix, Party A and Party B should each provide a bank guaranty.

第 23 条　违约方责任

23.1　甲乙双方任何一方未按合同第 9 条的规定按数额投资时，从逾期第 30 个银行工作日算起，每逾期一天，违约方应缴付投资额的＿＿%的违约款给予守约的一方。如逾期 90 天仍未提交投资额，除累计应交付投资额的＿＿%的违约罚款外，守约方有权按本合同第 22 条终止合同，并要求违约方赔偿损失。

23.2　由于一方的过失造成本合同及附件不能履行或不能完全履行时，由过失的一方承担责任。如属双方的过失，根据实际情况由双方分别承担各自应负的违约责任。

23.3　为保证本合同及附件的履行，甲乙双方应提供履约的银行担保书。

Article 24　Arbitration

24.1　Should any dispute arise from the implementation of or relating to Contract, both Parties shall resolve them through friendly negotiations. If the discrepancies cannot be solved by negotiations, they should be submitted to the Arbitration Committee of the International Chamber of Commerce for solution, whose decision shall be final and legally binding upon both Parties.

24.2　During the process of arbitration, the Contract should be executed with no interruption, except for those parts relating to discrepancies under arbitration.

第 24 条　仲裁

24.1　凡因执行本合同所发生的或与本合同有关的一切争执，双方应通过友好协商解决。如协商不能解决分歧，应提交国际商会仲裁委员会解决，仲裁裁决是终局的，对双方都有约束力。

24.2　在仲裁过程中，除双方有分歧正在进行仲裁的部分外，本合同应继续履行。

Article 25　Applicable Law

The signing, validity, explanation and implementation of this contract should abide by the laws of the People's Republic of China.

第 25 条　适用法律

本合同的签订、效力、解释和履行均受中华人民共和国法律的管辖。

Article 26　Force Majeure

26.1　If an event of Force Majeure occurs, to the extent that any contractual obligation such as war, fire, serious flood, typhoon, or earthquake of either Party cannot be performed as a result of such event, such contractual obligation shall be suspended while the event of Force Majeure subsists and the due date for performance thereof shall be automatically extended, without penalty, for a period equal to such suspension.

26.2　The Party encountering Force Majeure event shall promptly inform the other Party in writing and shall furnish appropriate proof of the occurrence and duration of such Force Majeure event.

26.3   In the event of Force Majeure, the Parties shall immediately consult with each other in order to find an equitable solution and shall use all reasonable endeavors to minimize the consequences of such Force Majeure.

第 26 条　不可抗力

26.1   如果双方中任何一方，由于发生如战争、火灾、严重水灾、台风或地震等不可抗力的事故，其后果达到不能履行合同责任的程度，在不可抗力事故继续存在时，合同责任就应推迟。应当执行合同责任的日期就应自动延长，不用罚款。延长时期与不可抗力继续存在的时期相等。

26.2   遭遇不可抗力事故的一方应立即以书面形式通知另一方，并出具事故发生及这一不可抗力事故持续时间的适当证明。

26.3   不可抗力事故发生时，双方应立刻彼此协商，以便寻找解决的办法，并使用一切合理的方法来减少这一不可抗力事故的后果。

Article 27   Trade Union

27.1   The employees of the Joint Venture Company shall have the right to establish a trade union and to participate in the activities of such trade union in accordance with the *Trade Union Law of the People's Republic of China* and the Joint Venture Regulations. The trade union of the Joint Venture Company shall represent the legitimate interests of the employees of the Joint Venture Company and shall be prohibited from carrying out any activities which are deemed by the Joint Venture Company to be detrimental to the Joint Venture Company's interests.

27.2   Any employee who ceases to be employed by the Joint Venture Company due to retirement, dismissal or resignation shall also lose his right to participate in the activities of the trade union in the Joint Venture Company.

27.3   In accordance with the relevant laws, the Joint Venture Company shall allocate an amount equivalent to two percent (2%) of the aggregate amount of wages of the PRC employees of the Joint Venture Company to the trade union as trade union funds. The trade union shall use such funds strictly in accordance with the *Rules for the Management of Trade Union Funds*.

第 27 条　工会

27.1   根据《中华人民共和国工会法》及合营公司的规章规定，合营公司的雇员有权建立工会，并参加这一工会的活动。合营公司的工会代表合营公司雇员的合法利益。禁止进行合营公司认为有害于合营公司利益的一切活动。

27.2   任何因退休、解雇或辞职而不再受雇于合营公司的雇员不再有权参与合营公司工会的活动。

27.3   根据有关法律，合营公司将分配给相当于合营公司中中华人民共和国雇员总工资额的 2%给工会，作为工会基金。工会应根据《工会基金管理规定》严格使用这笔基金。

Article 28   Versions

This contract is written both in Chinese and English. The contract in both Languages is of equal Validity. Should there be any discrepancy between the Chinese and English Versions, the text in the English language should be taken as standard.

第 28 条　版本

本合同以中、英文书就，中、英文本具有同等效力，中英文本如有不符，以英文为准。

Exercises

Ⅰ. Translate the following sentences from English into Chinese.

1. In accordance with this contract, Party B shall provide the Cooperation Venture Company with certain training.

2. In case, the Buyer fails to arrange insurance in time due to the Seller's not having faxed in time, all losses shall be borne by the Seller.

3. The guarantee period shall be 12 (twelve) months starting from the date on which the commodity arrives at the port of destination.

4. The Seller shall be liable for any dead freight or demurrage, should it happen that they have failed to have the commodity ready for loading after the carrying vessel has arrived at the port of shipment on time.

5. Both Parties have the responsibility to retain confidentiality regarding this Contract and no one is allowed to release any part of it to a thirty country without the consent of other Party.

Ⅱ. Translate the following sentences from Chinese into English.

1. 开具的信用证必须满足合同所规定的条款内容。
2. 信用证所列条件应准确、公正，卖方能予以承兑。
3. 广告费用应由乙方承担。
4. 买方须在签约后立即支付合同金额的 10%作为定金。
5. 管理公司须按规定收取物业管理费(含租金)。

Ⅲ. Choose the correct answer.

1. Please advise us what ____ are involved and the time ____ for delivery.
   A. procedures, need
   B. process, needed
   C. formalities, taken
   D. business, taken

2. Special instructions have been given to our dispatch department to send your orders on August 15 and September 15 separately, as ____ in your letter of July 15.
   A. was written
   B. ordered
   C. wishes
   D. specified

3. Sometimes, transshipment and partial shipments are____.
   A. permission　　B. permitted　　C. permitting　　D. permit

4. We wish to stress that shipment must be made within the prescribed time limit, as a further____ will not be considered by our endusers.
   A. expansion
   B. protract

C. prolong   D. extension

5. It is not necessary to indicate the name and address of the consignee on each package, since shipping marks comprise the ___ of the buyer's name.

     A. short time below   B. nickname for

     C. initials of   D. capital betters above

6. We will sign the contract on condition that the buyer's packing instructions are ____.

     A. obliged   B. observed   C. obeying   D. objected

7. We have not yet had precise shipping instructions and ____ your order until they arrive.

     A. are holding   B. have hold   C. hold   D. held

8. We have the goods you asked for in stock and will deliver as soon as we ____ your order.

     A. receiving   B. received   C. will receive   D. receive

9. Packing charges ____ in the price, and we can make delivery whenever you wish.

     A. included   B. include   C. is included   D. are included

10. We are sorry for the short delivery by 23 tons. This ____ you some difficulty in meeting orders of your clients.

     A. must have caused   B. must cause

     C. has caused   D. will be caused

Chapter 16 400 International Business English Sentences
国际商务英语 400 句

一、学习目的

    编者列出国际商务英语中常见的 400 句长句难句，it 句型，it 作形式主语，或形式宾语，以及特种定语从句等长句难句在其中都有反复应用，非谓语动词学会使用可以美化优化句子结构形式，表现出自己的外语水平及自己单位和自己国家的语言素养，提高自己单位和自己国家的工作人员的形象和信誉，以受到尊重。一些常用词组和惯用词组等学会灵活掌握也方便于读者的对外交流及参加经贸英语考试时在汉译英这个项目上多得些分数。

二、学习方法

    学前先复习一下自己的英语语法与句法知识，重要的条条框框也要熟记于心，英语的一些句法，从句、主句等的句法也需要先复习一下，再来学习这 400 句长句难句就容易理解与消化，然后就逐步能学会模拟、对照与使用，将自己的英语水平提高一个层次。要下好决心再学，然后才能有恒心，有信心，不会中途放弃。同样内容用不同词语和句子来表达的句子，也需要对比一下，常用词组、习惯英语等要刻苦记忆背诵，以求达到将自己的英语水平提高一个层次的目的。这样学生也一定会在参加任何经贸英语的考试考查时在最易丢分的汉译英项目中争得分数与名次，有助于通过考试。

    国际商务英语的掌握和使用是与英语系国家达成贸易交往的必要工具和手段，外经贸方面的资格考试大多也是英汉对译的词组、句子、段落等考题。针对很多学生不能很好地掌握英译对照的基础知识，也不能正确、顺利地与国际上的外贸人员进行交往的问题，本书列出 400 句外经贸英语的长句、难句、习惯用语、词组等方面的汉译英句子，并进行语法分析与讲解，便于学生阅读、研究与分析，并且熟读，甚至记忆，将汉译英技巧和水平提高一个层次。

1.   我们是中国最大的棉布出口商之一。
    We are one of the largest cotton exporters in China.
2.   我方感谢你方与我方在贸易方面的密切合作。
    We <u>thank you for</u> your <u>offering</u> (动名词)us close cooperation in <u>trading</u>(动名词).
3.   我方在平等互利、互通有无的基础上和世界各地的商人进行贸易。
    We trade with the merchants all over the world <u>on the basis of</u> (词组)equality, mutual benefit and exchange of <u>needed</u> (过去分词)goods.
4.   我们一直做纺织品进出口生意。
    We <u>have been trading (dealing, engaged)</u> (现在分词，现在完成进行时) <u>in</u> the line of

textile <u>importing and exporting</u>(动名词).

5. 我们经营各种纺织机械贸易。

    a. We<u> are engaged in </u>(现在时被动语态) <u>handling</u> (动名词)various kinds of textile equipment.

    b. We <u>are trading in</u> (现在分词，现在进行时) various kinds of textile equipment.

    c. We<u> are dealing in</u> (现在分词，现在进行时) various kinds of textile equipment.

    d. We<u> are handling</u> (现在分词，现在进行时) various kinds of textile equipment (常用表达方式).

6. 我们希望扩大我们的业务。

    a. We<u> are desirous of</u> (系词+表语) <u>enlarging</u> (动名词) our business.

    b. We are desirous of promoting sth.　　希望改进……

    c. We are desirous of developing sth.　　希望发展……

7. 如果你方能协助我方在欧洲获得一些贸易伙伴，我方将不胜感激。

    a. If you could help us in <u>obtaining</u> (动名词) some <u>trading</u>(动名词，定语，表方面) parterners in Europe, we <u>should</u> highly <u>appreciate</u>(原形动词，谓语) it/<u>should be</u> <u>indebted</u> (谓语，过去分词) to you/ should be grateful to you/be very much obliged.

    b. We shall appreciate it if you can…

8. 我们非常熟悉当地情况，并且与那里的许多公司都有很好的业务关系。

We are well<u> acquainted with</u> (现在时被动语态) the local conditions and <u>have</u> good <u>business connections with</u> many corporations there.

9. 在贸易圈内享有良好的声誉对生意人来说是最重要的事情。

    a. 用 It 句型

<u>It</u> (It 句型，作形式主语) is the most important thing <u>for</u> the merchants <u>to enjoy</u> (动词不定式，作 It 的逻辑主语) a good reputation in the <u>trading</u> (动名词作定语，表性质，功能) field.

    b. 用动名词短语作主语

<u>Enjoying</u> (动名词作主语) a good reputation in the <u>trading</u> (动名词，性质，功能) field is the most important thing for the merchants.

10. 中国国际贸易促进委员会已将贵公司推荐给我们。

Your Firm (Corporation/Company) <u>has been recommended to</u> (现在完成时被动语态) us by CCPIT(China Council for the Promotion of International Trade).

11. 在经营童装方面我方在全球范围内都享有很高的声誉。

    a. <u>Trading in</u> (动名词作主语) the children's garments <u>brings</u> us <u>high reputation</u> over the world.

    b. <u>Trading in</u> (动名词作主语) the children's garments makes us <u>enjoying</u> (现在分词宾语补足语) high reputation over the world.

12. 我们想了解贵国技术人员的就业情况。

We want <u>to acquaint with</u> (动词不定式作宾语) the employment position of the technical personnel in your country.

13. 我们的贸易政策是在平等互利、互通有无的基础上和各个友好国家进行贸易。

It (it 句型作形式主语) is our trade policy to do business with (动词不定式作 it 的逻辑主语) the friendly countries on the basis of equality, mutual benefit and exchange of needed goods.

14. 我们利用此机会表达我们在贸易方面和你们进行密切合作的愿望。

We avail of this opportunity to express (动词不定式作目的状语) our wish of making close cooperation with (动名词作 of 的宾语) you in our trading (动名词，宾语).

15. 我们希望了解你方电子计算机的市场情况。

We are in the hope (词组作表语) of acquainting with (动名词作宾语) the market condition of your electronic computers.

16. 通过相互努力我们一定能够扩大我们的贸易范围。

a. Through mutual efforts (By joint efforts) we are (系词) certainly in the position of enlarging (动名词作宾语) our business scope (field).

b. We are certainly able to enlarge (be able to do sth. 表示能够，指通过客观努力能做到某事，can 为主观方面能够)our business scope through mutual efforts.

17. 化学肥料属于上述公司的经营范围。

Chemical fertilizers fall within the scope of (come into the range of/lie within the scope of/stay within/remain within) business activities of the above-mentioned (过去分词，被动语态，作定语) corporation.

18. 我方得知你方作为经营绸缎制品的一家国有公司在中国是最有名望的。

We are given to understand (得知=被告知)that you are a state-run (state-operated)(过去分词，定语) corporation, being engaged in (现在分词作定语) the line of silk piece goods and enjoying (现在分词，定语) the highest reputation in China.

19. 我们之间多年的贸易往来有助于扩大我们的贸易范围，并增进我们的贸易利润。

Doing business (动名词作主语) between us for so many years has been contributing (现在完成进行时) much to the expanding (动名词作宾语) of our business fields and to the increasing (动名词作宾语) of our trade profits.

20. 扩大商业领域是从商者的共同任务。

Expanding (动名词) the trading fields is the common task of the traders.

21. 我们将以最新型的电器装备你的新居。

We shall furnish (将来时) your new house with the newest type of electric apparatus.

22. 请记着随时提供我们必要的信息。

Please bear in mind that you must furnish us with necessary information at all times.

23. 我们的产品质量在国际竞争中一直都符合标准，而且名列前茅。

The quality of our products is always up to the standard in the international competition and is (现在进行时) always standing in the first rank(分词作谓语).

24. 我们的国际贸易将对我国的经济发展大有帮助。

Our international trade will be (系词) helpful (表语)greatly for the economic development of our country.

25. 众所周知，我方的 B 系列产品在国际市场上是十分热销的。

It (形式主语) is well known that our products of B series are (现在时) warmly welcomed (被动语态作谓语) in the international market. (主语从句作 it 的逻辑主语)

26. 我方从美国大使馆商务参赞处得悉贵公司的名称和地址。

a. We have known (现在完成时) the name and address of your Company from the Commercial Counsellor's Office of the Embassy of U.S.A.

b. We have got (现在完成时) the name…

c. We have been informed of the (过去分词，现在完成时，被动语态，作谓语) name…

d. We have learned (现在完成时) the name….

e. The Commercial Counsellor's Office of the U.S. Embassy has informed (现在完成时作谓语) us of the name and address of your Company.

27. 本函的目的是探索和你方建立贸易关系的可能性。

The purpose of this letter is to explore (动词不定式作 is 的表语) the possibilities of establishing (动名词作宾语) the business relationship with you.

28. 我们给你们写信是希望探索从你方进口大量××型计算机的可能性。

We are writing (现在分词，现在进行时) this letter to you in the hope of exploring (动名词，宾语) the possibility of importing (动名词，与 of 一起作 possibility 的定语) large quantities of electronic computers Type ×× from you.

29. 我方有幸向你方自荐，期望有机会和你方合作并扩大业务。

We have the pleasure of introducing (动名词作宾语) ourselves to you with the hope of (词组) getting (动名词作宾语) an opportunity to cooperate with (动词不定式作目的状语，作定语也可) you and as well to extend (动词不定式作目的状语) our business.

30. 我们欣然给贵方寄上介绍信，希望这将是我们双方互利关系的前奏曲。

We are (系词) glad (表语) to send you this introductory letter, hoping (分词放在后面看作目的状语) it will be the prelude for the mutual beneficial relation between us.

31. 随着对外贸易的发展，我国国民经济已快步迈上了几个台阶。

In keeping with the expansion of the foreign trade, the national economy of our country has advanced (现在完成时) several steps further.

32. 我们很高兴通过长时间的函电往来，终于和你方达成了这次协议，这肯定会促进我们之间对外贸易的发展。

We are (系词) pleased (过去分词，表语) to have come to (动词不定式，完成时，表 pleased 的原因或方面) this agreement through protracted (过去分词，定语) correspondence, which would certainly promote the development of foreign trade between us.(特种定语从句，说明前面整个句子)

33. 鉴于我们之间的长期友好关系，并通过相互的巨大努力，我们终于达成了这次协议。这对于我国对外贸易营业额的增加将有所帮助。

In view of the long-standing (现在分词作定语) and friendly business relations between us and through our great mutual efforts, we have reached (现在完成时，谓语) this agreement, which will do a little bit to help the increase of our annual foreign trade turnover.

34. 我方希望你方今后能按常规办理我们之间的业务，这对发展和巩固我们之间的贸易是大有益处的。

It is our hope (It 形式主语) that you can follow our usual practices in doing (动名词，宾语) business trading (动名词，宾语) between us, (it 的逻辑主语从句) which (which 代表前面整个主句，故为特种定语从句) would be mutually beneficial to the developing (动名词) and (宾语) consolidating (动名词宾语) of our trading. (动名词，宾语)

35. 进行外贸时，我们一贯坚持平等互利、互通有无的原则。

We always adhere to the principle of equality, mutual benefit and exchange of needed goods in doing (动名词，宾语) foreign tradings(动名词转化为名词，宾语).

36. 你方为我们之间的贸易合作做了如此之多的工作，使我方十分感动，我方今后将进一步为我们两国之间的贸易发展添砖加瓦。

Your having done (完成时，动名词) so much work for the cooperation of our trade business has made us deeply touched (过去分词，被动语态作宾语补足语). In the days to come we would certainly do our little bit (表示愿望) further to help (动词不定式，目的状语) the development of the trade between our two countries.

37. 如你方欲购我方高质量产品，可以要求我方报价。

If you are (系词) in the market for (表语) our high quality products, you can ask us to offer (动词不定式，宾语补足语) you our prices.

38. 请向我方报男式衬衫的最低价。

Please make (原型动词，谓语，命令句) us your lowest quotation for men's shirts.

39. 你方瓷器报价太高，我方难以接受。

Your quotation of chinaware is too high for us to accept. (动词不定式，"太……，以致不能")

40. 我方一位美国客户希望购买你方××，请报给我们××的实盘价。

One of our clients from the United States is (系词) keen(表语) to purchase (动词不定式作状语，表方面) your ××, please offer us firm for them.

41. 我们殷切期待你方早日报来××的价格。

We are looking forward to (现在进行时) your early offer for ××.

42. 我方希望你方附寄一份你方产品价格单供我方参考。

We'd like you to enclose (动词不定式作宾语) us a price list of your products for our reference.

43. 随函附上我方产品价格单一份/我方产品价格单现附寄于此。

Enclosed (表语) here is (系词) a price (主语) list of our products.

(enclosed 作表语时，常放于句首。中间为系动词 is，主语在最后，为主系表倒装。此为"附寄"的习惯表达方式。)

44. 随函附上我方产品价格单一份，请查收。

Enclosed (宾语补足语) please find (谓语) a copy of the price list of our products.

(此为"附寄"的另一种习惯表达方式及习惯的英汉对译)

45. 我方希望收到你方开司米羊毛衫的详细信息及各种羊毛衫的价格单。

We wish <u>to receive</u> (动词不定式作宾语) your detailed information on your cashmere sweaters and your pricelist of various kinds of wool sweaters.

46. 如能附有照片及详细规格,我方将不胜感激。

We <u>shall appreciate</u> (将来时,谓语) it very much if you can attach photos and <u>detailed</u> (过去分词,被动语态) specifications to these materials.

47. 我方热切希望你方能针对你方的具体需求向我方提出询价。

We <u>are</u> (系词) keenly <u>desirous of</u> (表语) your <u>favoring</u> (动名词,宾语) us with inquiries for your specific requirements.

48. 如蒙询价,我方十分感激,并将立即办理此事。

We shall appreciate very much your enquiry and shall pay our prompt attention to it.

49. 我方很遗憾不能给你方提供此商品的报价,眼下我公司无现货可供。

We regret <u>being unable to offer</u> (动名词,宾语) you for this commodity, for <u>which</u> we are now out of stock (which 指前面整句,为特种定语从句).

50. 十分抱歉,我方不能考虑接受你方还盘。

Much to our regret, we <u>are not able to entertain</u> (作谓语) your counteroffer.

51. 你方询价之××型钢板现在已不属于我方经营之范围。

The steel plates Type ×× <u>for which you enquired</u> (which 前有介词的定语从句) <u>do not lie under the range of our business activities</u> (否定式,谓语) at present.

52. 你方报价碰巧和我方所盼望的价格吻合。

Your offer happens <u>to be</u> (系词) exactly <u>the same as</u> (表语)the price we expect.

53. 5% 的佣金将非常有助于推动你方产品的销售。

Five percent commission will <u>help</u> you very much <u>in pushing</u> (动名词作宾语) the sales of your products.

54. 永远保持适中的市场价格将会使你方商品总是获得卓有前途的市场。

<u>Keeping moderate market prices forever</u> (动名词作主语) will make your articles always <u>remaining (staying/lying) in</u> (现在分词作宾语补足语) the promising market (position).

55. 由于市场坚挺,我方建议你方抓紧这一商机,立即接受我方报盘。

<u>Owing</u> to the <u>strengthening</u> (动名词作宾语) of the market, we suggest that you <u>(should seize)</u>(虚拟语气 should 省略) firmly this trade opportunity and <u>(should accept)</u> our offer immediately.

56. 让我们各让半步,也许 5%的折扣会使你方满意?

Let's meet each other half way. Perhaps a 5% discount will <u>make</u> you <u>satisfied</u>? (过去分词宾语补足语)

57. 如果你们订×××打床单,我方同意给你方 2%的数量折扣。

<u>Provided</u> (过去分词,被动语态,条件状语) you order ××× dozen of bed sheets, we agree <u>to grant</u> (不定式,宾语) you <u>a 2% quantity discount</u>.

58. 等外品现在在打折(在降价)。

Off-grade qualities <u>are</u> (系词) now at <u>a discount</u>.(表语)

59. 重要的是你方报价必须在本月末以前到达我方，以便我方抓紧商机，获取最大利润。

<u>It is</u> (形式主语) rather important <u>that your</u> (主语从句，作逻辑主语) quotation <u>(should)</u> (虚拟语气，should 省略，不能写出) reach us no later than the end of this month <u>in order that we could grasp the business opportunity firmly in hands and obtain the biggest profits.</u> (目的状语从句)

60. 我方现在欲购××吨××，希望你方抓紧时间，尽快报价。要知道，商机是可遇不可求的。

We <u>are</u> (系词) <u>in the market</u> (表语) for ×× tons of ××, please cut things fine and send us your offer as soon as possible. As you know, the trade opportunity will <u>come by luck,</u> <u>not by searching</u>.(动名词，宾语，by searching 作方式状语)

61. 我们希望你们能立即给我们报来优惠的价格。

We hope you can quote us your favourable price <u>by return</u>.

62. 我方所附价格清单将使你方知道我们是努力将我们的报价保持在合理的水平上的。

a. Our <u>attached</u> (过去分词，被动语态作定语) price list will show you that we are <u>managing</u> (现在进行时) <u>to hold</u> (不定式作宾语) our quotations at the reasonable level.

b. … will make you <u>informed</u> (过去分词，被动语态，作宾语补足语) that we are managing to keep our quotations at…

c. … will make <u>it</u> (形式宾语) clear <u>that we are retaining our quotations at…</u>. (宾语从句作 it 的逻辑宾语)

63. 你方询价一定会得到我方的立即办理。

Your inquiry will certainly receive our prompt attention.

64. 我方发现你方报价合理，两三天内我方一定会给你方肯定答复。

We have found that your offer is reasonable and we will give you our definite reply in a couple of days.

65. 如果你方认为此报盘可以接受，请立即传真回复，以便我方确认。

If you think this offer <u>is</u> (系词) <u>acceptable</u> (表语) to you, please reply us by fax immediately for our confirmation.

66. 此报盘以货物未售出为条件。

This offer <u>is</u> (系词) <u>subject to</u> (表语) the <u>goods' being unsold</u>.

(being unsold 为动名词的被动语态，goods 为动名词的逻辑主语。)

67. 我们能以竞争性的价格提供男式衬衫的报盘。

We can <u>offer for</u> men's shirts at competitive prices.

68. 很遗憾，我方发现你方还盘与国际市场价格不符。

Much to our regret, we have found that your counteroffer <u>is not in line with</u> (not

<u>keeping in line with</u> (现在分词作谓语，现在进行时)/not remaining in line with) the international market price.

69. 我们很高兴收到你方的询价单，现确认我方今天的传真如下……

We <u>are</u> (系词) very <u>pleased</u> (表语) to receive your enquiry sheet and now we confirm our today's fax as follows: (动名词不定式作状语，表原因或方面)

70. 由于目前市场坚挺，价格上涨的趋势很大，我方建议你方立即接受我方报盘。

Owing to the <u>advancing</u> (现在分词作定语) market and the strong tendency of the price <u>increasing</u> (动名词，作宾语), we suggest you <u>to accept</u> (动词不定式，作宾语补足语) our offer immediately.

71. 如果订单数量达到 5000 打，我们可给予你方 5%～6%的数量佣金。

If the quantity of the order is up to 5,000 dozens, we can offer you a quantity commission of 5% to 6%.

72. 此报盘有效至本月底，你方立即接受此报盘一定不会使你方后悔。

This offer <u>is</u> (系词) <u>valid</u> (表语) <u>until the end of this month</u>(时间状语). Your immediate acceptance <u>will bring</u> (将来时) you no regret.

73. 在我方工艺品经营中，我们一般给予 3%或 5%的佣金，佣金超过 5%是不可能的。

In our art and craft business, we usually pay 3% or 5% commission. <u>Any commissions</u> (主语) over 5% <u>are</u> (系词) not <u>possible</u>.(表语)

74. 对你方所提的巨大数量的订货，我们可以给你方提供 4%的佣金，但无任何折扣，因为我们对此项产品的价格已属底盘价。

For the substantial quantity of the order you <u>mentioned</u> (一般过去时，主动，谓语), we can grant you 4% commission but with no discount, because the price of this article <u>is</u> (系词) already <u>at its rock-bottom</u>.(表语)

75. 由于此商品需求量大，市场价格变动也频繁，故此报盘有效期仅 10 天。

Owing to the heavy demand for this article and to the frequent fluctuations of the market price, this offer <u>is</u> (系词) <u>open</u> (表语) only for 10 days.

76. 根据你方要求，我方现报价如下，以我方最后确认为准。

At your request, we <u>are</u> now <u>offering</u> (现在分词作现在进行时的谓语) the following, <u>subject to</u> (补充说明) our final confirmation.

77. 请给我方报 30 吨红茶，CIF 伦敦的价格。

Please make us an offer CIF London for 30 tons of Black Tea.

78. 我方报给你方实盘，以 11 月 1 日、周二，我方时间上午 11 点以前收到你方答复为条件。

We offer you firm (句后省略了另一个 offer), subject to your reply <u>reaching</u> (现在分词作定语，定 reply) here by 11 a.m., Tuesday, November 1, our time.

(此句中可将 reaching 看成现在分词，作 reply 的定语；也可将 reaching 看成 subject to 的动名词，your reply 则为 reaching 的逻辑主语，因此最好用 reply's 作 reaching 的逻辑主语)

79. 行市正在上涨。

The market <u>is rising</u> (分词，作现在进行时) (stiffening, hardening, soaring).

80. 按照你方请求，我方已同意每笔交易提供你方 3%的折扣(回扣)。

<u>In compliance with</u> your request, we have agreed to give you a 3% discount (commission) for each transaction.

81. 根据形势发展需要，我方对绣花棉台布将提价 5%。

<u>In compliance with</u> (过去分词作定语，表被动) the requirement of the situation development, we shall increase the price of the cotton embroidered tablecloth for 5%.

82. 随函附上有关你方询价项目的报价单，收到此报价单后希望尽快回复你方接受与否，因为这些项目在国际市场上销售很快，而我方存货却又不多。

<u>Enclosed</u> (表语) <u>is</u> (系词) our quotation <u>sheet</u> (主语) <u>covering</u> (现在分词作定语) the items you <u>enquired</u> (过去时，谓语). We hope you can reply us your acceptability of it as soon as possible, because these items <u>have got</u> (现在完成时) <u>fast sales</u> in the international market without our rich stock.

83. 我方用户认为你方价格太高，我方也不能劝说他们接受你方价格，所以不得不向你方还盘如下。

Our end-users have found your price too high and we <u>are unable to persuade</u> (谓语) them much <u>to accept</u> (动词不定式，作宾语补足语) your price, so we <u>have to</u> make (不得不，固定用法) offer to you as follows.

84. 有否可能双方各让半步，从而达成这次交易？

Is there any possibility for us <u>to meet each other half way</u> (动词不定式作 possibility 的定语) <u>to conclude</u> (不定式作目的状语) this transaction?

85. 在中国不断出现了许多中日合资企业来组装日本牌子的电视机，使中国的组装电视机价格下降了，但日本品牌的原装电视机价格却始终居高不下。

In China there <u>have been appearing</u> (现在分词作现在完成进行时，作谓语) lots of Sino-Japanese <u>joint-ventured</u> (过去分词作定语) enterprises <u>to assemble</u> the (不定式作目的状语)TV sets of Japanese Brand <u>which</u> (which 作特定从句) <u>has been making</u> (现在完成进行时) <u>the prices of the TV sets</u> (过去分词作定语，定 sets) <u>packaged in</u> China <u>decreased</u> (过去分词作 price 的宾语补足语), but the prices of the Japanese Brand TV sets originally <u>installed</u> (过去分词作 TV set 的后置定语) in Japan <u>have</u> long <u>been occupying</u> (现在完成进行时) <u>the high position (have long been remaining</u> (现在完成进行时) <u>in the high side)</u> without any indication of price <u>lowering</u>(动名词作宾语).

86. 由于目前市场不断下跌，盼望你方认真考虑我方还盘，并早日给我们传来你方接受报盘的佳音。

Owing to the continuous <u>declining</u> (动名词，宾语) of the present market, we are <u>looking forward to</u> (现在进行时) your careful consideration of <u>accepting</u> (动名词作宾语) our counteroffer and to your <u>bringing</u> (动名词) us the favourable news of your acceptance of our offer.

87. 如果你方能降一些价格，比如降 2%，我方认为我们之间达成交易就有可能。

<u>Should you be able to reduce your price slightly</u> (条件状语从句), <u>say 2%</u> (举例说明),

we think we could <u>come to terms with</u> you.

88. 虽然我方很想和你方达成这次交易，但你方报价实在太高，我方无法接受。

   While (Although) we would like <u>to conclude this business with</u> (动词不定式作宾语) you, your offer is <u>too</u> high for us <u>to accept</u>. (不定式作状语，表程度)(While 后为状语从句)

89. 我们现在明白了这个市场价格流动的真实性。

   We <u>are</u> (系词) now <u>convinced of</u> (现在时过去分词，被动语态，表语) the truth of the market price fluctuation.

90. 你方应认真考虑价格低廉及质量优越的必要性。

   You must <u>take</u> both low <u>price</u> and excellent <u>quality into careful consideration</u>.

91. 我方报价是相当有竞争性的，国际市场价格又呈上升趋势，我方希望你方抓紧商机速战速决，立即接受，切勿犹豫。

   Our offer is rather competitive and in the international market <u>there</u> (定语) <u>is appearing</u> (现在进行时作谓语) an upward tendency. We hope you <u>will not hesitate in</u> (一般将来时，谓语) <u>seizing</u> (动名词宾语) firmly the business opportunity. We hope you will make your quick decision <u>to accept</u> (动词不定式，宾补，目的状语) our price and <u>to fight a quick battle</u> (目的状语) in the business field.

92. 我方将记住你方对××的询盘，一旦能接受新订单就会立即传真你方。

   We will keep your enquiry before us at table and will fax you as soon as we <u>are</u> (系词) <u>in a position</u> (表语) <u>to accept</u> (动词不定式，定语) new orders.

93. 虽然我方感激你方询盘，但很遗憾，由于国内外需求量太大，目前无法在今年接受新订单。

   <u>While (Although) we appreciate your enquiry</u> (让步状语从句), we <u>are</u> (系词) <u>regretful</u> (表语，表原因方面) <u>that</u> (宾语从句) this year we are not in a position to accept any fresh orders due to (owing to) the heavy demand both at home and abroad.

94. 你方此次报价略为偏高，但近期市场存货价格的下降趋势迫使我方不得不接受你方这次的报价。

   Your offer this time is slightly higher, but the stortening tendency of the recent market storage <u>pressed</u> (一般过去式，主动) us <u>to accept</u> (动词不定式，宾语补足语) your offer this time.

95. 如果你方有意购买我方其他货物，请告知具体要求，我方一定会立即办理你方的报价事项。

   If you should be interested in our other articles, please inform us of your specific requirement. We would <u>be sure to pay prompt attention to</u> (动词不定式，状语，表方面，特殊) your <u>offering</u>.(动名词，宾语)

96. 你方的价格不太能在国际市场上做得开，你方将面临的价格竞争是较为激烈的。降价 2% 如何？

   Your price will <u>not be</u> (将来时，系词) quite <u>workable</u> (表语) in the international market and the price competition you <u>will be faced with</u> (将来时，被动语态) will be rather fierce. How about a price reduction of 2%?

97. 我方十分感谢你方对我方要求降价 5%一事迅速回复。

We appreciate very much your immediate <u>response</u> (reply) <u>to</u> our request for a 5% reduction in price.

98. 你方迅速回复我方要求降价 5%一事，使我方十分感激。

Your immediate response to our request for a 5% reduction in price <u>made us</u> quite <u>obliged</u> (过去分词，被动，宾语补足语).

99. 我方认为除非你方修正价格，否则是做不成交易的。

We don't think we can <u>put</u> the business <u>through</u> unless you <u>revise</u> (一般现在时，第二人称) your price.

100. 我方报盘如下：床单，每条 CIF，纽约，××美元，订 800 打。

Our offer is as follows: Bed sheets, US $×× per piece, CIF New York, for an order of 800 dozens.

101. 如果你方愿意和我方成交，请给我方提供 2%的降价，也就是每打 18 美元。如何？是否可能做到？我方等候你方答复。

If you <u>are</u> (系词) <u>willing</u> (形容词，表语) <u>to close the business with</u> (动词不定式，状语，特殊) us, please make us a price reduction of 2%, i.e. US $18 per dozen. How about it? Is there any <u>possibility of doing it?</u> (动名词，宾语) <u>Waiting</u> (现在分词，省略 We are,现在进行时) for your reply.

102. 为了扩大我们之间的贸易范围，发展我们的友好关系以及我们的经济和技术，我方这次同意接受你方报价。

<u>For the purpose of expanding</u> (动名词作宾语) the trade scope between us and <u>to develop</u> (不定式，目的状语) our friendly relations, our economy and technique, we agree <u>to accept</u> (不定式宾语) your offer this time.

103. 让我们各让半步，以便达成此次交易。

Let's <u>meet</u> (原形动词，命令句) each other half way <u>in order to put this deal through.</u> (不定式，目的状语)

104. 我方所报的价格是没有任何折扣的，但你方从每笔订单中可以得到 2%的佣金。

Our offered price does not include any discount (There is no discount for our <u>offered</u> (过去分词，被动语态) price), but there is a 2% of commission <u>offered</u> (过去分词，被动语态) for each order.

105. 折扣或多或少会给我方推销产品一些鼓励，折扣越大，鼓励也越大。

Discount <u>will</u> more or less <u>encourage</u> (将来时谓语) us <u>in pushing</u> (动名词作宾语) the sales of the products. The <u>greater</u> the discount, <u>the more</u> the encouragement. (比较状语从句)

106. 你方 5%的佣金按扣除运费和保险费的发票金额为基础来计算。

Your 5% commission <u>will be</u> (将来时，被动语态) calculated <u>on the basis</u> of invoice value after <u>deducting</u> (动名词宾语) freight and insurance (after the deduction of freighted insurance).

107. 尽管我方再三请求，他们仍不同意增加折扣率。

In spite of our repeated (过去分词作定语) requests, they did not agree to increase (不定式作宾语) the ratio of discount.

108. 我方保证对你方的所有询盘将给予迅速办理。

We assure you of our prompt attention to all of your inquiries.

109. 你方必须稍微降低一些价格才能弥补你方价格和国际市场价格之间的差别。

It (it 句型) is necessary for you to make (不定式作逻辑主语) a slight reduction of your price to bridge the price gap between (不定式作目的状语) yours and that of the international market.

110. 按此价格成交是行不通的，因为这会使我方大为亏本。

It (形式主语) is not available to do (不定式逻辑主语) business at this figure, because such business will bring (将来时) us great short fall (loss).

111. 考虑到这个行业的初次交易，我们可给予5%的佣金。

With the view of initiating (动名词作宾语) business in this line, we are able to offer you 5% of commission.

112. 这种新式的羊毛衫使我们的用户甚感兴趣。

This new type of sweater is (系词) of great interest (表语) to our customers.

113. 至于我方的资信情况，请向中国银行查询。

As to our credit standing (financial condition) (动名词作宾语), please refer to (原形动词作谓语，命令句) the Bank of China.

114. 你方可向中国银行咨询我方资信情况。

You may refer to (原形动词，情态动词和 refer 作谓语) the Bank of China for our credit standing. (动名词作宾语，但也可看成是转化为名词的动名词)

115. 请你方参阅近日你我双方之间的往来传真。

We wish you to refer (不定式，宾语补足语) to the recent faxes exchanged (过去分词，被动语态作定语) between us.

116. 我方能提供你方所需的信息资料。

We are able to (谓语) supply you with the required (过去分词，作定语，被动语态) information.

117. 我方能接受你方订单。

a. We are (系词) in a position to (表语) accept your order.

b. We are able to (谓语) accept your order.

118. 我方不能接受你方订单。

We are not (系词) capable (表语) of accepting (动词不定式，作宾语) your order.

119. 我方能够满足你方十吨钢板的需要。

We can meet your requirement of 10 tons of steel plates.

120. 你方的意图正好和我们的期望一致。

Your intention happens to coincide (偶然，碰巧) with our wish.

121. 你方产品价格合理，品质优良，为我方大量向你方订购提供了很多有利的条件。

The prices of your products are reasonable and their quality is excellent, <u>which will offer us many favourable conditions for placing substantial orders with you</u>. (which 指前句所述情况，特种定语从句)

122. 我方有充分信心为我方产品找到很好的销路。

We <u>have full confidence in</u> <u>finding</u> (动名词作宾语) a good market for our products.

123. 按照要求，我方将于明日给你方寄去订单号为 105 号的样品一包，以供参考。

<u>As requested</u> (过去分词，被动语态), we are <u>sending</u> (现在进行时，表示不久的将来) you tomorrow a parcel of samples of Order No. 105 for your reference.

(As requested=As you requested 或 As we were requested)

124. 这种商品在欧洲市场是大受欢迎的。

a. This class of merchandize <u>is</u> warmly <u>welcomed</u> (过去分词，被动语态) in the European market.

b. This class of merchandize <u>has been enjoying</u> wide popularity (现在完成进行时) in the European market.

125. 你们的交货日期我们不能接受，请尽量提前到 5 月底。

Your delivery date is unacceptable. Please <u>try your best to move</u> (动词不定式，作宾语) it <u>up</u> (宾语补足语) to the end of May.

126. 如果你们要订货，必须尽快作出决策，否则一定会失之交臂。

If you intend <u>to place</u> (不定式作宾语) an order, you <u>must make up your mind</u> (情态动词+原形动词作复合谓语) immediately, otherwise you <u>will let slip</u> (将来时) such a golden opportunity.

127. 由于原材料的不确定性，我们不能接受任何新的订单。

We <u>are</u> (系词)not <u>in a position</u> (表语) <u>to entertain</u> (不定式) any fresh orders <u>on account of</u> the uncertainty of raw materials.

128. 你方大力推销我方产品促成了你我之间的几笔生意。

You <u>have made</u> great efforts <u>in</u> (现在完成时) <u>pushing</u> (动名词作宾语) the sales of our products, <u>which has resulted</u> (现在完成时)<u>in some transactions between us</u>.(特殊定语从句)

129. 你方的迅速决定一定会给你方带来一笔赚钱的买卖。

Your quick decision <u>will</u> (将来时) certainly <u>bring</u> you some profitable <u>businesses</u>.

130. 目前我方库存有限，市场需求又很活跃，看来你方早日作出决策还是有必要的。

At present our <u>stock is limited</u> (过去分词，被动语态，现在时)(is low) and the market need <u>is</u> (系词) rather <u>brisk</u> (表语). It seems <u>that your early decision is quite necessary for you</u>.(表语从句)

131. 最大码黑色裤子已售罄，但有其他尺码可供选择。

The black trousers in the biggest size are all sold out, but the other sizes <u>are</u> all <u>waiting</u> (现在进行时，谓语) for your choosing.

132. 你方这次的试订单必然会使我们之间的生意继续进行和扩大，这将带来我们之间贸易额的迅速上升和贸易的蓬勃发展。

Your trail order of this time <u>will</u> certainly <u>result in</u> (将来时) the <u>continuing</u> (动名词作宾语) and <u>expanding</u> (动名词作宾语) of our business, <u>which</u> (特殊定语从句) <u>will bring</u> (一般将来时) about a quick increase to our turnover and <u>will lead to</u> (一般将来时) a brisk development of our business.

133. 买方敦促卖方在一个月内生产大量的产品。

   The seller <u>was pressed to manufacture</u> (被动语态，被迫做某事) a substantial quantity of products in one month.

134. 对此商品我们已做成了大量的交易。

   We <u>have done</u> considerable businesses (现在完成时) in this type of articles.

135. 这一品牌的丝绸女裙颜色鲜艳、设计美观，在国际市场上肯定会大受欢迎。

   This brand of silk blouses <u>are</u> brightly <u>colored</u> (过去分词表被动) and beautifully <u>designed</u> (过去分词表被动), <u>which will surely meet</u> (将来时) <u>with great favour in the international market</u> (特种定语从句).

136. 我们深信这种绣花台布在国内外都会十分适销。

   a. We deeply believe that such kind of <u>embroidered</u> (过去分词作定语，表被动) tablecloth <u>will</u> (将来时) surely <u>be</u> (系词) <u>salable</u> (表语) both at home and abroad.

   b. We <u>have deep</u> (现在时) <u>confidence in</u> the salability of such kind of <u>embroidered</u> (过去分词作定语表被动) tablecloth both at home and abroad.

   c. We <u>are</u> (系词) <u>deeply confident</u> (表语) of the salability of…

137. 有否可能把数量增加到100公吨？

   Is <u>it</u> (形式主语) possible <u>to increase</u> (动词不定式，it 的逻辑主语) the quantity to 100 metric ton?

   (增加到多少，用 "to"，指增加的终点)

138. 有否可能把数量增加20公吨？

   Is <u>it</u> (形式主语) possible <u>to increase</u> (不定式逻辑主语) the quantity <u>by</u> 20 metric ton?
   (增加多少用 "by")

139. 你方采取必要的步骤加快订货将会使你方在这次交易中获利更多。

   Your <u>taking</u> (动名词作主语) the necessary steps in <u>pushing</u> (动名词作宾语) your prompt <u>ordering</u> (动名词，宾语) will <u>make</u> your <u>profits</u> (宾语)<u>increased in</u> (过去分词，被动语态，作宾语补足语) doing this transaction.

140. 请尽快给我方回信，以便我方为你方保留这些产品。

   Please <u>reply</u> (命令句) us your acceptability at your earliest convenience <u>for our reserving</u> (动名词作宾语与 for 一起作目的状语) these articles for you.

141. 我们利用这次市场坚挺的机会为我们的公司订购了大批的货物。

   We <u>have availed</u> (现在完成时) ourselves of this opportunity of the <u>advancing</u> (现在分词，定语) market <u>to place</u> (不定式，目的状语) a large quantity of goods for our corporation.

142. 利用现在的坚挺市场，我方将向你方订一大笔钢板的货。

   <u>Taking advantage</u> (分词作目的状语或条件状语) of the present strengthening market

we shall place with you a substantial order for steel plates.

143. 你们不必期望货物不予售出的可能性。

It is not necessary for you to expect the likelihood of the goods' being (动名词被动语态作宾语，goods' 为后面动名词的逻辑主语) unsold.

(being unsold 为动名词的被动语态，前面是逻辑主语 goods')

144. 感谢你方为我方利益着想提出如此良好的建议。

Thank you for your offering (动名词作宾语) us such good suggestion in our interest.

145. 我方愿意尽一切努力劝说我方用户将他们的购货转向你方。

We are (系词) willing to do (表语) every effort to persuade (不定式作目的状语) our users to divert (动词不定式，作宾语补足语) their purchases to you.

146. 通过长期的函电往来，达成首笔交易的日子终于来临，使我们的心情大为轻松愉快。

Through protracted exchanges of correspondence, the day of our finalizing this initial transaction has at last come, which (特种定语从句) made us both pleased and relaxed.

147. 他们的用户转而从我方购货，为此我们很高兴，因为这次的生意谈成与否不仅牵涉到赚钱多少的问题，而且也牵涉到我们能否在此地开辟贸易新战场的问题。

Their users' diverting (动名词) their purchases to our side made (将来时) us rather pleased (过去分词，作宾语补足语), because the finalizing (动名词作主语) of this transaction involves not only the problem of how much money we can win (宾语从句), but also the problem (宾语) of our opening up a new battle (动名词作宾语) field of trading in this area.

148. 由于库存短缺，这次我方不能接受你方如此量大的订单，特致歉意。

Owing to the shortage of stock, this time we are unable to accept (谓语) such large orders of yours. Please accept our apology.

149. 眼下原材料涨价，供应情况不稳定，接受你方如此大量的订单将使我方冒不能及时交货的风险。

At present, the prices of raw materials have been (现在完成时，过去分词，被动语态) raised and the supply conditions have been staying (现在完成进行时，现在分词) with uncertainty. To accept (不定式，宾语) your such large orders will make us involved (过去分词作宾语补足语) in the risk of being unable to (动名词作宾语) make the punctual delivery of the goods.

150. 由于此女裙绣花图案的风格适合当地客户的口味，毫无疑问，它们一定会马上在北欧地区得到惊人的速销。

Due to the suitableness of the embroidery designing (现在分词，定语) style of the skirts to the taste of the local customers, there will be no doubt that they will (将来时) immediately get surprisingly fast sale in the northern European district.

151. 我们之间的业务关系悠久而且融洽，商务发展前景光明，因此请放心，仓库里一旦有存货，我方将重谈此事，并立即传真你方。

The business relationship between us is (系词) both long-standing (现在分词作表语)

and perfect and the prospect for our business development is brilliant. So please <u>rest sure</u> (命令句) <u>that</u> (状语从句，表方面(特殊)) as soon as the supplies come into stock, we <u>will,</u> (将来时) certainly, <u>revert to</u> (动词原形，命令句) this matter and <u>fax</u> (动词原形，将来时)you immediately.

152. 一旦原材料来源稳定，我方将立即恢复正常生产，之后就有能力接受大批新订单。

Once the source of our raw materials supplying <u>comes to</u> (动名词，作宾语) its stable position, we <u>will restore</u> (将来时) our normal production and then we <u>will be</u> (将来时) <u>able to accept</u> large hatches of fresh orders.

153. 对你方寄来的样布剪样，我方甚感满意，但对你方产品品牌我方用户不太熟悉，建议你方多做广告和销售方面的工作，以便立足于我方市场。

We <u>are</u> (系词) quite <u>satisfied with</u> (过去分词作表语) your sample <u>cuttings</u> (动名词转为名词) you sent us, but our customers <u>are not</u> (系词) quite <u>familiar with</u> (形容词，表语) your brand. We suggest you <u>to do</u> (不定式，宾语) much work in your advertising and <u>canvassing</u> (动名词，宾语) in order to <u>get a footing</u> (名词) in our market.

154. 我方已订购30公吨苦杏仁，CIF，上海到岸，每公斤×××美元，9月发运。

We <u>have ordered</u> (现在完成时) for 30 metric tons of Bitter Apricot Kernel, at US ××× per mt CIF Shanghai, for shipment in September.

155. 我方很高兴地确认已与你方达成了1000台计算机的生意。

We <u>are</u> (系词) <u>pleased</u> (过去分词) <u>to confirm having</u> (不定式表状语，表方面，原因) <u>concluded with</u> (动名词作宾语) you a transaction of 1,000 sets of computers.

156. 你方必须执行我们之间的首次订单，否则我们之间的贸易发展将受到影响。

<u>It</u> (形式主语) is necessary for you <u>to execute</u> (逻辑主语) satisfactorily your first order between us, otherwise the development of the trade between us <u>will be affected</u> (过去分词，将来时，谓语，被动语态).

157. 仔细审查你方昨天寄来的布样之后，我方发现你方印花府绸的质量是一流的，这引起了我方从你方购买这种印花府绸的兴趣。

After perusal of your cloth sample <u>sent</u> (过去分词，被动语态，定语) by you yesterday we found the quality of your <u>printed</u> (过去分词，定语，被动语态) poplin <u>is</u> (系词) <u>of first class</u> (表语), <u>which</u> (特种定语从句) attracts our <u>interest in purchasing</u> (动名词作宾语) this <u>printed</u> (过去分词，定语) poplin from you.

158. 我方在此通知你方，如果你方可以按所提供价格现货供应下列项目，我方愿意向你方订货。

Here we inform you that we <u>are willing to place</u> (谓语) order with you for the following items <u>on the understanding</u> (动名词作宾语)(在理解，知道……之后) that they <u>will be supplied</u> (过去分词，被动语态，将来时，谓语) from stock at the <u>mentioned</u> (过去分词作定语，被动语态) prices.

(on the understanding that...如果……，以……为条件)

159. 我方很高兴地确认，已订购下你方1000吨钢板。

We <u>are pleased</u> (谓语) <u>to confirm having booked</u> (完成式动名词，作宾语) your order for 1,000 tons of steel plates.

160. 关于××号合同的执行问题，请迅速给我方寄来你方销售确认书。

Referring to (分词，常用语，涉及) the executing (动名词，宾语) of the Contract No. ××, please immediately send us your Sales Confirmation.

161. 你方也许会有兴趣知道，此地对我方绣花制品的需求量甚大，而且销售价格也高于欧洲市场。

You may (谓语) be interested in (过去分词，被动语态) knowing (动名词，宾语) that there is a brisk demand for our embroidered (过去分词，定语，被动语态) makes, and the prices are higher than those in the European market.

162. ××的平均年产量达××吨。

The average annual output of ×× amounts to (数量达到，谓语) ×× tons.

163. 此事涉及一系列问题，如专利、设备定价、产品销售额等。

This matter involves a series of problems, such as patent, equipment pricing (动名词，可看作同位语，指 pricing 等), product sales volume, etc.

164. 这批产品的质量一定会使你方大为满意，并带来双方之间订单的大量增加。

The quality of these shipments will surely meet with your satisfaction and lead to a great increase of our orders.

165. 我方检验了你方棉衬衫的规格及价格单后十分想向你方订货。

After examining (动名词，宾语) the specifications and the pricelist of your cotton shirts, we wish very much to place orders (宾语) with you.

166. 你方是否能尽快拟制订单，并于一两天之内给我们寄来，以便我们及早组织生产？

Is it (形式主语) possible for you to make up (形式主语) your order sheet as soon as possible and send us in a couple of days in order to enable (目的状语，不定式) us to organize (不定式，宾语补足语) our manufacturing? (动名词，宾语)

167. 今天我方传真你方，希望你方抓紧市场坚挺的机会并迅速作出决策，立即向我方订货。

Today we have faxed you in the hope of your seizing (动名词，宾语) firmly the opportunity of the strengthening (现在分词，定语) market and promptly making (动名词，宾语) your decision to place orders (不定式，目的状语) with us.

168. 我们一贯尊重合同，遵守信用，这对每个企业来说都是十分重要的。

We always abide by (谓语) the contract and keep good faith, these two points are very important for every enterprise.

169. 我们保证准时执行你方订单。

We assure you of our punctual shipment of your order.

170. 我们将妥善、迅速地处理这一订单。

Our best and prompt attention will be given to (将来时，过去分词，被动语态) the execution of this order.

171. 这些衣服的设计图案和你方样衣的设计图案不一致。

The design of these dresses do not match with (否定式，谓语) that of your sample.

172. 重新制作这些衣服是为了保证使其质量达到合同规定，此点可以证明我方对产品供货方面的要求是很严格的。

Remaking (动名词，主语) these dresses is (系词) to ensure (表语，不定式) their quality's keeping (动名词，宾语补足语) in accordance with (按照，根据，词组，表语) the stipulations of the contract, which shows our strict requirements to our product supplying(动名词，宾语).

173. 上个月新产品促销的收入款项达 200 万英镑。

The proceeds of the promotion of the new products last month amounted to £2,000,000.

174. 工程项目的一些部分在合同规定中有详细规定，虽然在图纸中没有注明，承包商也应执行。

Some parts of the project which have been stipulated in (现在完成时，被动语态) the contract but have not been shown (现在完成时，被动语态) in the drawings, should be performed (过去分词，被动语态，谓语) by the contractor as well.

175. 如果质量不合格，我方有权拒收，如退回你方，费用由你方负担。

We have the right to reject (不定式，定语) the goods in case they are (系词) unqualified (表语)(过去分词，被动语态) and return (前面省略 to，不定式作 right 的定语) them to you, the expense will be born (将来时，被动语态) by you.

176. 我方愿意了解你方关于进行业务的条件条款信息。

We would like to receive (动名词，宾语) your information on your terms and conditions of business conducting.

177. 每天需要处理的大批信函使我们从早到晚忙忙碌碌，以致耽误回信，实在抱歉。

A great number of correspondences necessary (形容词，定语)to be dealt (动词不定式，表方面，原因) with everyday make us bustling in and (现在分词，宾语补足语) out from morning till night, resulting in (现在分词，结果状语) our delay in replying (动名词) your letter. Please accept our apology.

178. 你方确认这些条件条款以后，我们将起草正式协议并在北京签订。

We would draw up (将来一定会做……)a formal agreement on receipt of your confirmation of these terms and conditions and sign (谓语，前面省略 would) it in Beijing.

179. 我方认为你方最好在专业杂志上广泛宣传你方的商品。

It (形式主语) appears to us that (逻辑主语从句) you had better give wide publicity to your commodities in the specialized (过去分词作定语) journals.

180. 我方将在我方展览室展览你方全部产品，并随时向来访者演示对设备的操作。

We shall exhibit all of your products in our showrooms and demonstrate the operation of the equipment to the visitors at all times.

181. 这份协议草案极不完善，需要修订。

This draft agreement leaves (现在分词，谓语，单数第三人称) much (形容词，名词) to be desired (不定式，被动语态，定语) and needs to be improved (不定式，被动语

态，宾语).

182. 协议草案现附寄于此，请提意见，并尽快返回，以便定稿。

Enclosed (表语) here is (系词) the draft agreement (主语) for your comments. Please return us as soon as possible for our finalization.

183. 我们打算按优惠条款向你方订一些家用电器。

We intend to place (不定式，宾语) some orders for household electric apparatus on favorable terms.

184. 有关商业当局已批准了贵公司的营业执照。

The relative commercial authorities have already approved (现在完成时) the business license of your corporation.

185. 如有发现任何损坏或不正常的情况，请立即通知我方，以使我方放心。

In case (动名词，宾语) of your finding any damage or unusual conditions, please inform (命令句) us at once in order to make (不定式，目的状语) us rest assured (过去分词，固定用法，作宾语补足语).

186. 以不可撤销的信用证进行付款是我方的惯例。

It (形式主语) is our usual practice (custom) to effect (逻辑主语) payment by irrevocable L/C.

187. 这个信用证必须修改，否则我方无法议付汇票。

This L/C must be amended (复合谓语，被动语态), otherwise we will not be able to negotiate our draft.

188. 你方进口许可证已经得到我方有关当局批准。

Your Import License has been approved (现在完成时，被动语态) by our relative authority.

189. 我方很高兴通知你方，你方信用证已经到达我方。

We are pleased to inform you that your letter of credit has already reached us here.

190. 一旦我方得到进口许可证和外汇，我方将立即寄出以你方为收益人的不可撤销的信用证。

Once (习惯用法) have we got (现在完成时，主语放 have 后时间状语从句或条件状语从句) our import license and foreign exchanges, we shall send you immediately our irrevocable L/C in your favor (以你方为收益人). (以 Once 开头的句子，其主语与助动词倒装)

191. 至于上述货物，我方准备给你方寄去一式两份的形式发票，你方可凭此形式发票向当局申请进口许可证。

As to the above-mentioned (过去分词，被动语态，定语) goods, we are sending (现在分词，现在进行时，表很近的将来) you our proforma invoice in duplicate, with which (which 前有介词的定语从句 which 定形式发展) you can apply to your relative authorities for import licence.

192. 鉴于我们之间长期的(悠久的)贸易关系，这次我们给予你们分期付款的优惠条款。

In view of our long-standing (现在分词，定语) business relations we offer (谓语) you our favourable terms of installment payment this time.

193. 根据规定的条款条件，我们将于一周之内开立以你方为收益人的信用证。

According to the stipulated (过去分词，定语) terms and conditions we should establish (复合谓语) our L/C in your favour within one week.

194. 我们将设法给你们分期付款的优惠条件。

We shall see our way of giving (动名词，宾语) you the favorable terms of installment payment.

195. 考虑到你方原材料供应的困难，我方同意将交货日期推迟两周。

Taking (现在分词，条件状语，原因状语) your difficulty in getting (动名词，宾语) the raw materials into consideration, we agree to postpone your delivery date for two weeks.

196. 我方深信你方一定会准时交货的。

We are deeply convinced of (过去分词，表语) your delivery on time.

197. 我方希望你方立刻修改信用证，以使我方在8月交货。

a. We hope you to amend (不定式，宾语) the L/C immediately to enable us to deliver the goods in August.

b. We are (系词) very desirous of (表语) your immediately amending (动名词，宾语) of the L/C to enable us to (不定式，宾语补足语) make August delivery.

198. 我方欲知承兑交单的付款条件你方是否同意，请传真回复。

We would like to be informed (不定式，宾语，被动语态) whether the payment terms of D/A would be (系词) agreeable to (表语) you. Please reply us by fax.

199. 新税法要到明年才生效。

The new tax law will not take effect (将来时，否定) until next year.

200. 必须充分理解，我们这样做是下不为例的(不是在创造先例)。

It (形式主语) must be (复合谓语，被动语态) clearly understood that in doing (动名词，宾语) this we are (形式主语，从句) not creating (现在进行时，谓语，否定) (establishing) any precedent.

201. 我们通常是不接受远期信用证的，但这次你们订单量大，交货期也不是太急，所以经多次研究之后，决定破例给予你们接受远期信用证支付的优惠条款。

Usually we don't accept (谓语) time L/C, but this time your order is rather large and the delivery date is as well not so close (谓语，否定), so after many times' considerations we have decided (现在完成时) to grant (不定式，宾语) you our favourable terms of payment effecting (动名词，宾语), that is (补充说明) by time L/C as an exception.

202. 由于资金占压很大，造成我方经济拮据。

Owing to the funds' being tied up (动名词，被动语态，定语，funds'为其逻辑主语) in numerous amounts our funds are rather tightened (过去分词，被动语态).

203. 经济不景气及银行利率很高也是造成我方经济上发生严重问题的原因。

The difficult economic climate and the prevailing (现在分词) high interest rates are the causes of <u>bringing about</u> (动名词，宾语) our serious economic problem (are the causes of bringing about the serious problem in our economy).

204. 要求较为宽容的付款条件会帮助我们减轻经济压力。

　　The easier payment terms <u>will help</u> us (to) <u>lighten</u> (过去分词，宾语补足语) our economic pressure.

205. 上述提议实在也是我们不得已而为之的。

　　We <u>have</u> no alternative choice but <u>suggest the above-mentioned</u> (过去分词，定语) proposal.

206. 我们别无他法，只得提出如此建议。

　　We <u>are left no choice</u> (leave 的被动语态，谓语) but propose such suggestion.

207. 如蒙你方理解，我方十分感激。

　　We would very appreciate <u>it</u> (形式宾语，逻辑上指 if…的内容) if we could get your <u>understanding</u>(动名词，宾语).

208. 作为一项特殊照顾，我们这次接受 30 天的远期信用证。但必须认为这仅是一种例外，不是未来贸易的先例。

　　As a special accommodation, we accept time L/C at 30 days. But <u>it</u> (形式主语) <u>must be considered</u> (复合谓语，被动语态) only as an exception, not a precedent for future business.

209. 希望我们的拒绝改变付款条件不至于影响我们之间良好的贸易关系。

　　We hope our refusal of <u>changing</u> (动名词，宾语) our payment terms will not affect the good trade relations between us.

210. 很抱歉，改变我们的付款条件意味着改变我们的贸易惯例，这是十分困难的，希望谅解。

　　We regret to say that <u>to change</u> (不定式作主语)our terms of payment means <u>to change</u> (不定式作宾语) our usual practice in <u>trading</u> (动名词，宾语), <u>which</u> (特殊定语从句) would involve us in quite great trouble. We have to express our apology to you.

211. 我方将开立金额为××美元的信用证。

　　We will establish an L/C in the amount of US $××.

212. 我方将寄给你方金额为××美元的发票。

　　We will send you our invoice in the amount of US $××.

213. 我方将向你们订一笔金额为××美元的货。

　　We will place an order with you for the amount of US $××.

214. 我们必须弄清楚，接受凭单付款的方式只是鉴于我们之间长期互利的友好关系而已。

　　We should make <u>it</u> (形式宾语) clear <u>that payment against document is made only in the light of our long and mutually beneficial relationship</u>. (宾语从句作 it 形式宾语的逻辑宾语)

215. 感谢你方 10 月 2 日对 374 及 375 号合同请求凭单付款表示同意的来信。

　　Thank you for your letter of 2 October, <u>agreeing with</u> (现在分词作原因状语) the

Payment Against Documents (D/P) for Contracts No. 374 and No. 375.

216. 如果每笔交易涉及的金额不超过 1000 美元或 1000 美元的相对兑换率的等值的人民币，就可以采用凭单付款方式。此为例外，绝非先例。

If the amount <u>involved</u> (过去分词作定语) in each transaction is less than (is no more than) US$ 1,000 or the equivalent in RMB, payment against documents will be available. It <u>is</u> (系词) <u>effected</u> (表语) only as an exception, not a precedent.

217. 100 美元按现行兑换率折合多少人民币？

What is the equivalent of US$ 100 in RMB in present exchange rate?

218. 接到我方汇票，请你方立即支付。

You <u>must pay</u> our draft when we present it.

219. 上述付款条款已获得我方出口部门批准。

The above-mentioned payment terms <u>have been approved</u> (现在完成时，被动语态) by our Export Department.

220. 信用证的任何修改必须在发货以前进行，不然出口商就要冒汇票遭银行拒收的风险。

Any amendment of L/C <u>should be</u> (谓语) made <u>in advance of</u> the shipment of the goods, otherwise the exporter would <u>run the risk</u> of the draft's <u>being dishonoured</u> (动名词，被动语态，宾语) by the bank.

(honour v. 履行，照付；the drafts being dishoured 逻辑主语+动名词的被动语态)

221. 检查之后，发现信用证条款有差错，请将"不允许分批装运和转船"改为"允许分批装运及转船"。

On examination, we have found some discrepancies in your L/C terms. Please amend "With partial shipments and transshipment <u>prohibited</u>" (过去分词，被动语态，宾语补足语) as "<u>Allowing</u> (动名词，主动，宾语) partial shipments and transshipment".

222. 我方已收到你方 No. ×××信用证，但发现其中有下列不符之处。

We have received your L/C No. ××, but have found it <u>containing</u> (现在分词,宾语补足语，指 L/C No. ××) the following discrepancies.

223. 我方很遗憾地通知你方，信用证的某些地方和合同条款规定不符。

We <u>are</u> (系词) <u>regretful</u> (表语) <u>to inform</u> (不定式，原因状语或方面，特殊) you that certain points <u>are not in conformity with</u> (过去分词，定语) the terms stipulated in the contract.

224. 差错如下：

The discrepancies <u>are</u> (系词) as follows:(形容词，表语)

(1) 佣金 2%，非 3%。

Commission should be 2% , not 3%.

(2) 货物应于 5/6 月期间装运，不是 6 月 30 日或 6 月 30 日前。

Shipment is <u>to be made</u> (表语,不定式,被动语态) during May / June instead of " on or before 30 June".

(3) 货物应按发票金额的 110%投保，而不是 130%。

Goods <u>should be insured</u> (现在分词，被动语态) for 110% of the invoice value, not 130%.

225. 请将你方×××号信用证作如下修改：

Please amend your L/C No. ×××　as follows:

(1)　删除 1、3、5 项，代之以 NO. ×××　合同中所规定的 2、4、9 项。

Delete Items 1, 3, and 5, replace them with the items 2, 4, and 9 <u>stipulated</u> (过去分词，定语，被动语态) in the Contract No. ×××.

(2)　将单价从 6.8 美元增至 7.3 美元，总金额增至××美元。

<u>Increase</u> (原形动词，命令句) the unit price from US$ 6.80 to US$ 7.30 and the total amount to US$ ×××.

226. 我方十分焦急，不知你方是否同意信用证延期两周，我方期待你方回信。

We <u>are</u> (系词)very <u>anxious</u> (表语) about your agreement upon the two weeks' L/C extension. We are expecting your reply.

227. 我方今天发来此传真，目的是催促你方同意并答复我方要求推迟××号信用证有效期三周之事。

Today we send you this fax, <u>urging</u> (现在分词，目的状语) you <u>to agree</u> (不定式，宾语补足语) and <u>to reply</u> (不定式，宾语补足语) to our request of <u>extending</u> (动名词，宾语) the validity term of the L/C No. ×××　for 3 weeks.

228. 如果你方要求延长信用证期限，你方必须清楚诚恳地说明原因，以便首先取得进口商的谅解，然后取得其同意。

If you want to ask for the L/C extention, you must state your reasons clearly and sincerely <u>in order to</u> (目的状语，不定式) firstly get the importer's <u>understanding</u> (动名词，宾语) and then secondly <u>get</u> (省略 to，不定式，目的状语) the promise from him.

229. 要求延长信用证期限的原因可能是主观的，如货源不足、生产事故、运输脱节等；也可能是客观的，如自然灾害、社会动乱或进口商未能及时开立并发出信用证等。

The reasons for <u>asking</u> (动名词，宾语) L/C extension may be subjective, such as, the shortage of material sources, the accidents in production, <u>disjointing</u> (动名词，宾语)in transport, etc. And they may as well be objective, for example, natural disasters, social disturbances or the importer's <u>not being able to</u> (动名词，前面 disasters 等的同位语，举例) establish and to send his L/C in time, etc.

230. 请查阅你方××号信用证，该信用证规定不允许转船。

We refer you to your L/C No. ××, <u>which</u> (定语，指 L/C No. ××) prescribes that transshipment <u>is not allowed</u> (过去分词，被动语态，谓语).

231. 请尽快寄来信用证修改书，以免耽搁我方准时发货。

Please send us your L/C amendment with the least possible delay (<u>to avoid</u> (不定式，目的状语) the <u>delaying of</u> (动名词，宾语)) our punctual shipment.

232. 为了保证质量，请你方务必同意展延信用证的发货日期——从 7 月 5 日展延到 8 月 15 日。

In view of <u>ensuring</u> (动名词，宾语) the quality, we request your agreement on your

L/C extending (动名词，宾语) of the shipment date—from 15, July to 15, August.

233. 重新生产这些产品需要三周时间，务必请你方理解我方的困难，同意将信用证延期三周。

Reproducing (动名词，主语) these products needs a period of 3 weeks, we beg (谓语) your understanding (动名词，宾语) of our difficulties and offer (动名词，谓语) us your agreement to the L/C's extending (动名词，宾语) of 3 weeks.

234. 我方愿意你方按照规定开立信用证，以便我们双方能够维持友好的贸易关系。

We would prefer that you issue your L/C as stipulated (过去分词，被动语态，方式状语) so that we could continue (谓语，目的状语，从句)our friendly business relations.

235. 我们有责任通知你方，再次延期信用证是不可能的。

We feel it (形式宾语) our duty to inform (不定式，逻辑宾语) you that extending (动名词，主语) this L/C again is impossible.

236. 你方想要再一次延长信用证期限是不可能的，你们再次拖延发货肯定会大为影响我们之间未来的贸易，请慎重考虑。

Your intension of repeatedly extending (动名词，宾语) of the L/C is (系词) impossible (表语) to be realized (不定式，方面，被动) and your repeated delays in shipping (动名词，宾语) the goods will greatly affect the future transactions between us. We wish you to make your serious considerations.

237. 我方为耽误发货而致歉，并为你方修改信用证而致谢。

We apologize for our delay in shipment and thank you very much for your L/C amendment.

238. 你方可通过中国银行西安分行议付我方汇票。

You can negotiate our draft through the Xi'an Branch of the Bank of China.

239. 我方答应你方尽全力加速开立信用证。

You may have our assurance (名词) that we shall do our utmost to establish the L/C.(定语从句)

240. 你方信用证少开 US$ ×××。

Your L/C is (系词) short (表语)-opened to the amount of US$ ×××.

241. 本次订货的我方佣金少算×× 英镑。

Our commission on this order is (系词) short-calculated (过去分词，被动语态，表注意) by ￡××.

242. 这批货物的发票少开 RMB ￥×××。

The shipment is (系词) short-invoiced (过去分词，被动语态，表注意) by RMB ￥×××.

243. 我方发现你方信用证少开 US$ 100。

We have found your L/C short-opened (过去分词，被动语态，宾语补足语) to the amount of US$ 100.

244. 随函附上我方×××号贷方通知，这是我方少付的 US$ ×××。

Enclosed (表语) is (系词) our Credit (主语) Note No. ××× for our short-paid (过

去分词，被动语态，定语) amount of US$ ×××.

245. 请清偿这笔未清的账目，勿再拖延。

Please settle this long <u>outstanding account</u> (现在分词，定语) without further delay.

246. 我方附寄支票一份，清偿所欠全部佣金。

We enclose a check in settlement of all <u>commission owing</u> (动名词，宾语).

247. 我方对在信用证中所犯的错误致以最深切的歉意。

Let us <u>tender</u> (宾语补足语，省略 to) our deepest apology to you for the mistakes <u>made</u> (过去分词，被动语态，定语) in our L/C.

248. 5%的保付货款佣金是否能使你方满意？

Will 5% of del credere commission make you <u>satisfied</u>? (过去分词，宾语补足语，被动语态)

249. 只有得到订货人的付款之后我方才支付佣金。

Commission <u>will be paid</u> only <u>after we have received</u> (现在完成时) <u>payments from the customers</u>. (时间状语从句)

250. 支付佣金的货币只能是订货人支付的货币。

The commission payments will <u>be effected</u> (将来时，被动语态，谓语) only in the currency of the payments from the customers.

251. 我方付款条件为凭单付现，你方对此定会欣然接受。

Our terms of payment <u>are</u> (系词) <u>cash against documents</u> (表语). We think you <u>will</u> (助动词，将来时) certainly <u>be</u> (系词) <u>agreeable</u> (表语) to it.

252. 我方在付款条件方面的通常做法是要求即期信用证。

As to our payment terms, our usual practice is <u>to ask</u> (不定式，表语) for sight L/C.

253. 我方信用证的有效期截止到 8 月 30 日，请千万注意。

Our L/C will expire on 30 August, <u>to which</u> (which 前带介词的定语从句，which 指整个前句为特殊定语从句) you <u>must pay</u> (复合谓语) close attention.

254. 我方的按时发货将使你方完全满意。

Our punctual shipment will give you entire satisfaction.

255. 我方坚持你方按原规定日期交货。

We insist on your <u>delivering</u> (动名词，宾语) the goods <u>according</u> (介词) to the <u>stipulated</u> (过去分词，被动语态，宾语) time.

256. 如果你方能在收到我方订单以后一个月之内交货，协助我方及时完成项目建设，我方深信我们双方之间的贸易关系将得到大大的巩固和发展。

a. <u>Should</u> you <u>be able to effect</u> delivery within one month after <u>receiving</u> (动名词，宾语) our order and help us <u>to fulfill</u> (不定式，宾语补足语) our project construction in time, we <u>would</u> (表愿望) deeply believe that the trade relationship between our two parties would be greatly <u>strengthened</u> (过去分词，被动语态，谓语) and developed. (条件从句中句首 if 省略，主语 you 与 should 倒装；主句谓语用 would，表示"一定"的意思)

b. If you <u>should</u> (条件句) be able… we would <u>be</u> (系词) deeply <u>confident</u> (表语) that the…

257. 我方很高兴地知悉我方所订购的货物已由你方发运。

We are glad to know (不定式，原因) that the goods we ordered (过去分词，被动语态，谓语) have already been dispatched (现在完成时，被动语态) by you.

258. 这些货物受损是由于野蛮装运所引起。

The damage of these goods was resulted (过去分词，被动语态) from rough handling (动名词，宾语).

259. 我方很高兴通知你方，你方上个月的订货已由东风号轮船发出。

We take the pleasure of informing (动名词，宾语) you that the (宾语从句) goods you ordered last month (过去分词，被动语态，定语) have already been shipped (现在完成时，被动语态) by "East Wind".

260. 分批装船和转船是不允许的。

a. Transshipment and partial shipments are not allowed (过去分词，被动语态).

b. Transshipment and partial shipments are not permitted (过去分词，被动语态).

c. Transshipment and partial shipments are prohibited (过去分词，被动语态).

261. 鉴于忙季来临，你方必须加快你方的交货步伐。

Considering (现在分词，原因状语) the approaching (动名词，宾语) of the busy season it (形式主语) is necessary for you to step up (逻辑主语) (to rush) your delivery.

262. 我们无法再加快交货。

We can't see our way clear (成语) to advance (不定式，目的状语) our delivery.

263. 发运方面的任何延误都会有损于我们未来的交易。

Any delay in shipment would be harmful to our future transactions.

264. 依照规定的条款条件，你方不经我方同意，自行改变我方要求的运输唛头是违反合同规定的。

In compliance with the stipulated (过去分词，被动语态，定语) terms and conditions your changing (动名词，主语) the shipping (动名词，表性质，用途) marks required (过去分词，被动语态，定语) by us without our agreement has infringed (现在完成时) the rule of the contract.

265. 我方从政府当局获得进口许可证的批准需要较长时间，所以你方最好从现在起就开始生产制造方面的组织工作，这样你方就能够在得到我方获得进口许可证的信息后很快进行交货。这就像中国谚语所说的："磨刀不误砍柴工。"

It (形式主语) will take a considerable time for us to get (不定式，逻辑主语) the approval of the import license from the governmental authorities. So it (形式主语) is better for you to start (不定式，逻辑主语) the manufacturing (动名词，表性质，方面) organization work from now on in order to enable (目的状语) you to effect the delivery of the goods as soon as you get the information on our obtaining (动名词，宾语) the import license. This is just like the so-called (过去分词，被动语态) Chinese proverb "Grinding (动名词，主语) a chopper will not hold up the work of cutting (动名词，宾语) firewood." (或者 "Chopper grinding (动名词，宾语) should not delay the firewood <u>cutting</u>(动名词，宾语，目的或条件状语从句").)

266. 请特别注意货物的包装，以免货物在运输途中损坏。

Please <u>pay special attention to</u> (原形动词，命令句) the <u>packing</u> (动名词，宾语) of the goods, lest the goods <u>should be damaged</u> (过去分词，被动语态，谓语) during transit.

267. 我们希望你们能在规定时间内准时交货。

We hope your punctual delivery of the goods <u>will be effected</u> (过去分词，被动语态，谓语) within the <u>prescribed</u> (过去分词，被动语态，定语) time.

268. 我方有信心按时发运，使你方完全满意。

We <u>are</u> (系词) <u>confident</u> (表语) <u>that we would effect punctual shipment to your entire satisfaction.</u>(状语从句，表原因或方面)

269. 需要强调的是，运输唛头的印刷必须符合我方的要求。

Emphasis <u>must be laid</u> (过去分词，被动语态) on the point <u>that</u> (定语从句) the <u>printing</u> (动名词，主语) of the shipping marks <u>should be kept</u> (过去分词，被动语态，谓语) in accordance with our requirements.

270. 这批货是两种不同的货物组成，将立即包装并发往你方目的港。请做好验收工作。

This shipment is <u>made up</u> (现在时，被动语态) of two different kinds of articles, <u>which</u> (定语从句) will be immediately <u>packed</u> and <u>dispatched</u> (过去分词，谓语，被动语态) to your destination port. Please <u>make</u> (命令句) your preparation to do your <u>accepting</u> and <u>inspecting</u> (动名词，定语，表性质，方面) work well.

271. 因为市场上对此产品的需求量很大很急，预订舱位也十分困难，如果你方不提前做好准备，我方将无法实现按时交货。

There is a great and urgent <u>need</u> (主语，名词) of this article in the market and <u>booking shipping</u> (动名词，主语) space will as well meet with great difficulty. So in case of your not <u>making</u> (动名词，宾语) an early preparation, our punctual delivery <u>will not be realized</u> (否定，将来时).

272. 一旦你方将货物备妥待运，舱位也已订妥，请即电邮我方，我方当立即电汇全部货款。

As soon as you get your goods ready for shipment and make your freight space <u>booked</u> (过去分词，宾语补足语), <u>please E-mail</u> (原型动词，谓语，命令句)us at once and we <u>will</u> immediately <u>remit</u> (将来时，谓语) you our full amount by T/T (Telegraphic Transfer).

273. 为确保一切程序的进行，请再三确认已完成安装及尚未完成安装的机器之间的缺口。

<u>In order to ensure</u> (不定式，目的状语) <u>the carrying</u> (动名词，宾语) out of all the processes, please <u>make sure</u> (原形动词，命令句) again and again the gap between the <u>installed</u> (过去分词，被动语态，定语) and the <u>uninstalled</u> (过去分词，被动语态，定语) machines.

274. 知道已安装及未安装机器之间的缺口可以使我们了解还需要作出多大努力以及需要多长时间才能完成生产任务。

Knowing (动名词，主语) the gap between the installed and uninstalled machines will help (将来时) us (to) master (动词不定式，宾语补足语，to 可省略) how great efforts (名词) we should make and how long we should take to fulfill (不定式，目的状语)this production task.

275. 在装运订单货物方面的任何延误都将使我方陷入向客户交货的困境，这将会影响我公司的声誉。

Any delay in shipping (动名词，宾语) our order will involve (将来时)us in the trouble with the buyers, which (特种定语从句) would affect our firm standing (动名词转换为名词) and high reputation.

276. 我方等待你方早日回复。如蒙早日回复，我方将不胜感激。

We are waiting for (现在分词，现在进行时) your early reply, which (特种定语从句) will be highly appreciated (过去分词，被动语态，将来时) by us.

277. 我方习惯的做法是：将货物先运到香港，然后转船至伦敦。需花费的时间大约为两周。

Our usual practice is (系词) to ship (表语) the goods firstly to Hong Kong, then make (前面 to 省略，表语) a transshipment to London. It (表时间) takes about two weeks' time.

278. "波士顿"号于 5 月 3 日或 3 日左右到达你港，请注意到货通知。

SS "Boston" will arrive at your port on/about 3, May. Please pay attention (命令句，谓语) to the advice of the goods' arrival at the port.

279. 请在规定的时间内装运我方订货。

Please ship our order within the time prescribed (过去分词，被动语态，定语).

280. 衬衫用盒子包装，每盒两件。

Shirts are packed (过去分词，被动语态) in boxes of 2 pieces each.

281. 螺丝用木箱包装，每箱内装 100 盒。

Screws are packed in wooden cases, each containing (现在分词，状语，补充说明)100 boxes.

282. 每件衬衫装一个塑料袋，6 袋装一盒。

Each shirt is packed in a poly bag and 6 to a box.

283. 所有货物在包装前均已逐个检查，目的是使货物安然无恙地抵达你方目的港。

All items were individually examined (过去分词) before being packed (动名词，被动语态) with the purpose of their successful arrival at your destination port.

284. 货物到达你方目的港之后，希望你们立刻开箱验货。如发现任何损坏，请于 15 天之内通知我方。

After the goods' arrival at your destination port, we wish that you unpack and examine them. In case of any damage, please inform us within fifteen days. (宾语从句)

285. 你方立即进行装运与交货是我方最期望的事情了，希望你们立即处理此事。

Your prompt shipment and immediate delivery are the most desirable matters to us. We hope you will pay (将来时) your prompt attention to this matter.

286. 这批货必须在许可证期满前运到，否则你方即为违约。

This shipment must arrive here before the expiration of the license, otherwise you <u>will breach</u> (将来时) the contract.

287. 屡次完不成按时交货的任务会导致买方撤销订单。

<u>Not finishing</u> (动名词，否定，主语) the task of effecting prompt delivery repeatedly <u>will result</u> (将来时) in the <u>buyer's</u> (动名词的逻辑主语) canceling his order.

288. 我方已在前一封传真中通知你方，你方耽误发货将影响到我方设备的准时安装及按时投产。

As you have been informed in our last fax, your delay in shipment will affect our punctual installation of the equipment and as well the equipment's punctually going into operation.

289. 尽管我方再三提醒，你方还是没有妥善包装货物并按时交货，这使得我方陷入极大的困境之中。

In spite of our <u>repeated</u> (过去分词) reminders, you <u>are</u> still <u>failing in</u> (现在进行时，谓语) your good <u>packing</u> (动名词，宾语) and your punctual <u>delivering</u> (动名词，宾语) of our goods, <u>which involves us in great trouble</u>. (特定定语从句)

290. 我方用户出于对所订货物的需要，正催促我方保证及时供货，使我方不得不再三给你方发传真催货。

In view of the urgent need of their <u>ordered</u> (过去分词，定语) goods, our customers <u>are</u> now <u>pressing</u> (现在进行时，现在分词) us <u>to ensure</u> (否定式，宾语补足语) our punctual supplying of their items. So we <u>have to</u> (不得不) fax you repeatedly <u>to urge</u> (不定式，目的状语) you <u>to effect</u> (不定式，宾语补足语)your delivery.

291. 由于港口拥挤，我们未能为你方××号订单的货物订上舱位，因此十分焦急，担心这次我们会耽误货物发运，希望你方对此有所准备。

Owing to the congestion of the port, we <u>were not able to book</u> the <u>shipping</u> (动名词，表功能，性质，定语) space for the goods of your Order No. ××. So we are now very anxious about our possible delay in our shipment of the goods. We think you <u>must get</u> (过去分词，被动语态，谓语) prepared for this.

292. 一旦无法海运，可否改为部分空运、部分陆运？如你方同意，即请传真确认，并更改信用证有关条款。

Once if <u>it</u> (形式主语) will not be possible <u>to effect</u> (逻辑主语) maritime <u>transporting</u> (动名词，宾语) of the goods, how about <u>making</u> (动名词，宾语) partial air transportation and partial land transportation? In case of your agreement on <u>taking</u> (动名词，宾语) such measures, please <u>fax</u> (命令句) us your confirmation and <u>make</u> (命令句) amendments to the relative terms of the L/C.

293. 由于此笔交易是以装运港船上交货价格成交的，你方必须在纽约将货物装上我方指定的船只。

Since the purchase is made on FOB basis, please <u>arrange</u> (命令句，原形动词) the shipment of the goods from New York on our <u>designated</u> (过去分词，定语) ship.

294. 由于此货物的性质极易受到震动、潮湿及高温的影响，所以你方一定要对之采取三防包装，即防震、防潮、防爆。

As the nature of these goods <u>is</u> (系词) <u>susceptible</u>(表语) to shock, dampness and high temperature, <u>it</u> (形式主语) is necessary <u>to insure</u> (逻辑主语) them of the "three proofs" <u>packing</u> (动名词，宾语), that is, shock proof, damp proof and explosion proof.

295. 请在这些包装件上用金属模板印上"小心轻放"的字样。

Please print the <u>following</u> (形容词，定语) words on these packages with metal stencil: "<u>HANDLE WITH CARE.</u>"(命令，提醒)

296. 你方遵守这些发运指示定会减少货物在运输途中的损失，切盼。

Your observation of these <u>shipping</u> (动名词，定语，表性质，功能) instructions will certainly reduce the losses in transit.

297. 这里是一些有关搬运、装卸、起吊等方面的警告性标志，如：此端向上！小心搬运！保持干燥！此端开启！置于阴凉处！等等。

Here are some <u>warnings</u> (动名词，主语) for <u>handling</u>, <u>lifting</u>, <u>loading</u>, and <u>unloading</u>, etc.: (动名词，宾语)

THIS SIDE UP

HANDLE WITH CARE

KEEP DRY

OPEN THIS END

<u>TO BE</u> (不定式，被动语态) KEPT COOL

298. 如果你方发现有破碎或其他损坏，请立即告知我方。

If you find any breakage or other damages, please inform us at once.

299. 我方希望货物顺利到达你方，并能使你方满意。

<u>It</u> (形式主语) is our hope <u>that</u> (逻辑主语，被动语态) the goods <u>will reach</u> (将来时) you in good condition and <u>meet</u> (将来时，前面省略 will) your satisfaction.

300. 我方担心我方将不得不支付较大的指定包装的费用，因为它需要额外的劳动和费用。

We <u>are</u> (系词) <u>afraid</u> (表语) that we shall <u>have to</u> (将来时，状语从句，表原因，方面，不得不) charge more for the <u>designated</u> (过去分词，被动语态，定语) <u>packing</u> (动名词，宾语), <u>as it calls for extra labor and cost.</u> (原因状语从句)

301. 剩余的货物将于下月初由第一班便利轮船发运。

The remaining goods <u>are going to</u>(现在进行时，表将来) <u>be shipped</u> (过去分词，被动语态) by the first available steamer at the beginning of next month.

302. 如蒙你方通知我方有关货物包装的细节，我方即可拟制相应保险单，并尽快给你方寄去。

In case of your <u>informing</u> (动名词，宾语) us of the details of your shipment <u>packing</u>, (动名词，宾语) we <u>may make up</u> (谓语) relative policy accordingly and send it to you as soon as possible.

303. 你方耽误交货，已使我方陷入困境。

Your delay in delivery <u>has put us</u> (现在完成时) to a predicament.

304. 由于这些货物容易破损，建议你方用集装箱船只装运。

As these goods <u>are</u> (系词) <u>apt to break</u> (表语), we suggest you to <u>ship</u> (动词不定式，宾语补足语) them by container vessel.

305. 直至目前我方尚未收到信用证，结果我方没能按时装运。

Up till now we <u>haven't received</u> (现在完成时，表否定) your L/C and, in consequence, we were not able to effect shipment in time.

306. 短缺的货物将与你方下一批订货一起发运。

The short-shipped goods <u>will be forwarded</u> (过去分词，被动语态，将来时) together with your next order.

307. 他们发传真解释××号订单名下的货物短缺的原因。

They faxed <u>to account for</u> (目的状语) the short-delivery of the goods under the Order No. ××.

308. ××号货物短缺的问题可能是在运输途中发生的，非我方所能控制，请直接与运输公司联系。

The short-delivery of the goods under the Order No. ×× <u>might have occurred</u> (情态动词，表可能，完成式) during transit, <u>which</u> (特殊定语从句) is a matter out of our control. You may directly <u>come into</u> (不定式，谓语) connection with the shipping company.

309. 请采取一切可能的步骤，立即发出这次未装运的设备零件，否则会耽搁我方的装配工程。

Please <u>take all</u> (命令句) necessary <u>steps to effect</u> (不定式，目的状语) immediate shipment of our equipment parts short-shipped by you, otherwise our project installation may <u>be delayed</u> (过去分词，被动语态).

310. 不恰当的包装会使货物在运输过程中受损，务必注意。

Improper <u>packing</u> (动名词，主语) will result in the damage in transit, <u>to which</u> (特殊定语从句，which 前有介词) you should pay attention.

311. 这种出口物资必须用 5 层包装纸，现在只用了 3 层，这是不够坚固的，不能承受粗暴装卸。

This kind of substance for export <u>should be packed</u> (过去分词，被动语态) with 5-ply paper <u>packing</u> (动名词，定语，表性质) bags, but you <u>had packed</u> (过去完成时) them in 3-ply paper bags only, such <u>packing</u> (动名词，主语) <u>was</u> (系词) not strong <u>enough to bear</u> (表语，不定式) the rough <u>handling</u> (动名词，宾语).

312. 你方所谓的我方的货物短缺问题，实际是你方包装不当而造成的漏破导致的，这种情况是不应由我方负责的。

Your <u>so-called</u> (过去分词，定语) our "short shipment" <u>was</u> (系词), in fact, the <u>breakage</u> (表语) or leakage <u>caused</u> (过去分词，定语) by your improper <u>packing</u> (动名词，宾语). Such <u>so-called</u> (过去分词，定语) our " short shipment" <u>should</u> (谓语) not lie within our responsibility.

313. 这里我们附寄一份 8 号货箱所装货物的清单一份，供你方用以与你方订单及发票副本核对。

Enclosed is our list of the contents of Case No. 8 for you <u>to check</u> (不定式，目的状语) this with our order and the copy of your Invoice.

314. 主要商品由卖方按发票金额 120% 投保一切险。

Insurance <u>is</u> (系词) <u>to be effected</u> (表语)(to be covered) by the seller on the subject article against All Risks for 120% of the invoice value.

315. 这些机器必须妥善包装，以便防湿、防潮、防锈和防震。

These machines <u>must be</u> well <u>packed</u> (过去分词，被动语态) <u>to protect</u> (不定式，目的状语) against dampness, moisture, rust and shock.

316. 我方很抱歉地通知你方，本月无直达班轮，第一艘可供装运的轮船在下月初。

We regret <u>to inform</u> (不定式，宾语) you <u>that</u> (宾语从句) there is no direct liner available this month, the first available steamer will be in the <u>beginning</u> (动名词，in 后为表语) of next month.

317. 你方××号订单的货物装运已定于下月开始，分 2 次均装于香港轮船。预计×× 到达你港。

The shipment of the goods for your Order No. ×× <u>is</u> (系词) <u>to be effected</u> (不定式，被动语态，表语) in two equal lots, <u>beginning</u> (现在分词，定语，时间状语，说明 to be effected) from next month. The estimated time of arrival (ETA) at your port <u>will be</u> (系词) <u>at ××</u> (表语) <u>with transshipment in Hong Kong</u> (介词短语，词组，作 be 的补充说明).

318. 我方一收到你方信用证，将立即利用第一艘可利用的班轮运出你方货物。

As soon as your L/C reaches us here, we shall effect the shipment of your goods by the first available steamer.

319. 我方现在欣然地通知你方，为应你方要求，我方经过巨大努力，将原计划 8 月中旬装运你方 XX 订单的货物提前到 7 月底装运。

We are pleased to inform you that as you <u>requested</u> (谓语，过去时) and through our great efforts, we <u>are</u> (系词) <u>successful</u> (表语) in <u>advancing</u> (动名词，宾语) the shipment of your goods for Order No. ×× from the middle part of August to the end of July.

320. 我方必须重申，如果你方错过这次东风号班轮，必然使我方货物耽误至少半个月到港，这将会影响我方设备安装。

We <u>have to reiterate</u> (不得不，不定式) that in case of your <u>losing</u> (动名词，宾语) this steamer "East Wind", the arrival of our goods at our port <u>will be delayed</u> (过去分词，被动语态) for at least half a month, <u>which</u> (特殊定语从句) will affect the installation of our equipment.

321. 如果你方要求我方提前交货，分批装运你方货物是唯一的办法。可否一半货物 9 月份装运、一半货物 10 月份装运？如果你方同意，请立即传真确认。

If you ask for shipment <u>advancing</u> (动名词，定语), the only way is <u>making</u> (动名词，

表语) partial shipments of the goods. How about <u>making</u> (动名词，宾语) a partial shipment of half of the goods in September and half in October? Please fax us immediately your agreement.

322. 你方××号订单的货物早已备妥待运，请选派船名并尽快通知我方船名。

The goods for your Order No. ×× <u>are</u> (系词) <u>ready</u> (表语) for shipment for quite a long time, please <u>designate</u> (命令句) a steamer and <u>inform</u> (命令句) us its name as early as possible.

323. 你方迄今为止未发来信用证，致使我方延误发货，这个责任应该由你方来负。

Up till now you <u>haven't</u> (现在时，否定) sent us your L/C, <u>resulting in</u> (现在分词，放句末表结果状语) our shipment delay, and the responsibility for <u>which</u> (which 后句子指 shipment delay 定语从句，which 前有介词) should be put on your shoulder.

324. 按装运条件规定，付款必须在收到信用证以后 7 天内进行。

According to the <u>stipulated</u> (过去分词，定语) terms, payment <u>should be effected</u> (被动语态) within 7 days after arrival of the L/C.

325. 信用证规定这批货的装运日期为 10 月 3 日，所以我们必须尽快联系运输公司订好船舱。

<u>It</u> (形式主语) <u>has been stipulated</u> (现在完成时，被动语态) in the L/C <u>that</u> (逻辑主语，从句) the shipment date of these goods will be on 3 October, we <u>must contact</u> (谓语) with the <u>shipping</u> (动名词，表性质) company for the <u>shipping</u> (动名词，表功能) space as soon as possible.

326. 货物运到你方目的港以后 10 天之内在出口商所在地的国家和城市到有关银行议付汇票。

The negotiation of the draft <u>should be effected</u> (被动语态) in the city and country of the exporter within 10 days after the goods' arrival at your destination port.

327. 出口商品的包装必须十分坚固，以便承受粗暴装运可能引起的货物损坏。

The <u>packing</u> (动名词，主语) of the exported commodities should <u>be</u> (系词) <u>strong enough</u> (表语) <u>to withstand</u> (不定式，结果状语) rough <u>handling</u> (动名词，宾语) <u>which</u> (定语从句，说明 rough handling) may result in the damage of the goods.

328. 我方感到甚为抱歉，由于供应商方面的耽搁，使我方无法按合同规定在下月上旬将货备妥待运。我方已于昨日将此意传真你方。

We should apologize to you that owing to the delay on the part of our supplier, we are unable to get the goods ready for shipment before the early part of next month according to the stipulations of the contract. Yesterday we already <u>faxed</u> (过去时) you that effect.

329. 从你方开立信用证到我方货物备妥待运并抵达你港，正常需要 4 个月左右的时间。

<u>It</u> (表时间) normally takes <u>about a time</u> (宾语) <u>of 4 months from</u> (to 的动名词，宾语) your <u>establishing</u> (动名词，介词，宾语) the L/C to our goods' being ready for shipment and reaching your port.

330. 这种有纠纷的事情应提交仲裁。

This matter in dispute <u>should be submitted</u> (被动语态，谓语) to arbitration.

331. 我方已登记"胜利"号的舱位，准备下月底发运货物。收到货后请务必检查货物到港情况。

   We <u>have</u> already <u>booked</u> (现在完成时，过去分词) the <u>shipping</u> (动名词，表用途，定语) space in SS "Victory" and <u>are planning</u> (现在进行时，谓语) <u>to effect</u> (不定式，宾语) shipment by the end of next month. Attention <u>must be paid</u> (谓语) to the inspection of the goods after their arrival at your port.

332. 我方××号订单货物的投保包括破碎险，额外保险费将由我方负担。

   Our insurance <u>placing</u> (动名词，主语) for the shipment of Order No. ×× includes the risk of <u>breakage</u> (动名词，宾语). The extra premium <u>shall be</u> (将来时)for our account.

333. 对于按 CIF 价格出售的货物，我们一般投保一切险和战争险，按发票金额的 100% 加 20%。

   For the goods <u>sold on</u> (过去分词，定语) CIF basis, we generally effect insurance against All Risks and War Risk for full invoice plus 20%.

334. 需要时你方必须从检验机构获取检验报告，然后与中国人民保险公司联系以商定解决方法。

   If necessary, you <u>have to obtain</u> (谓语) your survey report from your <u>surveying</u> (动名词，定语，表性质功能) institution and then <u>approach</u> the PICC (与 to obtain 等同) (People's Insurance Company of China) for settlement.

335. 由于你方所发之货质量低劣，我方不得不向你方提出索赔。

   Owing to the poor quality of your shipments, we <u>have to lodge</u> (谓语) our claim against you.

336. 如果纠纷无法谈判解决，就需要诉诸仲裁。

   If the dispute is not negotiable, <u>resorting</u> (动名词，主语) arbitration may be necessary.

337. 这批货的检验证明说明货物在发运时情况是良好的。

   The Inspection Certificate covering this shipment states the shipment's <u>staying in</u> (动名词，宾语) good condition when <u>shipped</u> (过去时，谓语，也可看作是过去分词).

338. 这证明意外损坏是在运输过程中发生的，应由运输公司负责赔偿。

   This proves <u>that</u> (宾语从句) the accidental damage has happened during transit and the <u>shipping</u> (动名词，表性质、功能) company should take the responsibility of <u>making</u> (动名词，宾语) compensation for the losses.

339. 涉及本合同以及因执行本合同所发生的一切争执应通过友好协商予以解决。

   All disputes in connection with this contract or the contract execution thereof <u>should be</u> (被动语态) settled amicably by negotiations.

340. 我方逐个检查，发现每个都有不同程度的泄漏。

   We <u>have examined</u> (现在完成时) one by one and found that each of them <u>was leaking</u> (过去进行时，谓语) more or less.

341. 如果对这批货物提出索赔，需要提交足够的证据。

In case of claiming for (动名词，宾语) compensation in respect of this consignment, sufficient evidences should be supported (被动语态).

342. 若争议无法通过双方谈判解决，可提交仲裁。

Disputes may be submitted (被动语态) for arbitration in case (条件状语从句) no settlement can be obtained (被动语态) between both two parties.

343. 货物的投保将由我方以 CIF 价的 110%投保。如果要求投保附加险，额外保险费将由买方自理。

Insurance of the goods to be covered (不定式，定语) by us for 110% of the CIF value and any extra premium for additional insurance, if required, (条件从句，required 前省略 you are) shall be born by the buyers.

344. 我方按发票金额的 110%投保目的港。

Our insurance coverage is for 110% of invoice value up to the port of destination.

345. 我方如果要求投保附加险，所需额外保险费将由买方支付。

Should additional coverage be required (谓语，被动语态), the extra premium incurred (过去时，定语) would be (系词) for (表语) the buyer's account.

346. 我们一般对按 CIF 价出售的货物向中国人民保险公司投保。

We shall insure with (谓语) the People's Insurance Company of China for the goods sold (过去分词，定语) on CIF basis.

347. 你方愿意按发票金额加 10%投保。我们正在洽办中。

You wish to insure (宾语，不定式) shipment for 10% above invoice value, which (特种定语从句) is having (现在进行时) our due attention.

348. 水渍险和破损险适合你方货物投保。

WPA and Risk of Breakage suit (谓语) your consignment.

349. 我方希望按 CIF 价格卖货，但对这笔交易我方希望由你方在你处投保。

We prefer selling (动名词，宾语) on CIF basis, but for this transactions, we would like you to effect (不定式，宾语) insurance on your side.

350. 额外运费及额外保险费应由买方负责。

Extra freight and extra insurance premium shall be (系词) for the buyer's (表语) account.

351. 我方对这种商品不投保破碎险，请将破碎险字样从信用证保险条款中删除。

We do not cover Breakage for this article. Please delete (命令句) the word "Breakage" from the insurance clause of the L/C.

352. 这里的保险公司以 5%的免赔率承保这种险。

The insurance company here insures (谓语) this risk with 5% franchise.

353. 保险商拒绝支付索赔不是因为未投保破碎险，而是因为此险有 10%的免赔率。

The underwriters declined to pay (不定式，宾语) the claim not because (原因从句) the breakage was (系词) uncovered (表语), but because the risk was insured (被动语态，过去时) with 10% franchise.

354. 兹告知你方，根据我国海洋货物运输条款，我方承保上述一切险的现行费率为 1%。

For your information, our present rate <u>being charged</u> (现在式分词，被动语态) by us against ALL Risks is 1%, <u>subject</u> (条件状语) to our own Ocean Marine Cargo Clauses.

355. 我方想请你方将我方一笔从大连运往上海的玻璃器皿及手工艺品的货物进行投保，险种为平安险、水渍险、破碎险及 TPND 附加险。

We would like you to <u>arrange</u> (动词不定式，宾语) the insurance on our shipment of Glasswares and Hand crafts from Dalian to Shanghai. The kinds of insurance we would like <u>to cover</u> (不定式，宾语) are FPA, WPA, Breakage and the additional insurance of TPND.

356. 请按发票价值的 110%投保。

Please insure for 110% of invoice value.

357. 根据国际法他们答应了这项要求。

The request <u>was granted</u> (被动语态，谓语) in accordance with the international law.

358. 我方可以提供这种保险服务，但保险费率较高。

We can offer you such coverage, but at a slightly higher premium.

359. 由于你方货物未能按时到港，我方现在向你方提出由此而遭受的全部损失的索赔。

As a consequence of your failure <u>to deliver</u> (不定式，定语) the goods to our port on time, we now lodge a claim against you for all the <u>losses incurred</u> (过去分词，后置定语).

360. 兹就大米短重一事提出索赔如下。

We <u>are</u> now <u>lodging</u> (现在进行时) claims with you for shortweight as follows.

361. 我方现寄给你方第××检验证一份及我方金额为××××美元的索赔清单一份，请查收。

Enclosed please find one copy of Inspection Certificate No. ×××, as well as (together with) our Statement of Claims <u>amounting</u> (现在分词，定语) to US$ ××××.

362. 建议你方在 CIF 基础上和我方进行业务往来，并由我方代为保险。

We suggest you (you <u>are advised</u>) (被动语态) <u>to do</u> (不定式，宾语) business with us on CIF basis and <u>leave</u> (定语，leave 前省略 to) the insurance <u>to be effected</u> (被动语态，宾语补足语) by us.

363. 我方提货后发现货物短交 200 磅。

After <u>taking</u> (动名词，宾语) delivery of the goods, we found a short delivery of 200 lbs in weight.

(磅，重量单位)

364. 按你方一般惯例，你方只按发票价格加价 10%投保，因此额外保费由我方负担。

According to your usual practice, you <u>insure</u> (谓语) the goods only for 10% above invoice value, therefore the extra premium will <u>be</u> (系词) <u>on</u> (表语) our account.

365. 中草药很怕受潮，受潮后会变质，长期置于露天或不通风处，都会引起霉变。

The medicinal herds <u>are</u> (系词) <u>afraid</u> (表语) of dampness and deterioration is usually <u>caused</u> (被动语态，现在时) by <u>dampening</u> (动名词). <u>Putting</u> (动名词，主语) them in the open air or in the badly <u>ventilated</u> (过去分词，宾语，被动语态) place for a no short time will <u>make the herbs mildewed</u> (过去分词，被动语态，宾语补足语).

366. 发运前中国商品检验局检验了所有货物，签署的收据及提单也都能证明我们的货物在发运前是良好的，可能货物在运输过程中遭受淡水雨淋或被置于不通风的船舱。如果你方投保了淡水雨淋险，可向保险公司提出索赔。

Before shipment China Commodity Inspection Bureau <u>has inspected</u> (现在完成时) all the goods. The mate's receipt and the Bill of Lading can as well give evidence <u>in our goods'</u> (动名词，逻辑主语) <u>being in good condition</u> (动名词，宾语) before shipment. <u>It</u> (形式主语) was possible <u>that</u> (主语从句) the goods <u>had suffered</u> (过去完成时) fresh or rain water damage or <u>had been put</u> (过去完成时，被动语态) in the bad <u>ventilated</u> (过去分词，被动语态，定语) cabin. If you <u>have covered</u> (现在完成时) insurance against fresh and /or rain water damage risk, you <u>may lodge</u> (定语) your claim against the Insurance Company.

367. 请注意上述货物必须在 6 月 18 日前装出，保险须按发票价格的 120%投保一切险。

Please <u>see to</u> (命令式) it that the above-<u>mentioned</u> (过去分词，被动语态，定语) goods <u>are</u> (系词) <u>to be</u> (表语，被动语态) shipped before 18, June and the goods <u>are</u> (系词) <u>to be</u> (表语，被动语态) covered for 120% of invoice value against All Risks.

368. 如果出现损坏，贵方可在货到 30 天内提出索赔。

Should any damage <u>occur</u> (if 省略，条件从句), you <u>may put in</u> (谓语) a claim within 30 days after the arrival of the consignment.

369. 恭贺你方被委任为××地区的独家代理人。

<u>Congratulate</u> (习惯用语，也可看作是主语 we 省略) you on your <u>being appointed</u> (动名词，被动语态，宾语) as the sole agent of the territory ××.

370. 我方很高兴地任命你方为我方的业务代表，并深信我们一定会向着双方互利的贸易关系迈出前进的大步。

We are pleased to appoint you as our business representative and <u>are</u> (系词) deeply <u>confident in</u> (表语) our <u>marching</u> (动名词，宾语) big steps forward towards the mutually beneficial association.

371. 需要时你方必须从检验机构获取检验报告，然后与中国人民保险公司联系以商定解决方法。

If necessary, you have to obtain your survey report from your surveying institution and then approach the PICC (People's Insurance Company of China) for settlement.

372. 你方××号订单项下货物的保险按发票价加 20%投保至目的港。

The insurance of your goods of Order No. ×× <u>is covered</u> (被动语态，谓语) for the invoice cost plus 20% up to the destination port.

373. 由于你方所运货物为容易腐烂的食品，你方最好投保腐烂变质险。

As your goods <u>to be</u> (不定式，定语，被动语态，表将来要) shipped <u>are</u> (系词) the foodstuffs easily <u>to be deteriorated</u> (不定式，are 的表语，被动语态), it's better for you <u>to insure</u> (逻辑主语) the goods against the risk of deterioration.

374. 索赔损坏货物的每一个诉讼都涉及三个方面：被保险人、承运人及保险人。

Each case of claim on <u>damaged</u> (过去分词，定语) goods <u>involves</u> (谓语) three parties,

国际商务英语（第3版）

i.e., the <u>insured</u>（被动语态）, the carrier, and the <u>insurer</u>（保险人）.

375. 我方××号订单货物的投保包括破碎险，额外保险费将由我方负担。

Our insurance covered for the shipment of Order No. ×× includes the risk of breakage. The extra premium shall be for our account.

376. 对于按 CIF 价出售的货物，我们一般投保一切险和战争险，按发票金额的 100% 加 20%。

For the goods sold on CIF basis, we generally effect insurance against All Risks and War Risk for full invoice value plus 20%.

377. 损坏的原因在保险单的范围之内，你方可向有关的保险公司提出赔偿。

The cause of damage <u>is</u>（系词）<u>within</u>（表语，介词短语）the coverage of the insurance policy, and you can lodge compensation from the insurance company <u>concerned</u>（过去分词，被动语态，定语）.

378. 这份劳埃德的鉴定证明货物的损坏是由于包装不足所引起的。

This certificate of Lloyd's surveyor can prove that the damage of the goods <u>has been</u>（现在完成时，被动语态）caused by poor packing.

379. 中国商品检验局出具的检验报告将作为最后的依据，对双方都有约束力。

The Survey Report <u>issued</u>（过去分词，被动语态，定语）by the China Inspection Bureau <u>will be taken</u>（谓语，被动语态，将来时）as final and <u>binding upon</u>（现在分词，作表语）both parties.

380. 鉴于我们有很丰富的经验及广泛的业务关系，我们希望你们能任命我们为该地区的独家代理人。

In view of our rich experience and extensive business connections, we hope you <u>will appoint</u>（将来时）us as your sole agent for this area.

381. 我方东南亚地区的代理空缺，有待今后委任。

Our representation in Southeast Asia <u>has been vacant</u>（现在完成时，形容词作 been 的表语）and is <u>to be appointed</u>（表语，被动语态）later.

382. 我们希望委任你为东北地区的代表并促进我们之间互利的联系和合作。

We wish <u>to appoint</u>（宾语）you as the representative of the Northeast area and we are <u>looking</u>（现在进行时）forward to the <u>promoting</u>（动名词，宾语）of our beneficial mutual association and cooperation.

383. 我方以前经营的××型计算机现在由××公司全权代表。

Our formerly <u>operated</u>（过去分词，定语，被动语态）×× Type Computers are now fully <u>represented</u>（现在时，被动语态）by ×× Company.

384. 你方申请担任我方电器产品独家代理三年，我们对此正在认真考虑。但我方总裁正出国在外，须等他回国后方能作出最后决定。我方延迟回复，致以歉意。

Your application for our sole agency on our electric apparatus for a period of three years is now <u>put</u>（现在时，被动语态，谓语）under our careful consideration. But because our President is now <u>being</u>（表语，动名词）abroad on business and the final decision must be made only after his <u>coming</u>（动名词，宾语）back from abroad, we here apologize (谓语) to you for our delaying (动名词, 宾语) in giving (动名词, 宾语) you our reply.

385. 你方担任我方驻英国伦敦的销售代理人的建议在一定程度上来说是可行的，因为我们知道你们在英国伦敦的商务活动范围很大，多年的老客户也比比皆是。

Your suggestion of being (动名词，宾语) our sales agent in London, Britain is (系词) feasible (表语) to a certain extent because we know that you have got (现在完成时)a wide field of business activities there and your many years' old customers can be found everywhere.

386. 请放心，你们要求担任我方驻京独家代理的建议我们会认真考虑的，一待我方总经理回国，我方将立即回复你方。

Please rest assured (命令句, 过去分词) that your application for being appointed (动名词，宾语，被动语态) as our sole agent in Beijing would be put into our careful consideration. We would reply you as soon as our General Manager comes back from abroad.

387. 你方能否被委派为我方驻伦敦的独家代理的问题有待于我方总经理和董事长的批准。

The problem of whether (宾语从句) you could be appointed (被动语态) as our sole agent in London depends (谓语，现在时) upon the approval of our General Manager and our President of the Board of Directors.

388. 此委任的试用期为 12 个月，佣金为所有销售净值的 5%。

The trial period of this appointment is 12 months, and the commission is 5% of the net value of all sales.

389. 根据代理协议的规定，代理商是不允许销售其他厂家的类似产品的。

According to the stipulations of the agency agreement, the agents are not allowed (否定，被动语态，谓语) to sell the (不定式，宾语) similar products of other manufacturers.

390. 鉴于你方承诺的营业额太低，代理问题仍在考虑之中。

The question of agency is (系词) still under (表语) consideration because the annual turnover you promised (谓语，过去时) is too low.

391. 如果你方愿意委任我方为你方亚洲地区的代理人，我方可以保证每年××美元的营业额。

Should you be prepared (条件从句，主谓倒装，被动语态，否定式，宾语) to appoint us as your agent in Asia, we would guarantee (谓语，表意愿) a turnover of US$ ×× each year.

392. 综合贸易公司经常担任银行和生产厂家及零售商之间的中间人。

The general trading companies often act as the intermediaries among banks, manufacturers and the retailers.

393. 请速将你方的推销计划及在你方市场可能的年营业额传真告知我方。

Please fax us immediately your plan for sales pushing (动名词，宾语) and the annual turnover you <u>may realize</u> (谓语) in your market.

394. 迄今为止，我们之间成交的生意并不很多，所以考虑你方为我方亚洲地区代理人的问题还为时过早。

Up to now, we haven't done more businesses between us, so we think <u>it</u> (形式宾语) premature for <u>us to consider</u> (逻辑宾语) you as our agent in Asia.

395. 当我们之间的业务发展能使我们双方都满意时我们再谈代理之事。

Let's <u>revert to</u> (宾语补足语, to 省略) this agency matter when the business between us <u>develops</u> (谓语) to our mutual satisfaction.

396. 如果你们能继续努力推销我方产品，把年营业额提高到××美元，我方将考虑任命你方为我方××地区代理商的问题。

If you are able to continue <u>paying</u> (动名词，宾语) your efforts <u>to push</u> (目的状语，不定式) the sales of our products and increase the annual turnover up to US$××, we'd like to put the question <u>of appointing</u> (动名词，宾语) you as our agency in ×× area <u>under our consideration</u>. (put…into 词组)

397. 在取得独家代理权以后，市场就会完全处于你方控制之下了。

After <u>holding</u> (动名词，宾语) the sole agency in hand, the market <u>will be</u> (系词) wholly <u>under</u> (表语) your control.

398. 经过我公司董事会的讨论和批准，你方从下月初起将可成为我方在东南亚地区的总代理人。

After the discussion and approval of our Board of Directors, you <u>will become</u> (将来时) our general agent in Southeast Asia, <u>commencing</u> (补充说明，分词) from next month.

399. 你方作为我方××地区独家代理人的期限为 12 个月，从××到××。如果你方年营业额有所增长，任期可延长 12 个月。

The period of your appointment as the sole agent in the territory of ×× is twelve months, from ×× to ××. In case of your increasing the turnover, the period of your appointment <u>may be extended</u> (被动语态，谓语) for another 12 months.

400. 代理商可从每笔订单得到按净发票售价 5%的佣金，该佣金在制造商收到每笔订单的全部货款后支付。

The agent shall receive commission of 5% on the net <u>invoiced selling</u> (过去分词，被动语态，定语) price from each order. The manufacturer <u>shall pay</u> (将来时) this commission after <u>receiving</u> (动名词，宾语) the full payment for each order.

附录 1　历届外贸英语口语试题题型

Ⅰ. Read the following passage aloud.

Fast Food Restaurants

The favorite food in the United States is the hamburger, a kind of round sandwich containing grilled ground beef. A favorite place to buy hamburgers is a fast food restaurant. At fast food restaurants, people order their food, wait a few minutes and carry it to their tables themselves. At some fast restaurants, people can order their food, pay for it and pick it up without leaving their cars. There are many kinds of fast food restaurants in the United States. Most of them sell hamburgers, French fries and milkshakes, which are traditionally popular foods among Americans. In addition, there are numerous fast food restaurants that serve Chinese food, Mexican food, Italian food, chicken, seafood and ice cream. The idea of the fast food restaurant is so popular that nearly every kind of food can be found in one.

Questions:

1. Please name some famous fast food restaurants that you know.
2. American fast food has already made inroads on China, and has gained much popularity among Chinese customers, both old and young. But its biggest attraction is its delicious taste, which has drawn millions of kids, rather than its nutrition. Because it contains too much fat, it has partially contributed to the fact that many young eaters grow fatter and fatter. What do you say to kids who like this kind of food?

Ⅱ. Translate the following sentences into Chinese orally.

1. It's very kind of you to come and meet me at the airport, Miss Wang.
2. We will do our best to ship the goods as early as possible, and we feel sure that the shipment will be satisfactory to you in every respect.
3. I believe that our pleasure cooperation over the years has proved us trustworthy partners.
4. Talking about food, I have two favorites: one is Chinese food, the other is French food.
5. My secretary will send the contract with my signature to your hotel at 2:00 this afternoon.

Ⅲ. Translate the following sentences into English orally.

1. 如果能安排我参观你们的制造厂，那就太感谢您了。
2. 很高兴能有机会向贵公司介绍我们新开发的产品。

3. 如果你们的条件合适，我们将很乐意做你们的代理。

4. 明天晚上是否有空？我们经理想为您举办一个晚宴。

5. 你们必须明白，国际市场上同类产品的竞争是非常激烈的。

IV. Free talk

(If you don't like the topic given here, you can choose to answer the questions following the passage above. Remember, try to say as much as possible.)

(如果不喜欢这个交谈题目，可以对上面短文中的问题展开回答。)

To own a personal car would be a nice idea. Yet the fact is, even though a great number of Chinese customers have no financial problems to buy personal cars, most of them are still hesitating. Despite a potential market, sales are not encouraging, at least not so far. In your opinion, what are the reasons behind this?

附录 2　历届外贸英语试题题型

Ⅰ. Translation of terms.

A.　Translate the following terms into Chinese.
1. FCA
2. TRIMs
3. T.P.N.D.
4. composite index
5. G.A.
6. voyage charter
7. endorsement
8. straight bill of lading
9. rebate
10. auction

B.　Translate the following terms into English in full.
1. 议付
2. 保函
3. (代理业务中的)委托人
4. 无追索权
5. 市场准入
6. 电子商务认证
7. 领事发票
8. 循环信用证
9. 贸易壁垒
10. 北美自由贸易协定

Ⅱ.　Make the best choice for each of the following sentences.

1. Our corporation _____ foodstuffs.
   A. deals　　　　B. handles　　　　　C. handles in　　D. specializes
2. The consignment was shipped _____ on the SS Changfeng which left Shanghai for Singapore on June 16.
   A. clean　　　　B. cleaned　　　　　C. cleaning　　　D. cleanly
3. Mr. Wang _____ charge of our sales in Europe. All of the following can be used here EXCEPT____.
   A. has been put in　　　　　　　　　B. has taken

C.　is in

D.　is in the

4.　For your own＿＿＿ please expedite the L/C, which must reach us before August 7.

A.　advantage　　B.　benefit　　　　C.　consideration　　D.　profit

5.　Our illustrated catalog ＿＿＿＿ shows various types of bathroom fittings and the sizes available.

A.　also enclosed

B.　is also enclosed

C.　that also enclosed

D.　which also enclosed

Ⅲ.　Translate the following letter into English in a proper format.

Sanders Durables Pty. Ltd.

34 Queensland Road

Melbourne, 3,400, Australia

先生/女士：

很高兴收到你方 7 月 8 日来函，询问我公司能否提供 3000 套家用空调机(货号：TW0203)。很遗憾地告知，所提商品暂时无货。

为满足你公司需求，现推荐一种新款变频(Adjustable-speed)空调。在质量上它与你方所询问的分体式空调一样好，但性能更加稳定，能耗降低高达 15%且价格要低 20%。这种空调在中国非常畅销，相信也会在贵国市场受到欢迎。

随函寄上我公司出口价格和详细的交易条件。期盼收到你们的订单。

Ⅳ.　Fill in the contract form in English with information gathered from the following E-mails.

E-mail 1

Sender: Cathy Jones< cathy @ hotmail.com>

Receiver: Wang Feng < wangf@yahoo.com>

Subject: Teapots

Date: 12-05-15　　　　15:58:00

Shandong Eastern General Trading Co., Shandong, China

Dear Mr. Wang,

How are you?

I'm glad to tell you that our customers are very satisfied with your last shipment of brown ceramic teapots delivered to us two months ago. They have placed a new order for your teapots as follows:

Item # TP5203E/ J2 (2-cup capacity)　　　　　480 pcs, 48 pcs/ ctn

Item # TP5205E/ J2 (6-cup capacity)　　　　　1,680pcs, 24 pcs/ ctn

Item # TP5208E/ J2 (10-cup capacity)　　　　1,206pcs, 18 pcs/ctn

Do the prices remain the same? Could you advise your earliest date of delivery when confirming the order?

Thanks and best regards.

Unitrade Co., Ltd. / Cathy Jones

E-mail 2

Sender: Wang Feng < wangf@yahoo.com>

Receiver: Cathy Jones < cathy@ hotmail.com>

Subject: Teapots

Date: 12-05-16   09:53:00

Unitrade Co., Ltd.

Dear Miss Jones,

Thank you for your new order. I'm glad to say we can supply the teapots you require on the usual terms. Our prices remain unchanged, i.e.

Ceramic Teapots, Brown	FOB Qingdao
Item # TP5203E/ J2 (2-cup capacity)	@ USD 6.20/dz
Item # TP5205E/ J2 (6-cup capacity)	@ USD 10.16/dz
Item # TP5208E/J2 (10-cup capacity)	@ USD 22.06/dz

We can deliver them in July.

If the above is acceptable, please confirm.

Thanks for your kind cooperation!

Best. Regards

Wang Feng

For Shandong Eastern General Trading Co., Shandong, China

Ⅴ. Write a letter in English asking for amendments to the following letter of credit by checking it with the terms of the given contract.

Deutsche Bank AG

Date: April 9, 2012

To Bank of China, Guangzhou

We hereby open our Irrevocable Letter of Credit No. 6785 in favour of Guangzhou Textiles Corporation for account of Schmitz & GmBH, Hamburg, Germany up to an aggregate amount of EUP 24,000 (Say Twenty-four Thousand Euros Only) CIFC 2% Hamburg for 100% of the invoice value relative to the shipment of:

6,000 yards of Pongee Silk Art. No. 6103 at EUR4.80 per yard as per Contract No. 1122 dated February 15, 2002 from Guangzhou, China to Hamburg, Germany.

Drafts to be drawn at sight on our bank and accompanied by the following documents:

—Signed Commercial Invoice in triplicate;

—Full set of clean on board bills of lading made out to our order quoting L/C No. 6785 marked "Freight Collect";

—One original marine insurance policy or certificate for 130% of the invoice value covering All Risks and War Risks, with claims payable in Germany in the currency of draft(s).

Partial shipments and transshipment are prohibited.

Shipment must be effected not later than May 31, 2012.

Draft(s) drawn under this credit must be negotiated in Germany on or before June 5, 2012.

1122 号合同主要条款：

卖方：广州纺织品公司

买方：史密茨有限公司，德国汉堡

商品名称：府绸

规格：6103 号

数量：6 000 码

单价：CIF 汉堡每码 4.80 欧元(含佣金 2%)

总值：28 800 欧元

装运期：2012 年 5 月由中国广州运往德国汉堡，允许分批装运和转船

保险：由卖方按发票金额的 110%投保一切险和战争险

付款：按货物金额 100%开立以卖方为受益人的不可撤销的即期信用证，凭卖方汇票议付。

VI. Translation of passages.

A. From English into Chinese. (5 points)

Before obtaining a large order, an exporter must check that he has the necessary cash to finance the contract — he may not receive payment for the goods until some time in the future. In certain circumstances he may be able to ask for payment in advance of the order. However, in most cases he will have to produce the goods and deliver them to the market before being paid. Terms of payment are therefore important. An exporter must state the payment terms clearly and definitely and make sure that there will be no misunderstanding between exporter and importer, especially when the transaction involves a larger amount of money.

B. From Chinese into English. (5 points)

我们必须优化传统的出口商品结构，靠价格和数量竞争的时代已经一去不复返了。在当今激烈竞争的国际市场上，只有以质取胜和改善售前售后服务才能行得通。要通过精加工和深加工提高出口商品的附加值，要努力生产试销对路的名优特新产品和"拳头产品"打入国际市场。由于市场形势千变万化，出口产品必须不断更新换代，做到你无我有，你有我优，胜人一筹。

附录3 历届外销员从业资格 外经贸英语试题题型

Ⅰ. Translate the following terms.

1. From English into Chinese.
   (1) PNTR
   (2) Irrevocable Letter of Credit
   (3) Blank Endorsement
   (4) General Average
   (5) FAQ
   (6) DES
   (7) Franchise
   (8) FPA
   (9) Bill of Exchange
   (10) Auction

2. From Chinese into English.
   (1) 世界银行
   (2) 电子商务
   (3) 托运人
   (4) 进口许可证
   (5) 国际商会

Ⅱ. Choose the best answer for each of the following question.

1. We _____ to allow you a special discount if you increase your order to 5,000 pairs.
   A. have prepared   B. are prepare
   C. are prepared   D. were prepared

2. With computer users linked to the Internet growing _____ every year, business is trying to cash in on the worldwide network.
   A. at million   B. with a million
   C. with one million   D. by millions

3. _____ you fulfill the terms of the L/C, we will accept the drafts drawn under this credit.
   A. Provided   B. To provide
   C. In the case   D. Only if

4. Subject to satisfactory arrangements _____ terms and conditions, we should be pleased to act as your sole agent.

    A. as   B. as per

    C. as if   D. as to

We find that there is no stipulation of transshipment _____ in the relative L/C.

    A. allowing   B. which allows

    C. which allowed   D. being allowed

Ⅲ. Translate the following into an English letter in a proper form.

写信人：新路华贸易有限公司

地址：中国上海，兴达路 999 号金星大厦(Golden Star Mansion)33 层

收信人：James Brown & Sons，由日用品部(Daily Articles Department)办理

地址：#304-310 Jalan Street, Toronto, Canada

日期：2010 年 6 月 30 日

内容：

感谢你 6 月 15 日的来函和样品。

特告知，我方客户对你方样品的试用结果非常满意，但现在仍有些犹豫。

经与同类货物作仔细比较，我们发现你方报价有点高。当前的洗发精(Shampoo)市场充斥着各种各样的品牌，像 Rejoice、Pond's 等优质产品很容易买到。而且这些品牌都已得到我地市场的认可。就洗发精而言，很多消费者不愿接受新产品。你方产品作为新品牌，最大的卖点将是它的护发(hair care)功能；质量上虽然已经达到客户要求，但要想在我地市场打开销路，必须还要具备价格优势，否则是很难与一些老牌产品竞争的。

鉴于此，我方客户建议将原报价减 10%。请考虑并作及时答复。

Ⅳ. Fill in the contract form with information gathered from the following correspondences.

(1) Outgoing Letter

Beijing, November 5, 2009

Dear Sirs,

Thank you for your enquiry of October 30 for Women's Nylon Garments. In compliance with your request, we have enclosed a price list and an illustrated brochure. Although we still have certain amount of stock we can hardly keep them for a long time because of the heavy demand. Samples will be sent on request.

We are looking forward to our early reply.

                          Yours faithfully,

               Beijing Garments Imp/Exp. Corporation

(2) Incoming Letter

Dear sirs,

Many thanks for your quotation of November 5 and the samples of Women's Nylon

Garment.

We are satisfied with the quality and pleased to enclose our Order No. 333 for 3 sizes mentioned in your latest catalogue.

We note that you can supply these items from stock and hope you will send them before December 31. Our company will reserve the right to cancel this order or reject the goods for any late arrival.

For your reference, we with to effect payment by D/P 60 days. Please kindly let us have your confirmation.

ORDER

No. 333

Beijing Garments Imp/Exp. Corp.

Beijing, China

Please supply the following items:

Quantity (Doz)	Item	Size	Unit Price (Per doz) CIF London
15	Women's Nylon Garments	Small	US$75.00
16	ditto	Medium	US$110.00
14	ditto	Large	US$150.00

London Trading Co. Ltd.

Ⅴ. Write a letter in English asking for amendments to the following letter by checking it with the given contract terms.

London Bank

Irrevocable Documentary Credit No. LST150

Date and place of issue: 15 September 2011, London

Date and place of expiry: 15 December 2011, London

Applicant: London Im. Co. , Ltd

Beneficiary: South Export Corp. , Guangzhou

Advising Bank: Bank of China, Guangzhou Branch

Amount: GBP10, 000 (Say Sterling Pounds Ten Thousand Only)

Partial shipments and transshipment are prohibited.

Shipment from China port to London, latest 30 November 2011.

Credit available against presentation of the following documents and of your draft at sight for 90% of the invoice value:

——Signed commercial invoice in quadruplicate

——Full set of clear on board Bills of lading made out to order of London Bank marked freight prepaid.

——Insurance certificate or policy endorsed in blank for full invoice value plus 10%, covering all Rise and War Risk.

Covering 5/t Fresh Shrimps, first grade, at GBP2,000 per m/t CIF London as per Contract NO. 245B.

245B 号合同主要条款：

买方：伦敦食品进口有限公司

卖方：广州南方出口有限公司

5 吨一级冻虾每吨 CIF 伦敦 2200 英镑，2011 年 11 月 30 日前从中国港口用直达轮运往伦敦。保险由卖方按发票金额 110%投保一切险和战争险。凭不可撤销的即期信用证支付。

Ⅵ. Translate the following passage.

1. From English into Chinese. (5%)

In a foreign transaction, an open account is a convenient method of payment and may be satisfactory if the buyer is well established, has demonstrated a long and favorable payment record, or has been thoroughly checked for credit worthiness. Under open account, the exporter simply bills the customer, who is expected to pay under agreed terms at a future date. Some of the largest firms broad purchase only on open account.

2. From Chinese into English. (5%)

客户一旦接受了报盘，出口商就以一份合同来确认这笔买卖。在确认交易时，有的进出口公司使用销售合同，有的用销售确认书。通常，销售合同或销售确认书包括一般条款、条件，以及随商品不同而各异的一些特殊条件。但卖买方的姓名、产品说明、数量、单价、总额、付款条款、装运港和目的港等细节是必不可少的。

Keys to the Exercises
练习答案

Chapter 1

I.

Shanghai Import & Export Commodity Inspection Bureau

No. 13 Zhongshan Road, Shanghai, China

Tel: **Fax:**

E-mail: **Post Code:**

II.

China National Light Industrial Products   **18, March, 2015**
Import and Export Corporation
Guangzhou Branch
No. 87 The Bund, Guangzhou, China

Chapter 2

Keys to the Exercises (略)

Chapter 3

I. Translate the following sentences from English into Chinese.

1. 我们希望在平等互利的基础上和贵方建立业务关系。
2. 我们知道贵公司从事纺织品贸易已有十多年之久。
3. 我们很高兴地知道贵公司需要我们的大量童车。
4. 我方有意于扩大和你们的业务关系，并和你方达成更多的交易。
5. 贵方在国际市场上一直享有盛誉。

II. Translate the following sentences from Chinese into English.

1. The cooperation between our two parties will certainly be strengthened day by day.
2. Our two parties must carry out careful consultations and negotiations.
3. We have decided to entrust you with the sole agency for our products of ×××.
4. We shall be very pleased if you agree to reach the compensation trade agreement with us.
5. We hope to put some of our products on consignment in your Company.

Chapter 4

I. Translate the following sentences from English into Chinese.

1. 虽然我们愿意协助你们，但我们认为在我们的报价中已无再打折扣的余地，因为我方已将价格降到最低的限度。
2. 我方想问一问，对数量达到 1000 打的订货，你们能否给予 5% 的折扣。
3. 为了得到所需的信息，询价者必须简单、清楚地开列询价单。
4. 从所附发票你们可以看出，我方价格是完全处于你们所提出的最大数额之内的。
5. 我方报盘已于昨天传真你方，你方现在应该已经收到。

II. Translate the following sentences from Chinese into English.

1. We are pleased to have your inquiry of August 2 for our leather shoes.
2. We confirm having accepted your offer.
3. If you are able to reduce your price by 3%, we are willing to place orders with you.
4. We are airmailing you a parcel of dress samples. Please fax us your receipt of it immediately.
5. This offer is firm, subject to our final confirmation.

Chapter 5

I. Translate the following sentences from English into Chinese.

1. 我们希望你们对我们的选择感到满意，并希望你们的这次订货将使我们之间的业务进一步发展。
2. 你方销售经理昨天给我们发来传真，说我们的价格是可以接受的，并要求我们今后两年内为你们供货。
3. CIF 是一个价格条款，所指的价格包括货物的成本及将货物运到目的地的保险与运费。
4. 我方将给你方另封空邮样品，希望你方能发现样品令你方满意。
5. 如果我方被及时告知的话，是会为你们保留这些产品的。

II. Translate the following sentences from Chinese into English.

1. We have pleasure in enclosing a copy of our latest catalogue asked for in your letter.

2. We regret to inform you that we do not have in stock the goods you desired.

3. We have found with satisfaction that the quality of your products is high and the price is reasonable.

4. Please arrange our coverage of the goods through the Lloyd's broker.

5. The quality of our products will certainly reach the limits of your requirements.

Chapter 6

Ⅰ. Translate the following sentences from English into Chinese.

1. 在接受汇票以前，银行将要求你方出示提单、商业发票、装箱单证等。

2. 如果你方实现了信用证的条款，我方就会接受在此信用证项下所开之汇票。

3. 收到我方信用证以后，你方必须尽快发货。

4. 你方产品性能必须完全符合我方样品。

5. 必须提请你方注意你方信用证的开立问题，因为我方的发货日期已经临近。

Ⅱ. Translate the following sentences from Chinese into English.

1. The buyer's L/C should reach the seller one month before the shipment date.

2. We have been informed by the shipping company that SS "Victory" is due to sail for London on or about 20th this month.

3. It is a great pleasure to inform you that we have got all your ordered goods ready for shipment. Please establish your L/C at once.

4. We can ship immediately whatever we have on hand (in stock) instead of waiting for the whole lot to be completed.

5. We have faxed to you this morning to amend the L/C No. ×××.

Chapter 7

Ⅰ. Translate the following sentences from English into Chinese.

1. 我方已给发货部门发出特别指示，按照你方 7 月 15 日的信中特别说明的，将你方订单于 8 月 15 日及 9 月 15 日分别发出。

2. 我方希望强调，一定要在规定的时间范围内发货，因为我方用户不会考虑进一步延期的问题。

3. 没有必要在每个包装件上都标明收货人的姓名和地址，因为运输唛头已包括了买主姓名的首字母。

4. 为了向你们确保货物在完好无缺的情况下到达你方，所有货都装在专用的集装箱内。

5. 这一包装件的提货不属于保险公司的责任范围，所以你方可向保险公司提出索赔。

II. Translate the following sentences from Chinese into English.

1. Sometimes, transshipment and partial shipments are permitted, subject to the different kinds of goods.

2. We have the goods you asked for in stock and will deliver as soon as we receive your order.

3. Packing charges are included in the price, and we can make delivery whenever you wish.

4. We are sorry for the short delivery by 50 tons.

5. Your attention must be called to the delivery date of our order No. ××. We wish you to make out an arrangement as early as possible.

Chapter 8

I. Translate the following sentences from English into Chinese.

1. 耽误付款的利息从 5 月 15 日算起到支付日 12 月 15 日，年利率为 10%，总额为×××美元，应由你方付款。

2. 我方通知你方，如果所有样品不在 120 天之内返回，我方就将开发票给你方，请你方付款。

3. 我们期望有些订单能在以后两个月内支付，并请问你方：我们可否将你方账款的支付从 6 月 2 日推迟至 7 月 15 日。

4. 在今后的交易中，如果每笔金额不超过 5000 英镑，可按"付款交单"(D/P-Documents Against Payment)方式办理支付。

5. 请注意××号及××号合同项下的所有付款必须及时完成。

II. Translate the following sentences from Chinese into English.

1. We think it necessary to send the shipping documents by registered mail.

2. We shall fax you as soon as the goods are available.

3. This class of merchandise is usually sold on D/A (D/A- Documents Against Acceptance) terms.

4. We are pleased to inform you that we have effected the payment of 100 electronic Computers in accordance with the stipulations set forth in your L/C No. ××.

5. We have opened an irrevocable L/C No. ×× for US $ ××× in your favor.

Chapter 9

I. Translate the following sentences from English into Chinese.

1. 我方准备赔偿你方损失，并将通过电汇给你方寄去所索赔的金额××美元。希望我方此次疏忽不致损害我们的良好关系。

2. 关于我方×××号订单，我方将给你方寄去官方文件，表明发给我方的数量比所订的要少。

3. 对发生于从仓库至目的地的运输过程中的任何损坏，我方都没有责任。

4. 经检查发现，将近 20% 的包装件破包，这显然要归咎于包装不当。

5. 由于保险费随保险范围的大小而变化，额外保险费由买方负担。

II. Translate the following sentences from Chinese into English.

1. Insurance premiums will be added in invoice amount together with the freight charges.

2. If the buyer's country prevents performance of the contract, this kind of risk is called country risk.

3. If you want to cover Breakage Risk, you must pay for the extra premium.

4. Now we enclose you the above-mentioned insurance terms for your reference.

5. In accordance with the international practices we can provide you such coverage.

Chapter 10

I. Translate the following sentences from English into Chinese.

1. 投标文件所列供应和交付货物的总价为×××元人民币或×××美元。
2. 投标人根据文件的规定，承担执行合同的责任和义务。
3. 提供和交付的货物技术规范应与招标文件规定的技术规范相一致。
4. 卖方应按照要求一览表中买方规定的时间表交货和提供服务。
5. 所有外国制造厂家的投标必须经过其在北京注册的代表处提交。

II. Translate the following sentences from Chinese into English.

1. The Bid is valid for a period of sixty (60) calendar days from the date of bid opening.

2. We invite open tenders for the supply of power station equipment.

3. This corporation invites enterprises in China and abroad to participate in the tender for the extension of the container dock at the port of ××.

4. All bid documents are required to be formally signed virginals and must be sealed before mailing.

5. The result of this tendering is that the contract is awarded to ×× Corp. which made the second lowest bid.

Chapter 11

I. (略)

II. (略)

III.

1. A   2. C   3. A   4. C   5. A   6. B   7. D   8. C   9. A   10. C

Chapter 12

Ⅰ. (略)

Ⅱ.

1. C   2. B   3. C   4. D   5. C   6. B   7. A   8. D   9. B   10. A

Chapter 13

Ⅰ. (略)

Ⅱ. (略)

Ⅲ.

1. C   2. D   3. A   4. A   5. D   6. C   7. B   8. B   9. A   10. B

Chapter 14

1. B   2. D   3. D   4. B   5. A   6. B   7. B   8. A   9. B   10. C

Chapter 15

Ⅰ. Translate the following sentences from English into Chinese.

1. 按本合同,乙方应向合作经营公司提供一定的培训。
2. 如因卖方未能及时传真通知,致使买方不能及时投保,则卖方承担全部损失。
3. 自货物到达目的港起 12 个月为质量保证期。
4. 若承运船如期抵达装货港,卖方因备货未妥而影响装船,则空舱费及滞期费均由卖方承担。
5. 双方有义务对本合同保密,未经对方许可,任何一方不得将本合同内容透露给第三方。

Ⅱ. Translate the following sentences from Chinese into English.

1. The letter of credit must fulfill all the terms and conditions of this Contract.
2. The term of the letter of credit should be clear, fair and made payable to the Seller.
3. Advertising expenses shall be borne by Party B.
4. A deposit of 10% of the total price should be paid by the Buyer immediately after signing the Contract.
5. The management company collects property management charges (including rent) according to the rules.

Ⅲ.

1. C   2. D   3. B   4. D   5. C   6. B   7. A   8. D   9. D   10. A